BLISS

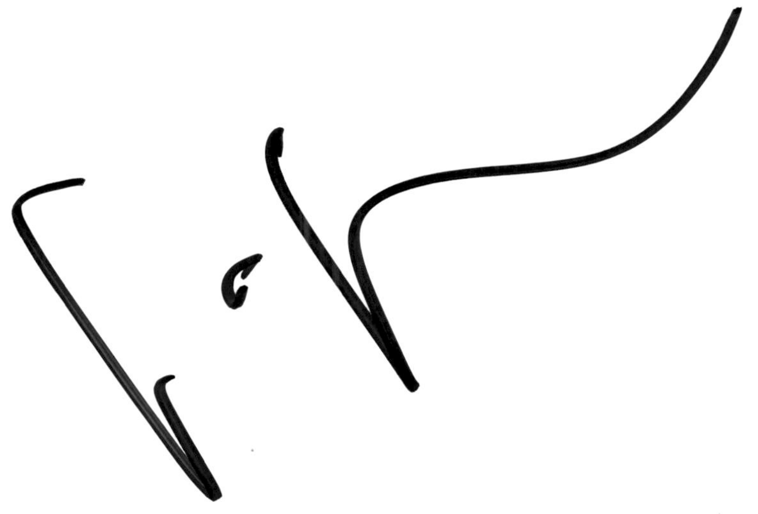

BLISS

Transformational Festivals & the Neo Hippie

Photographs by Steve Schapiro

Introduction by Theophilus Donoghue

Afterword by Wavy Gravy

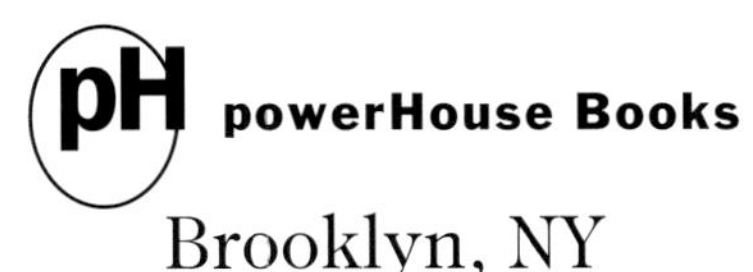

powerHouse Books

Brooklyn, NY

Introduction by THEOPHILUS DONOGHUE

This book is about transformational festivals and the subject of "Bliss" within the current hippie counter-culture movement. Although many people think that hippies were a phenomena of the 60s and early 70s, the movement never ended; it simply vacated the cities in order to live in eco-villages (hundreds throughout the States) and congregate for annual festivals, most notably the Rainbow Gathering. The summer hippie festivals are numerous, especially along the West Coast, and this book documents a niche within the current hippie generation which is characterized as "bliss ninnies." These are the hippies who are focused on God above all things and on radiating the feeling of that connection. Unlike the hippies of the past, the current generation is more inclined towards meditation, yoga, prayer, and ecstatic dance as means of entering altered states as opposed to the use of psychedelics. There's also a major focus on taking care of the body through a raw, organic, vegan diet.

The current hippie generation definitely still has a strong political awareness and activist spirit, but the "blissed out" portion of this "family" that these photos document are primarily concerned about spirituality as opposed to politics as being a means of improving the world. "Bliss" is a concept which is better expressed through imagery than words as the primary expressions of it are often non-verbally communicated whether it be through meditation, dancing, or silently looking into one another's eyes—a practice known as eye gazing or open-eye meditation. With this bit of understanding, the photos should speak joyfully for themselves…

Mystic Garden, Oregon

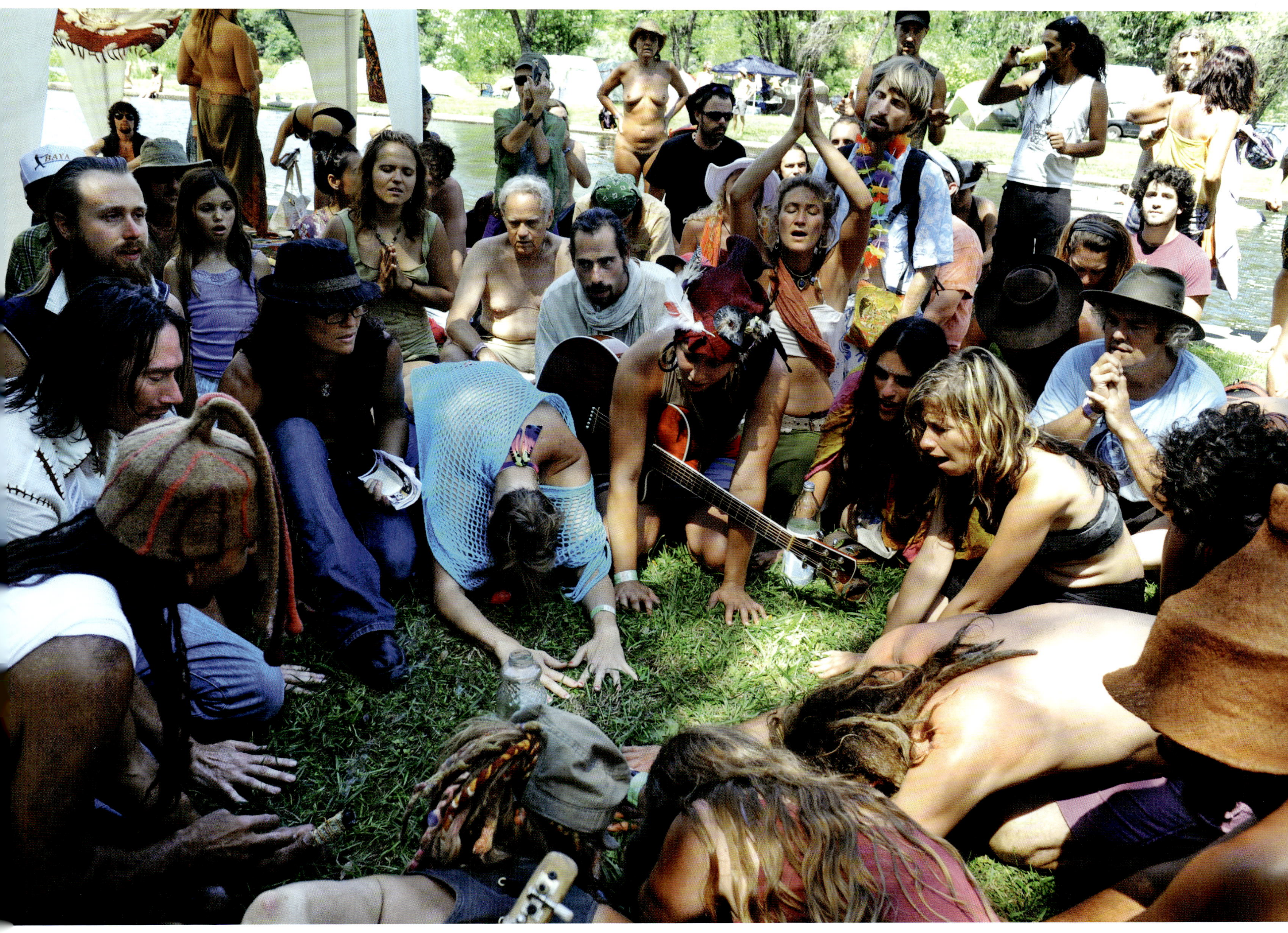

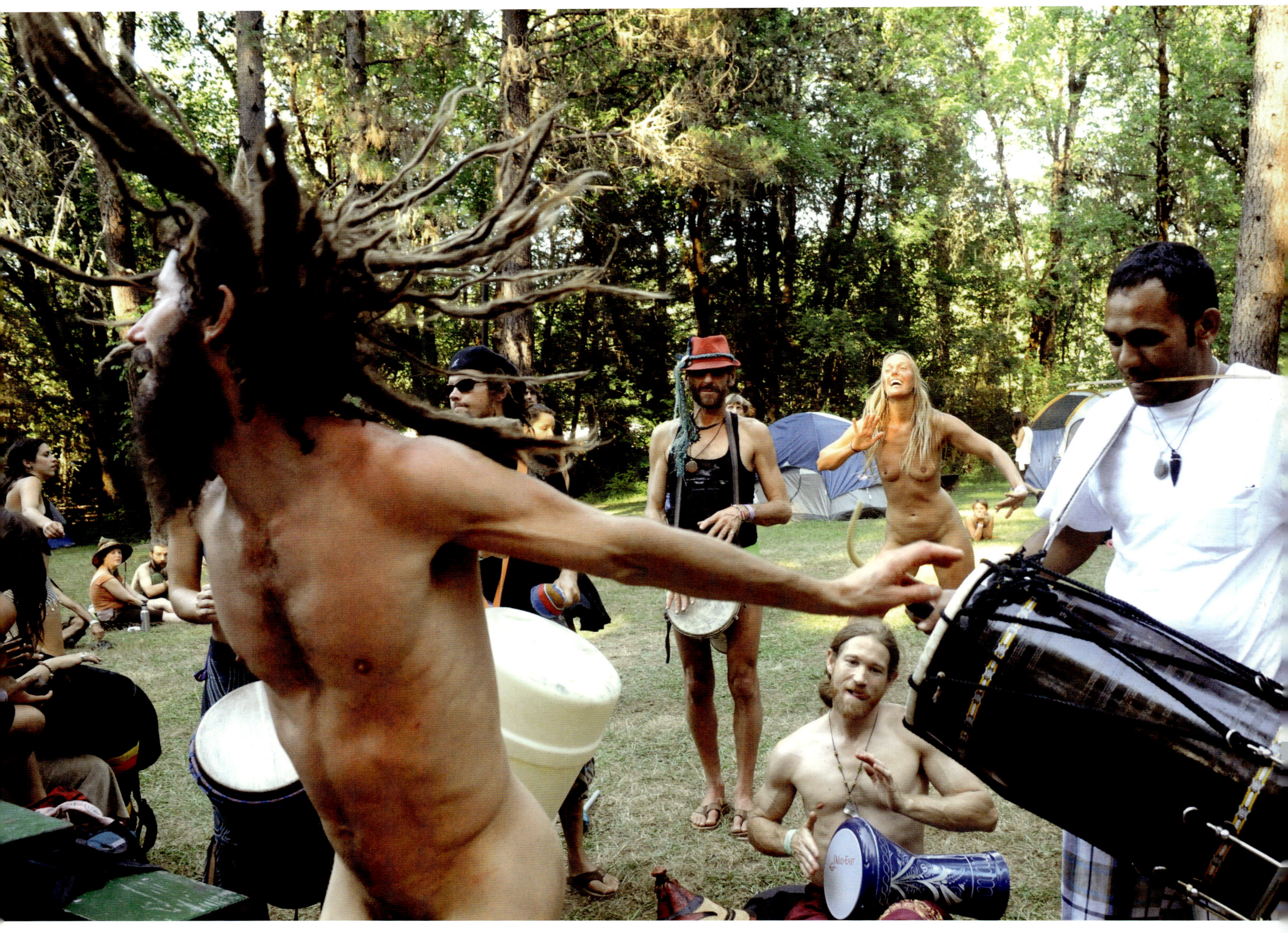

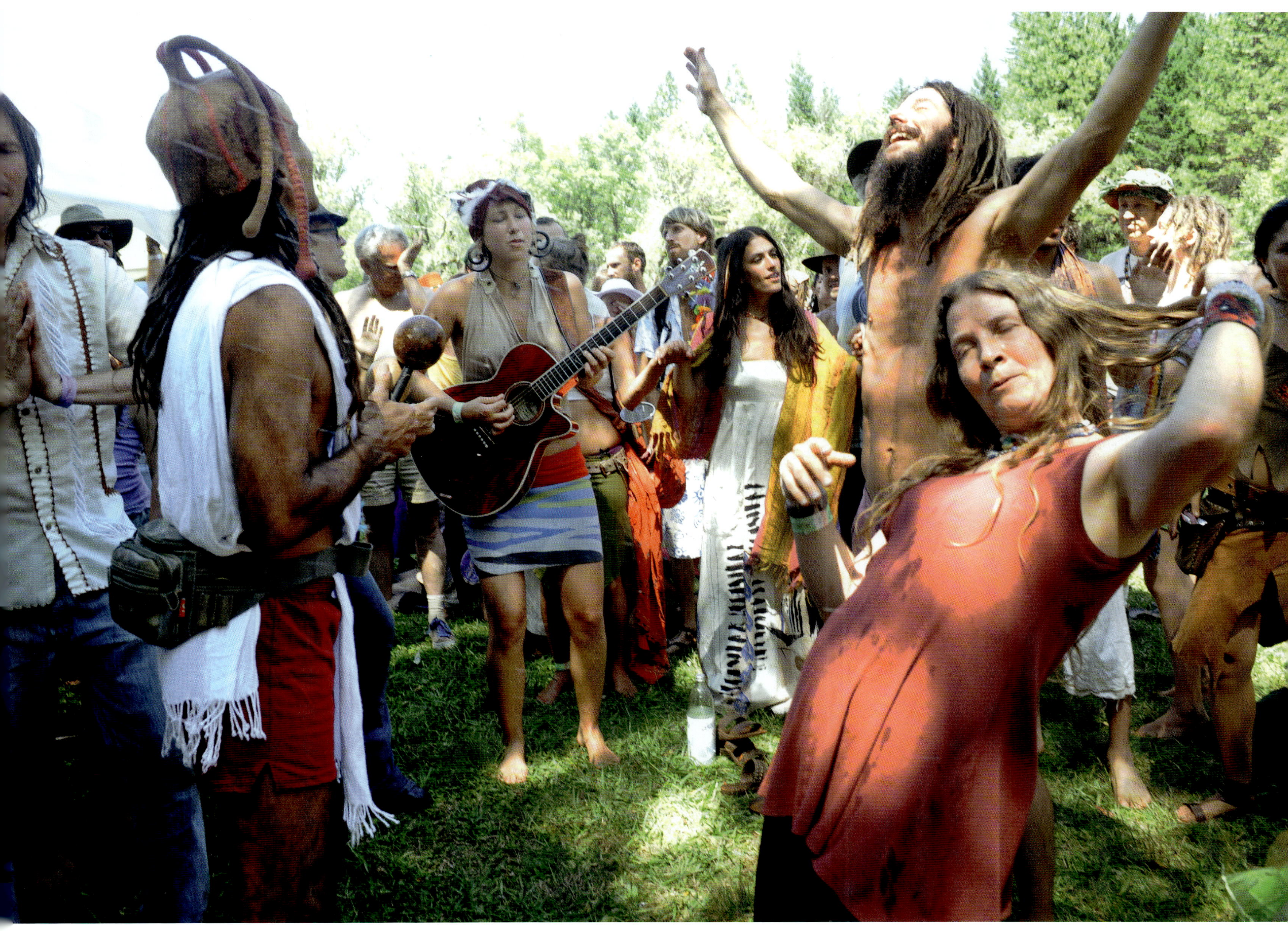

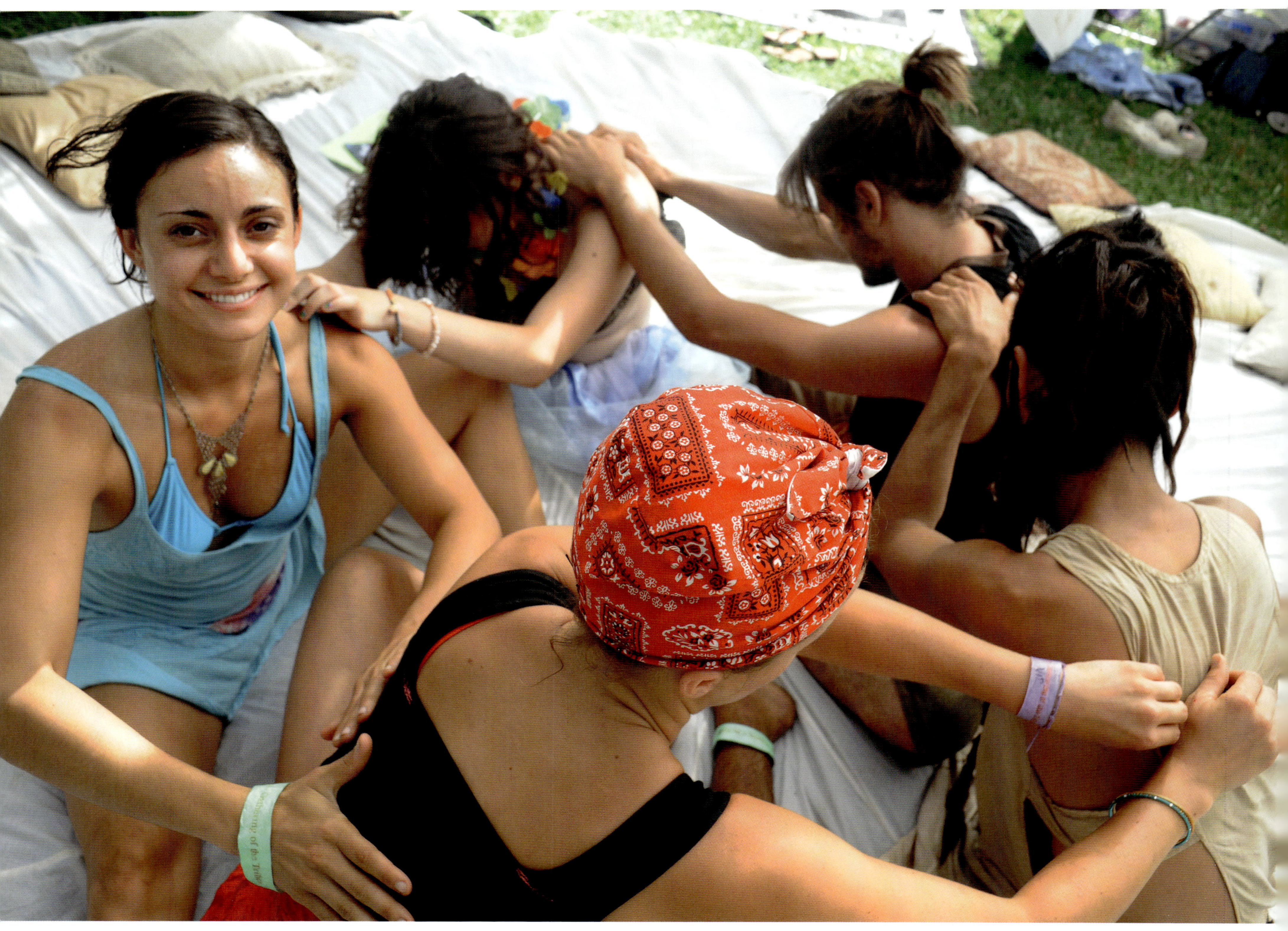

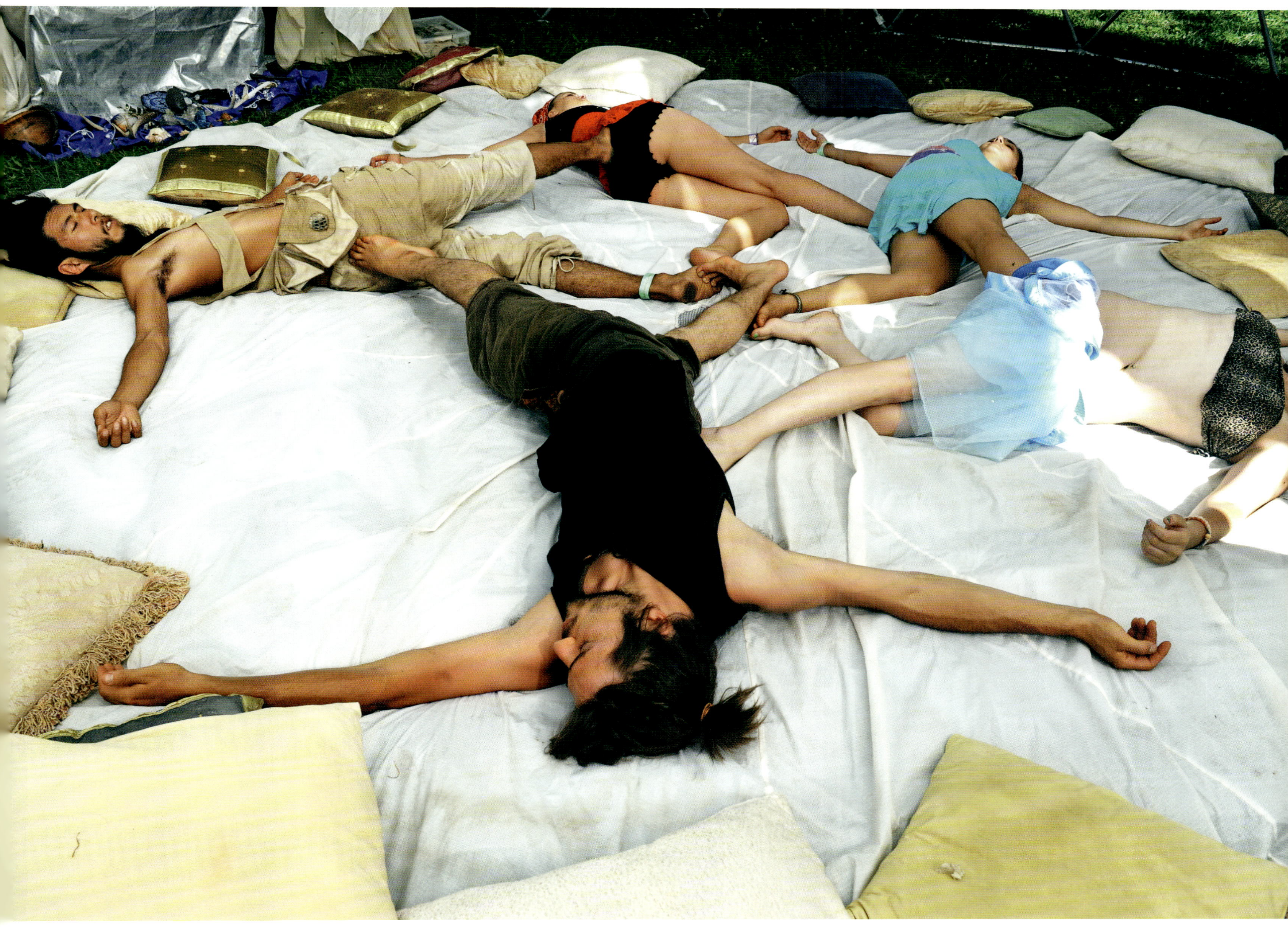

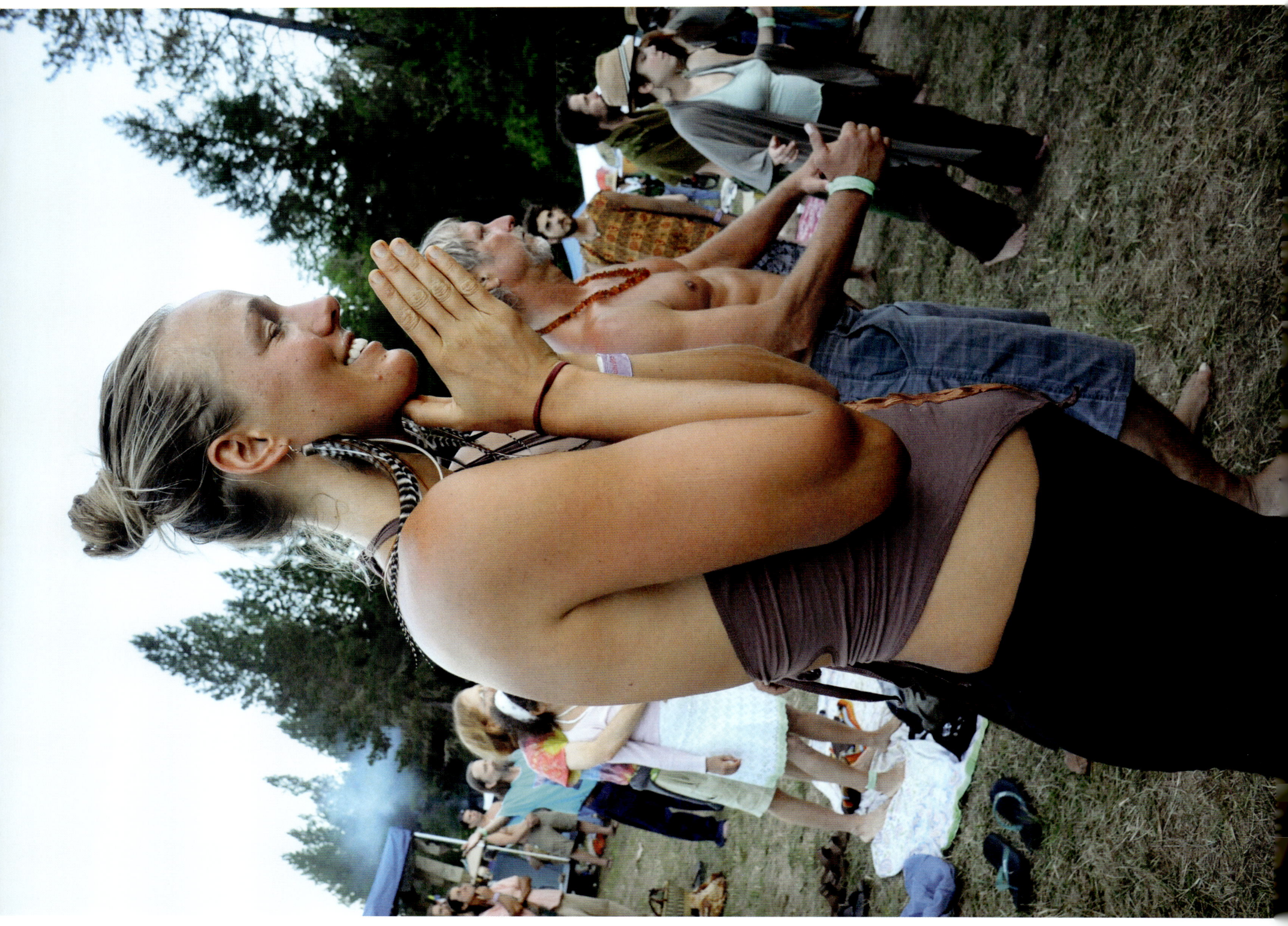

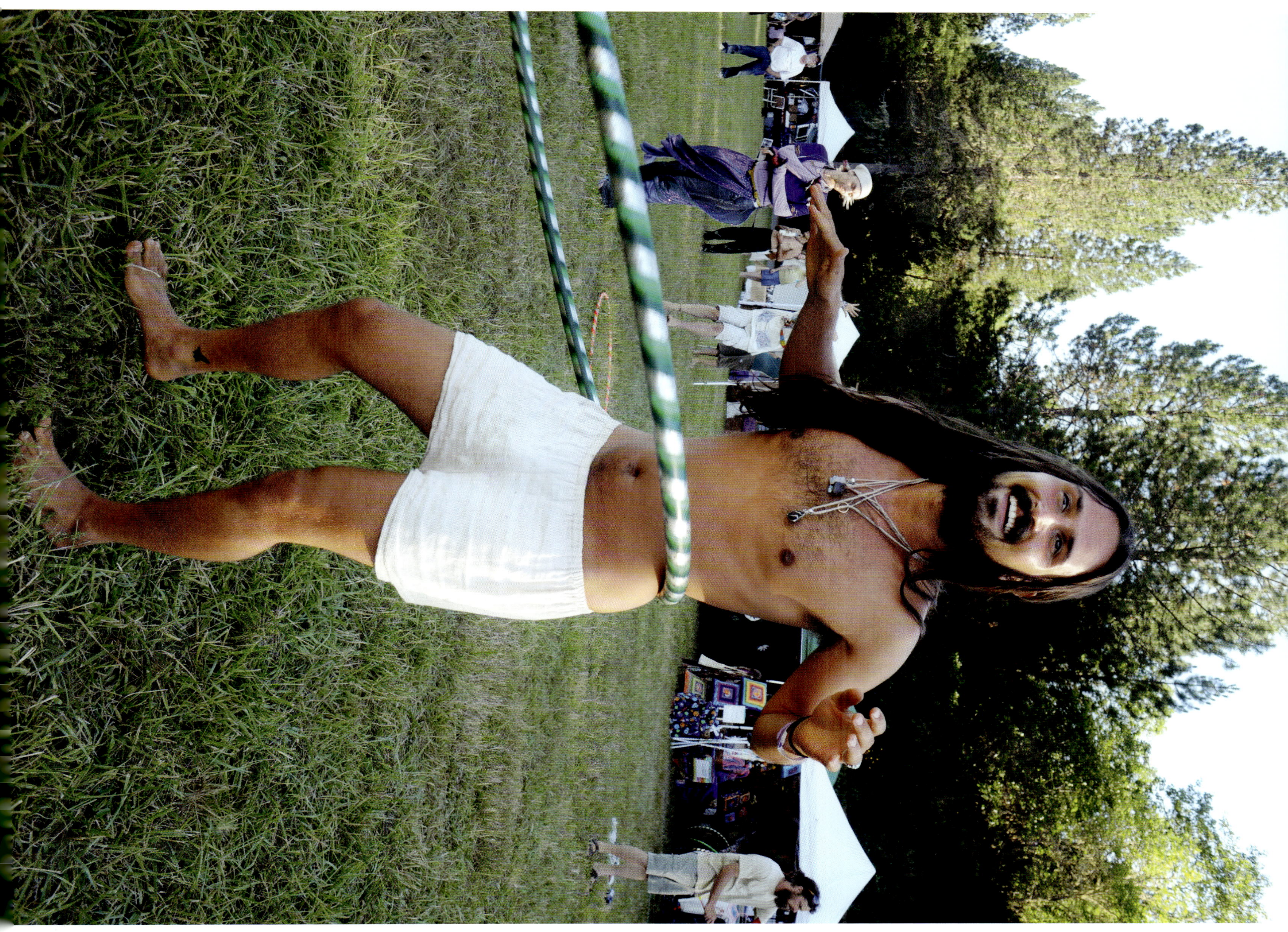

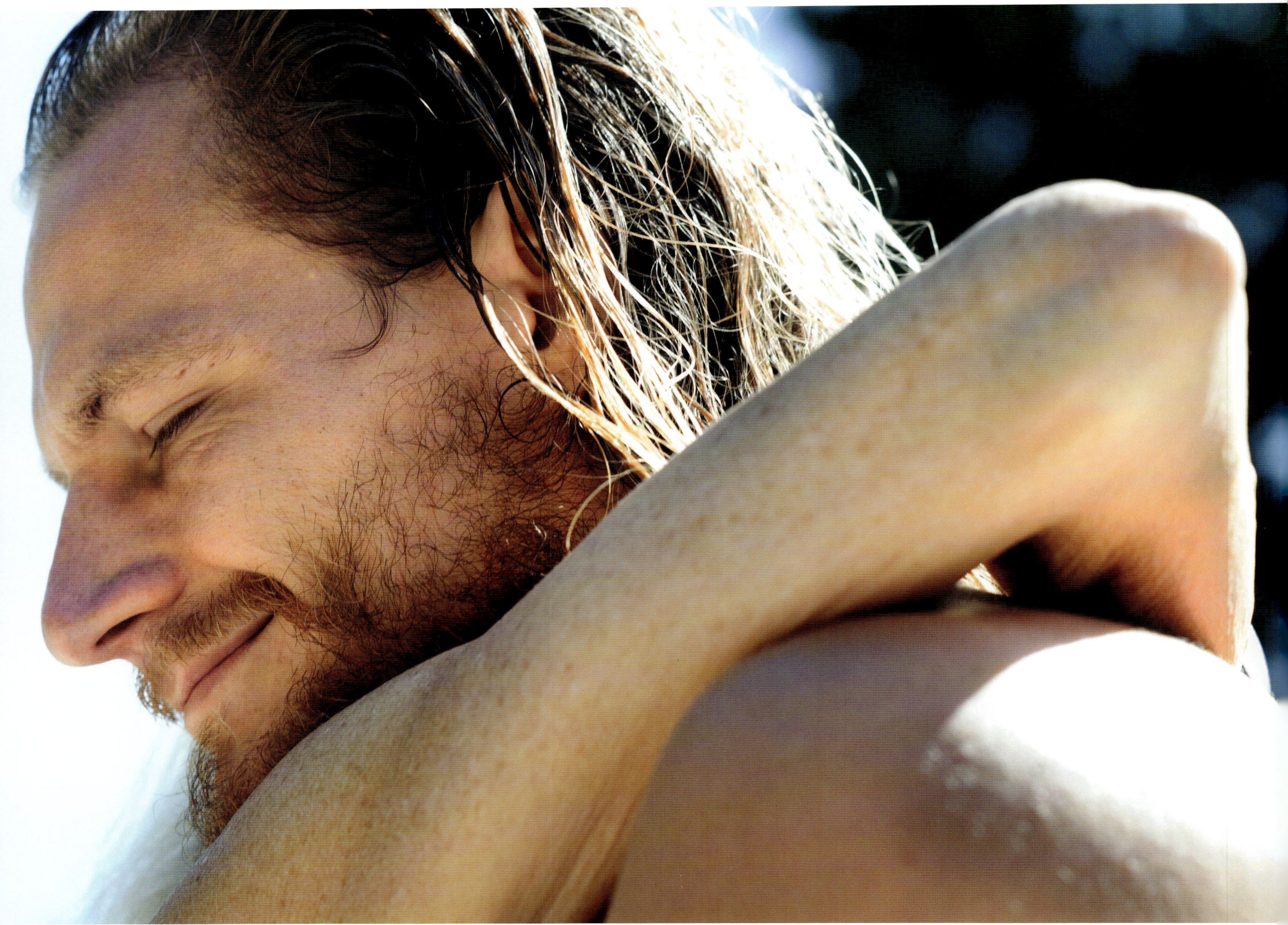

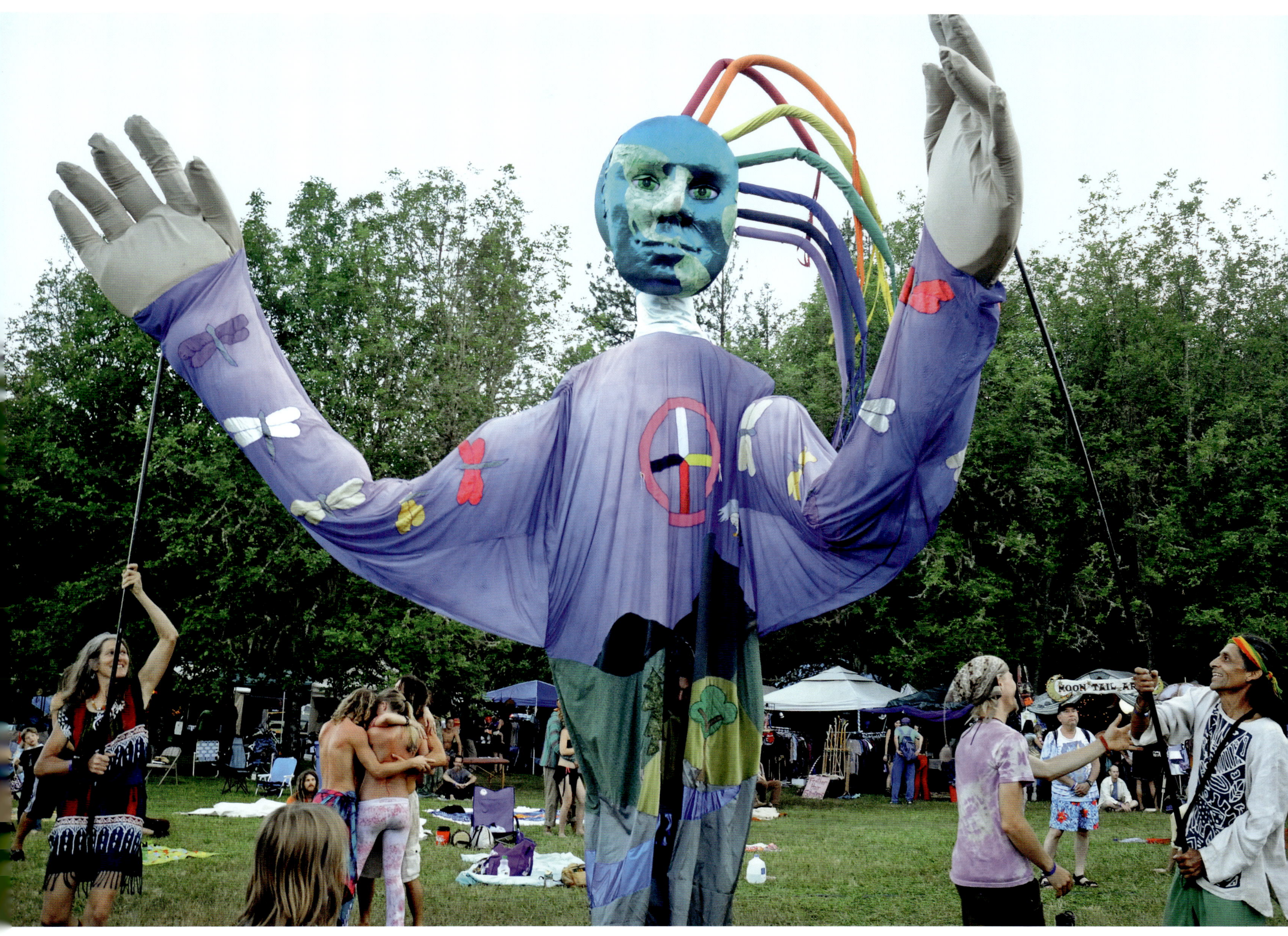
MOON TAIL

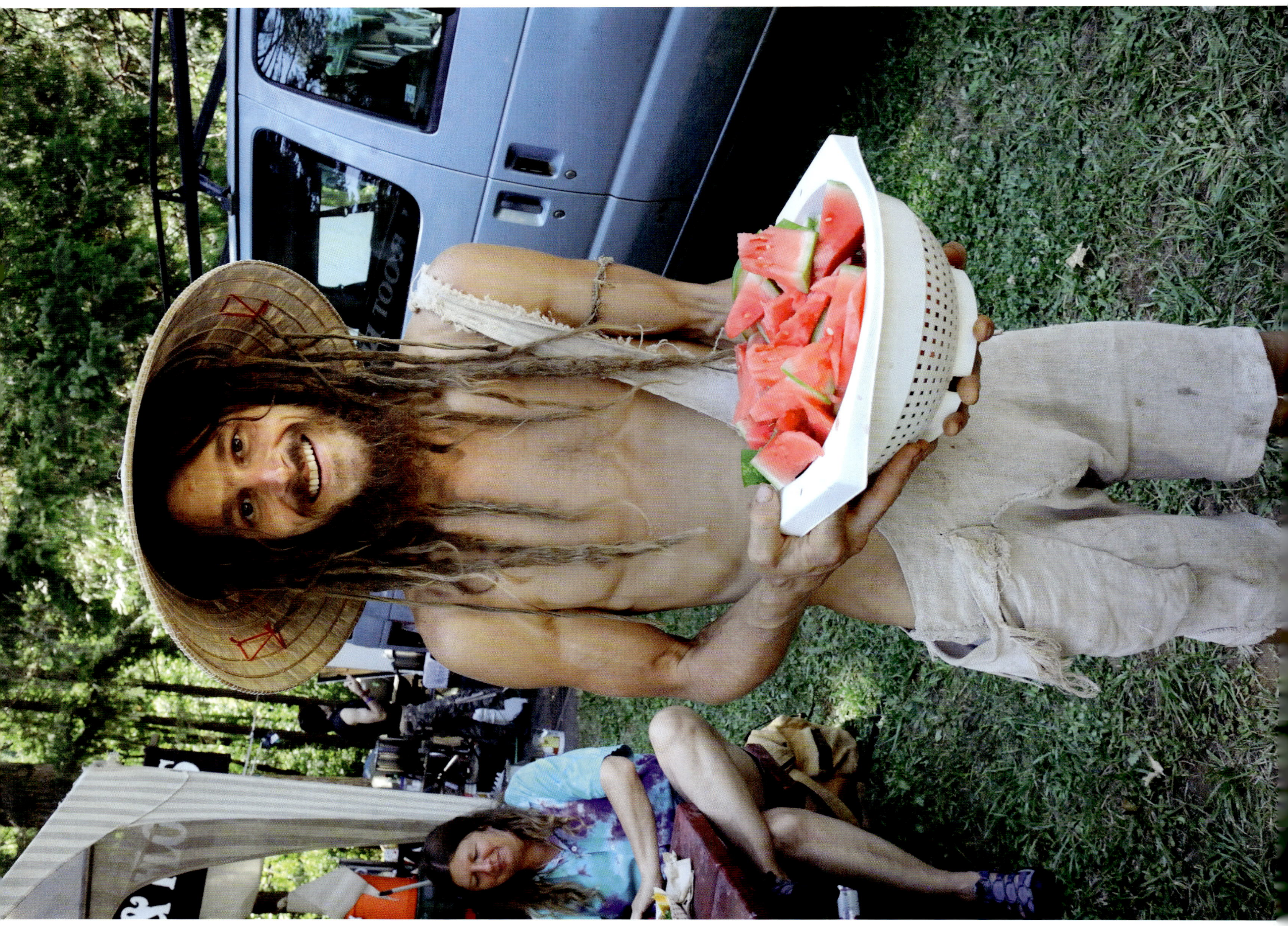

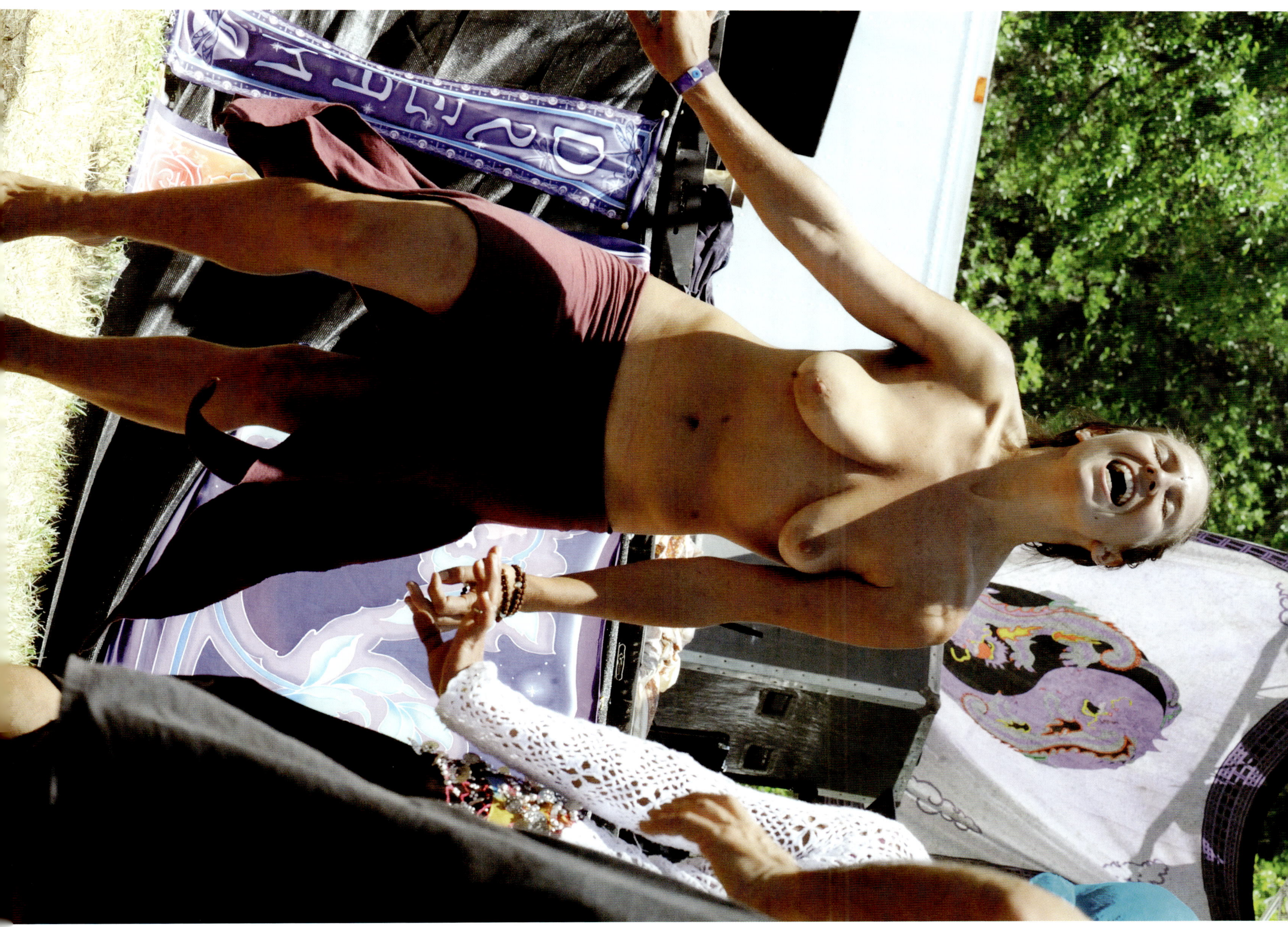

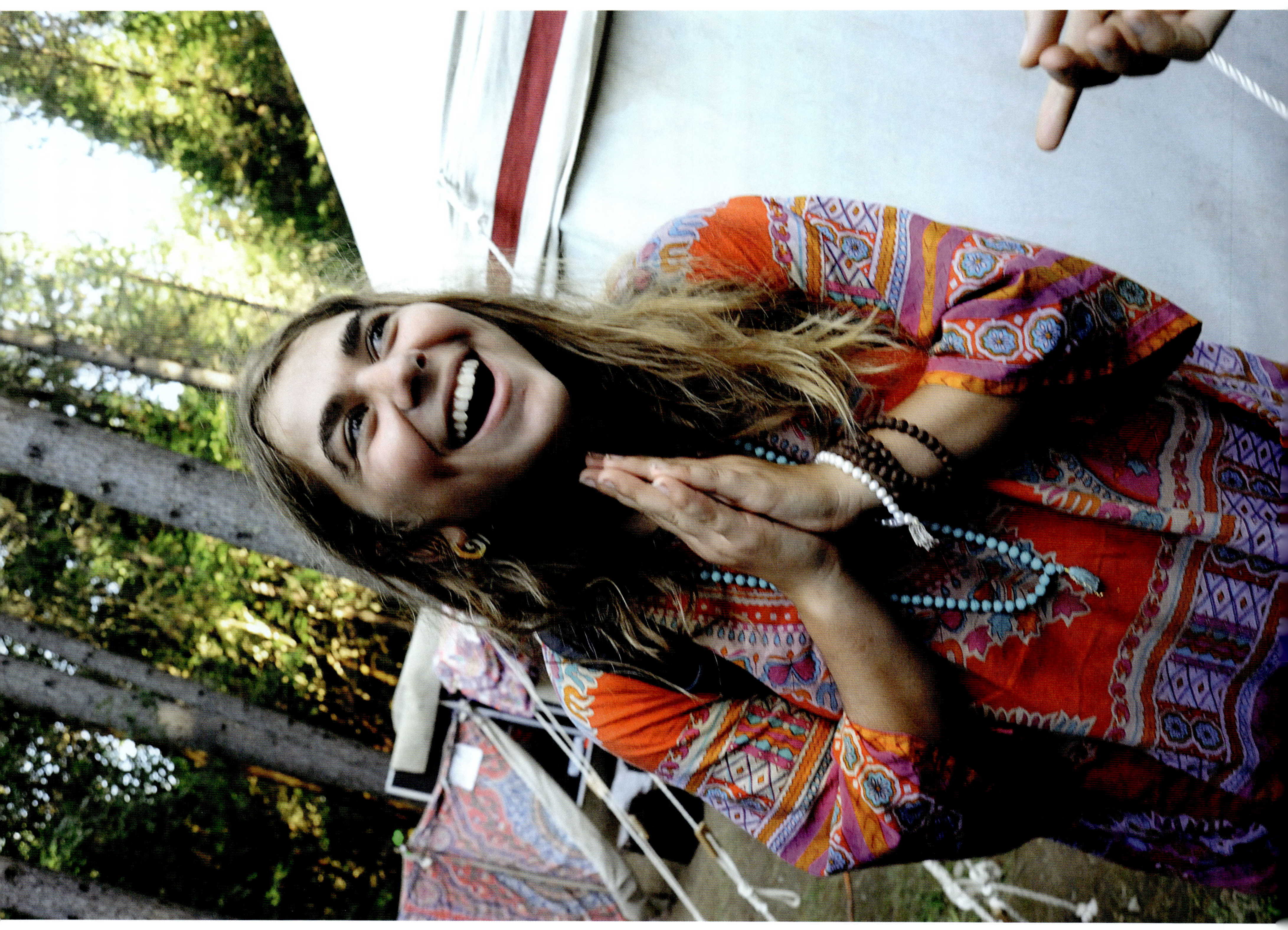

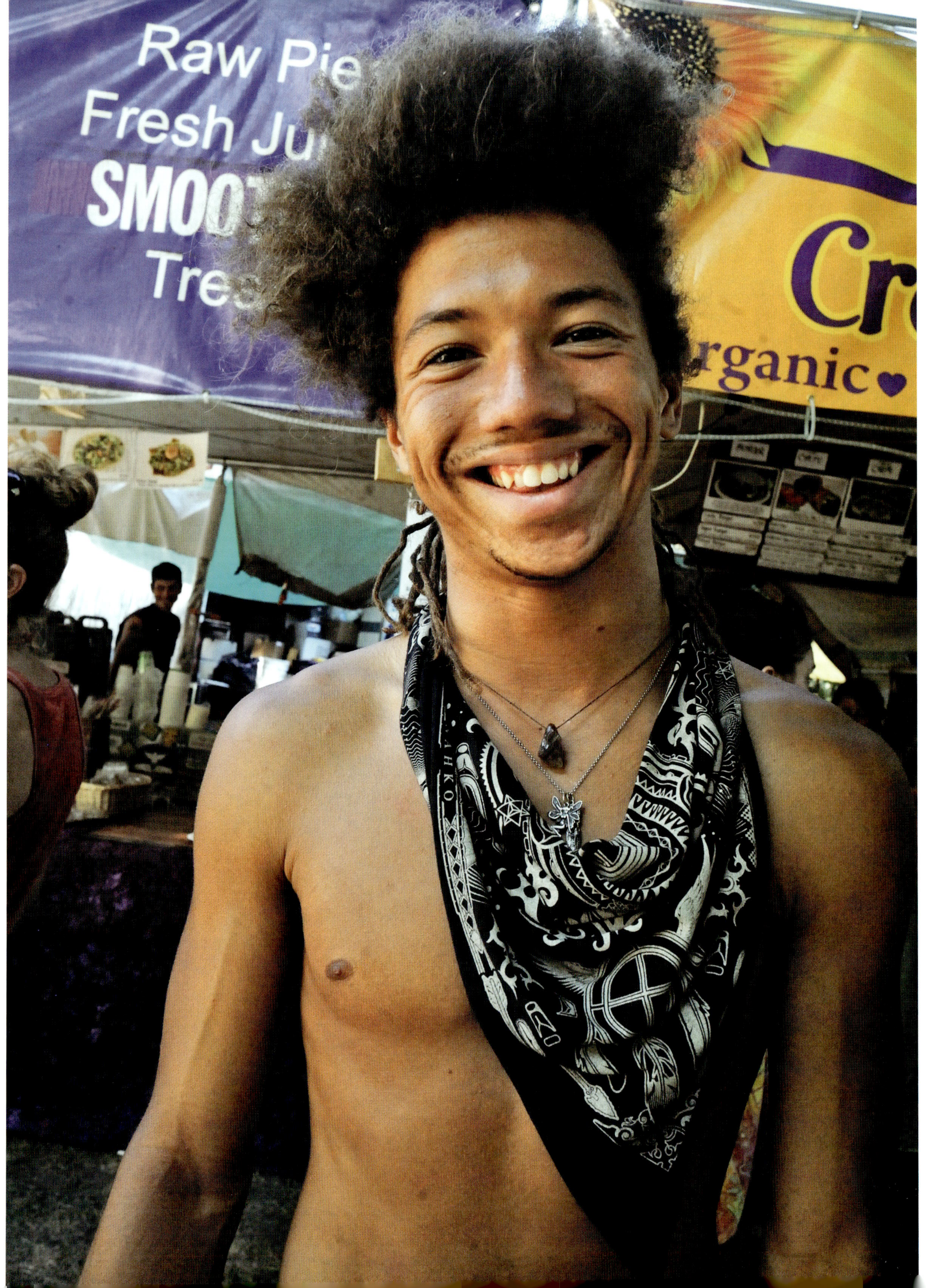

Raw Pie
Fresh Ju
SMOO
Tre
Cr
rganic ♥

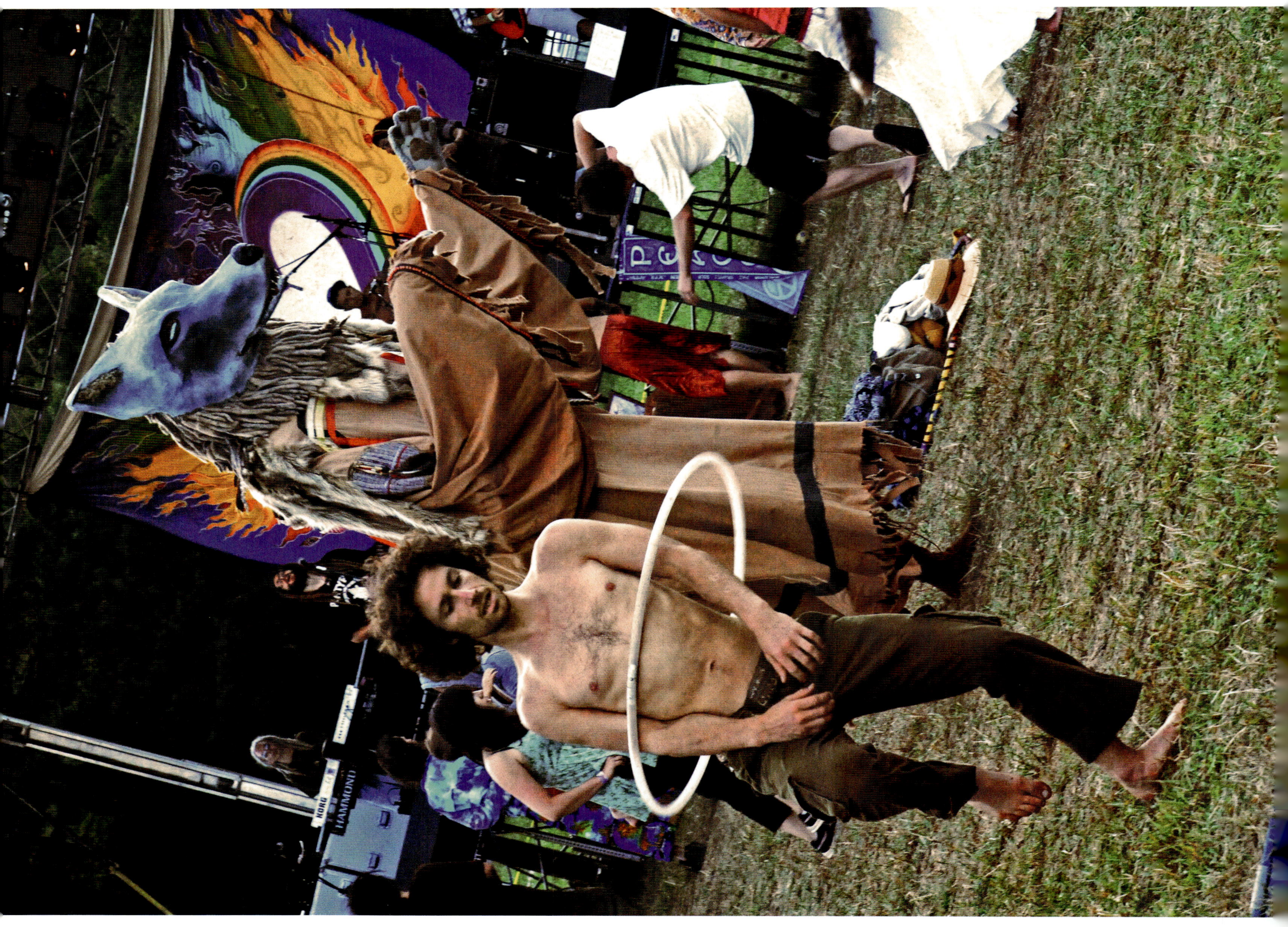

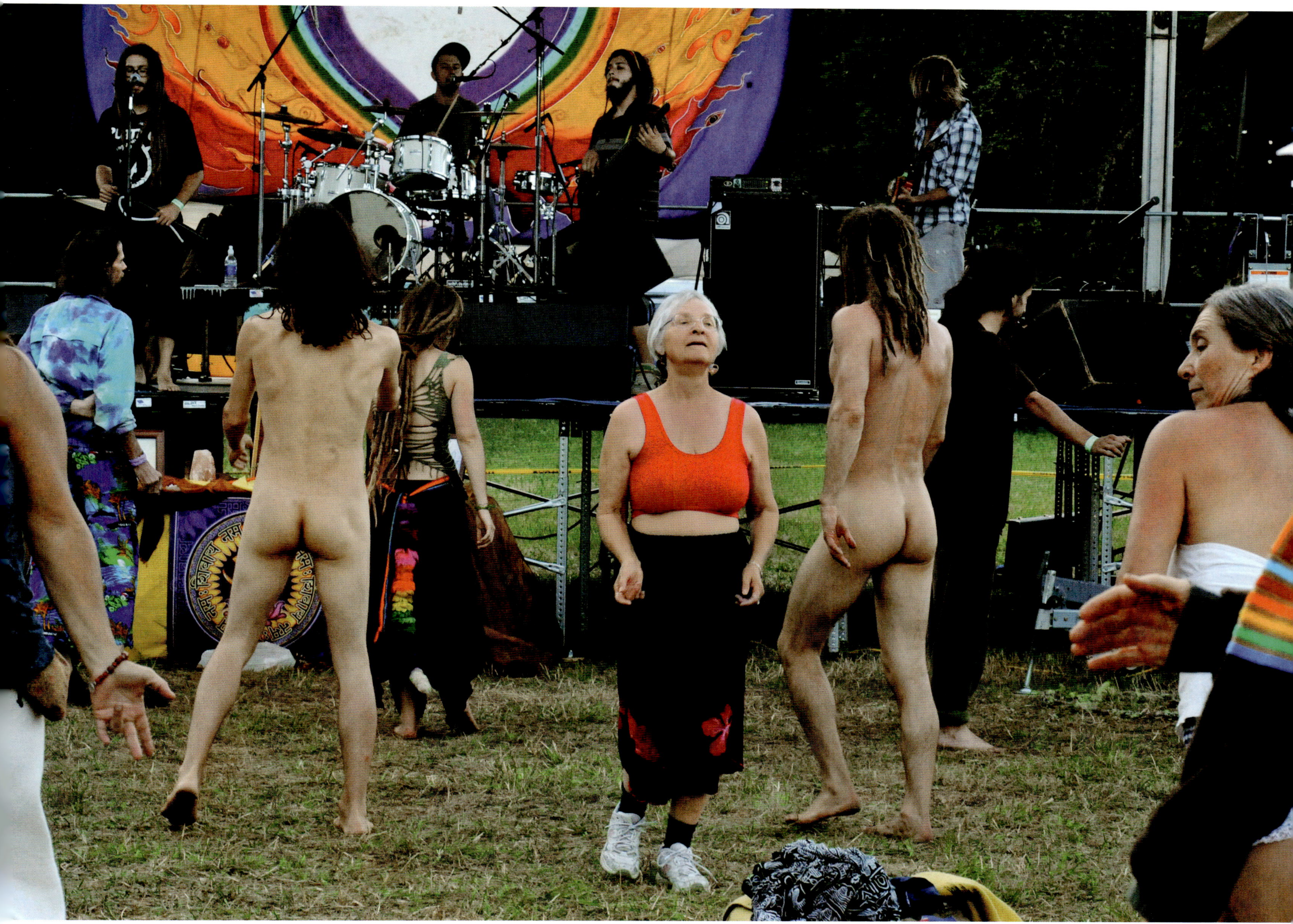

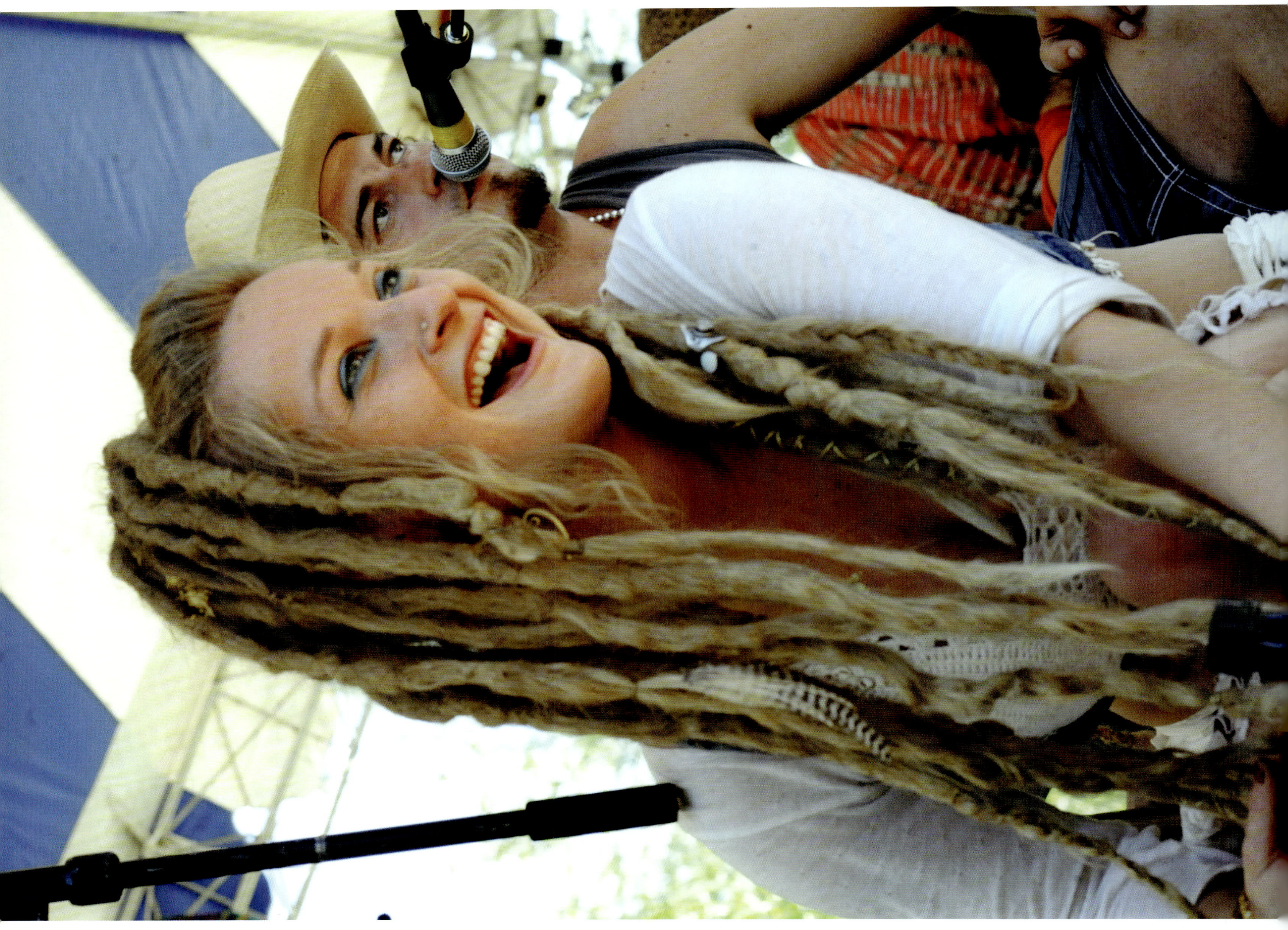

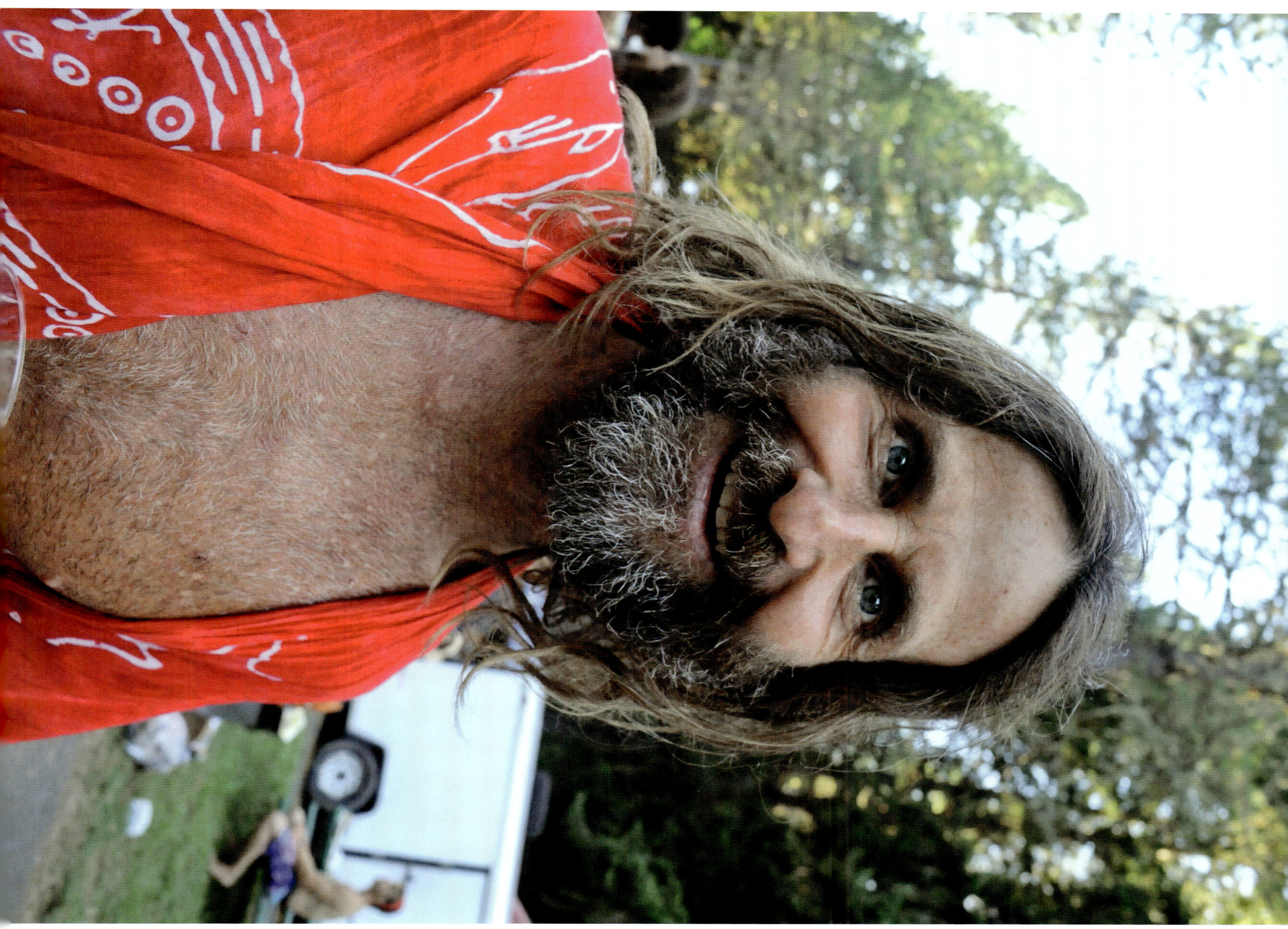

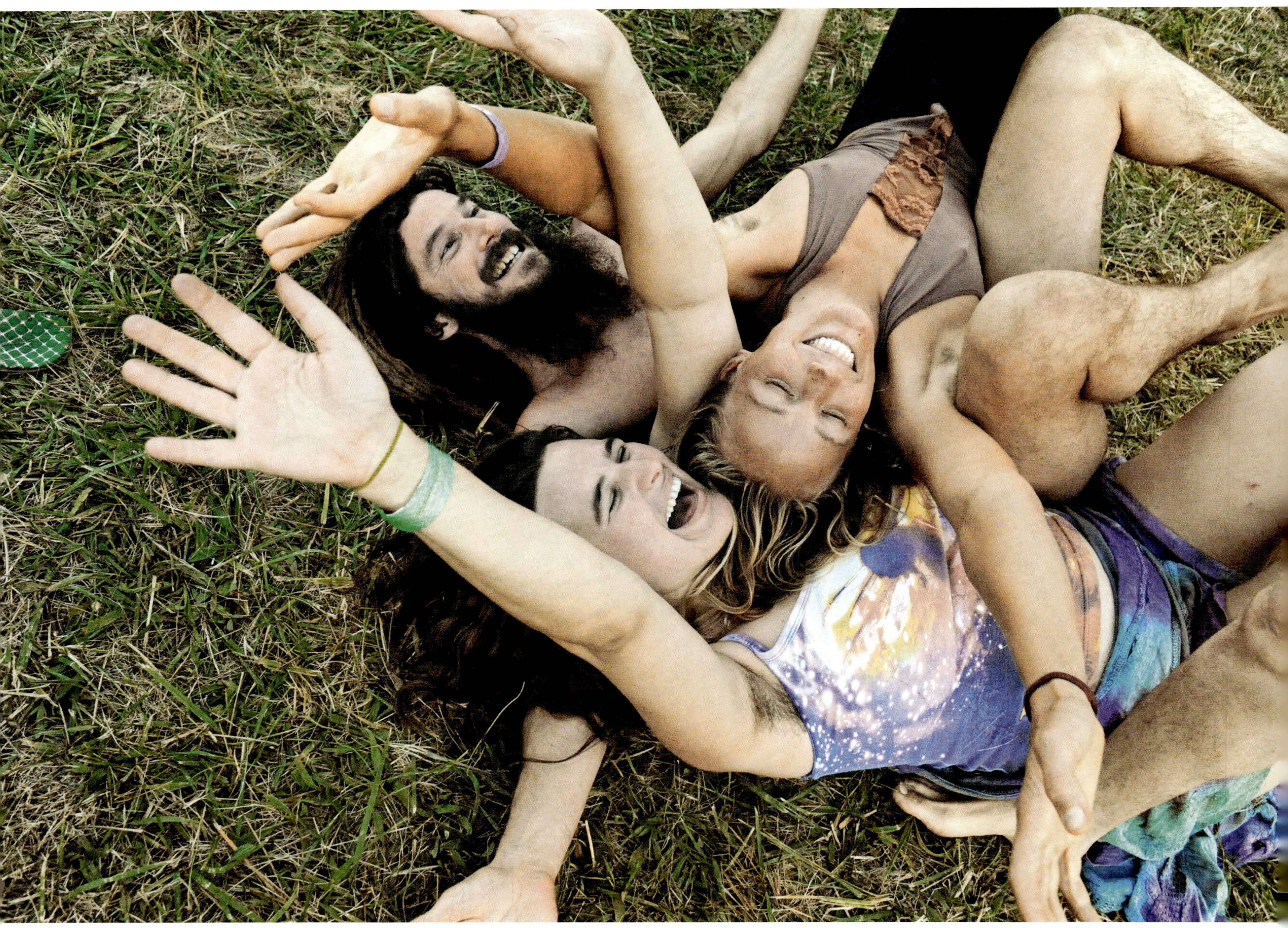

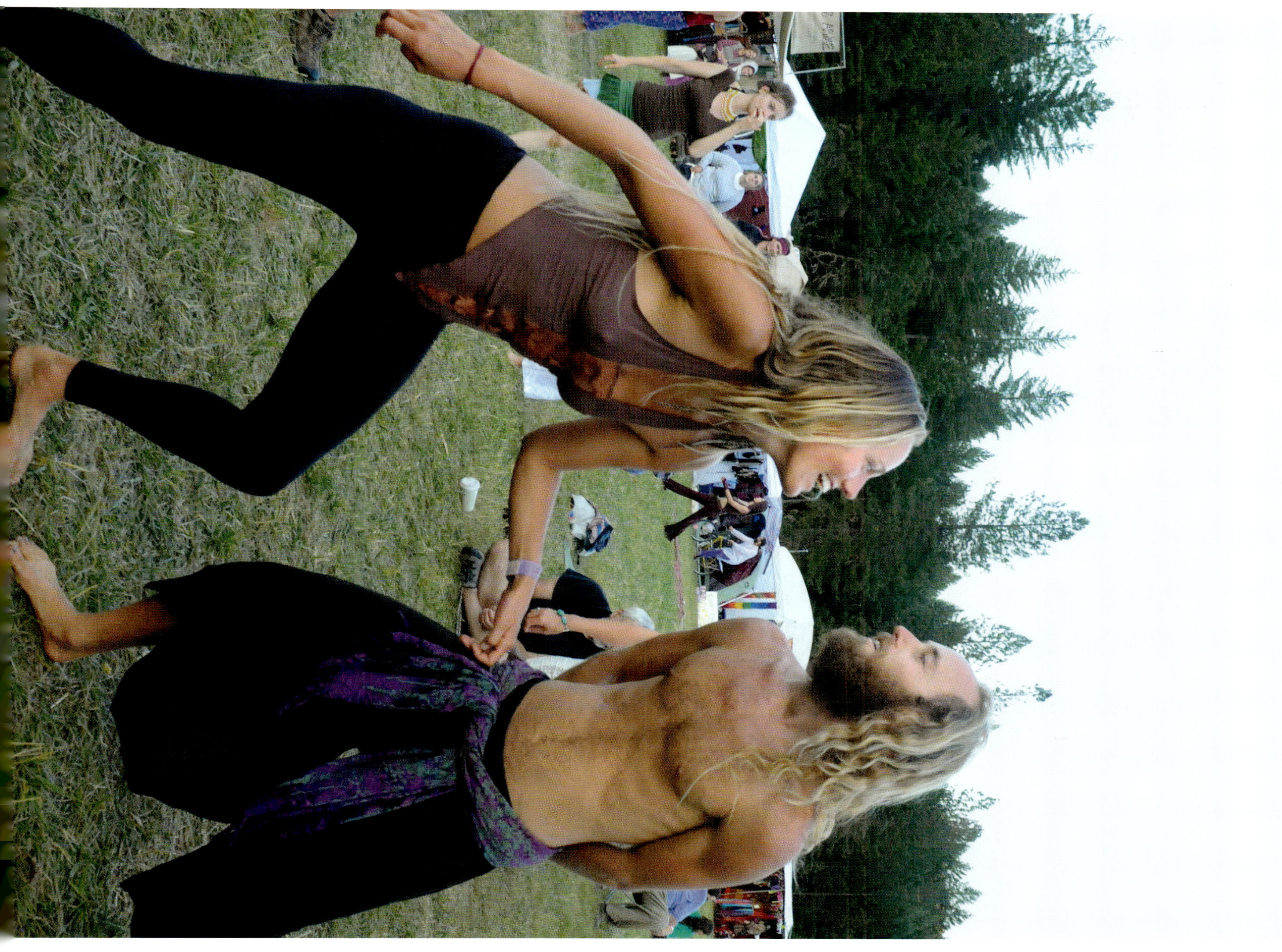

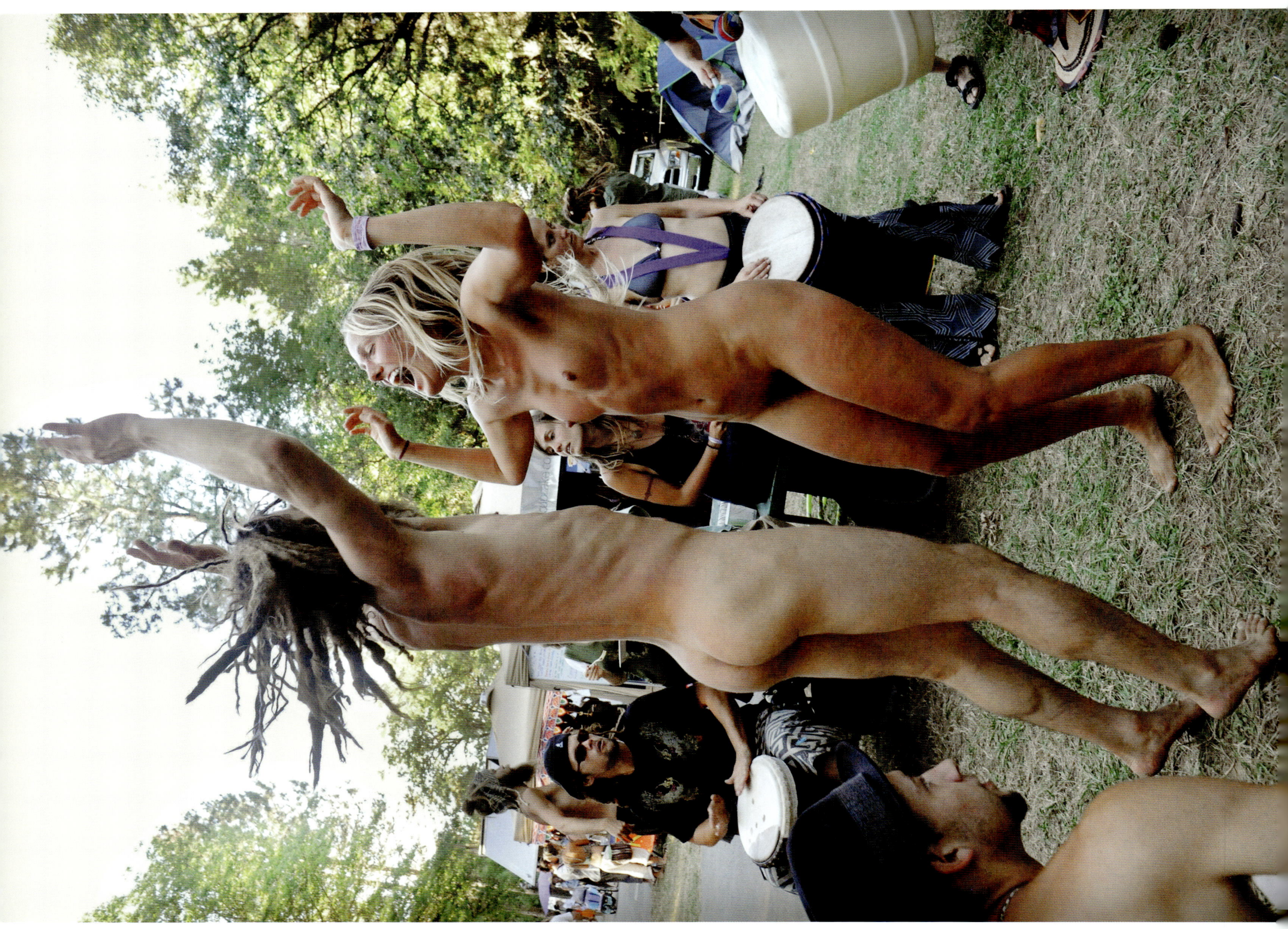

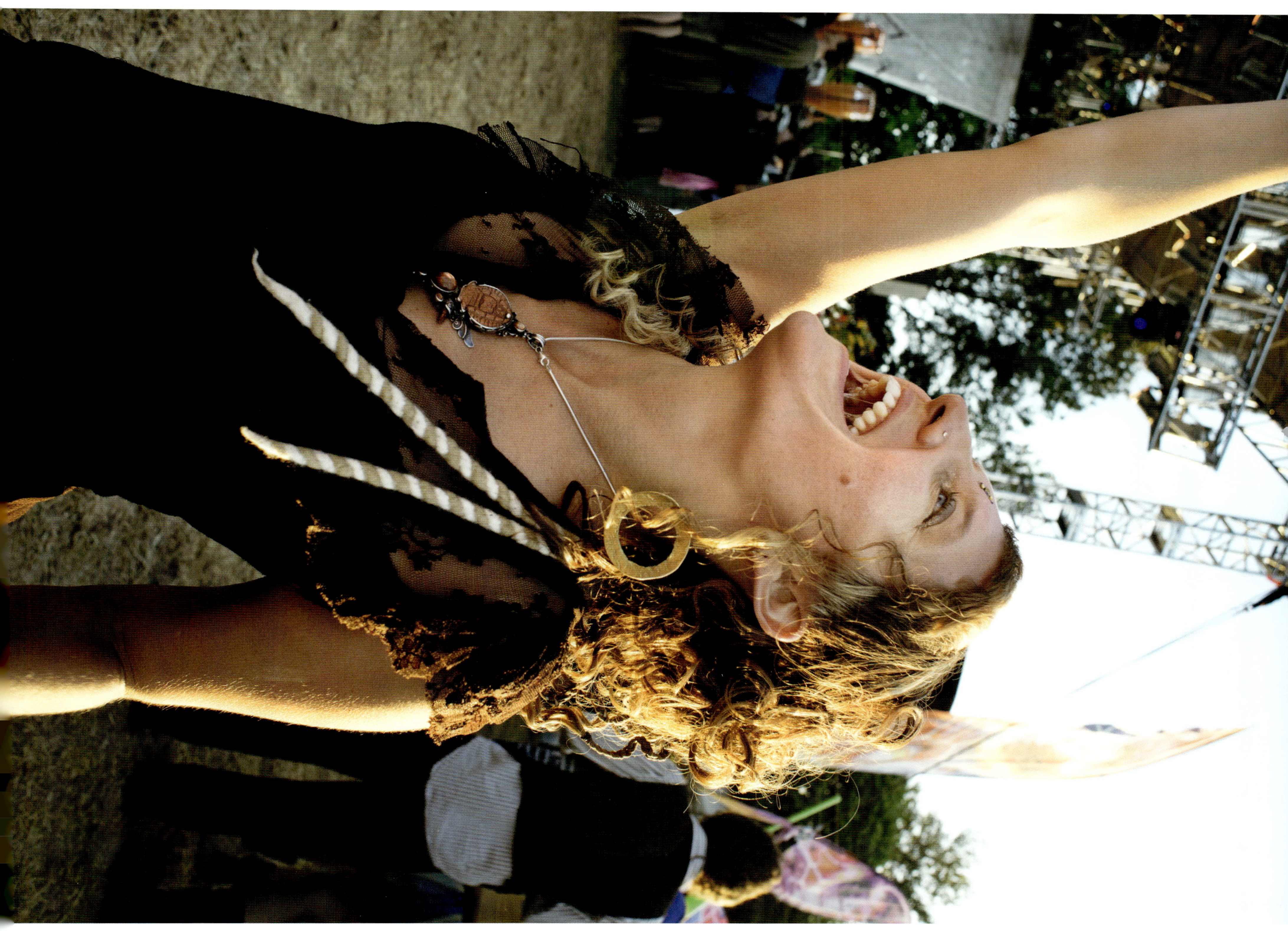

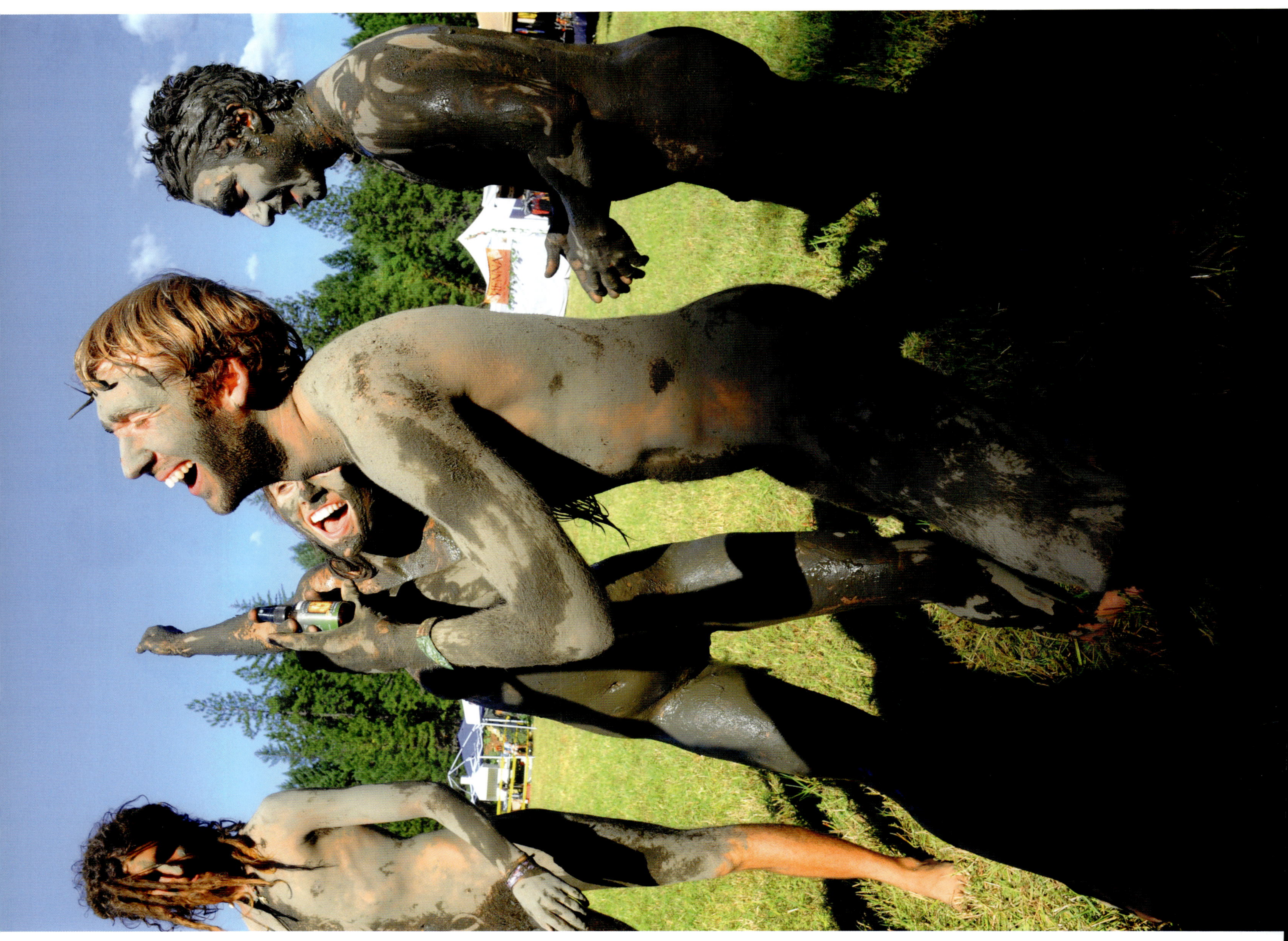

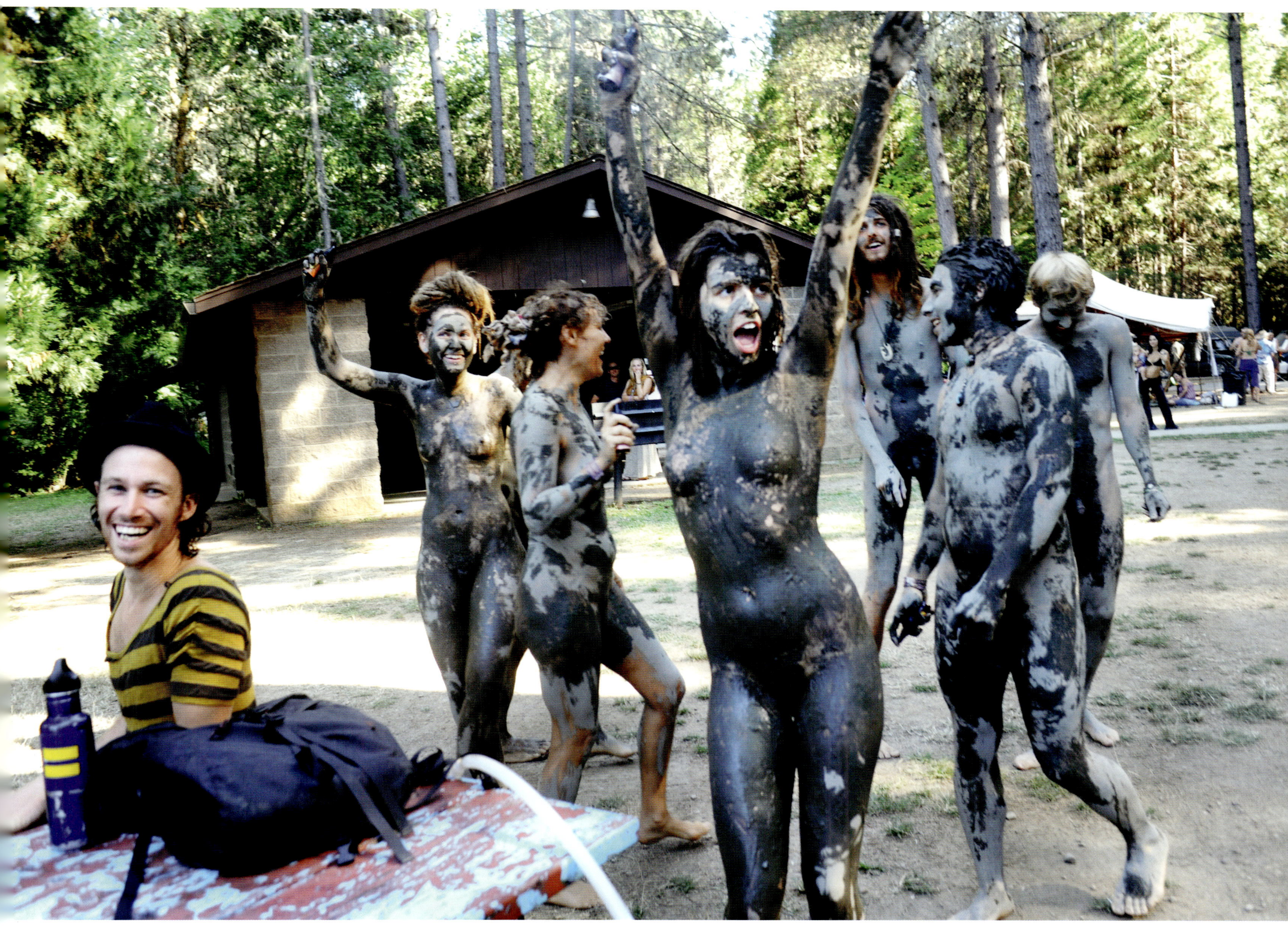

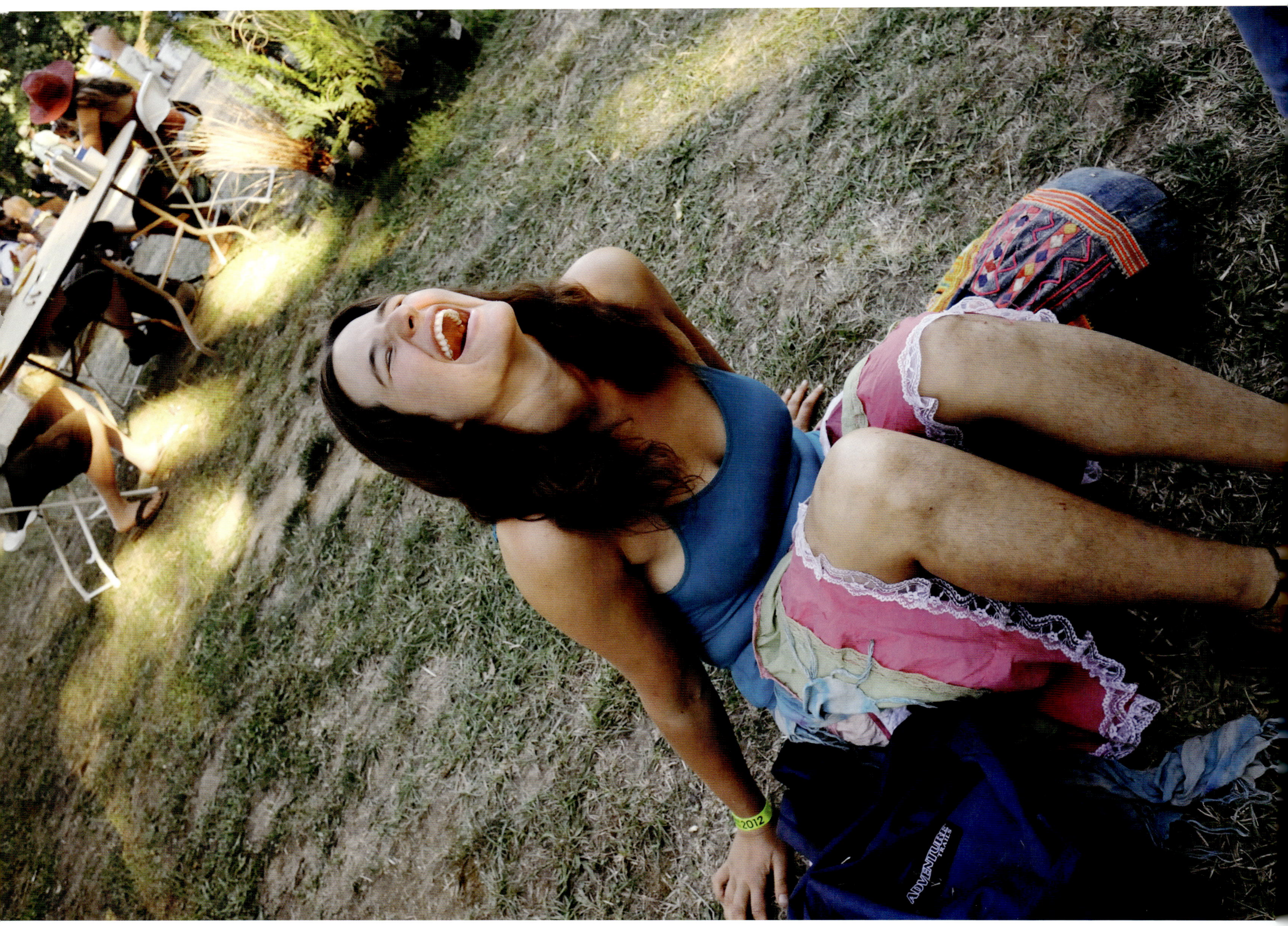

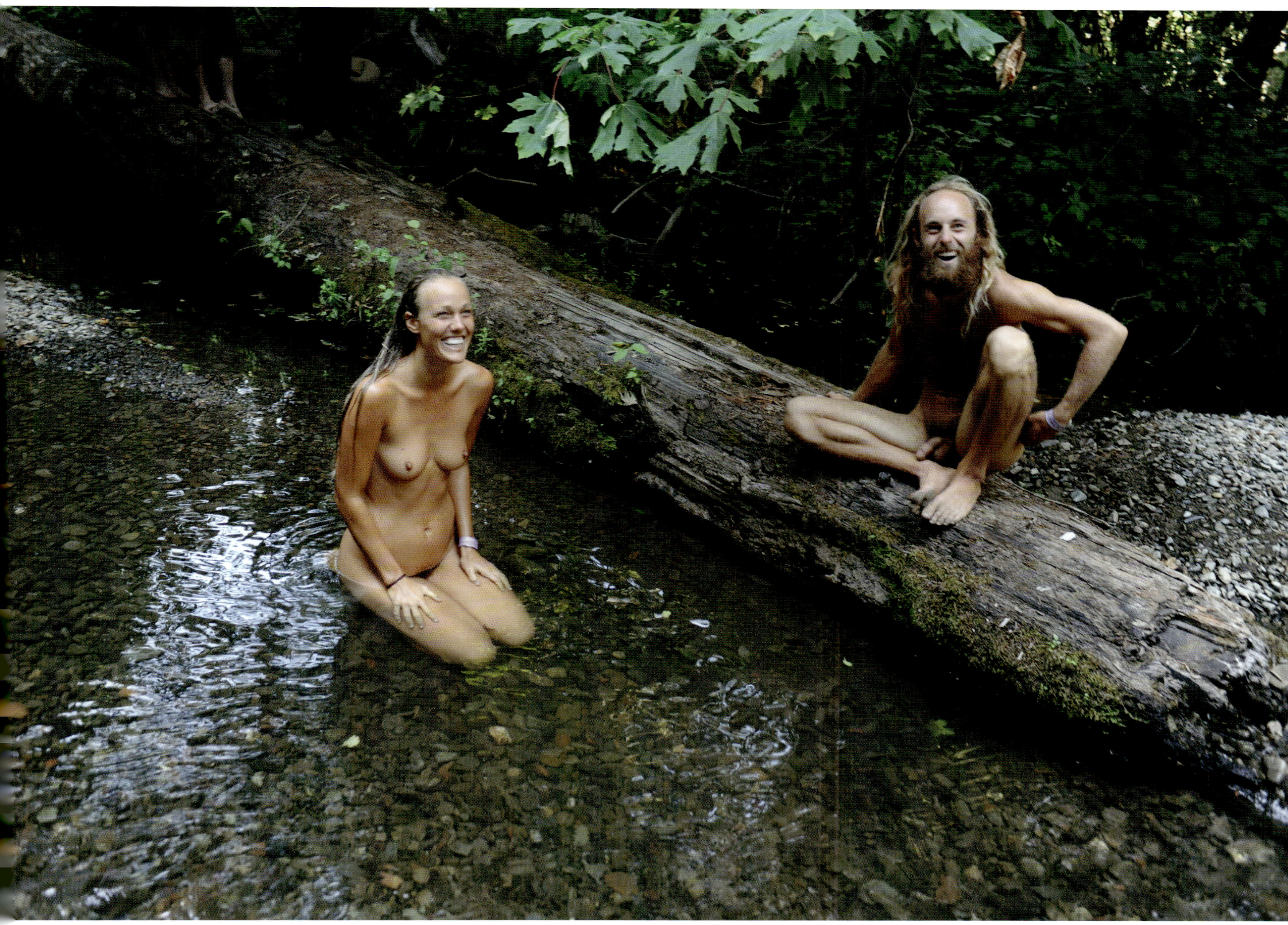

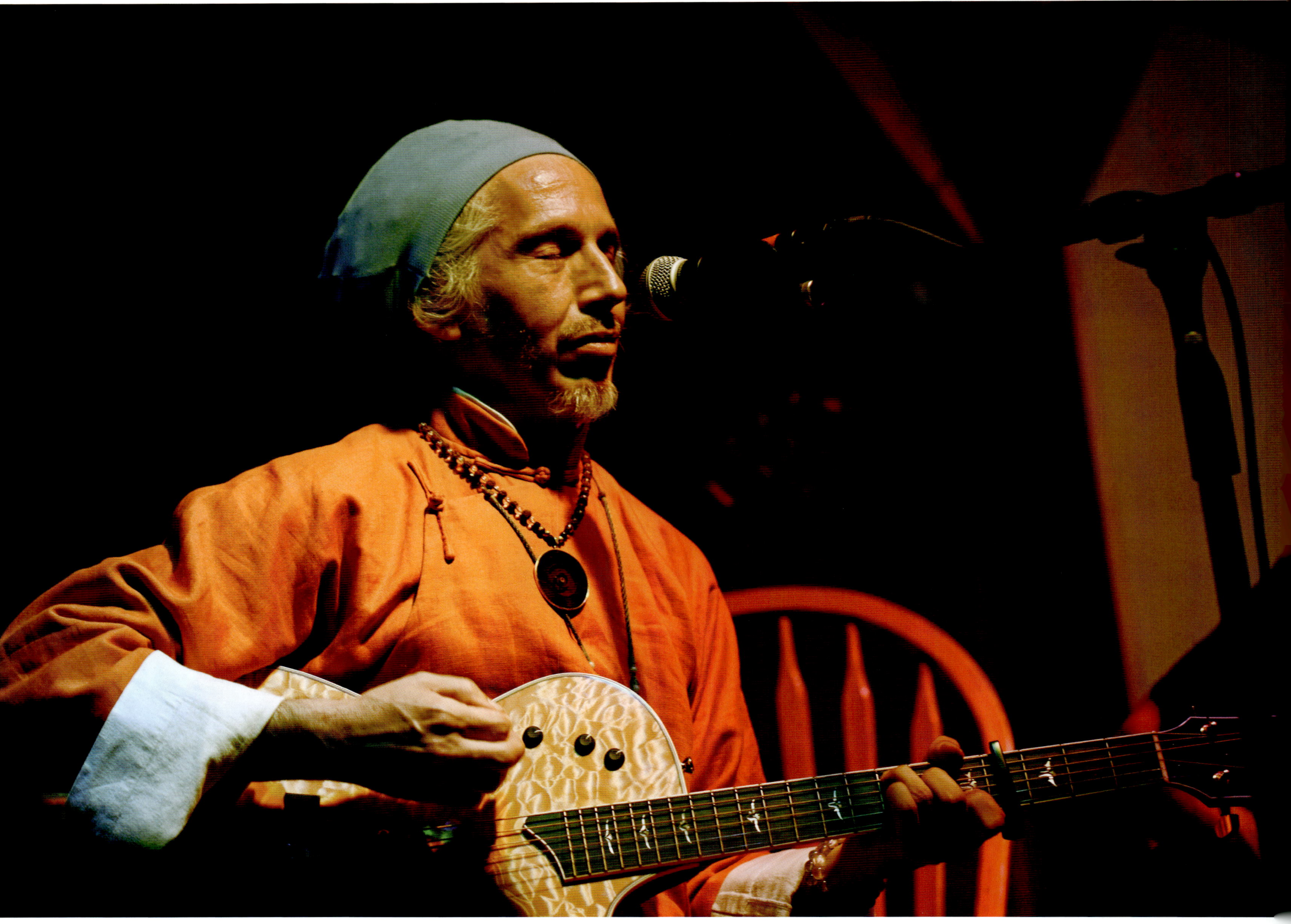

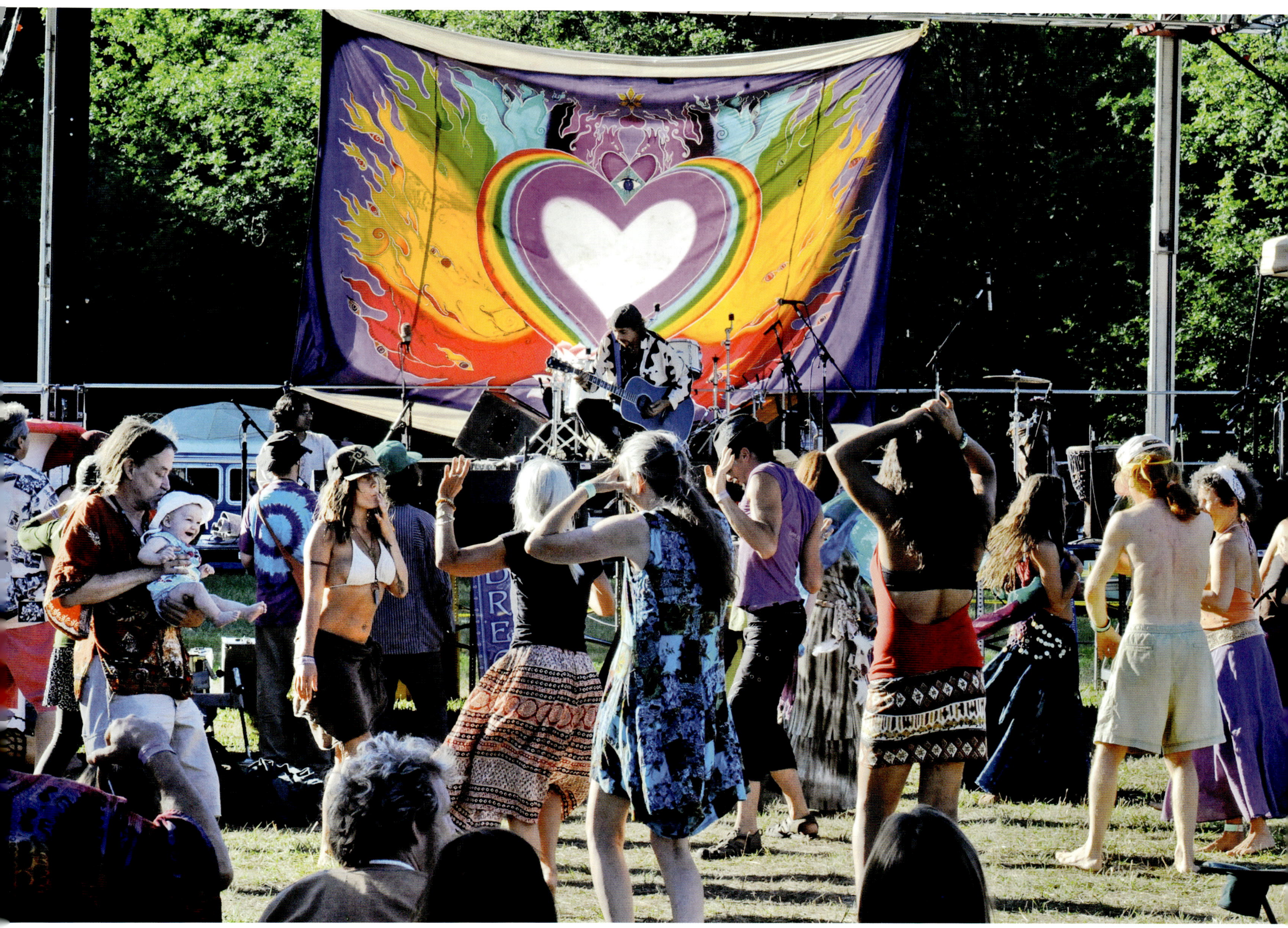

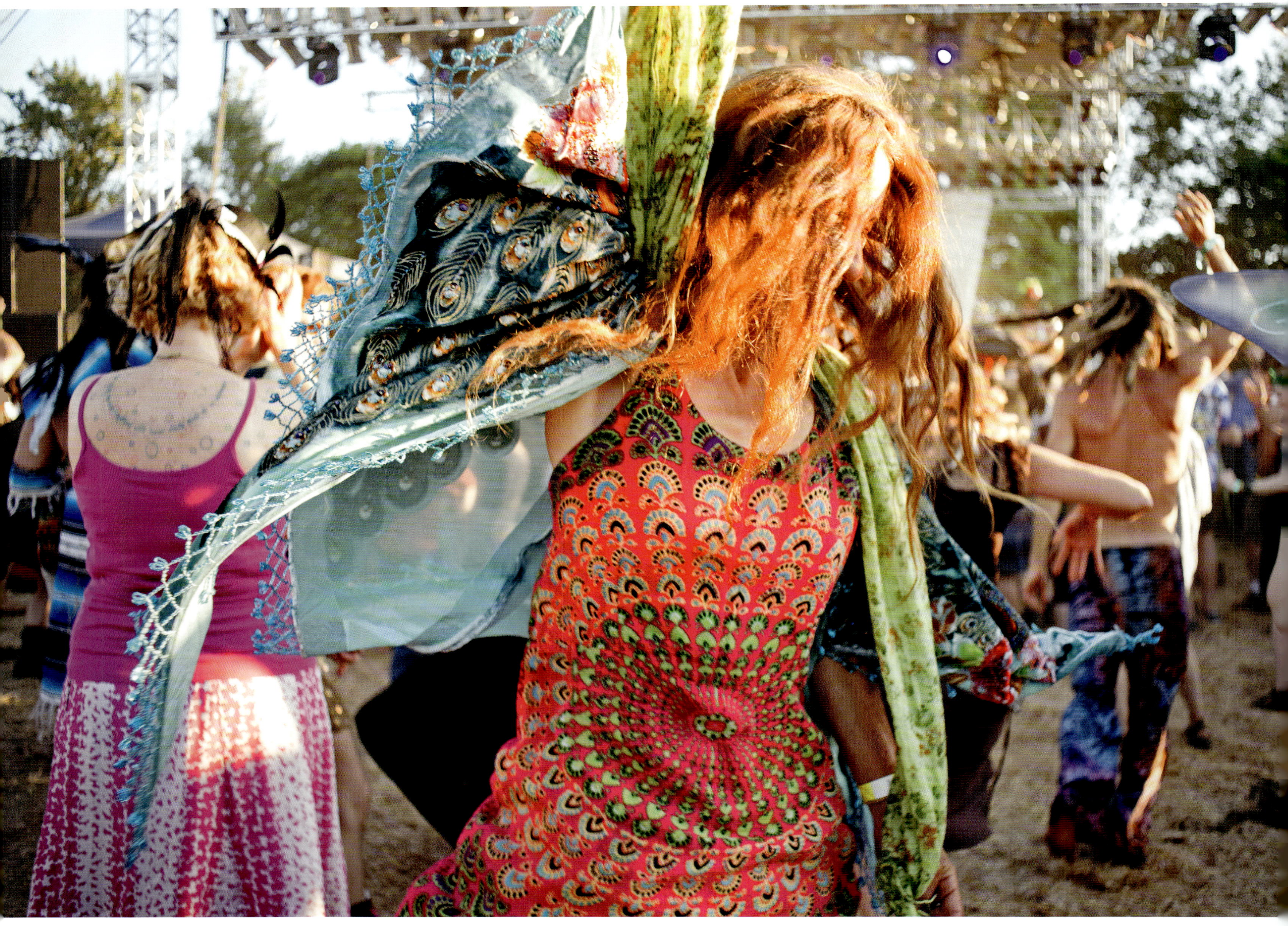

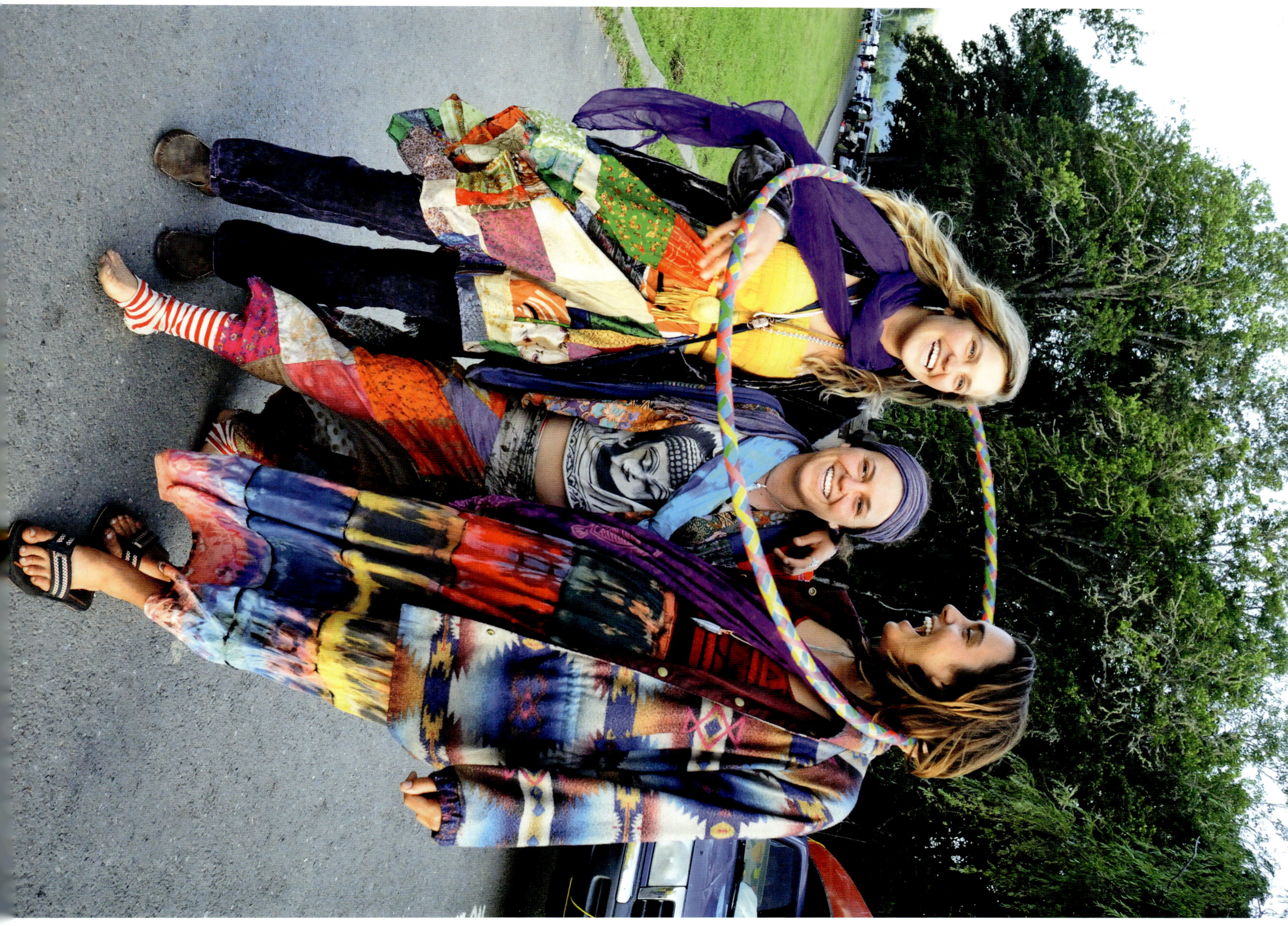

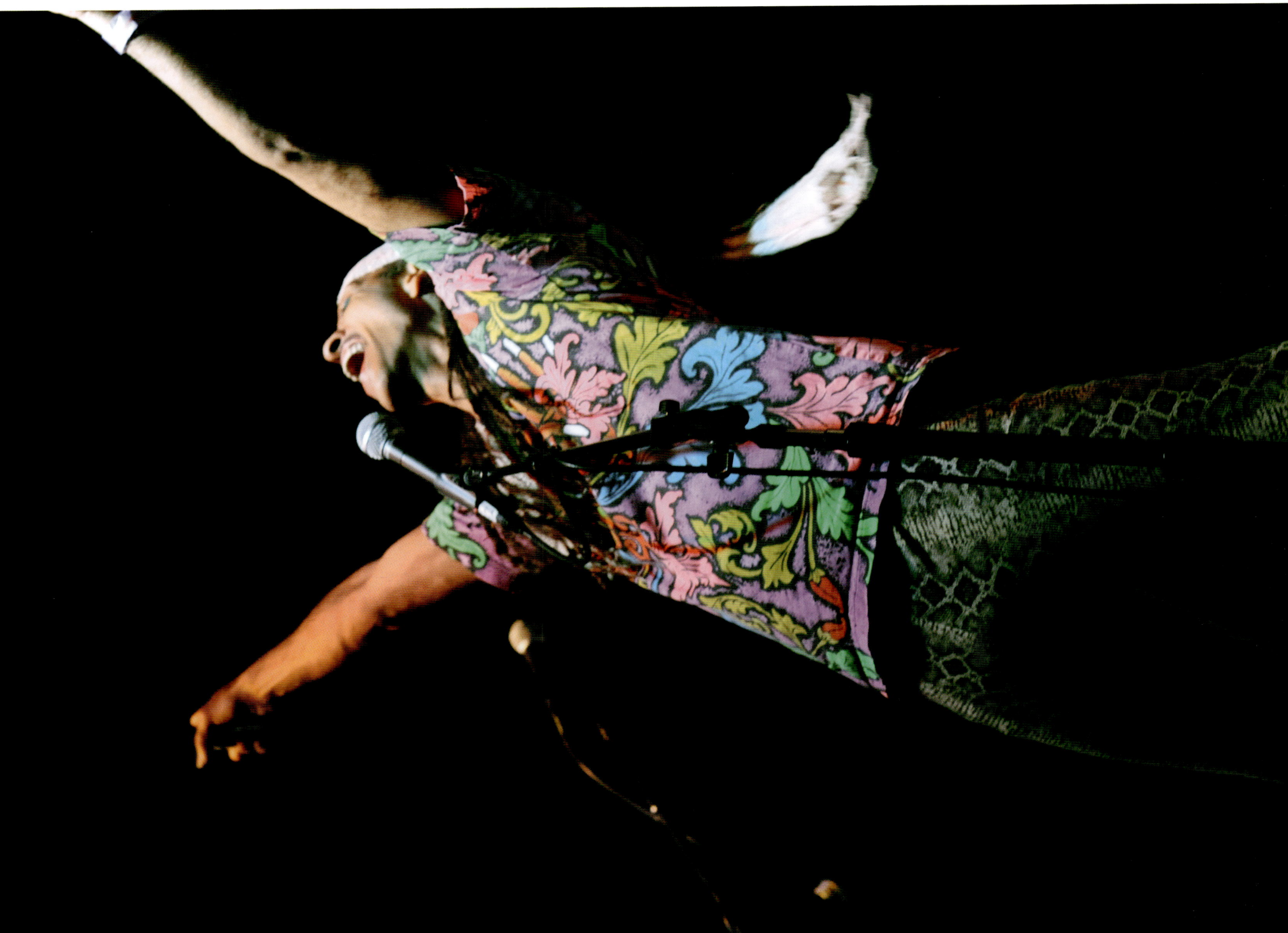

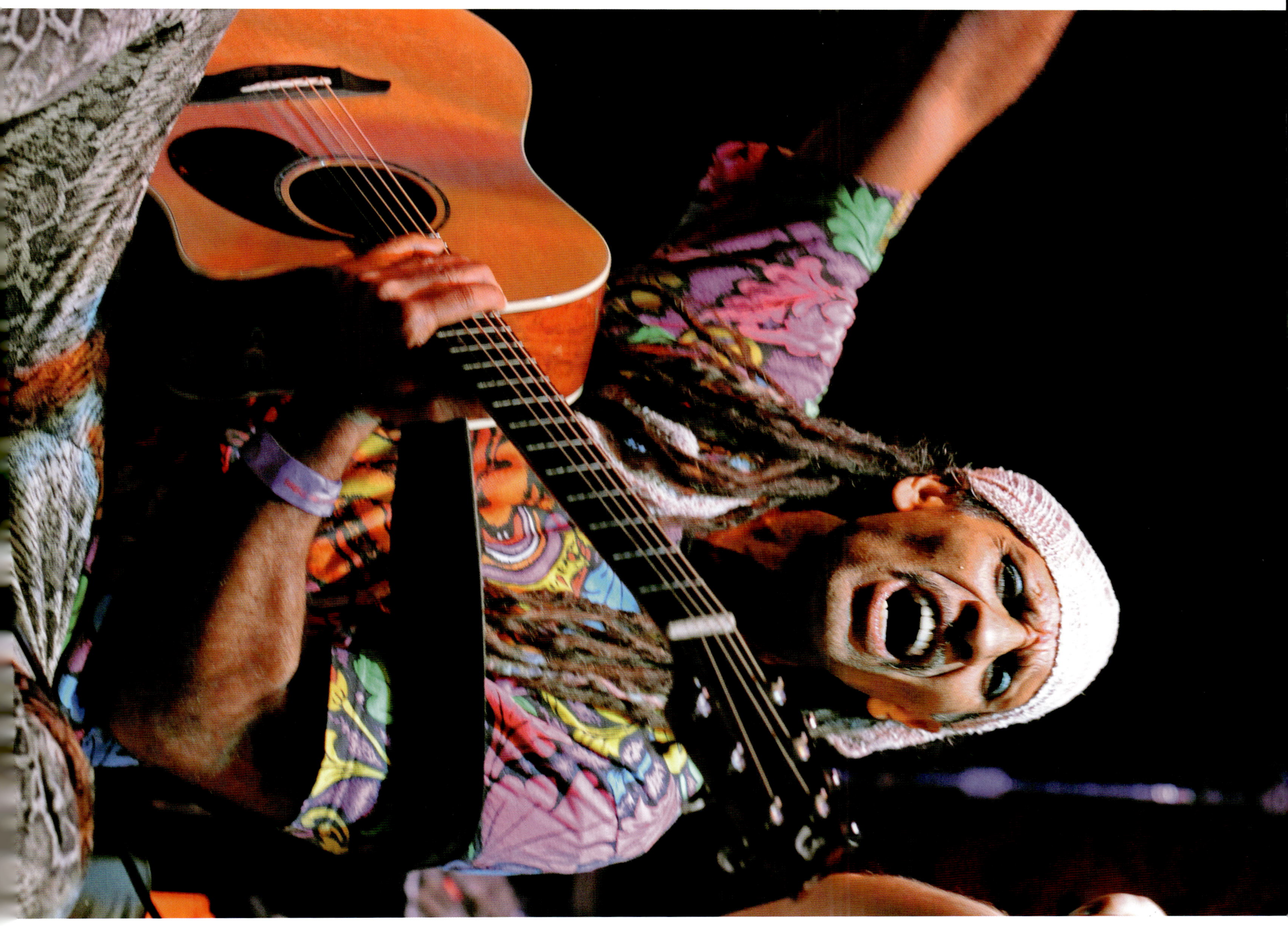

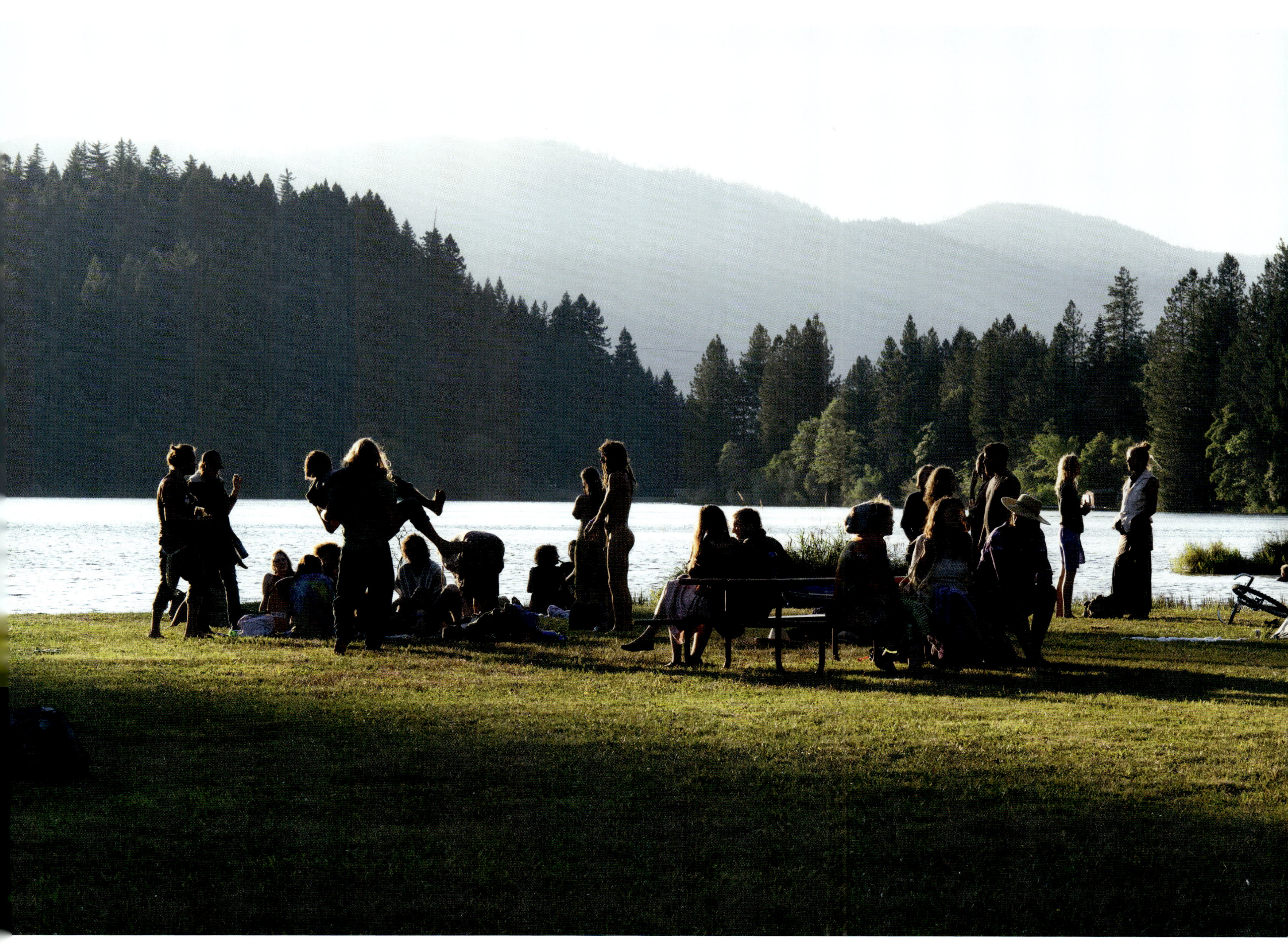

Shangri-La, Minnesota

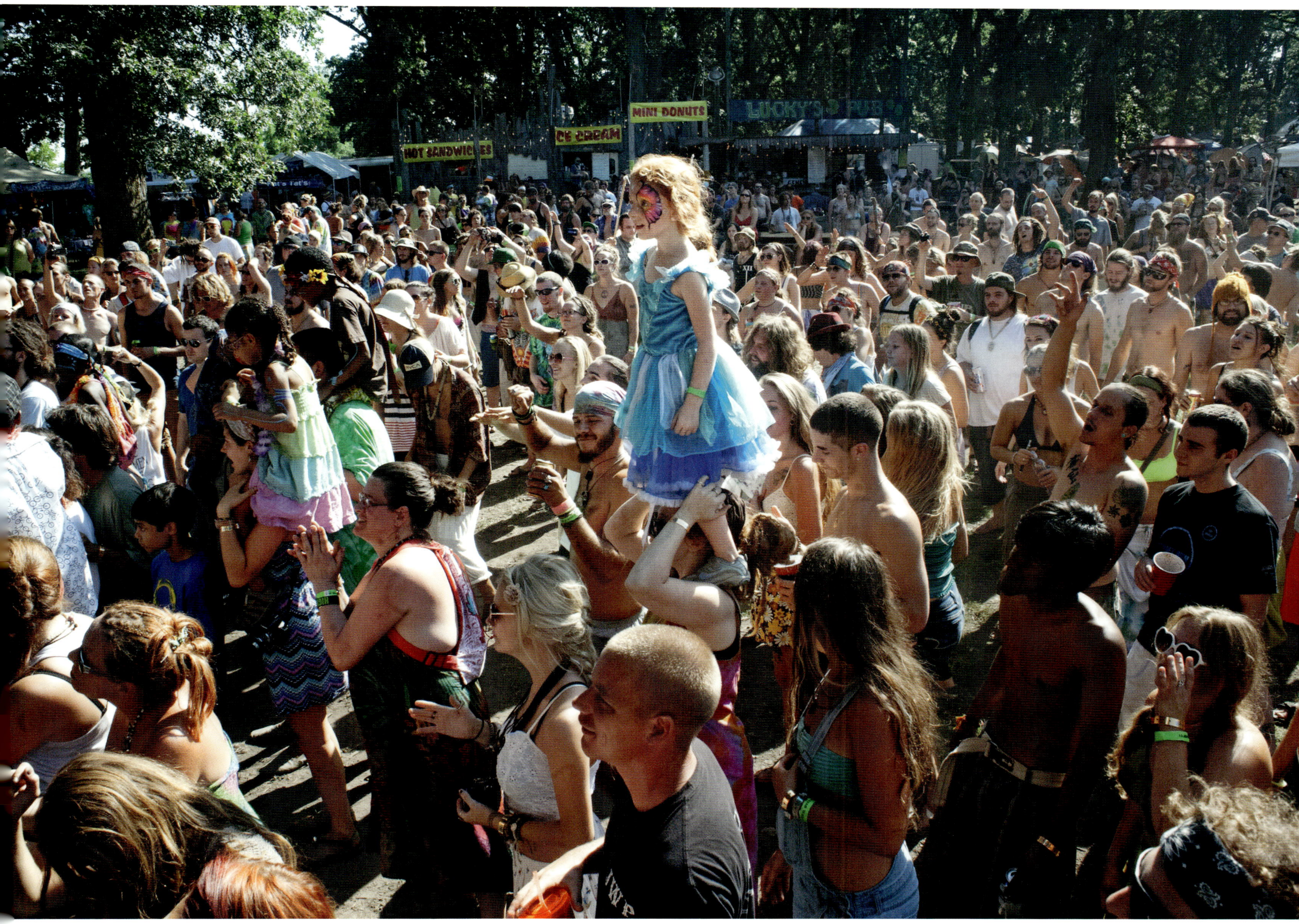

HOT SANDWICHES
ICE CREAM
MINI DONUTS
LUCKY'S PUB

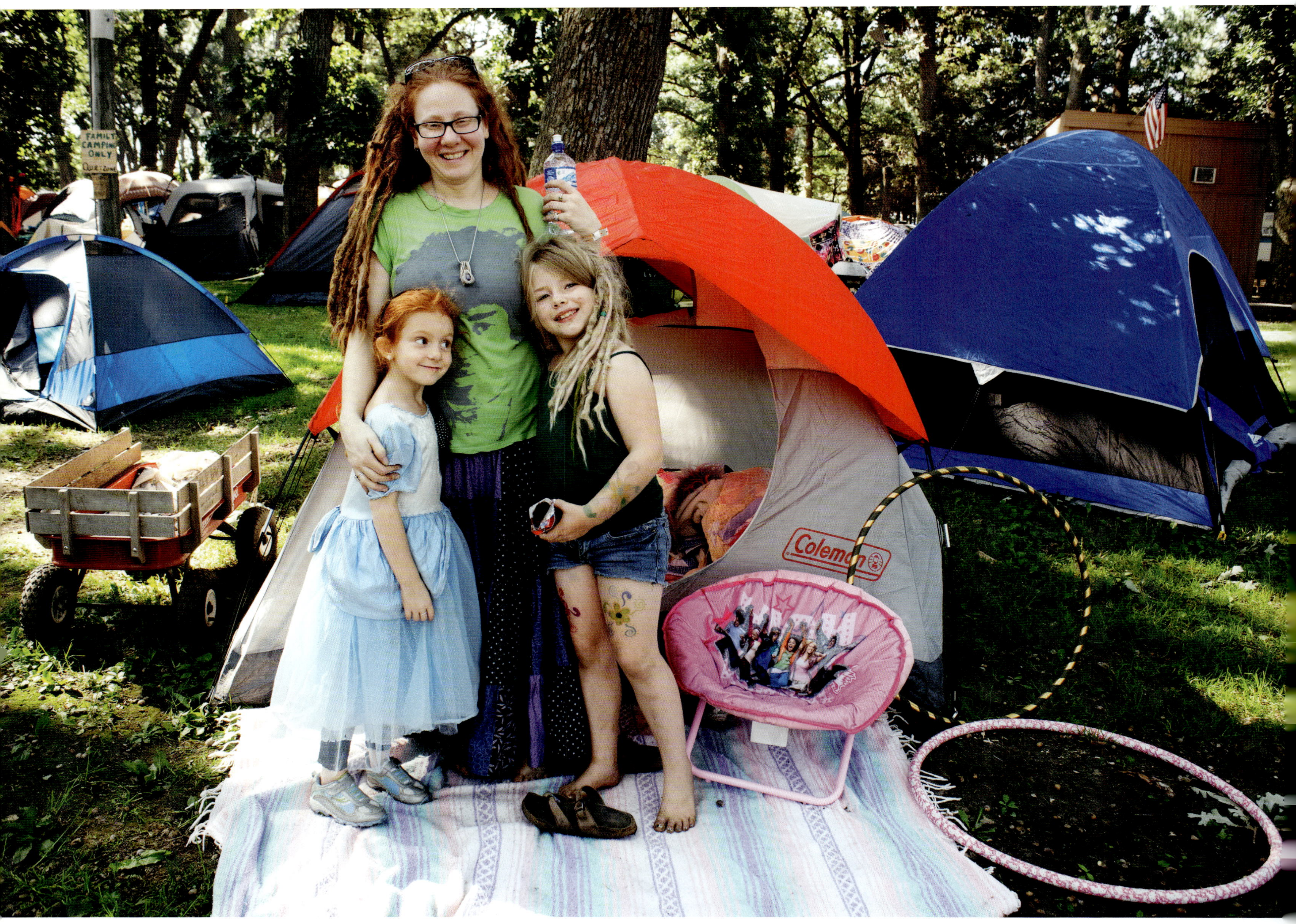

FAMILY
CAMPING
ONLY
Coleman

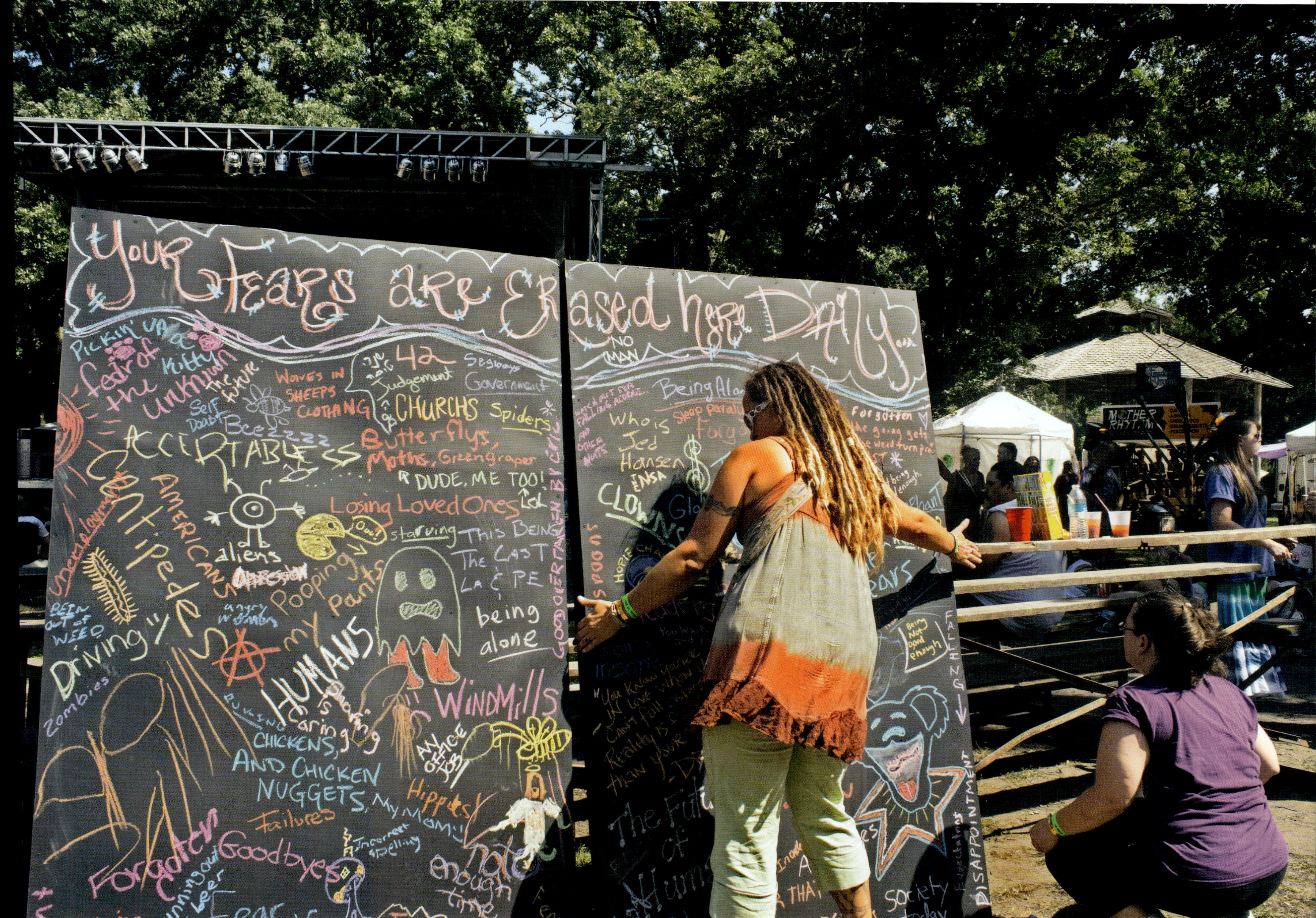

Your Fears are Erased here Daily
Pickin' up a fear of the unknown
kitty
Wolves in Sheeps Clothing
The future
Self Doubt
Bee
42 Judgement
Segways
Government
NO MAN
Being Alone
Who is Jed Hansen ENSA
Sleep Paralysis
Forgotten
When the going gets tough the weed turn pro
CHURCHS
Spiders
CLOWNS
Butterflys, Moths, Greengrapes
DUDE, ME TOO!
ACCEPTABLE
AMERICAN CENTIPEDES
Losing Loved Ones
starving
THIS BEING THE LAST LARGE PE
aliens
Oppression
Pooping my pants
being alone
Bein out of WEED
Driving
HUMANS
caring
Zombies
WINDMILLS
CHICKENS, AND CHICKEN NUGGETS, My Mom!
AN OFFICE OF
Hippies!
Failures
Forgoten
Goodbyes
running out of beer
Incorrect Spelling
not enough time
The Future of Humans
society today
DISAPPOINTMENT
FALLING
Being Not Good enough

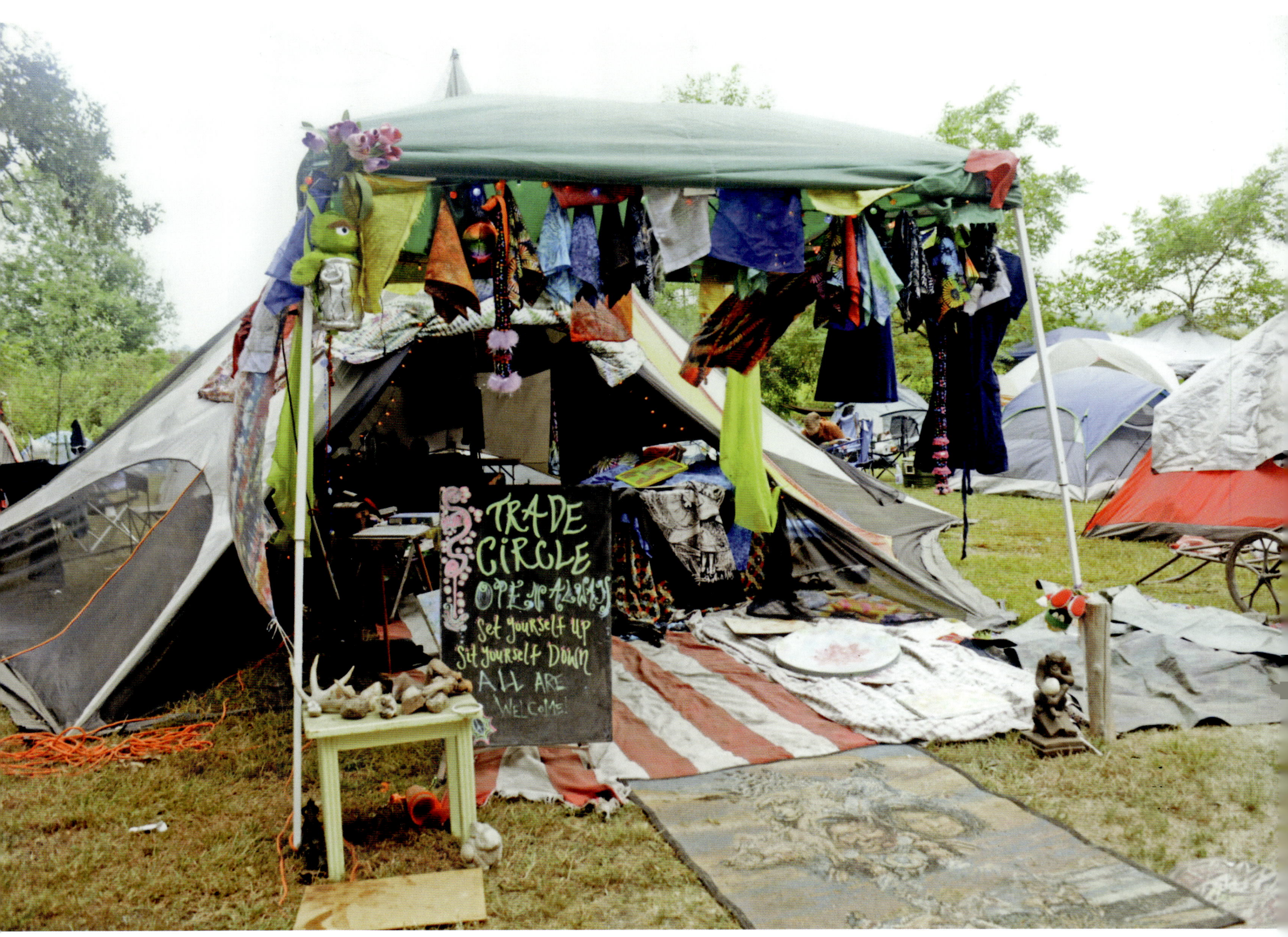
TRADE
CIRCLE
OPEN ALWAYS
Set Yourself Up
Sit Yourself Down
ALL ARE
WELCOME!

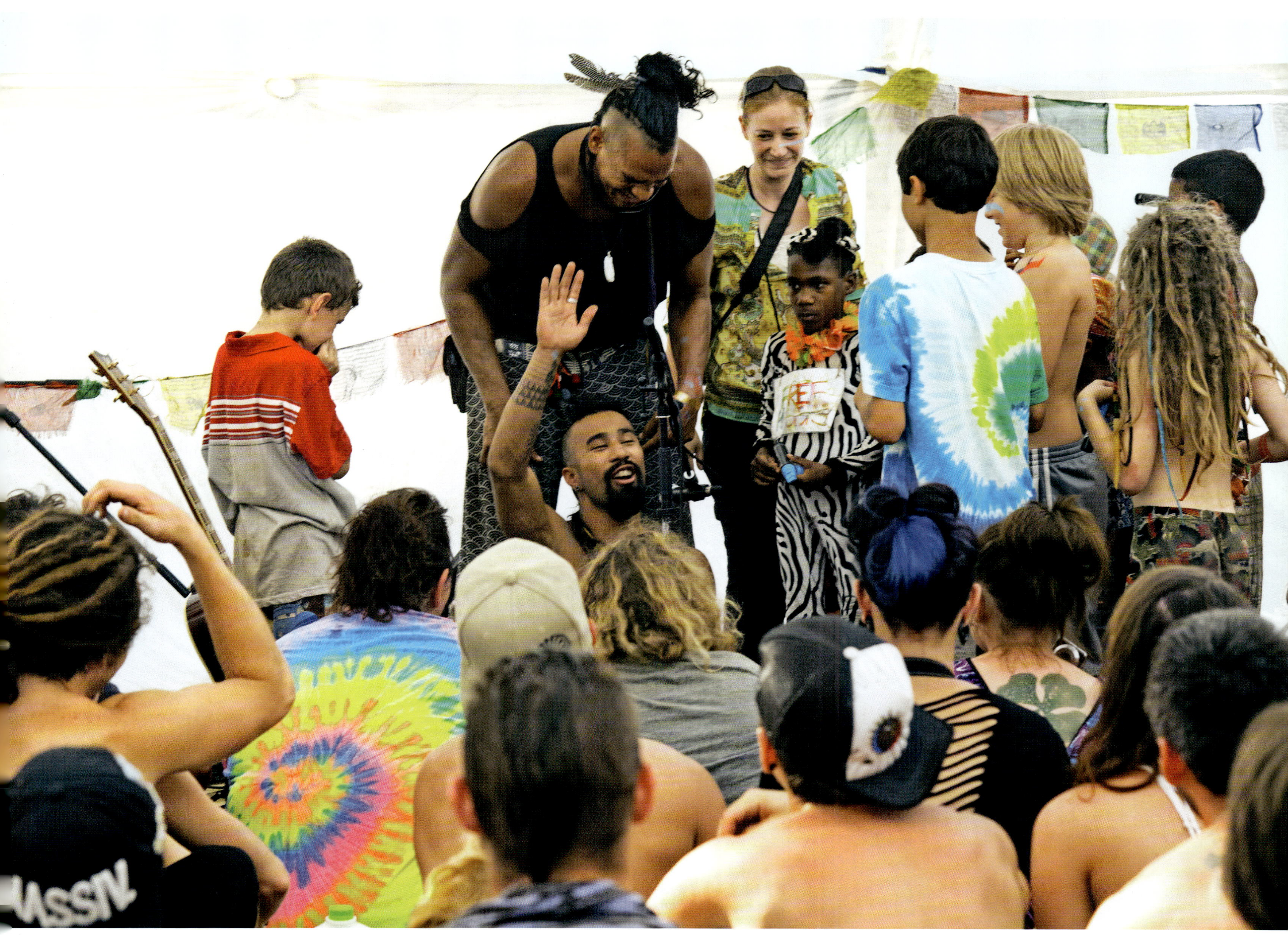

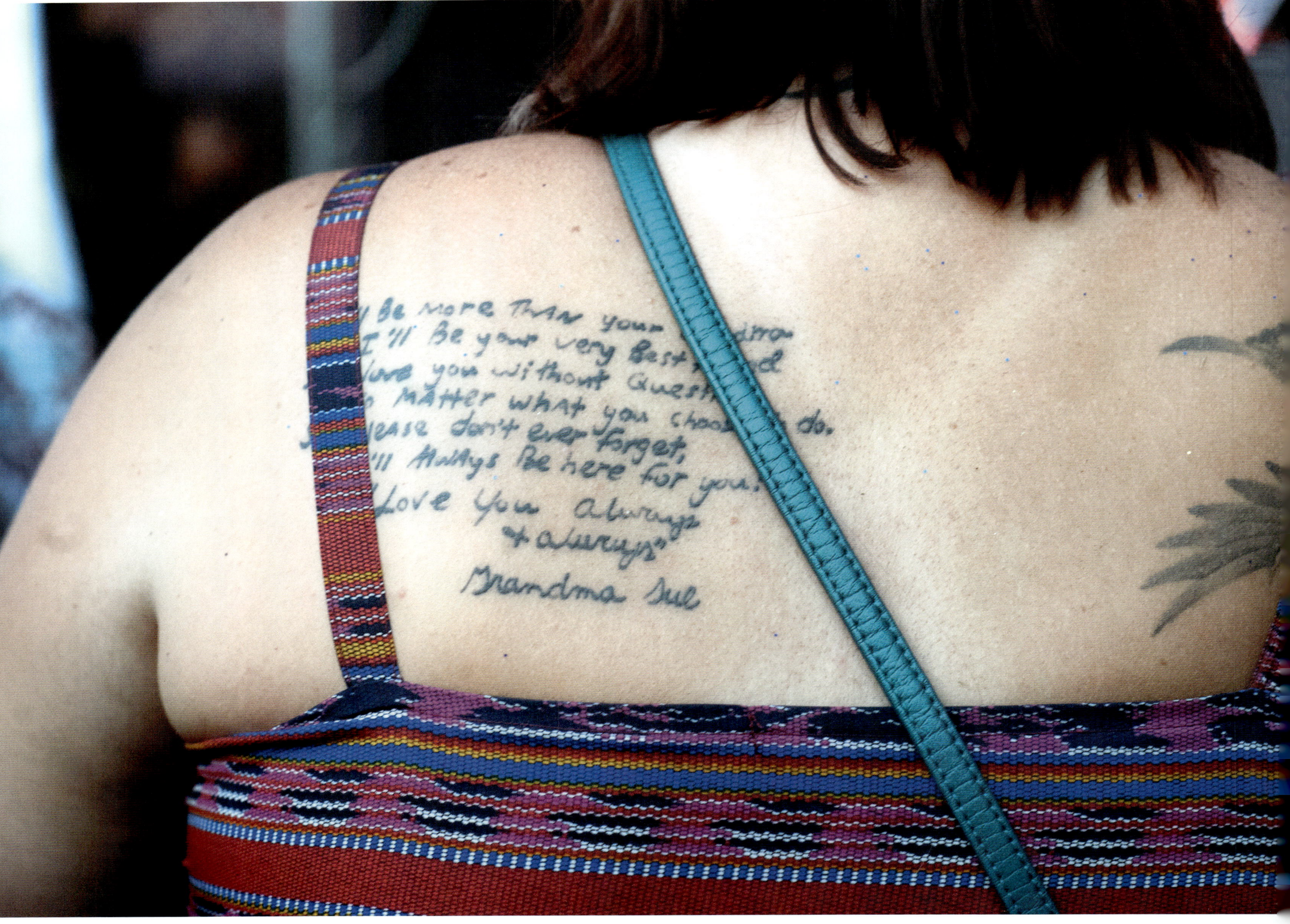
y Be more Than your
I 'll Be your very Best
love you without Quest
matter what you choo
ease don't ever forget,
'll Always Be here for you
Love You always
+ always"
Grandma Sue

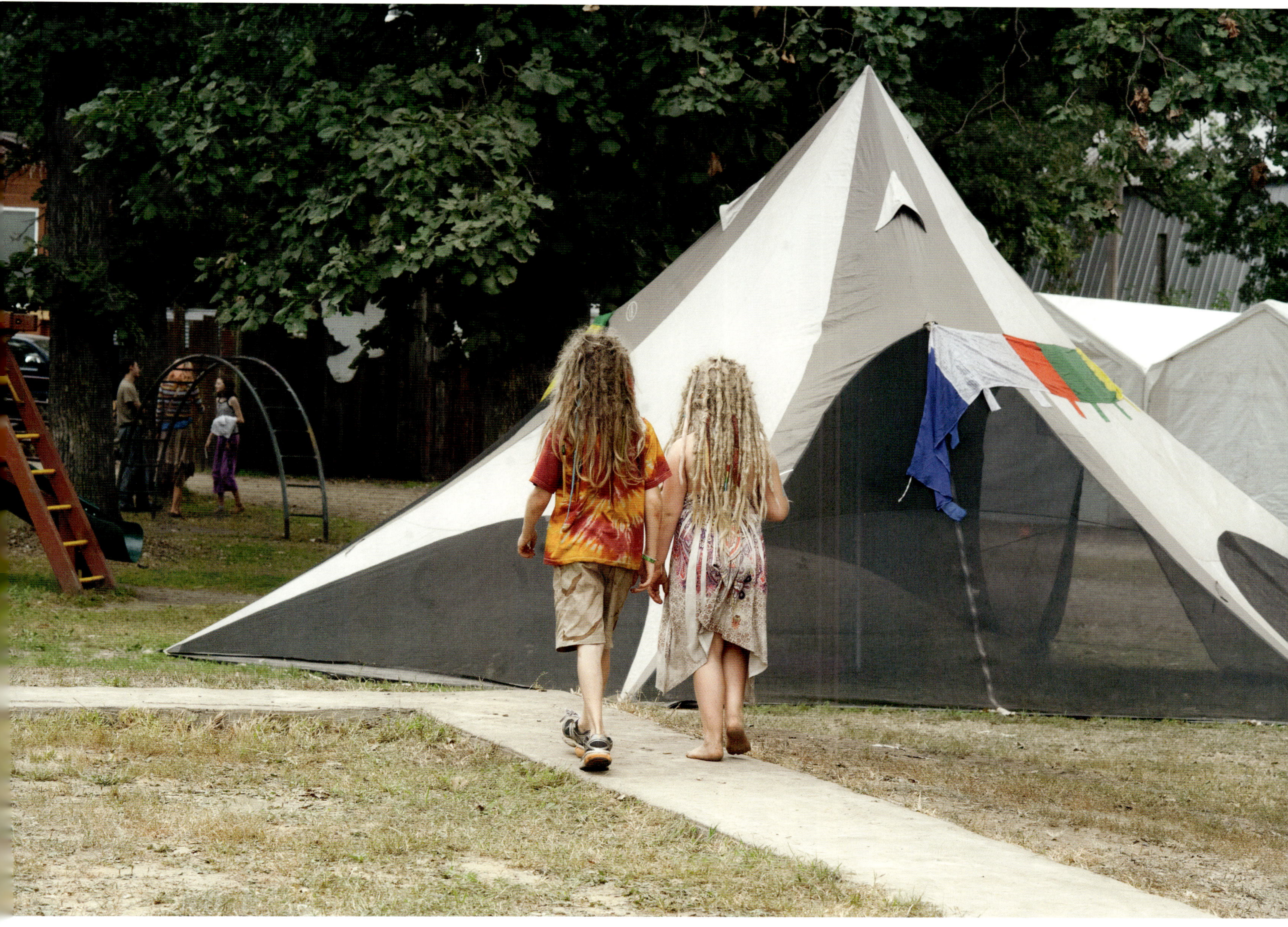

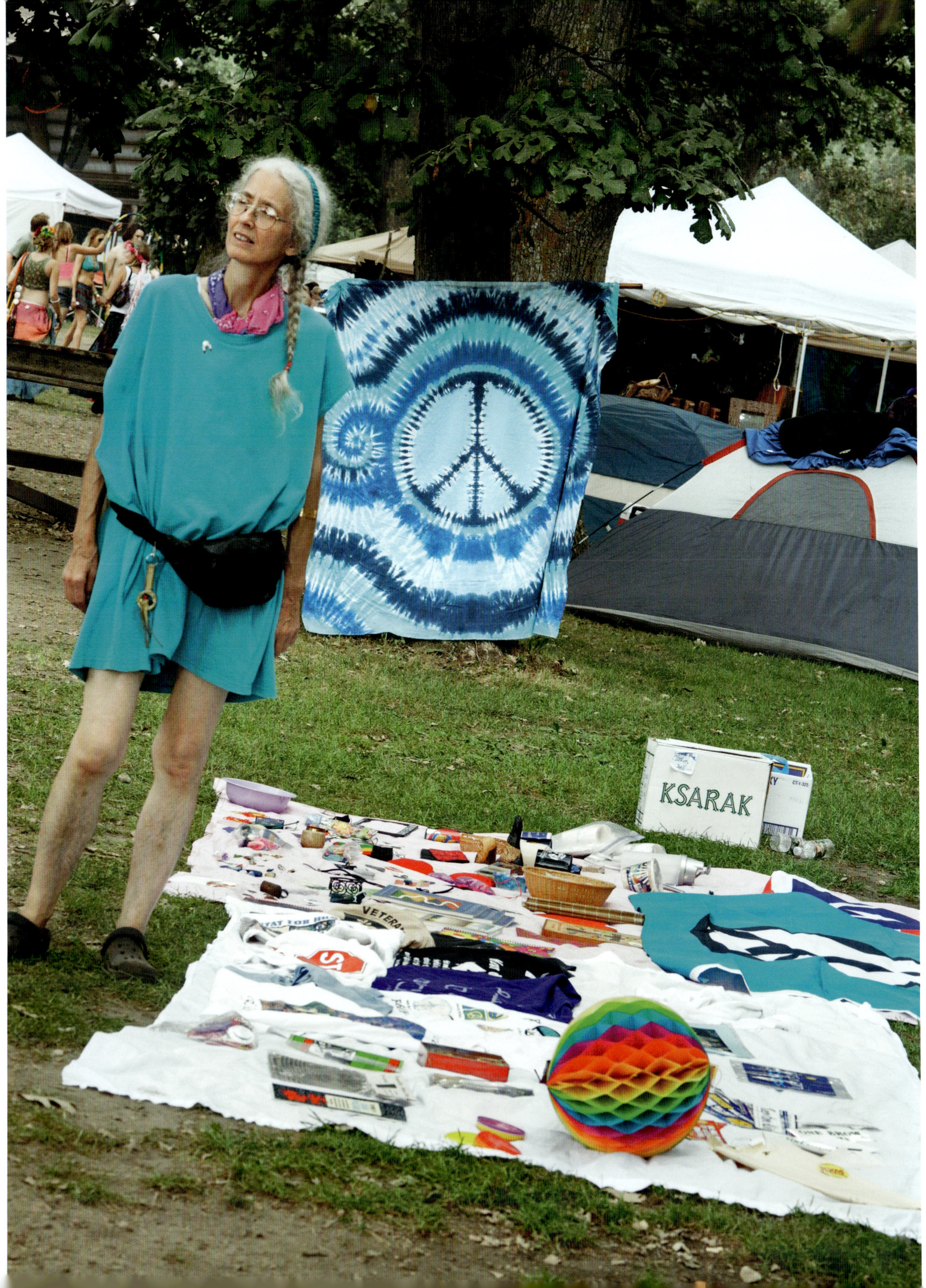
KSARAK

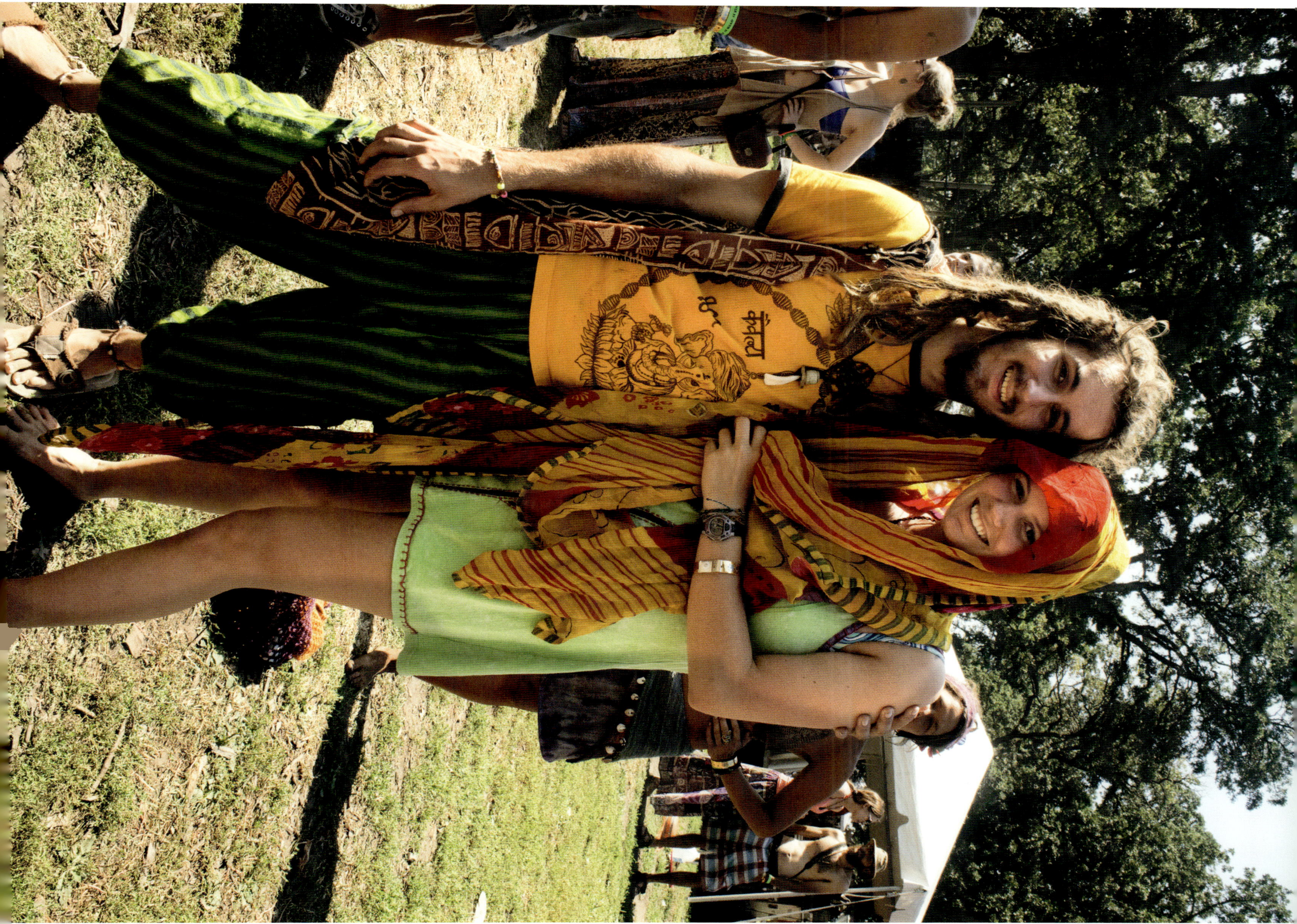

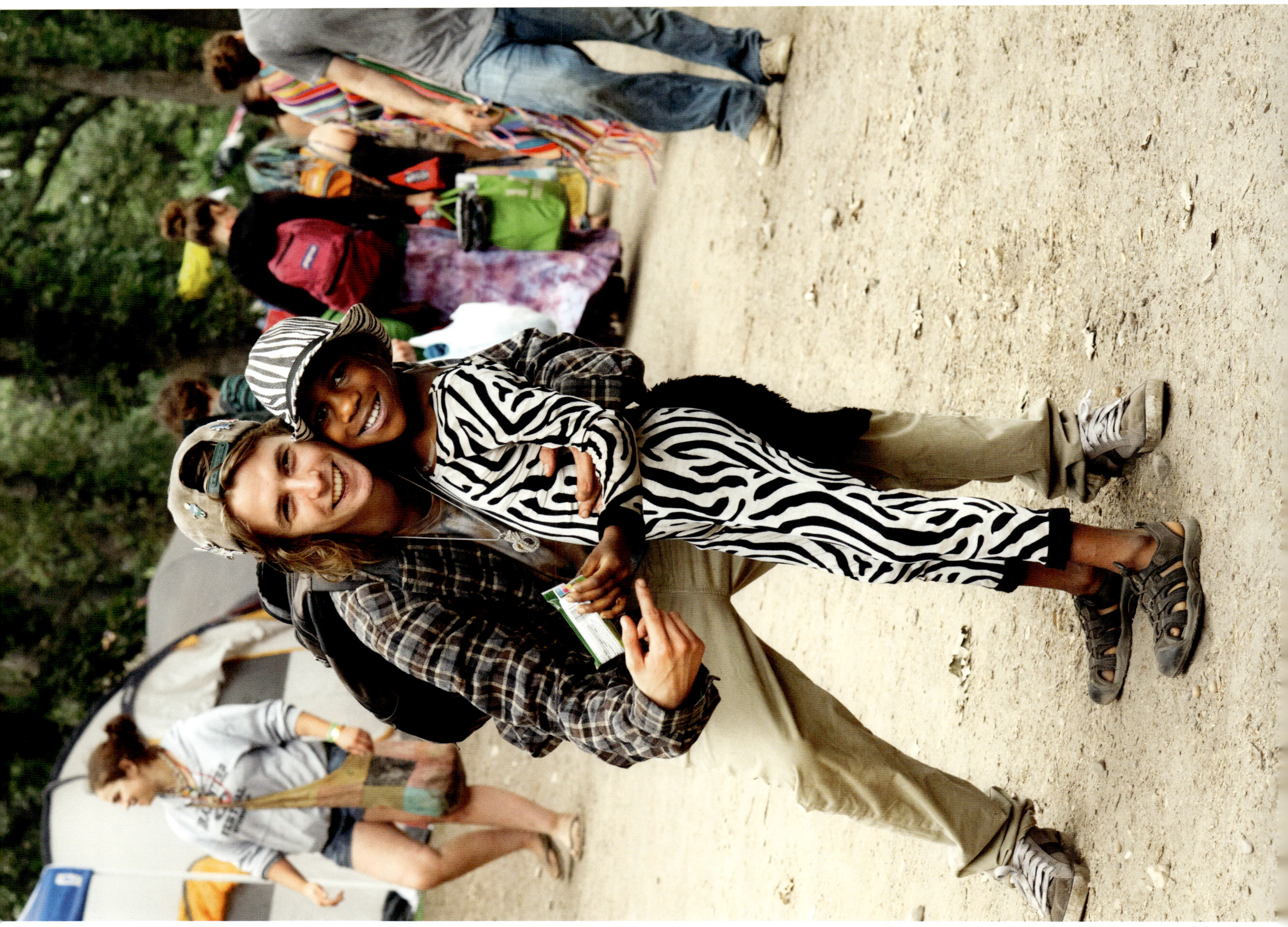

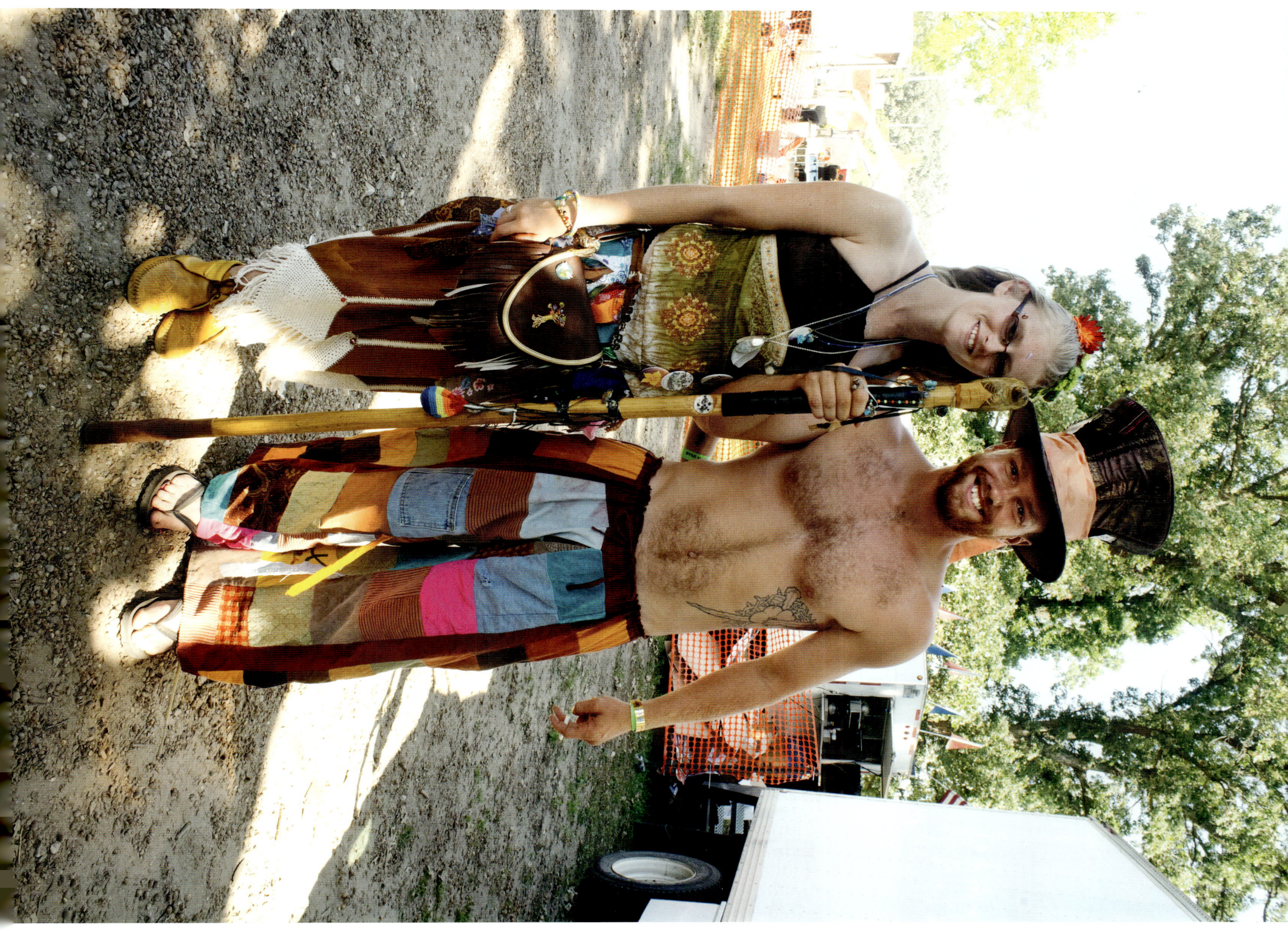

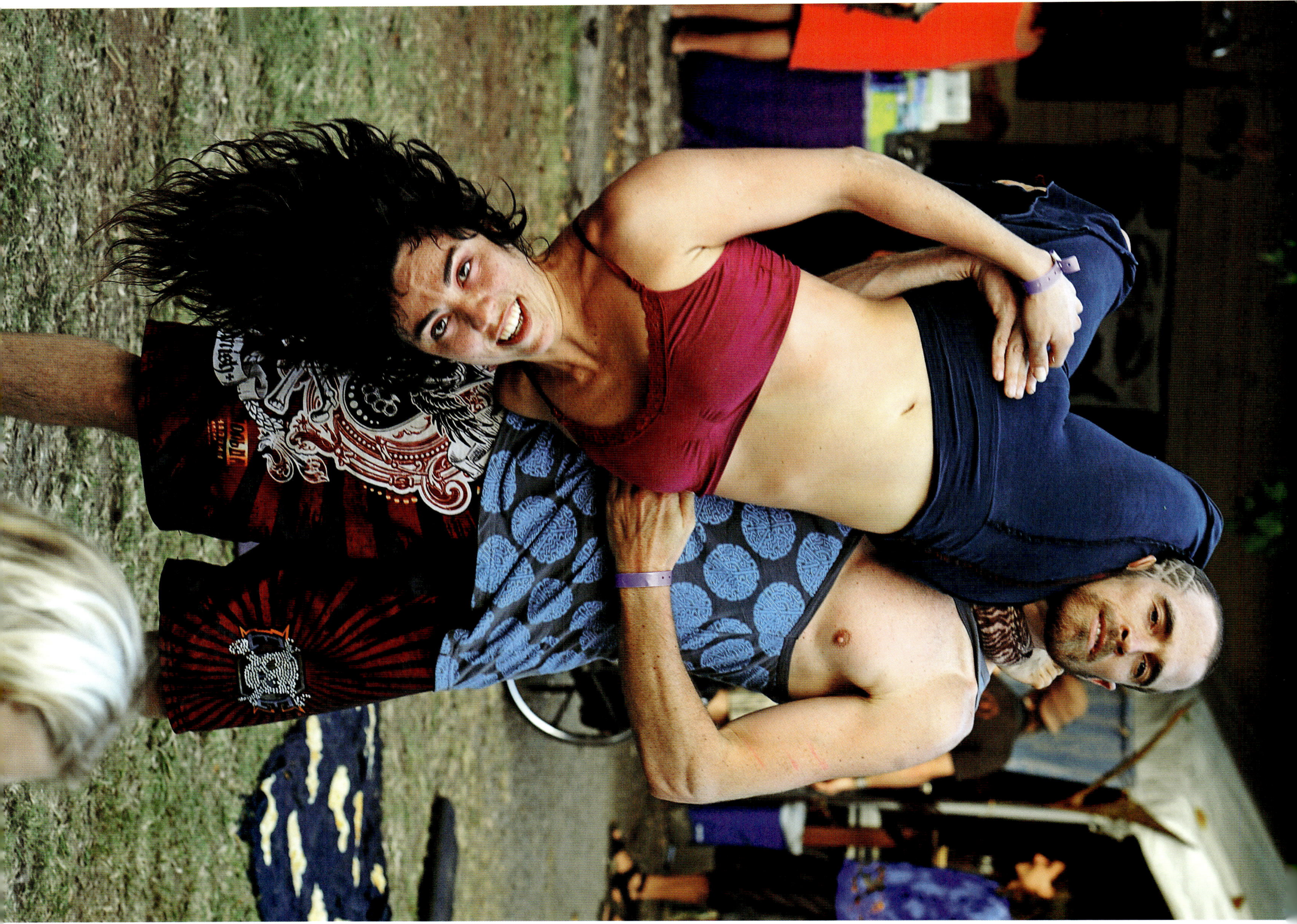

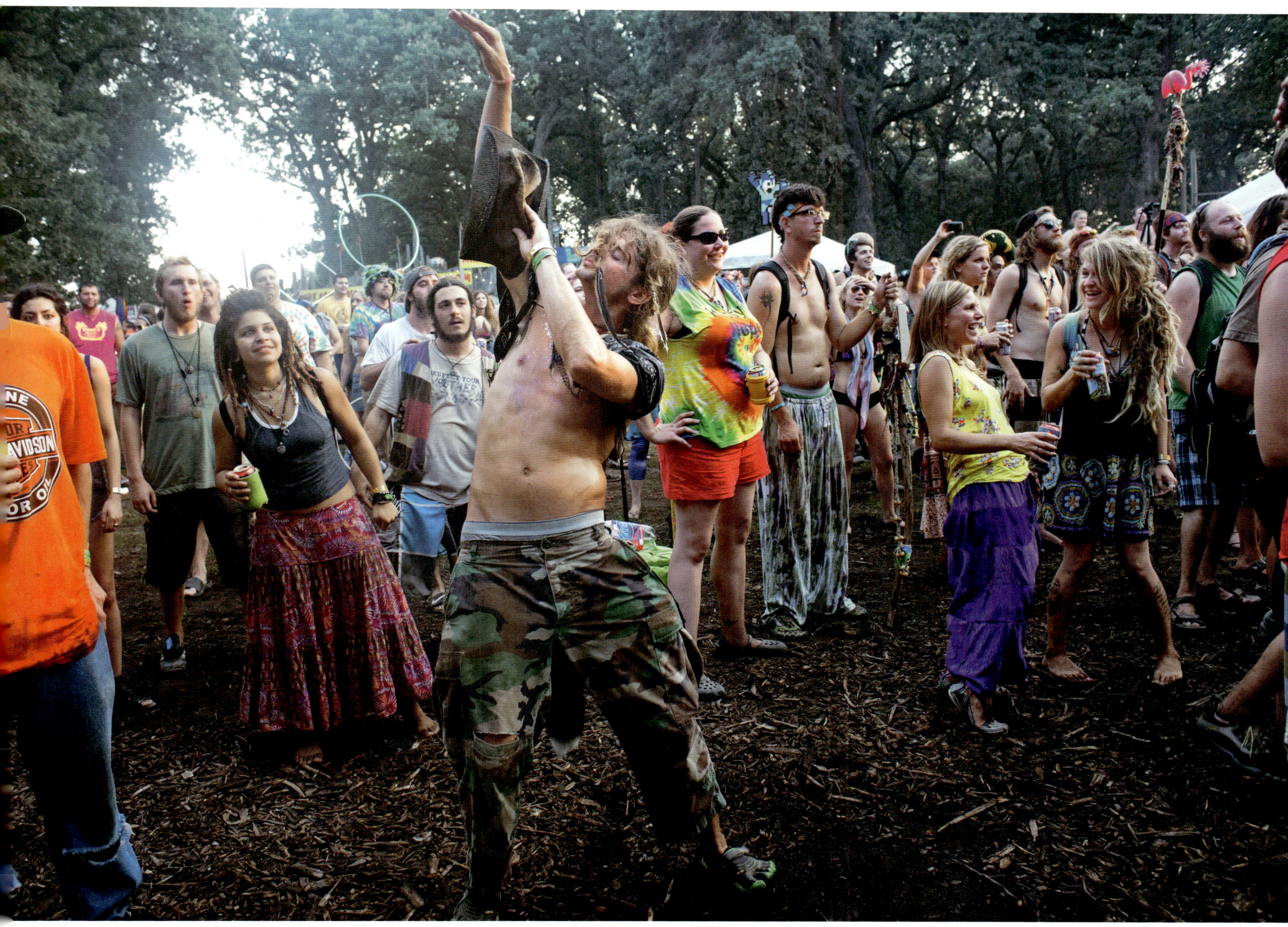

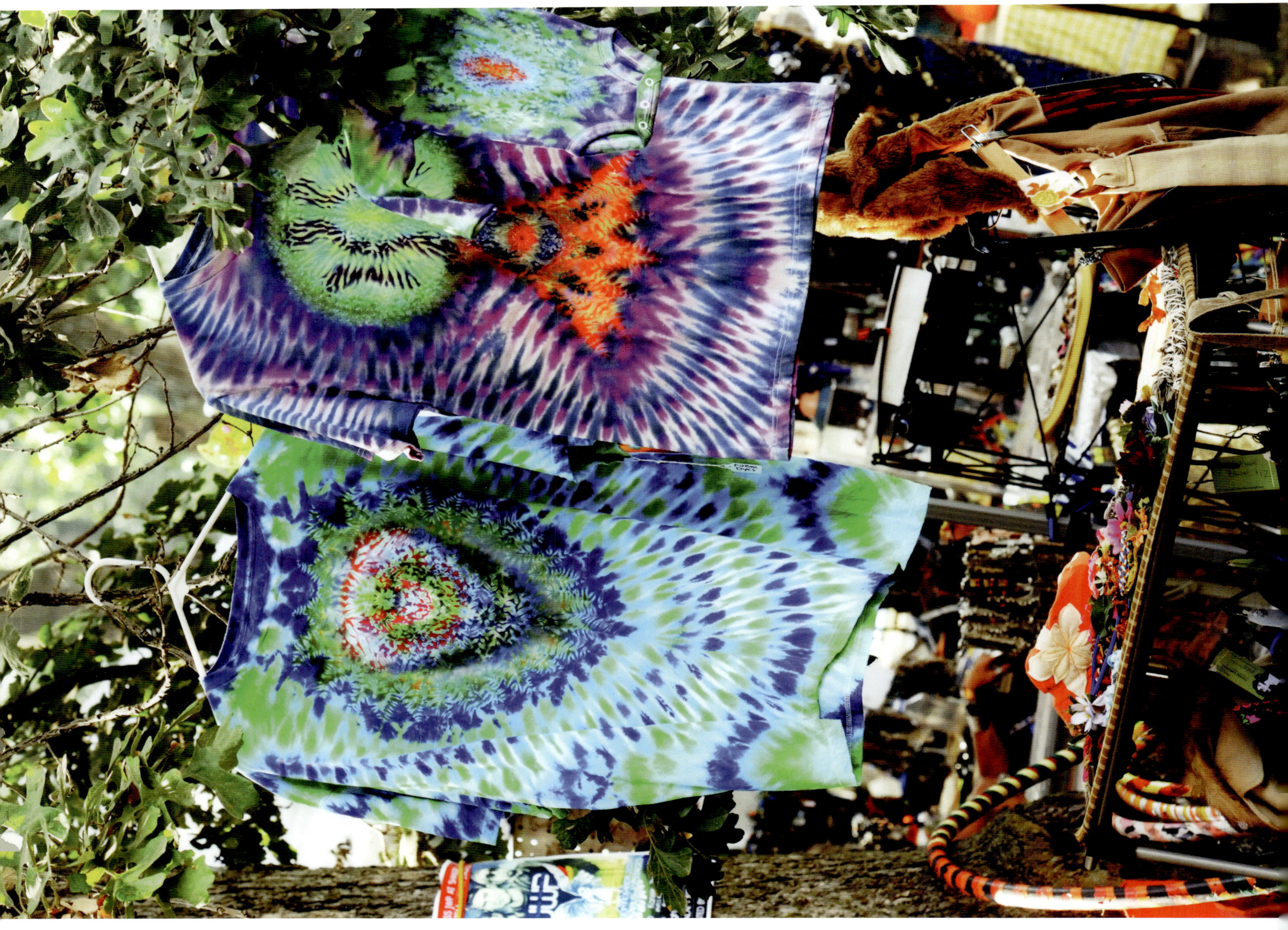

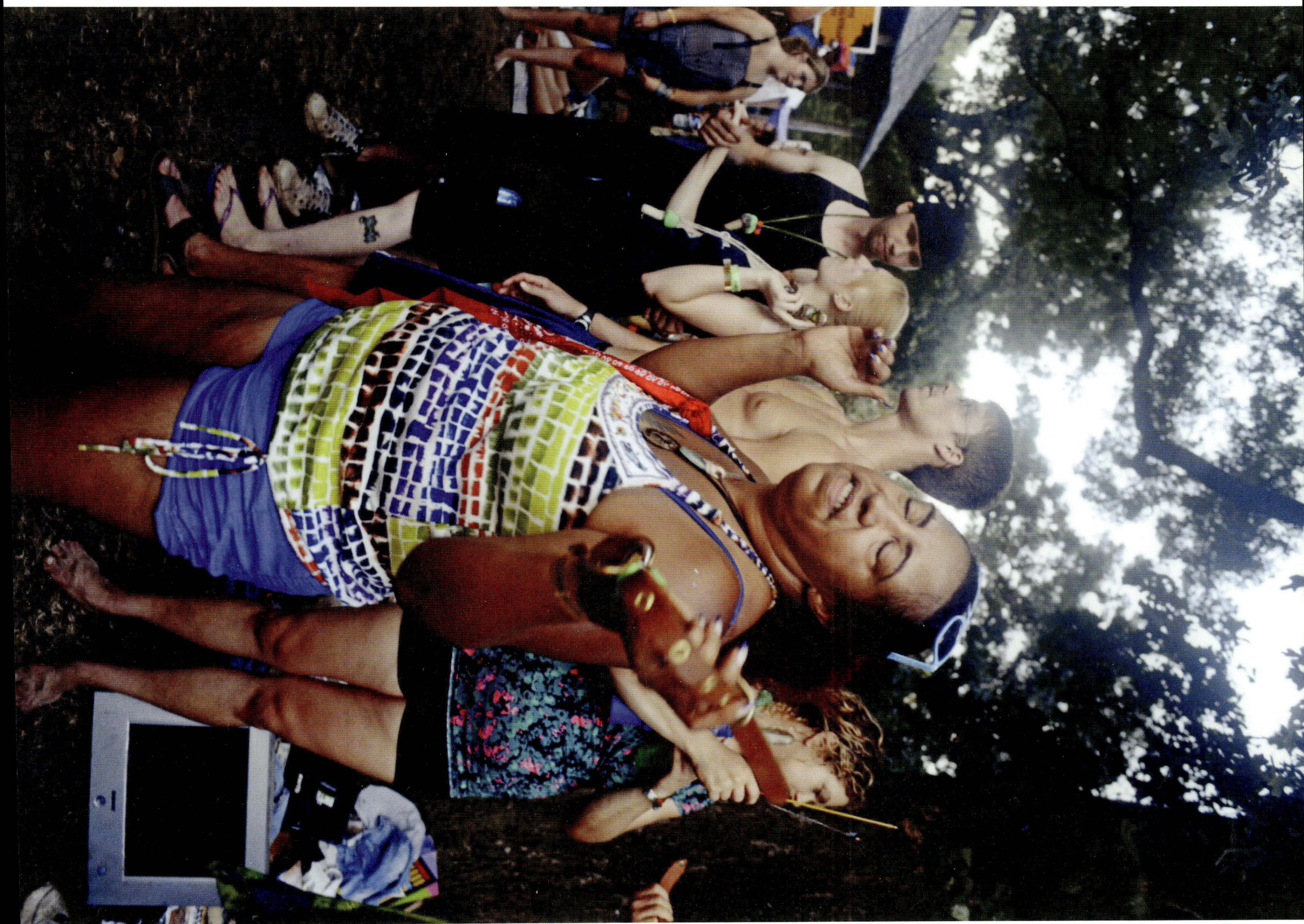

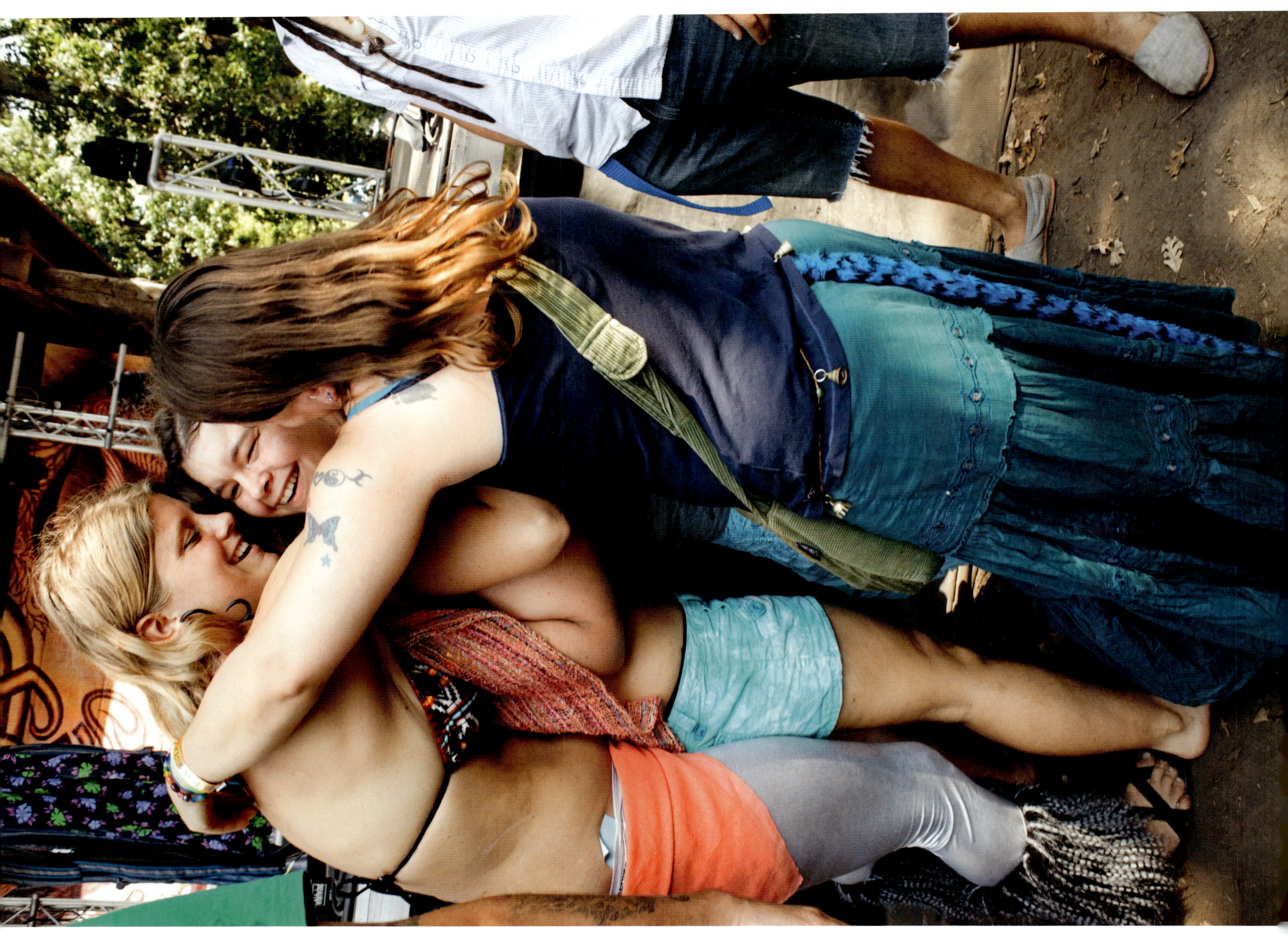

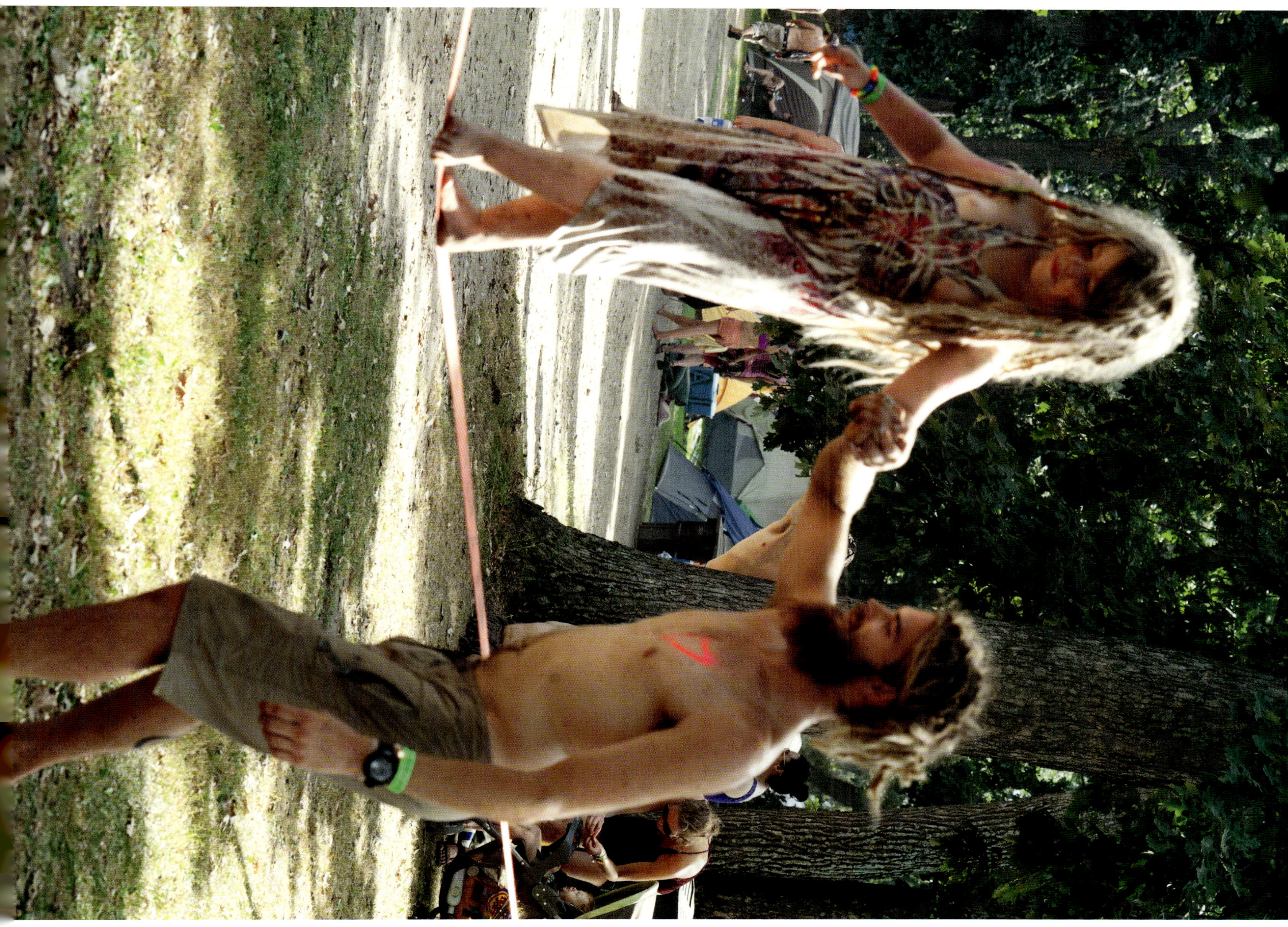

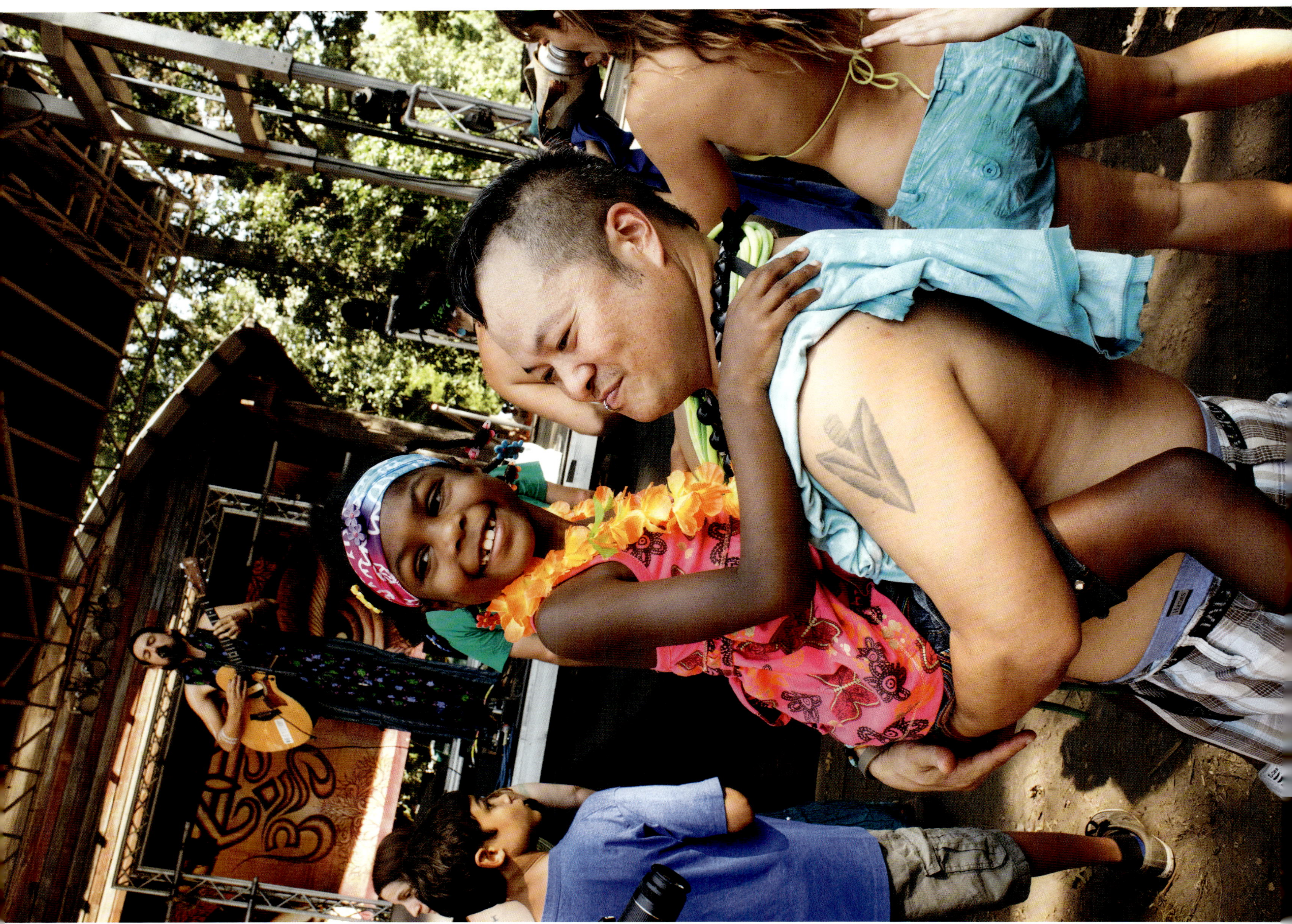

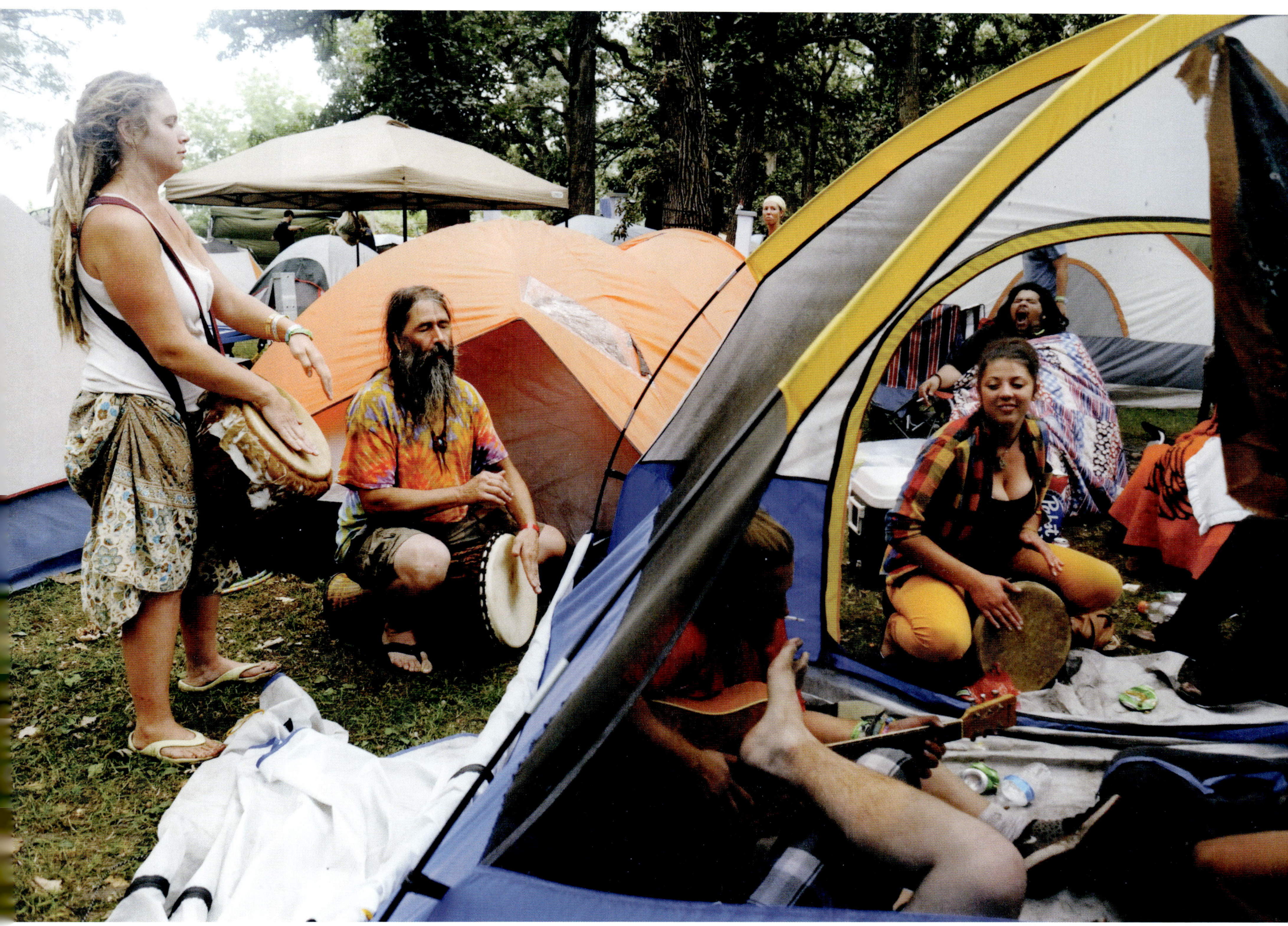

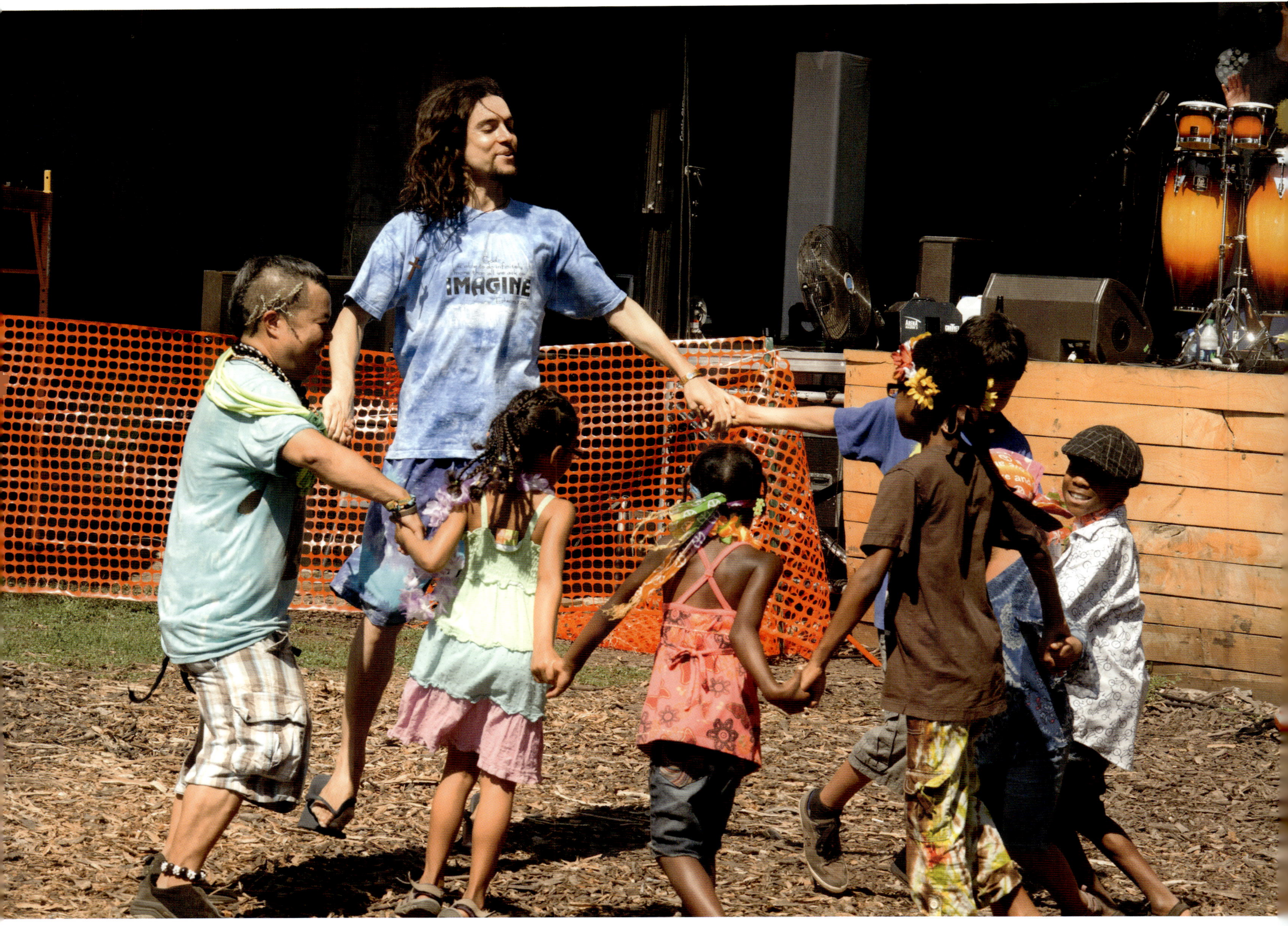
IMAGINE

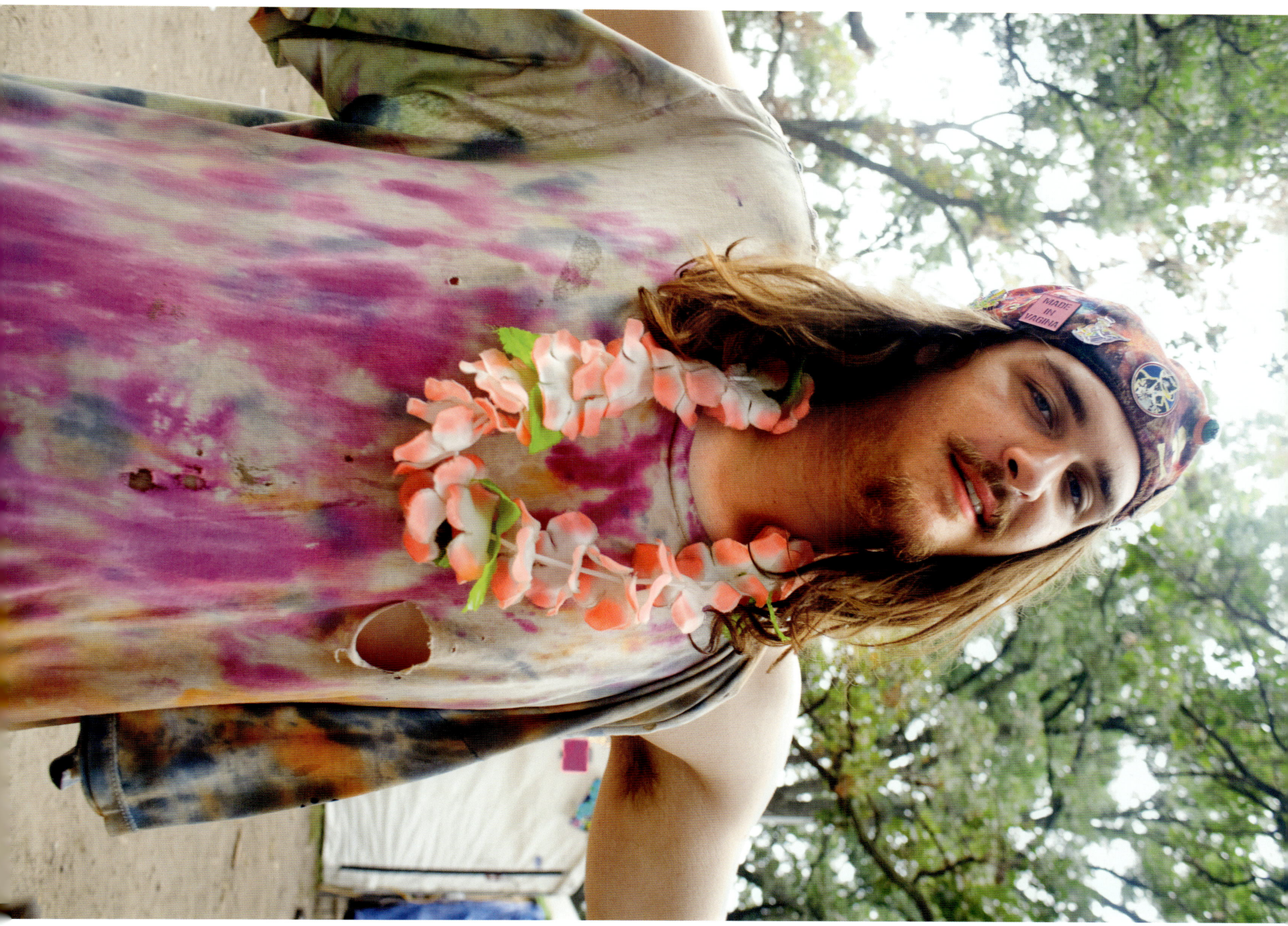
MADE
IN
VAGINA

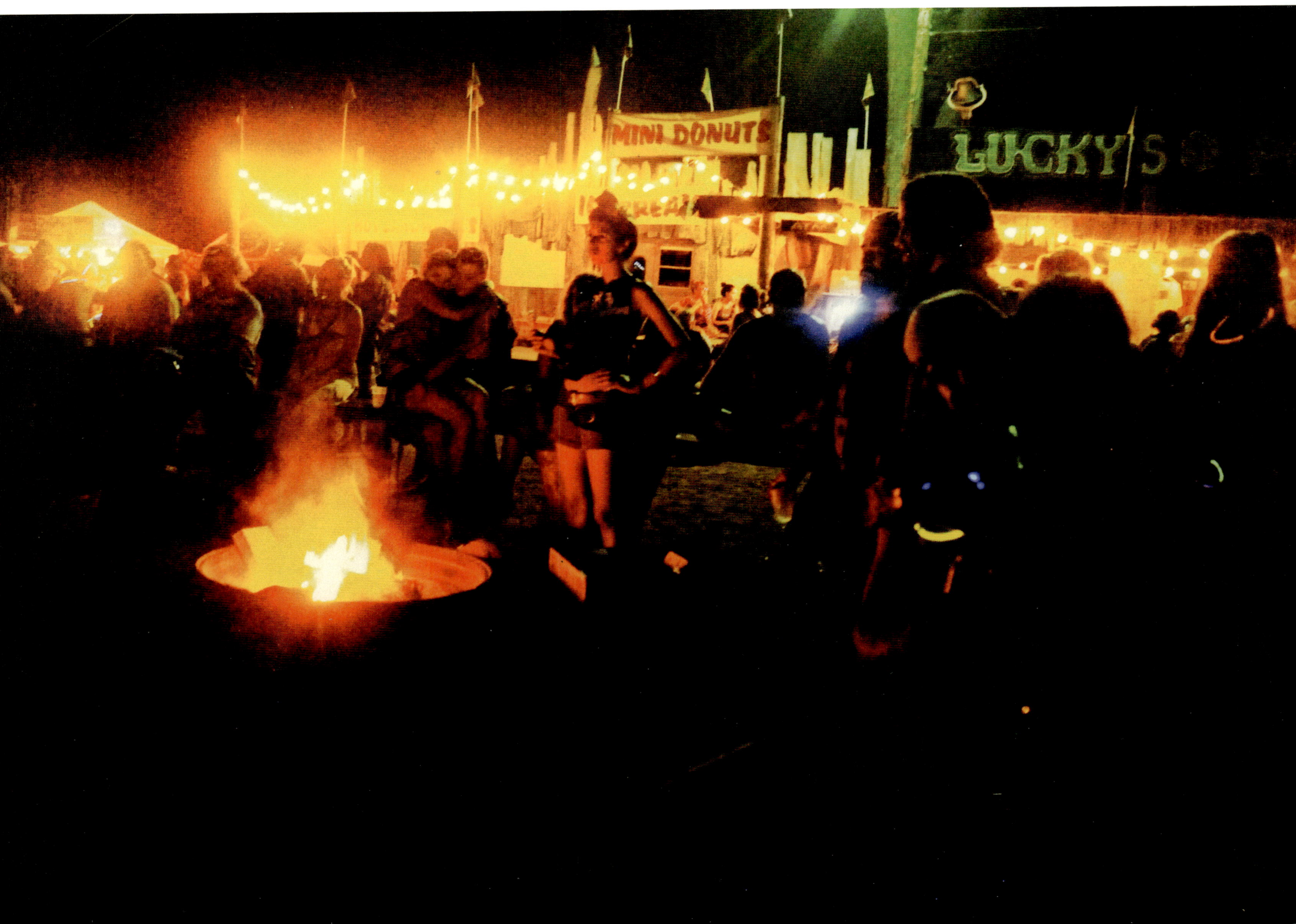

MINI DONUTS
LUCKY'S

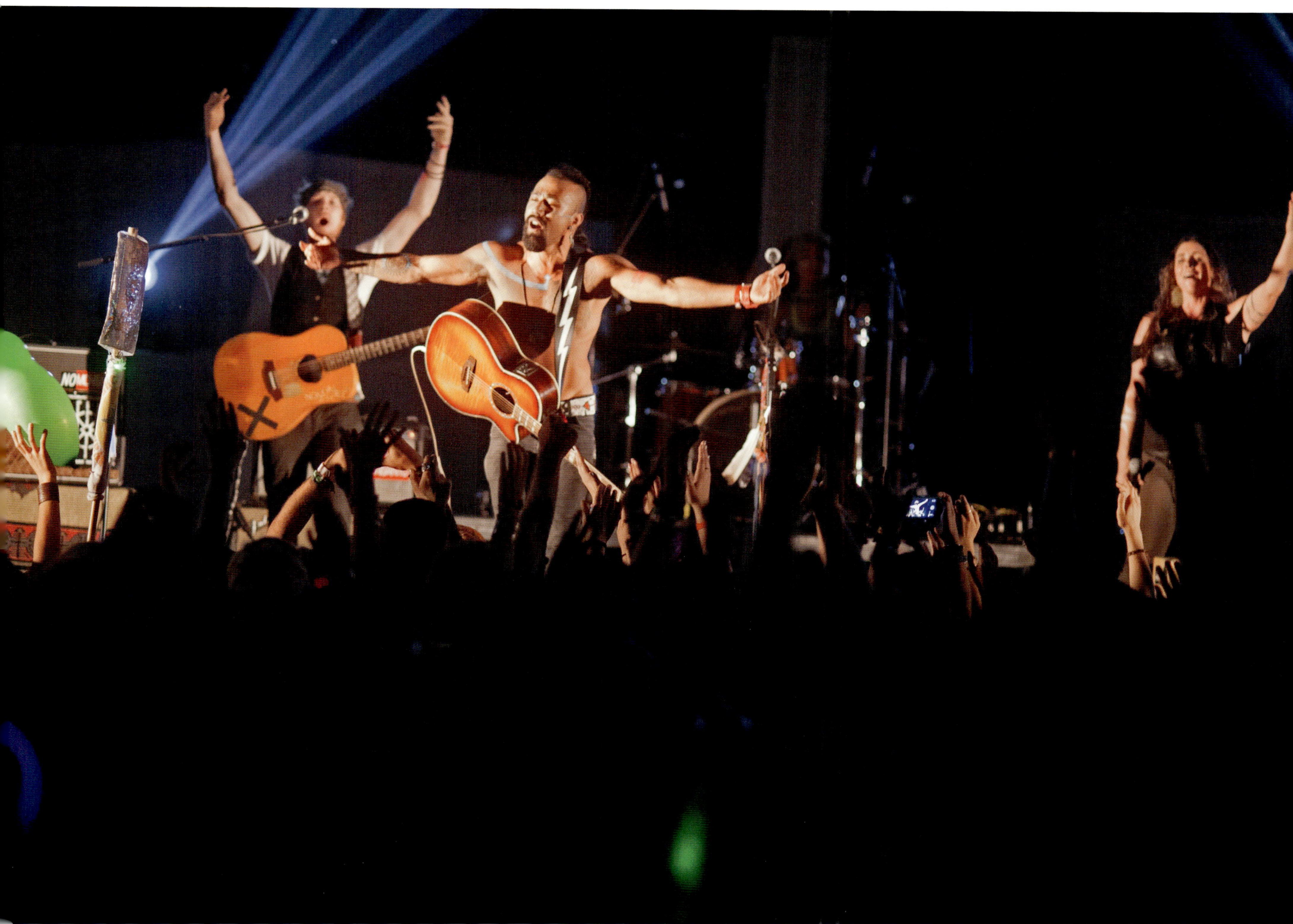

Hawaii

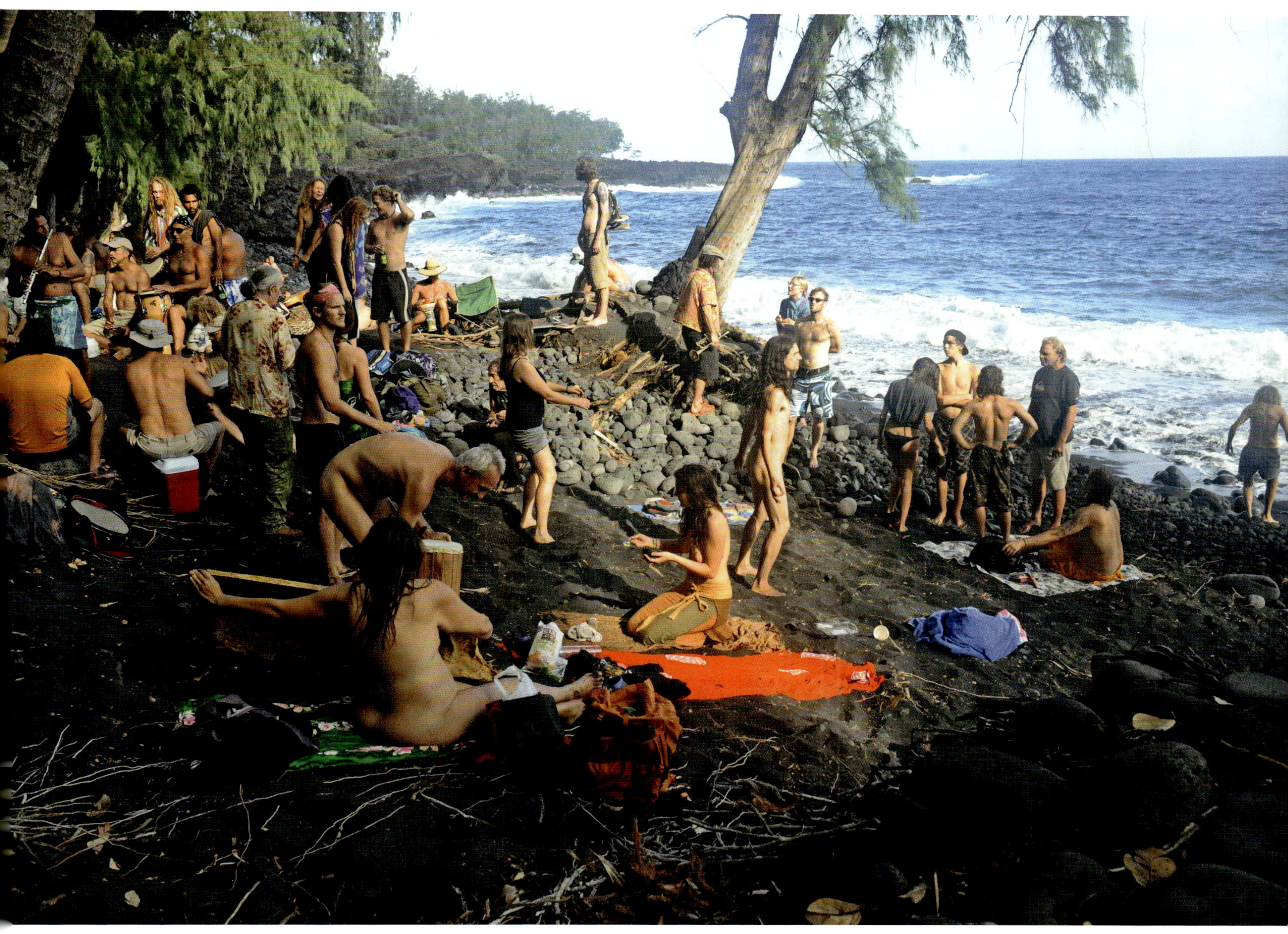

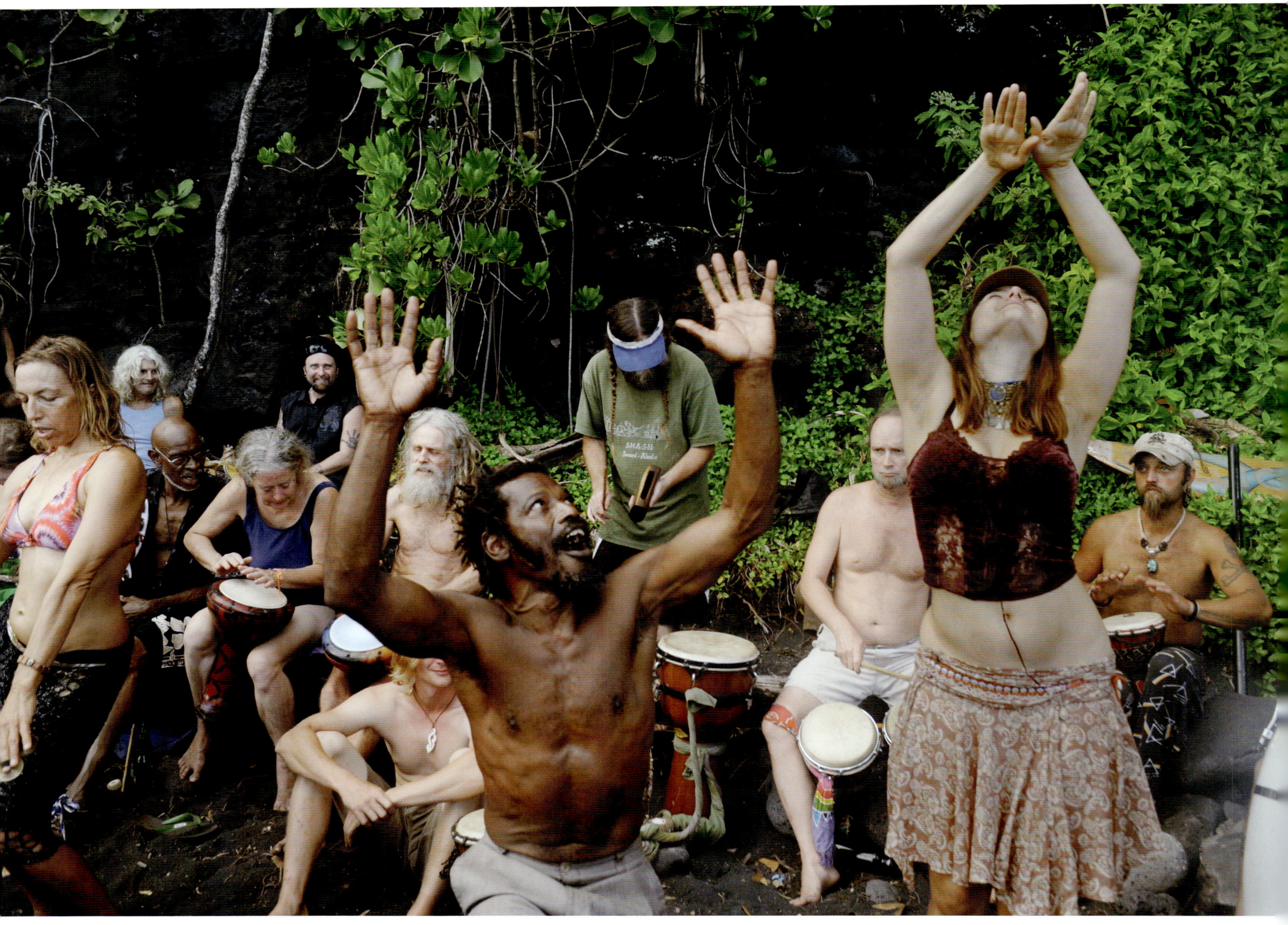

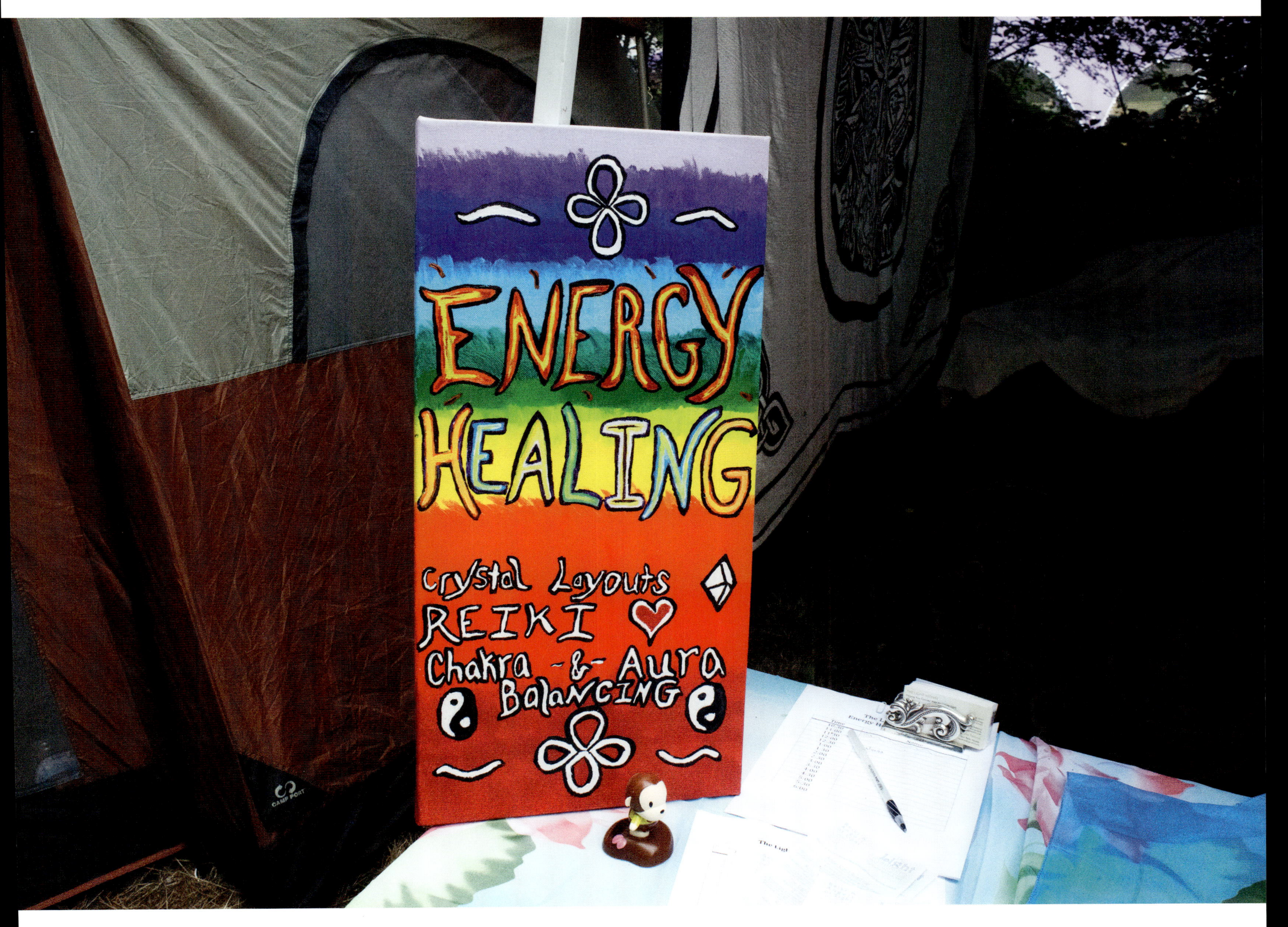
ENERGY
HEALING
Crystal Layouts
REIKI
Chakra - & - Aura
Balancing

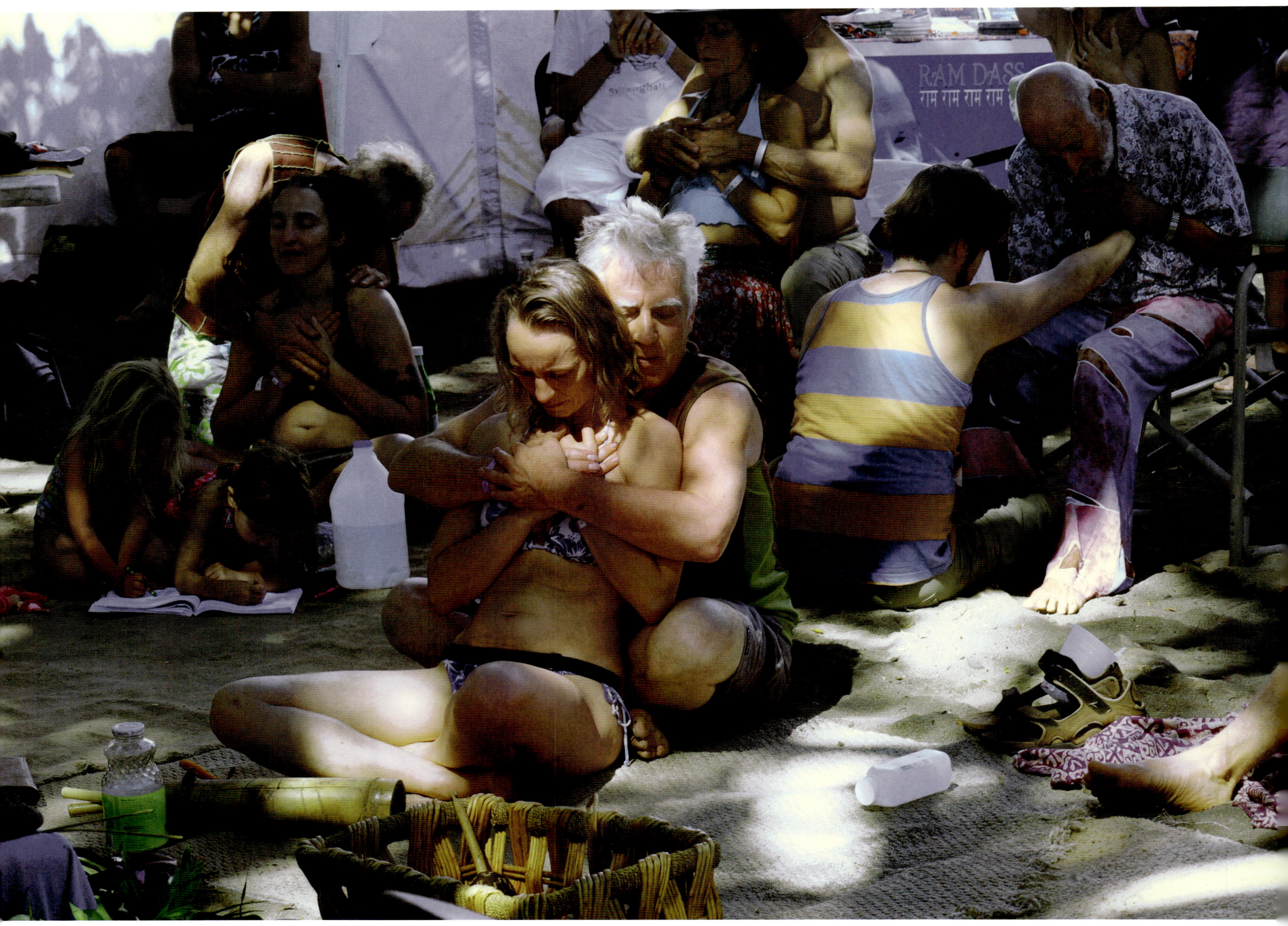

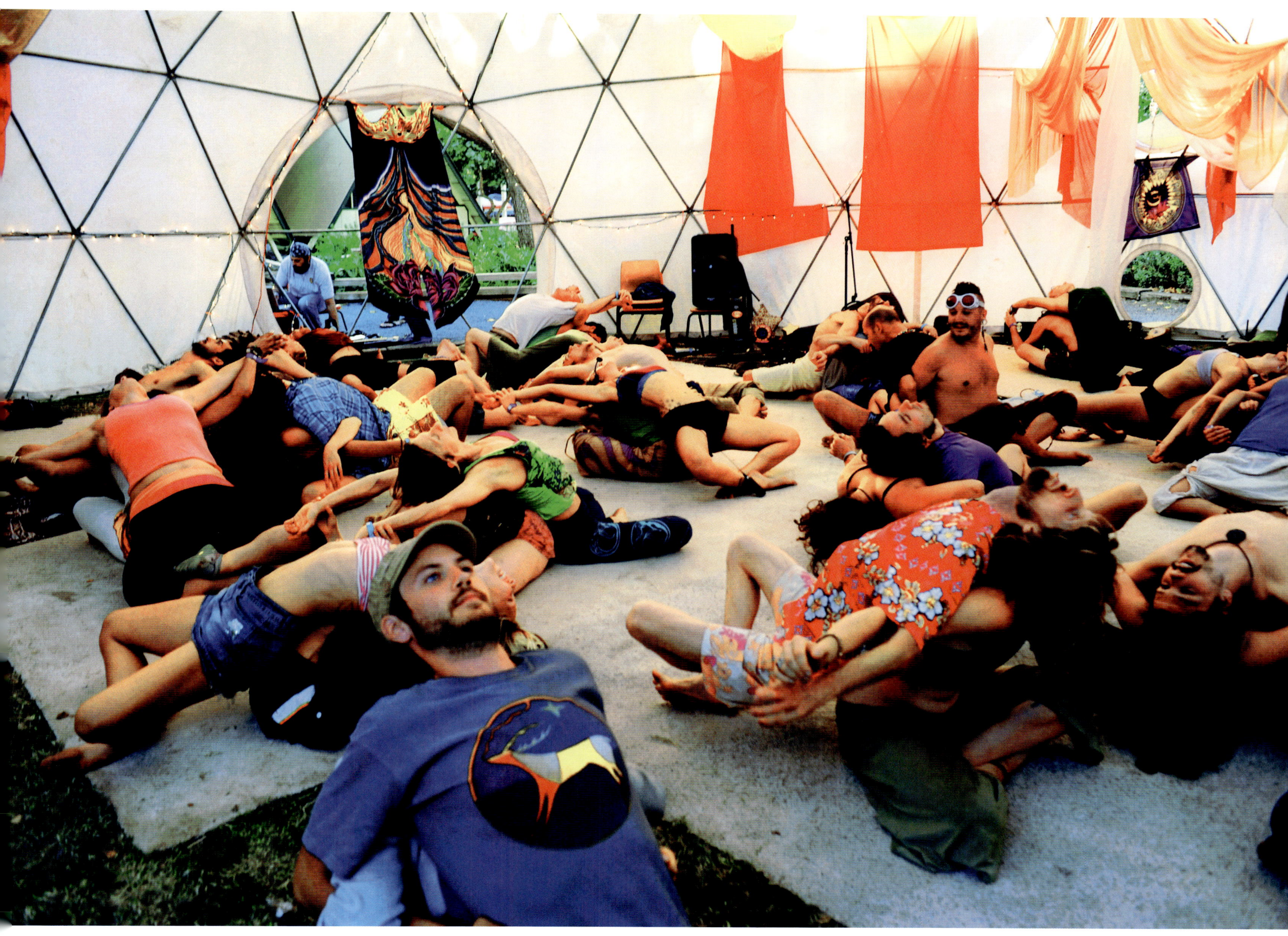

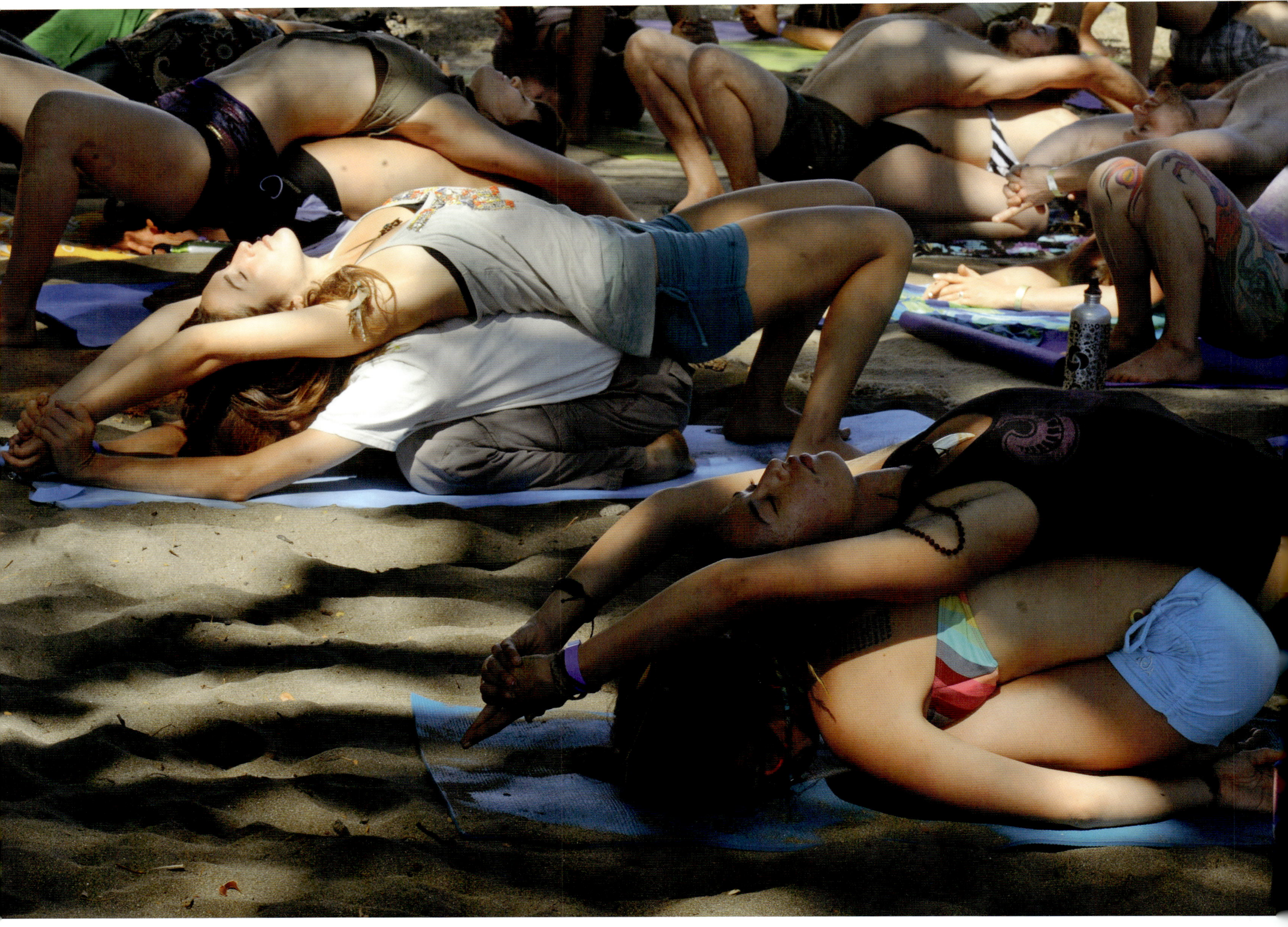

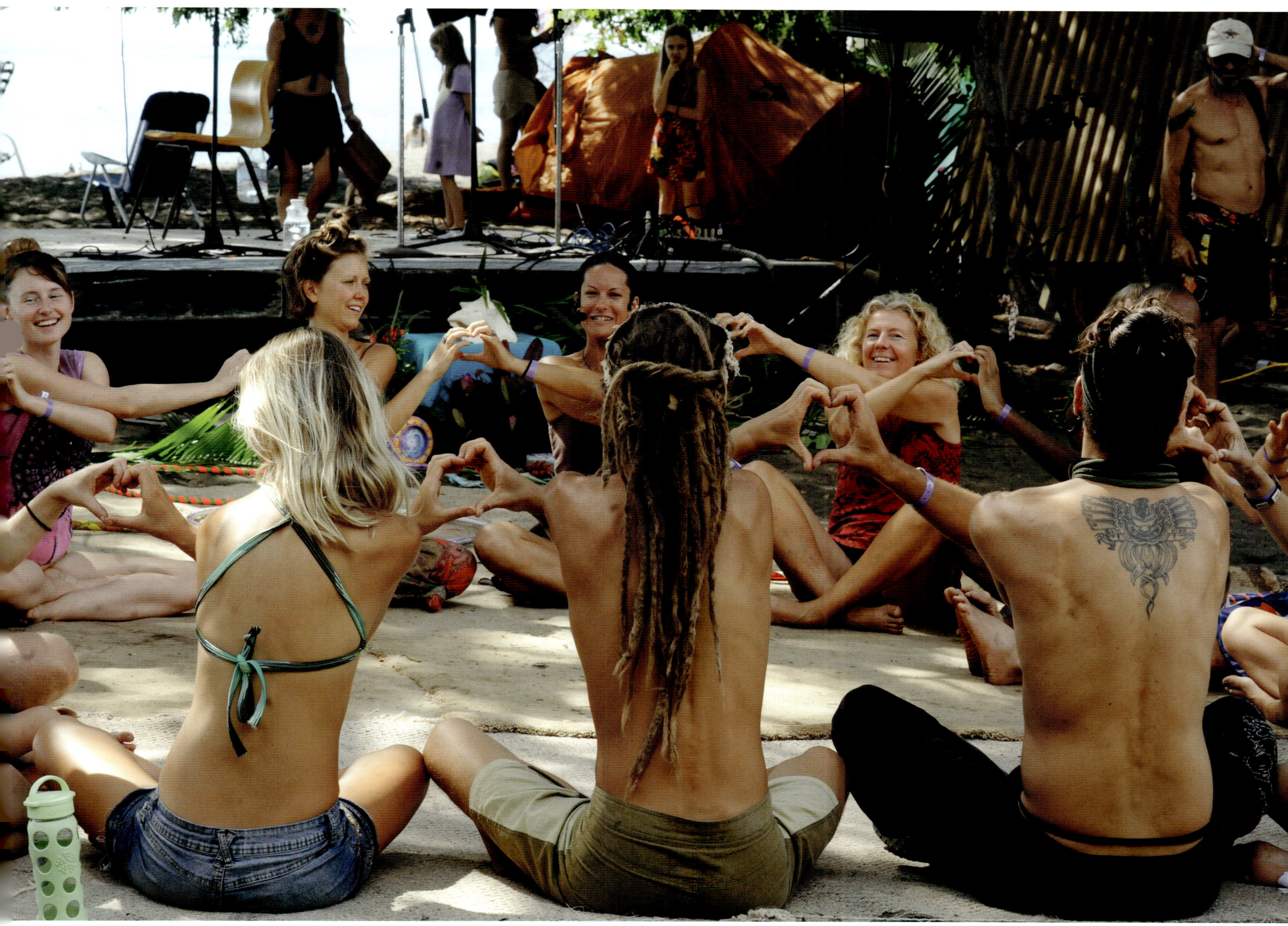

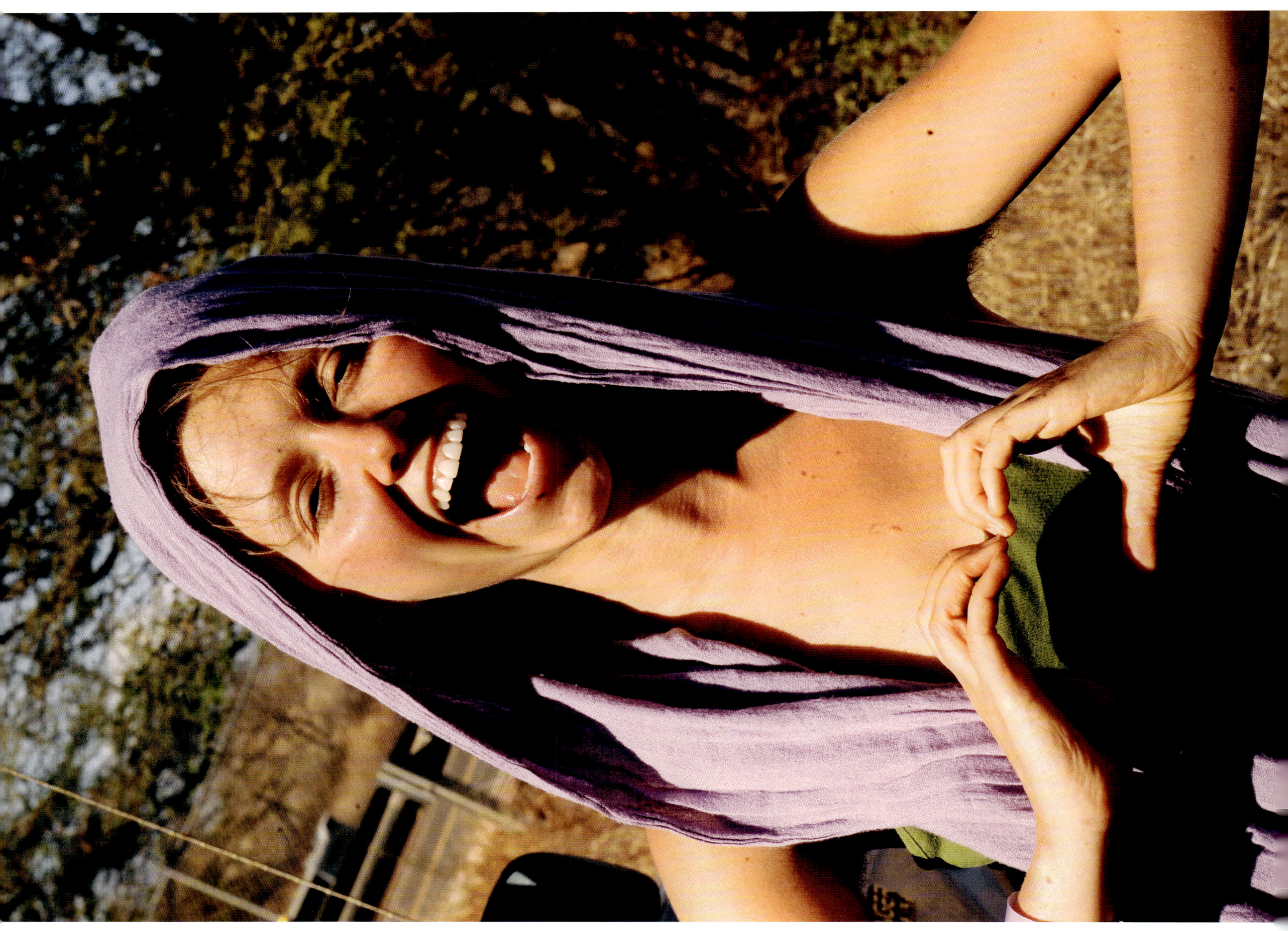

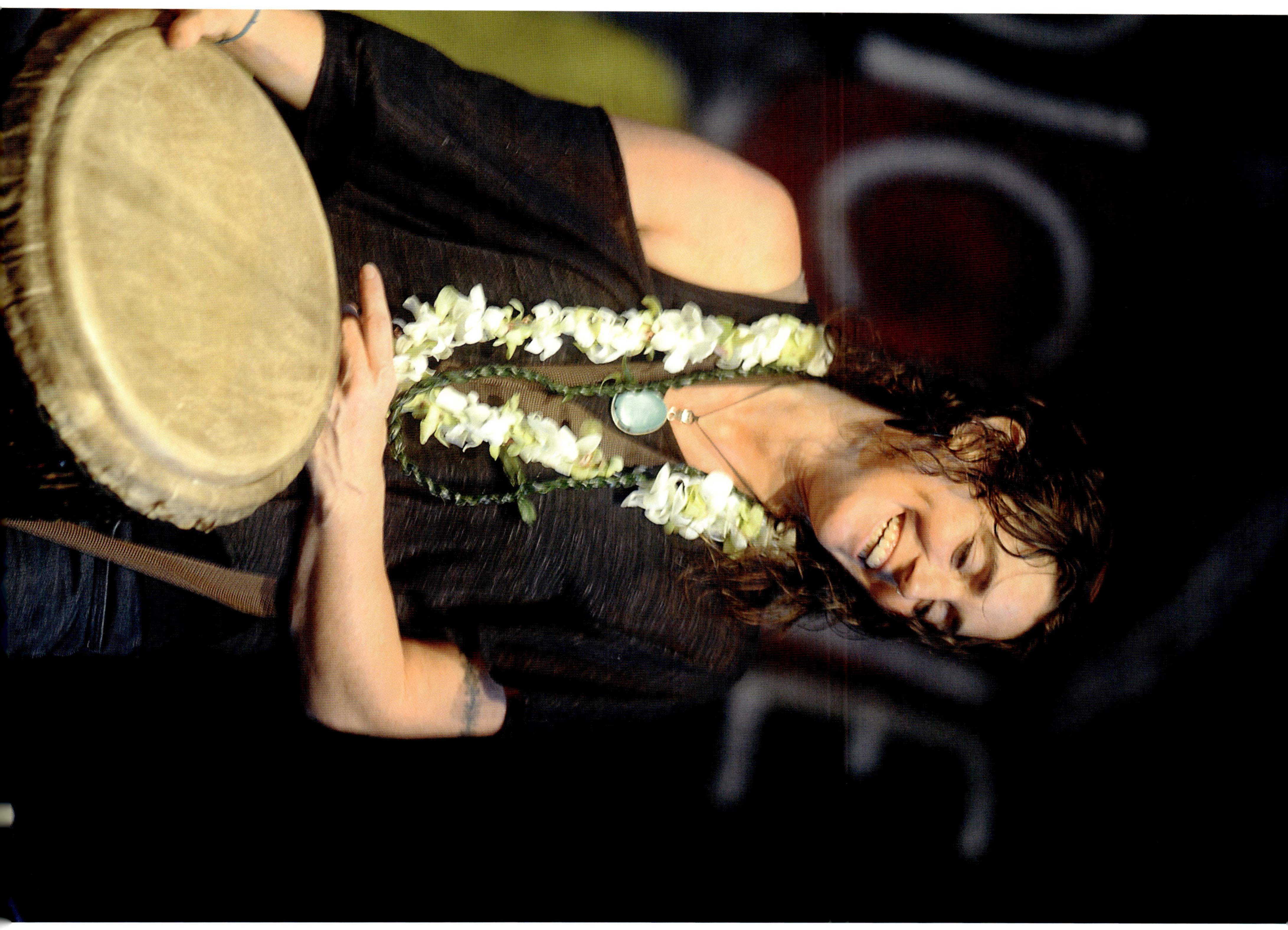

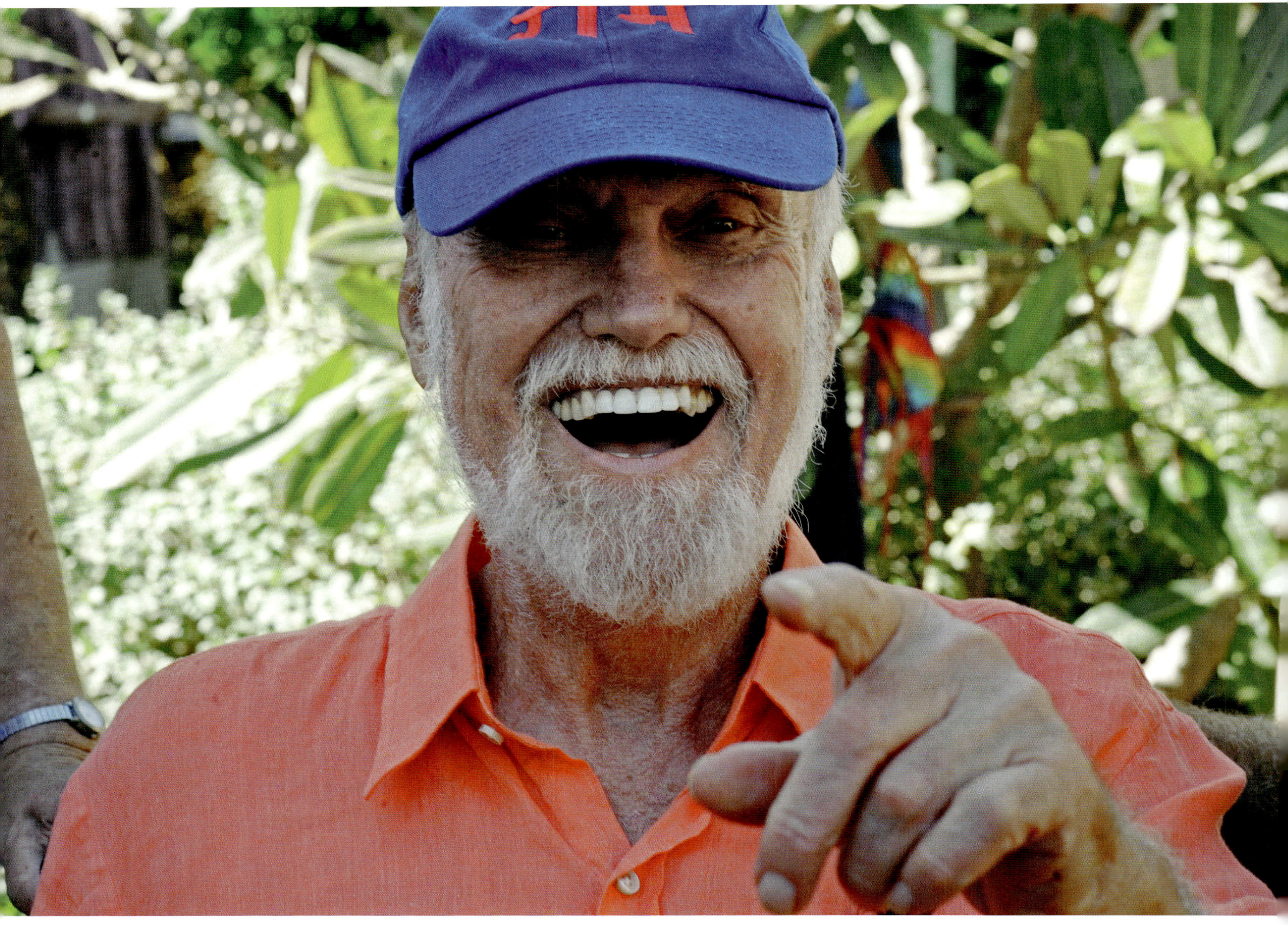

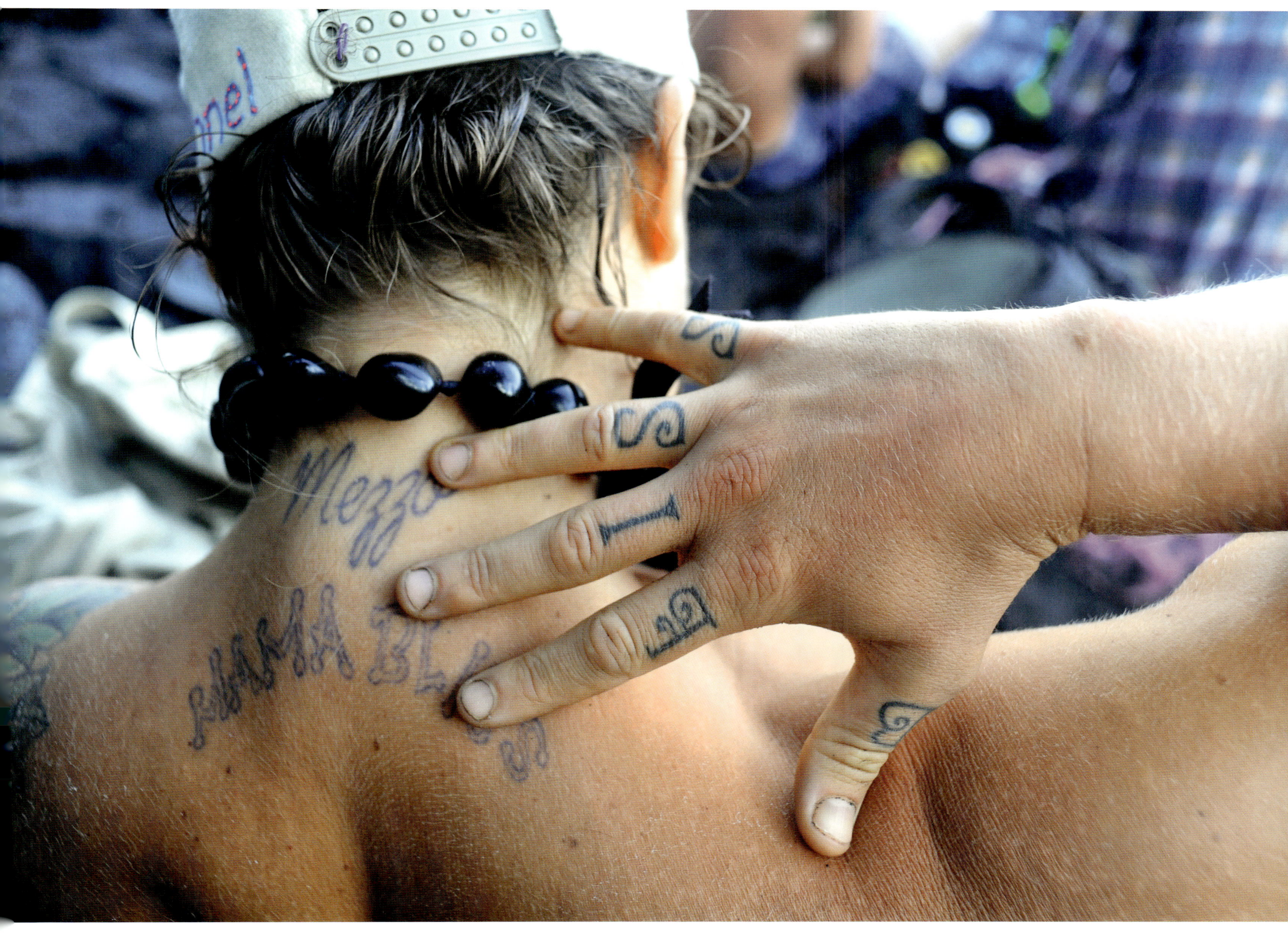

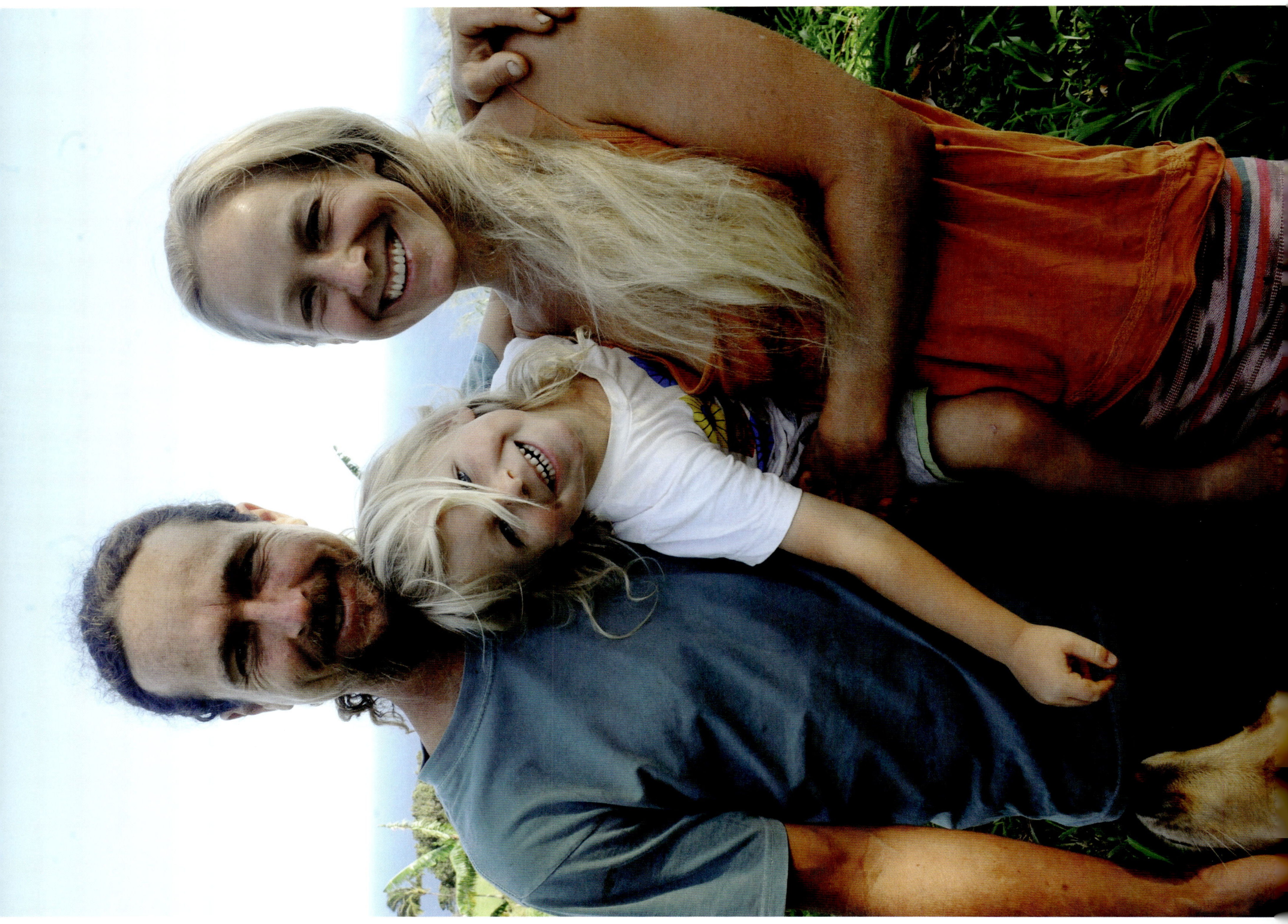

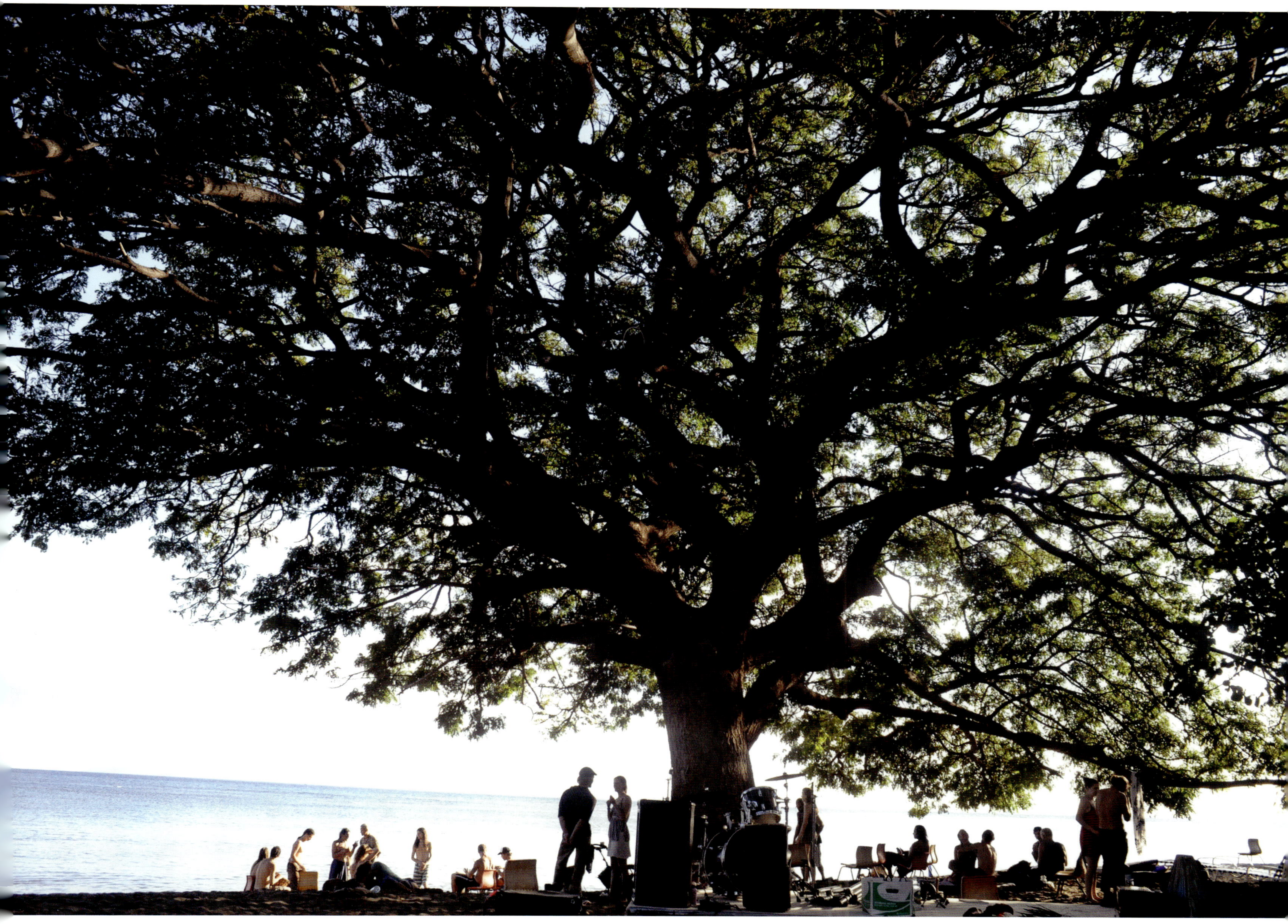

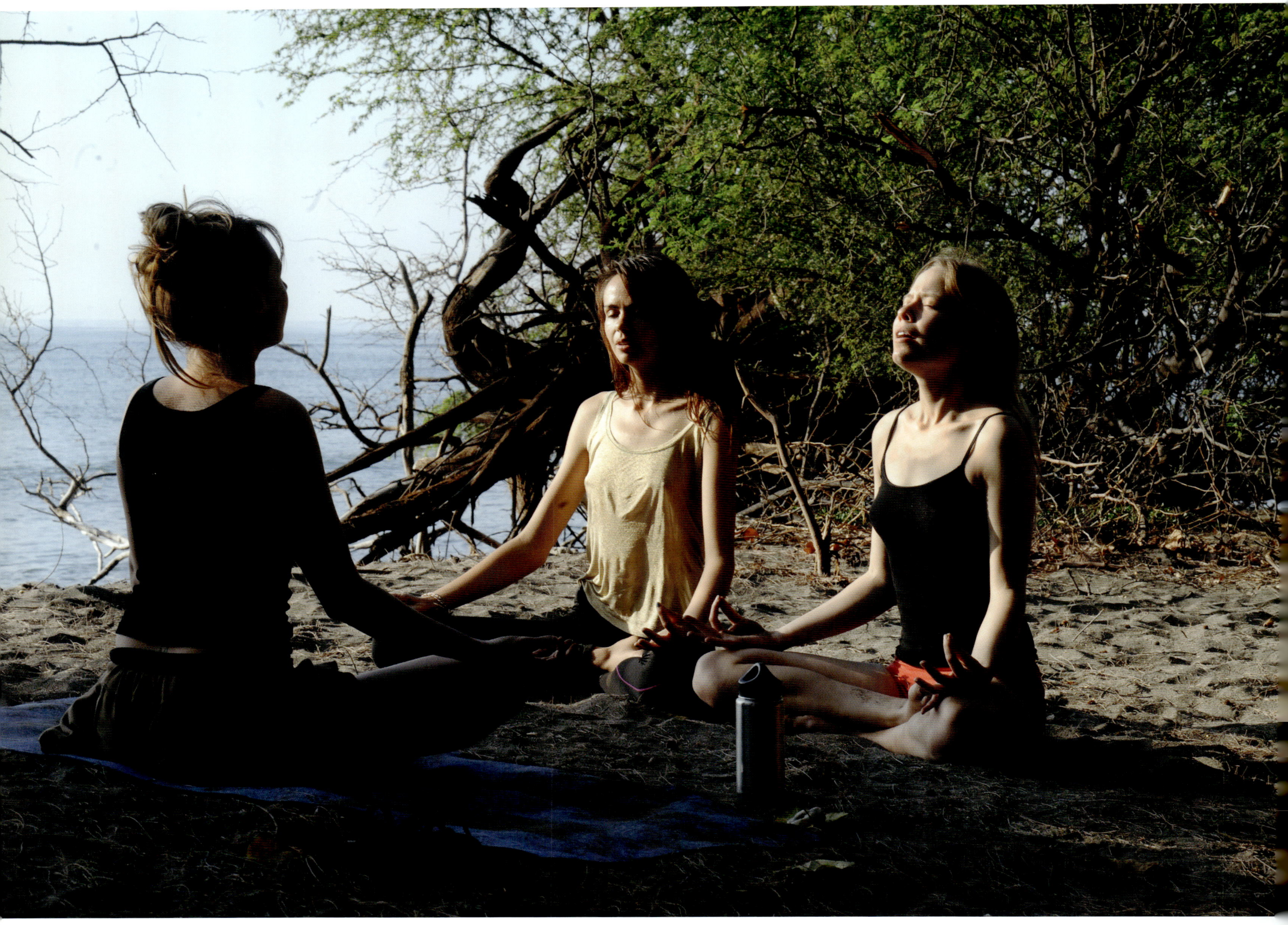

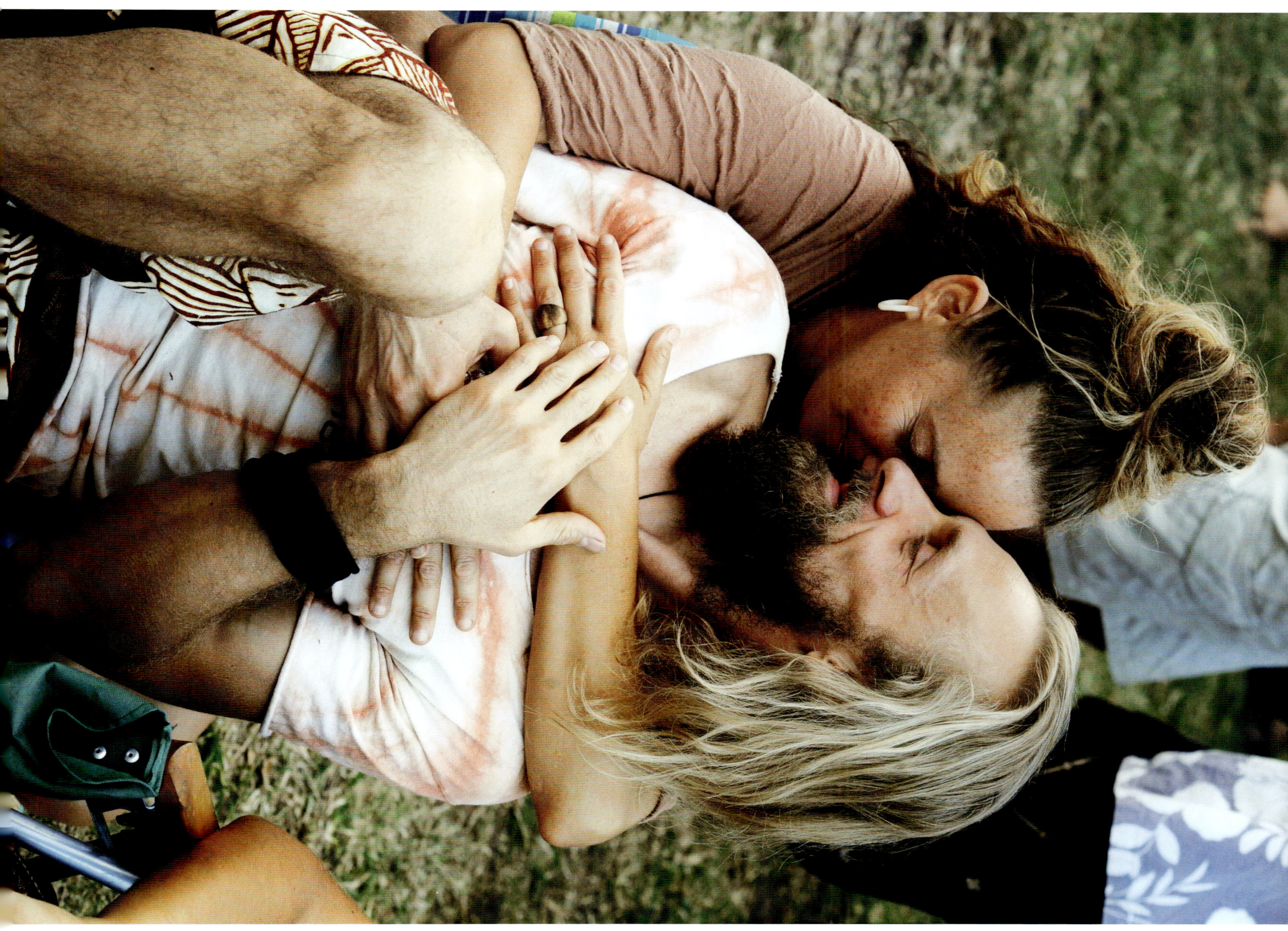

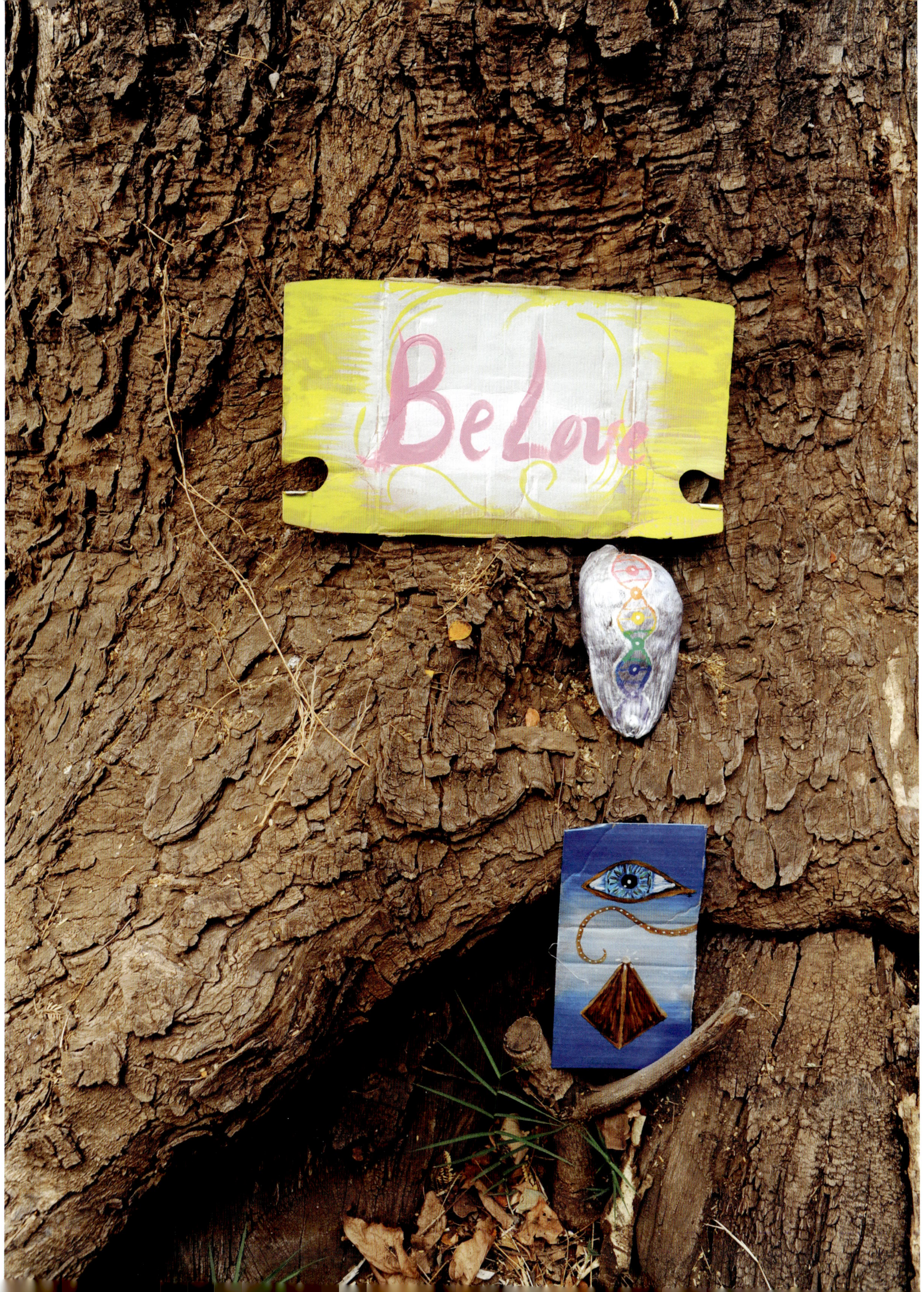

Be Love

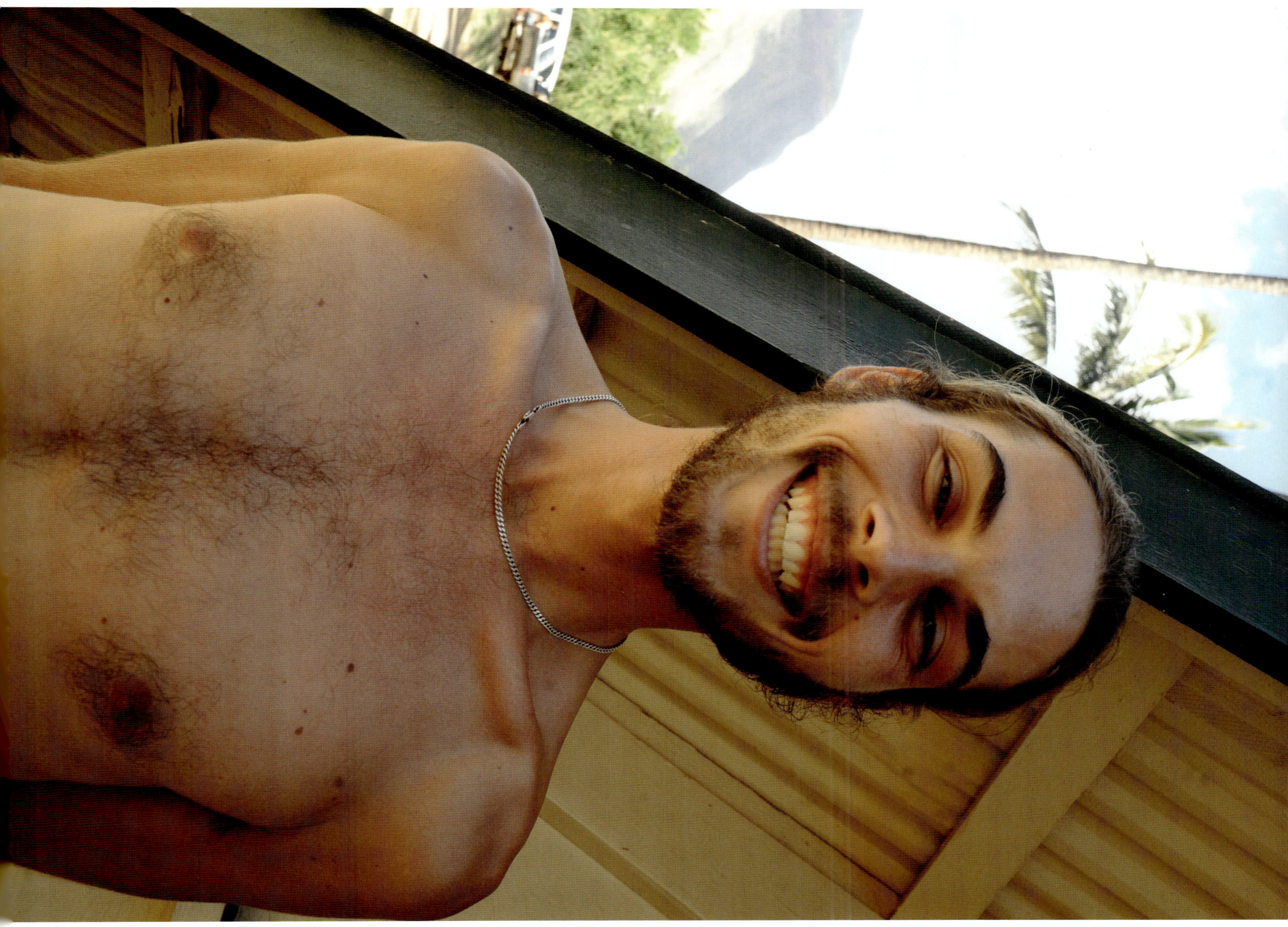

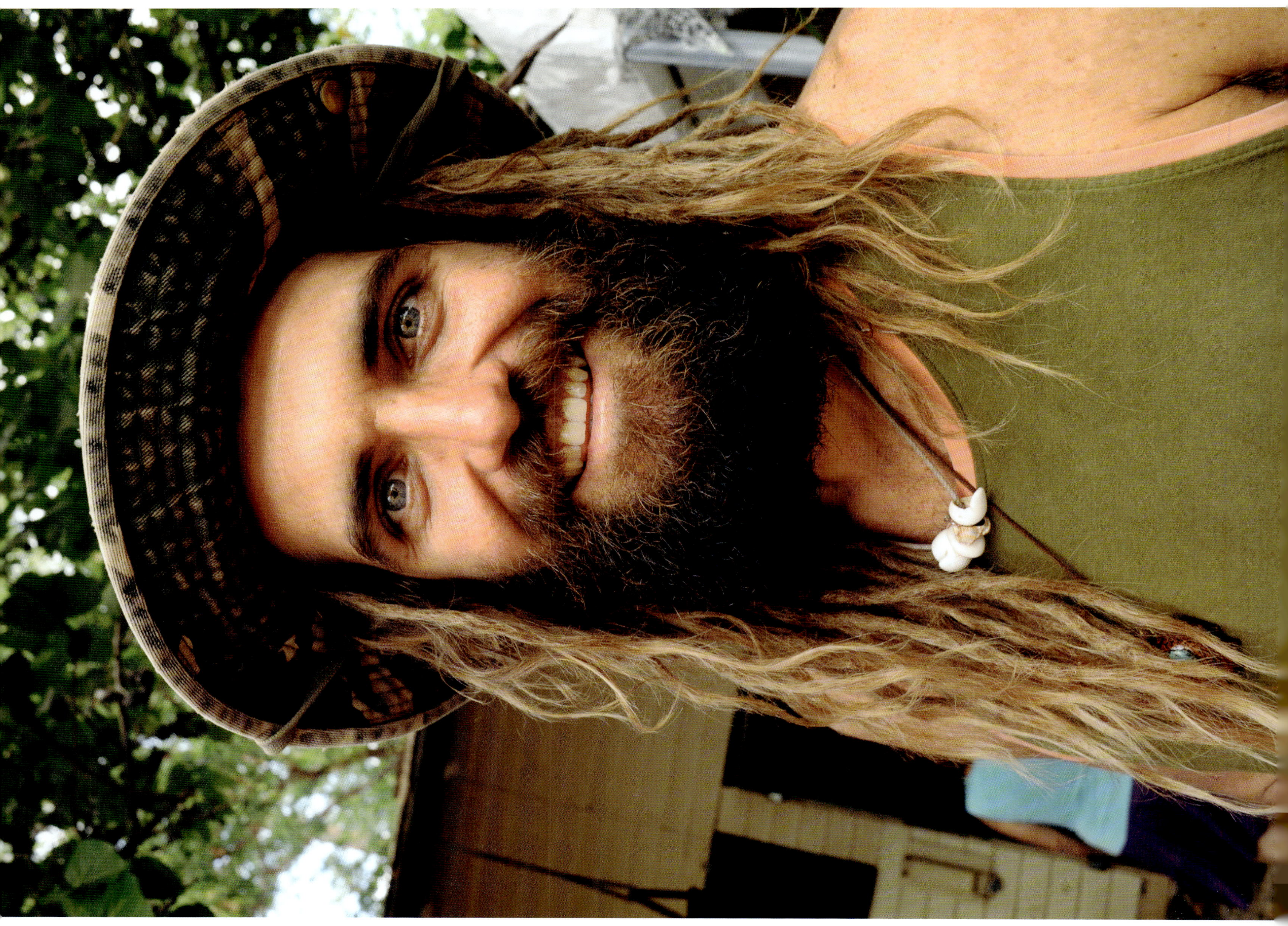

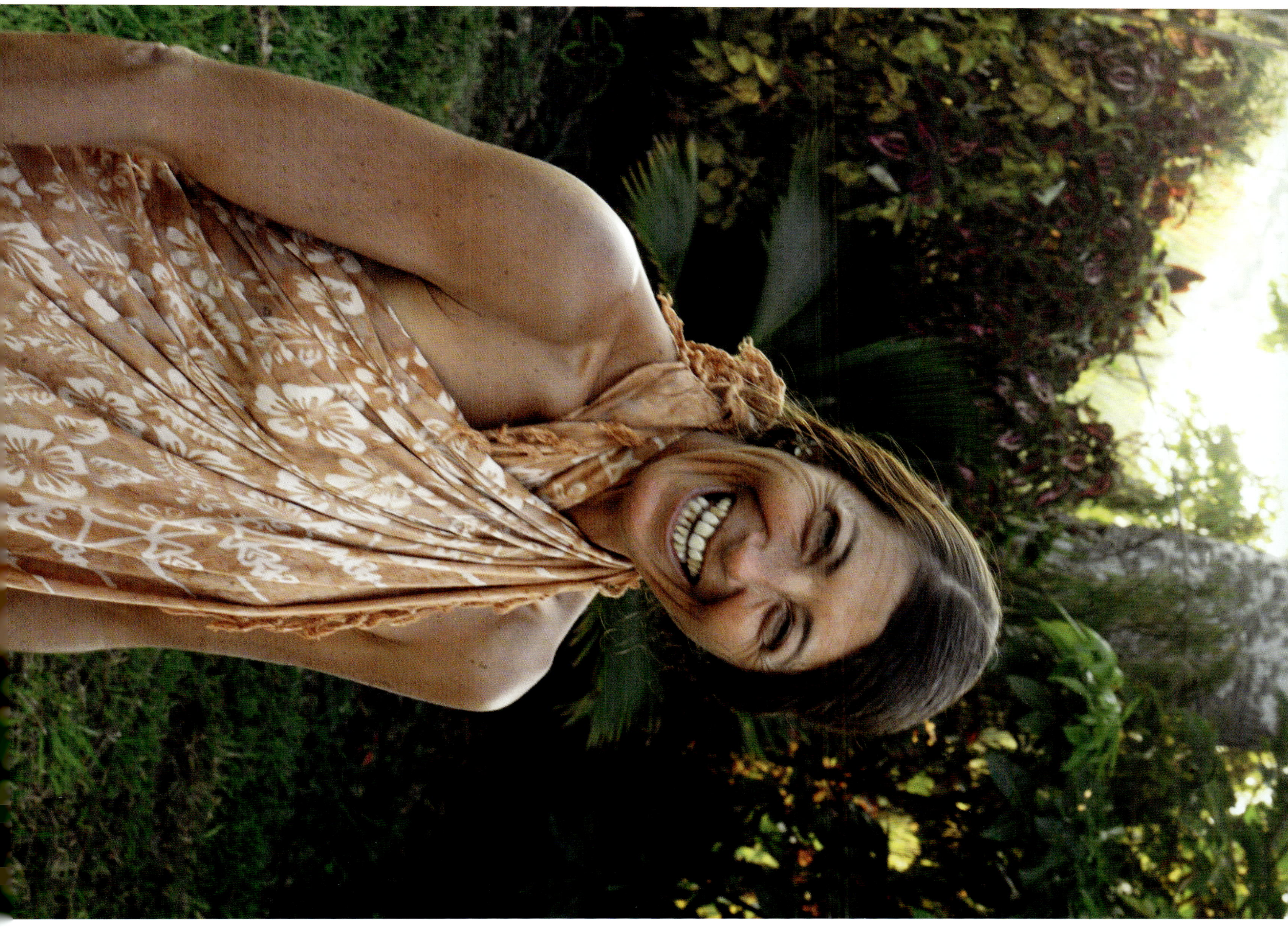

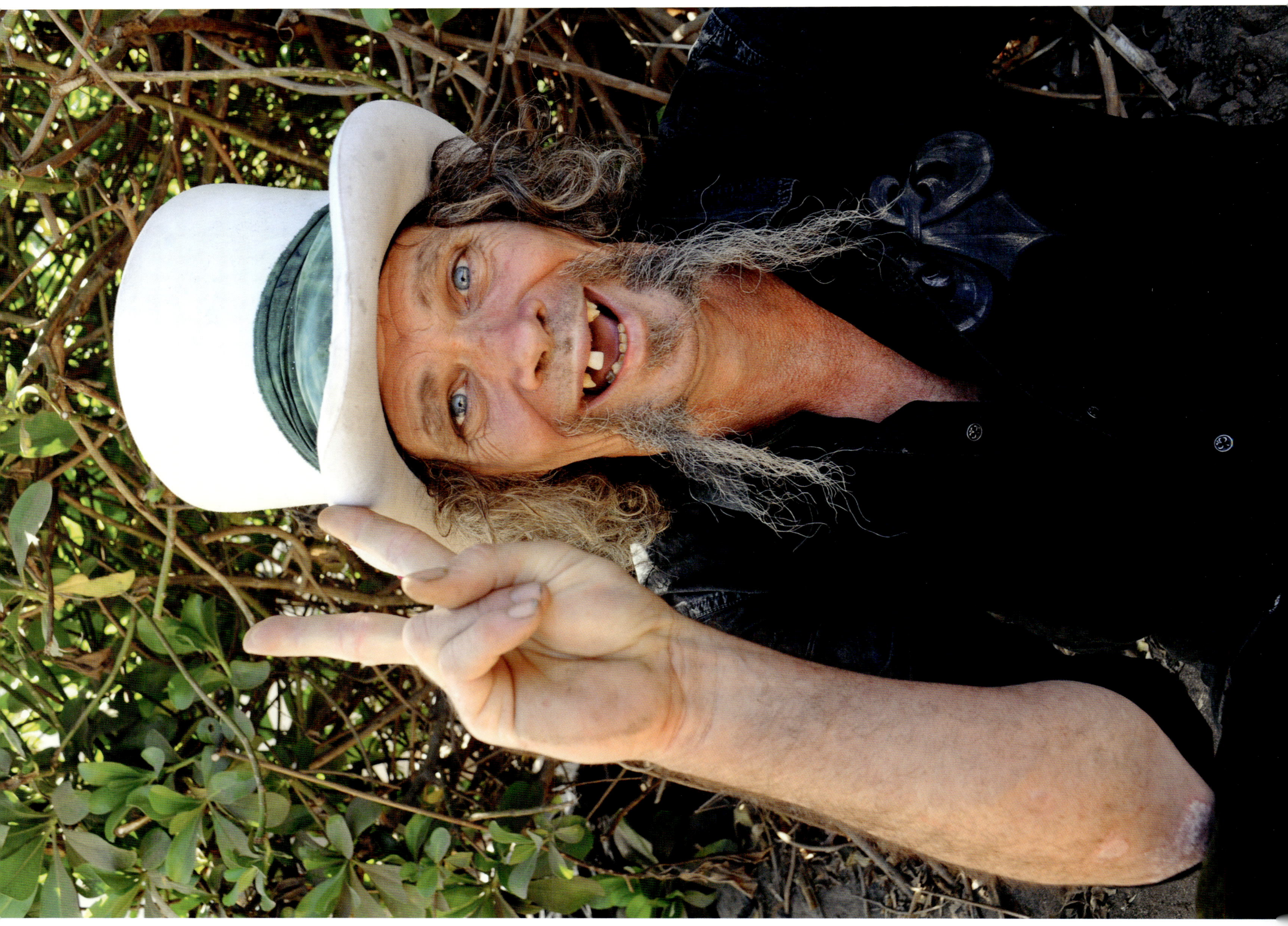

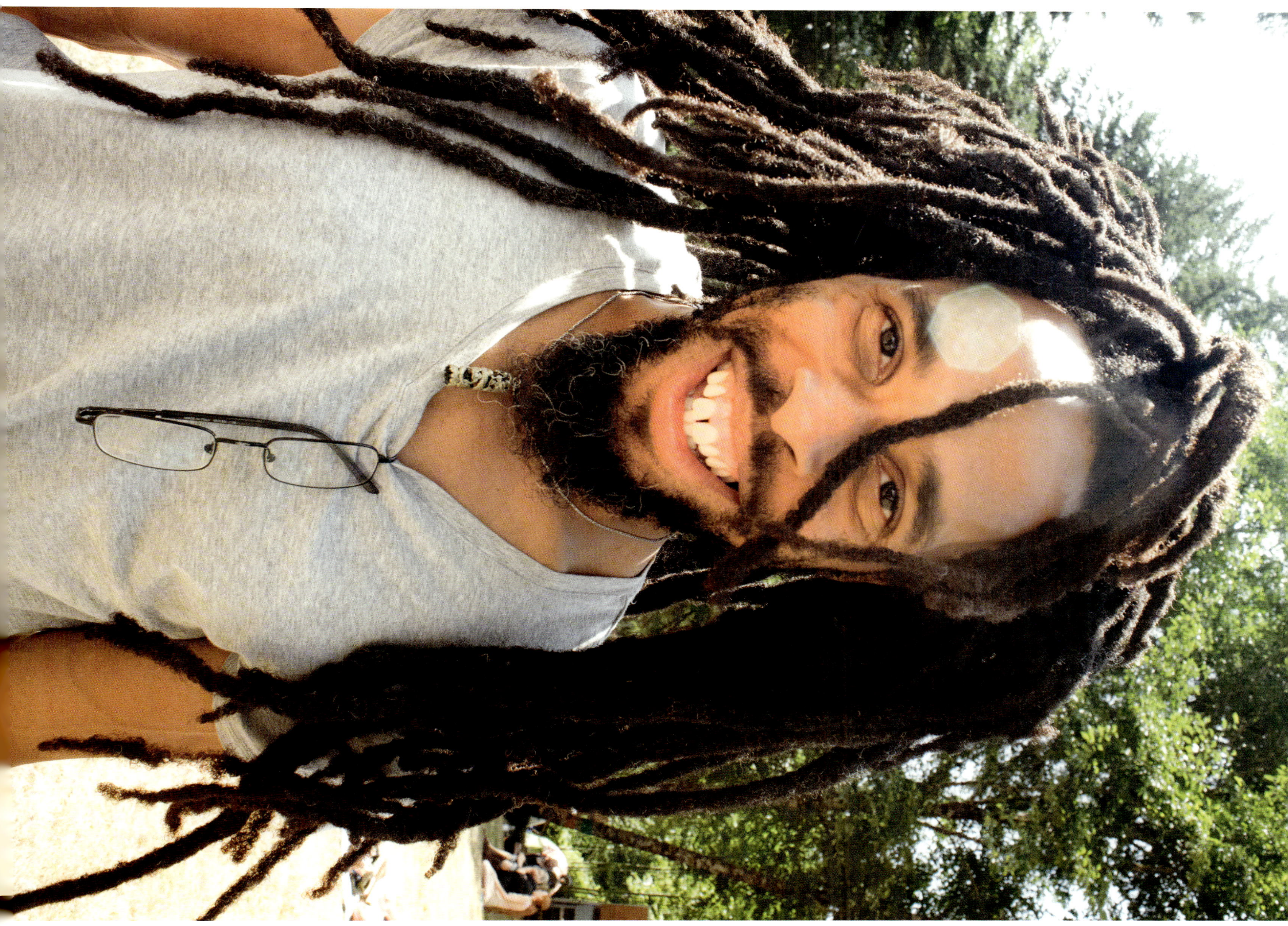

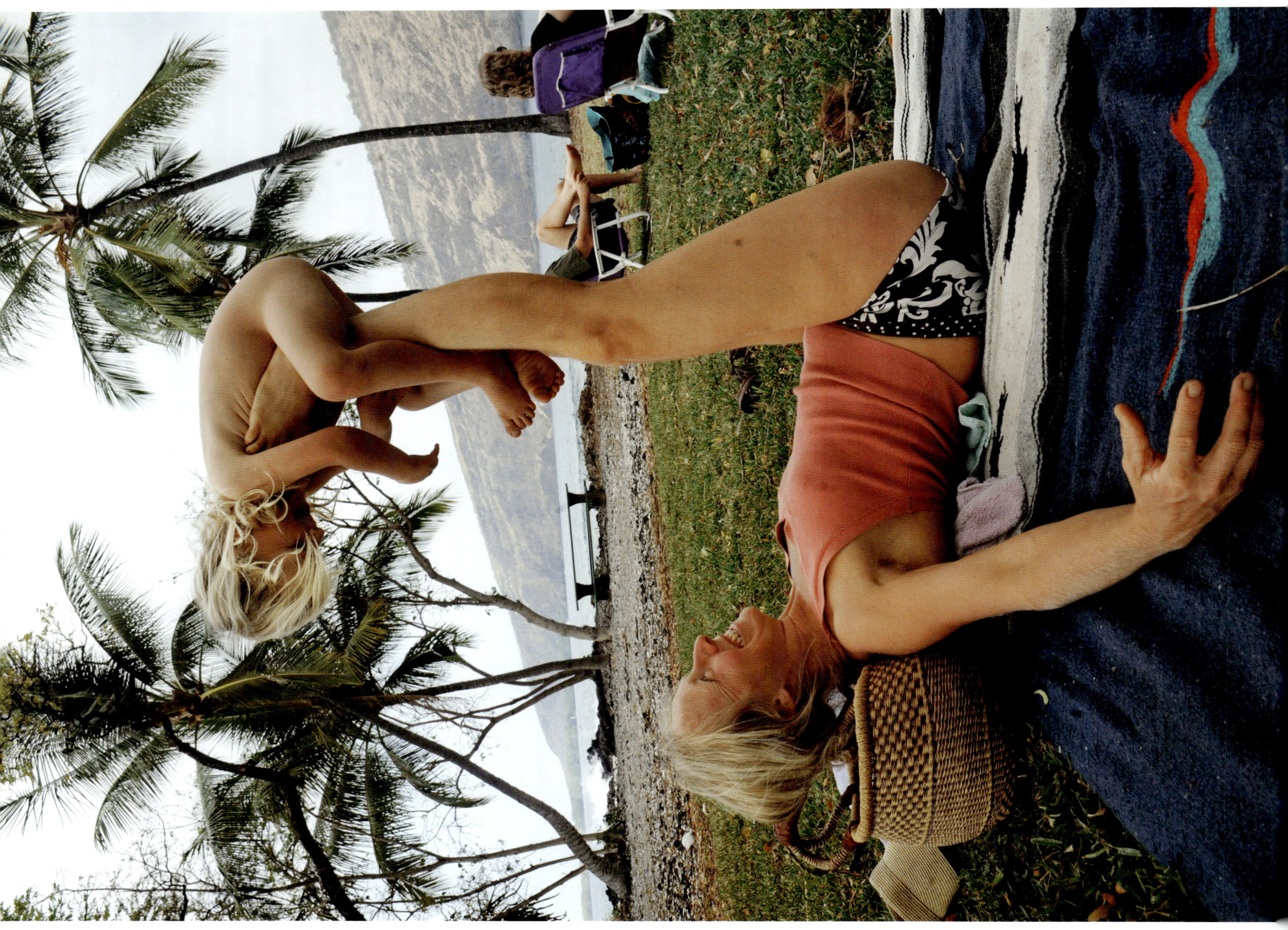

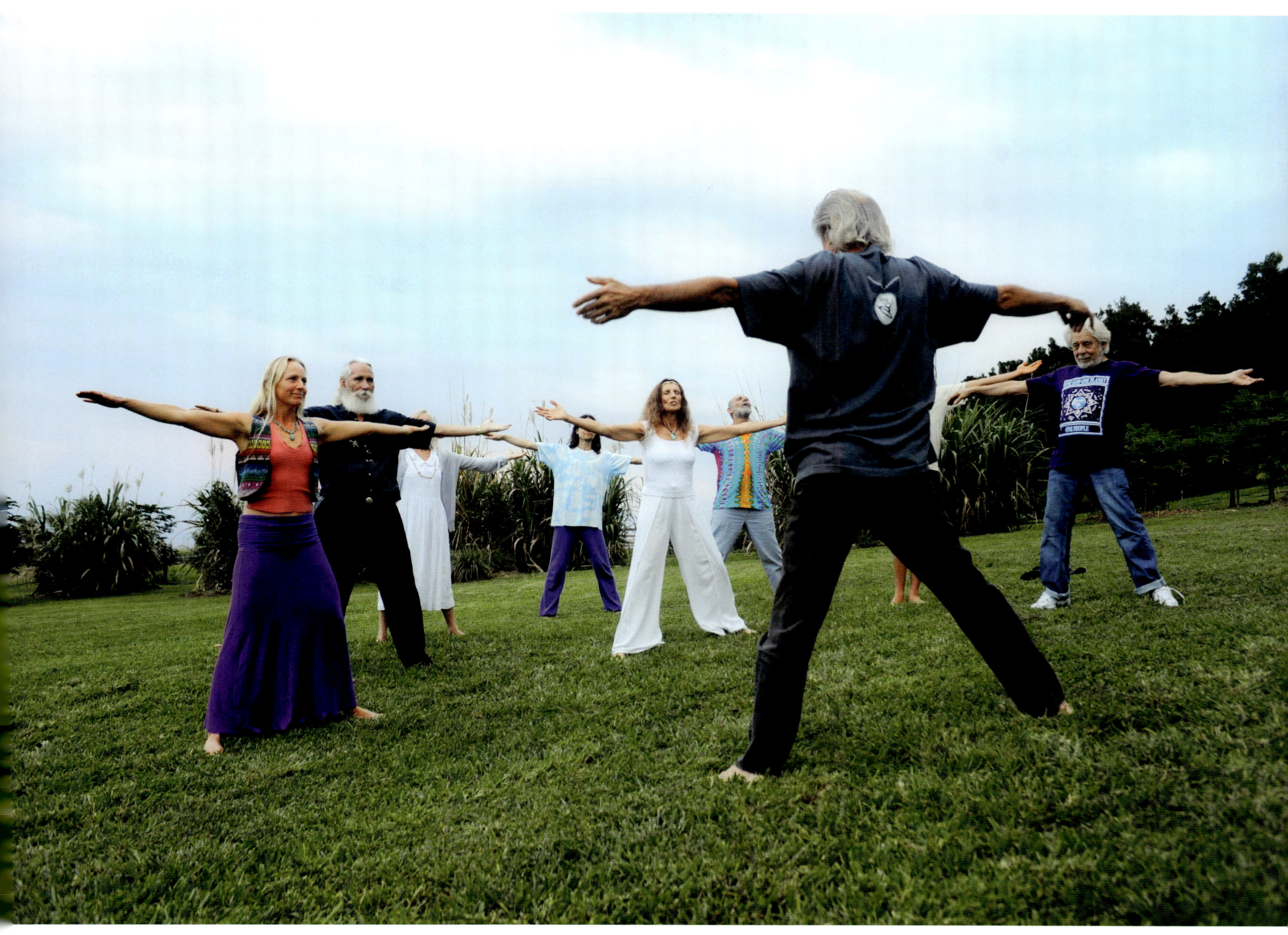

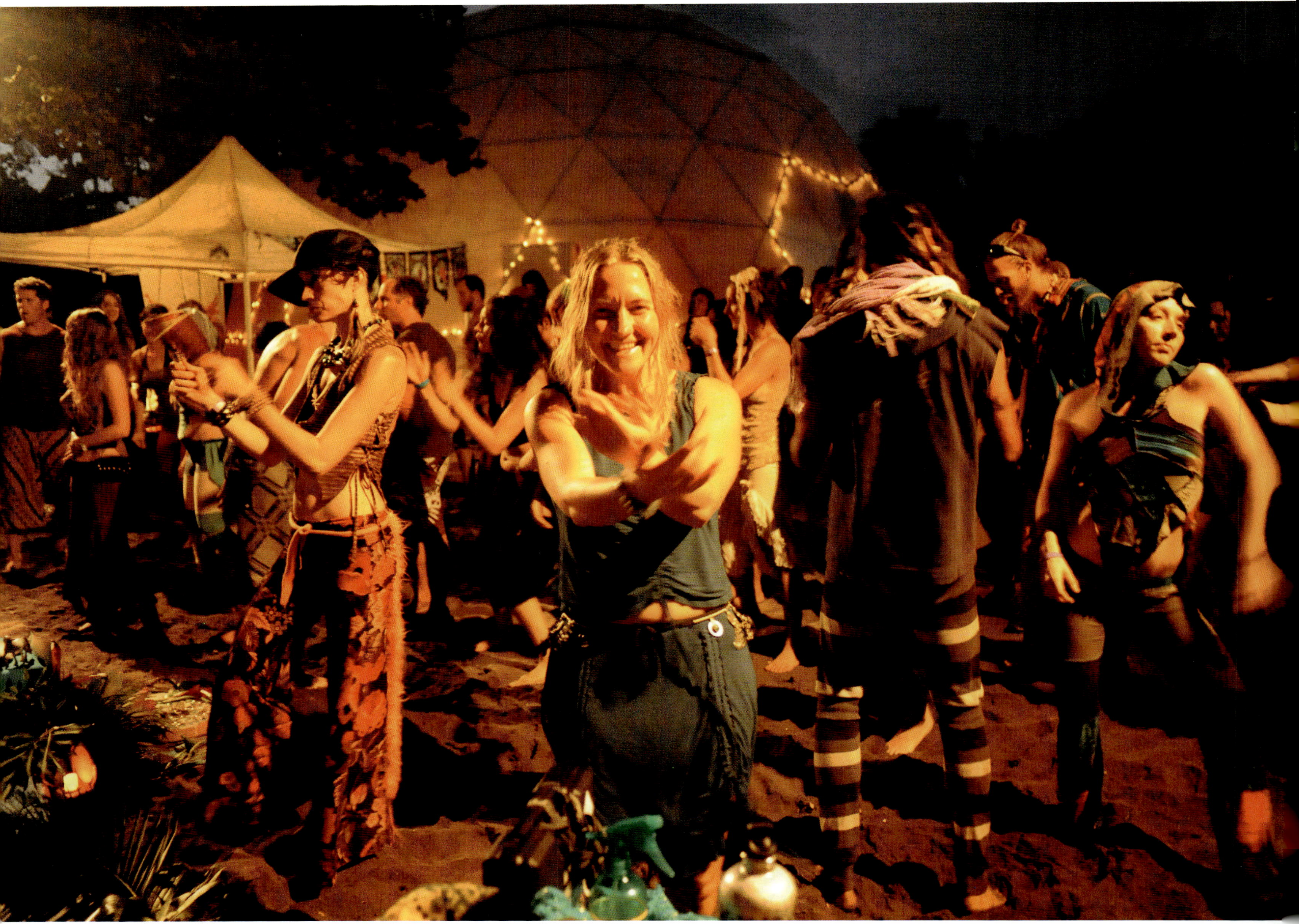

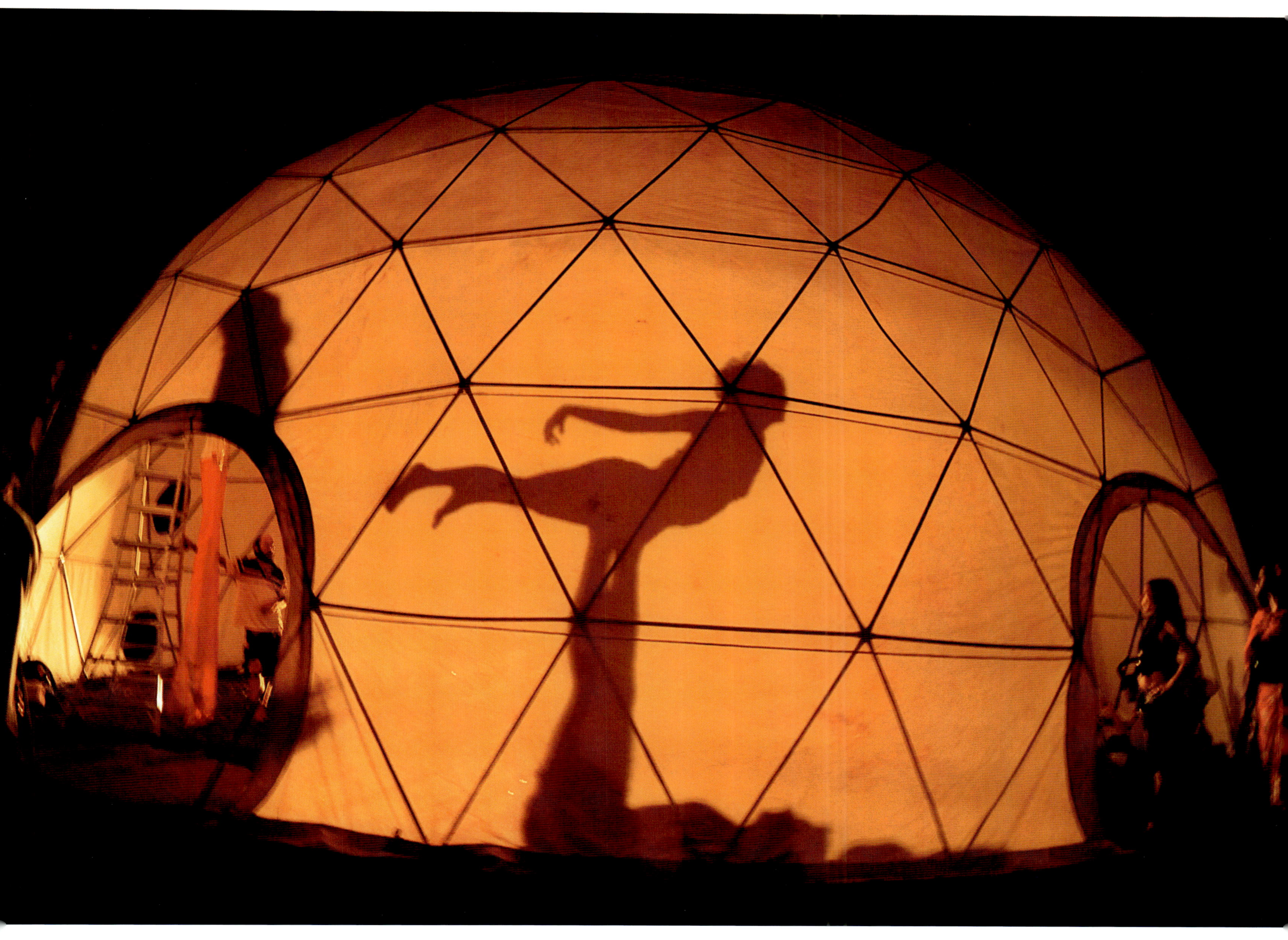

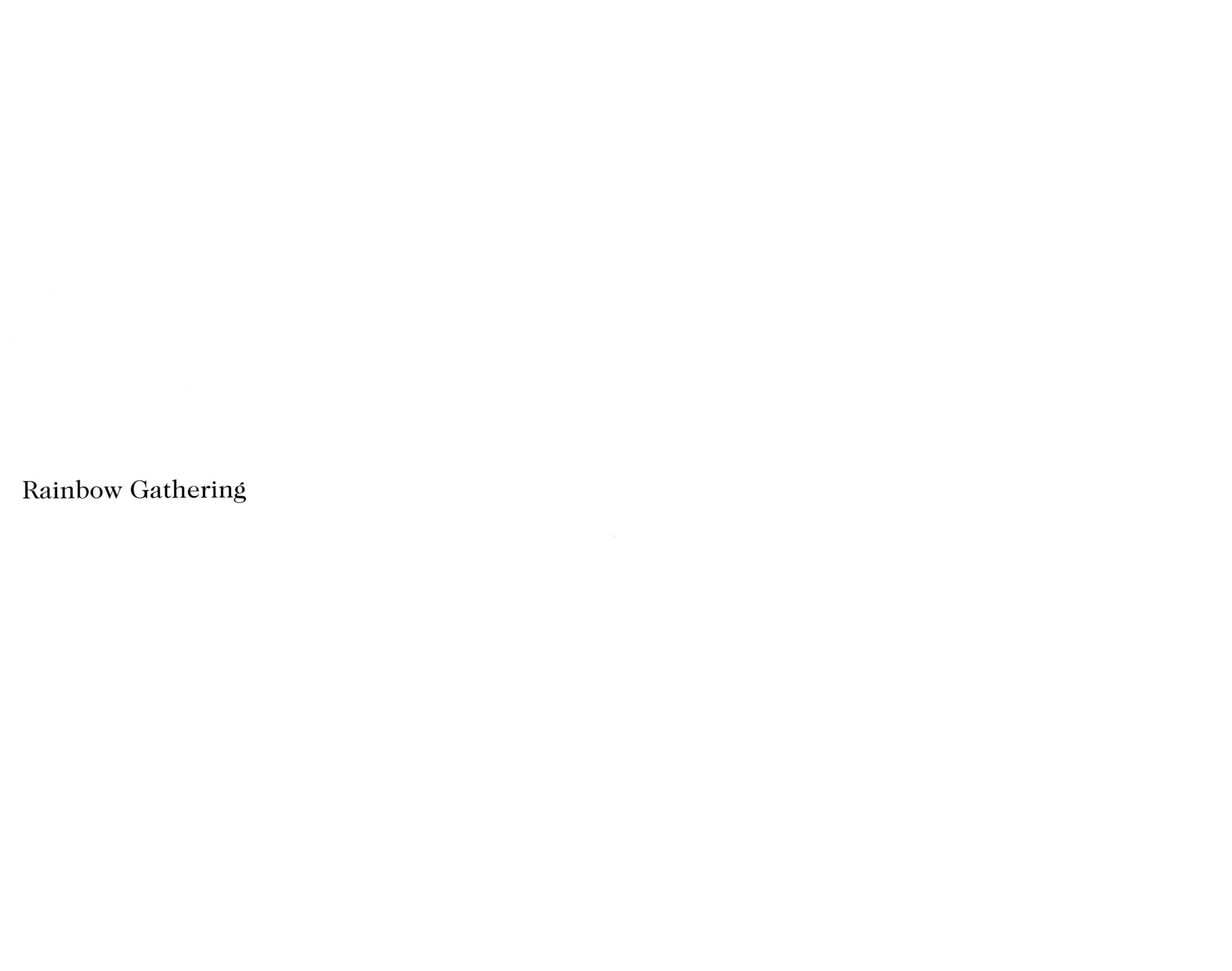

Rainbow Gathering

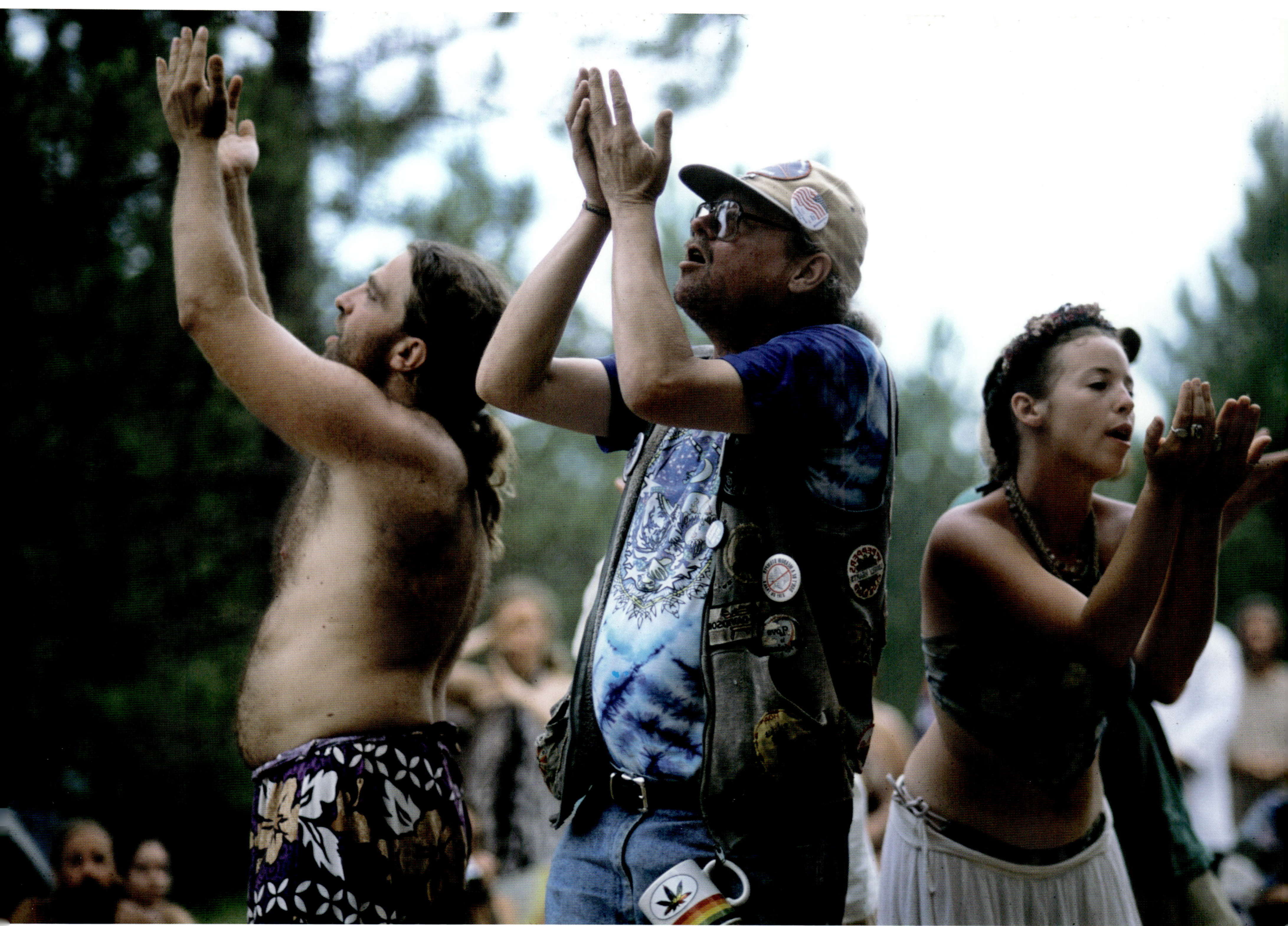

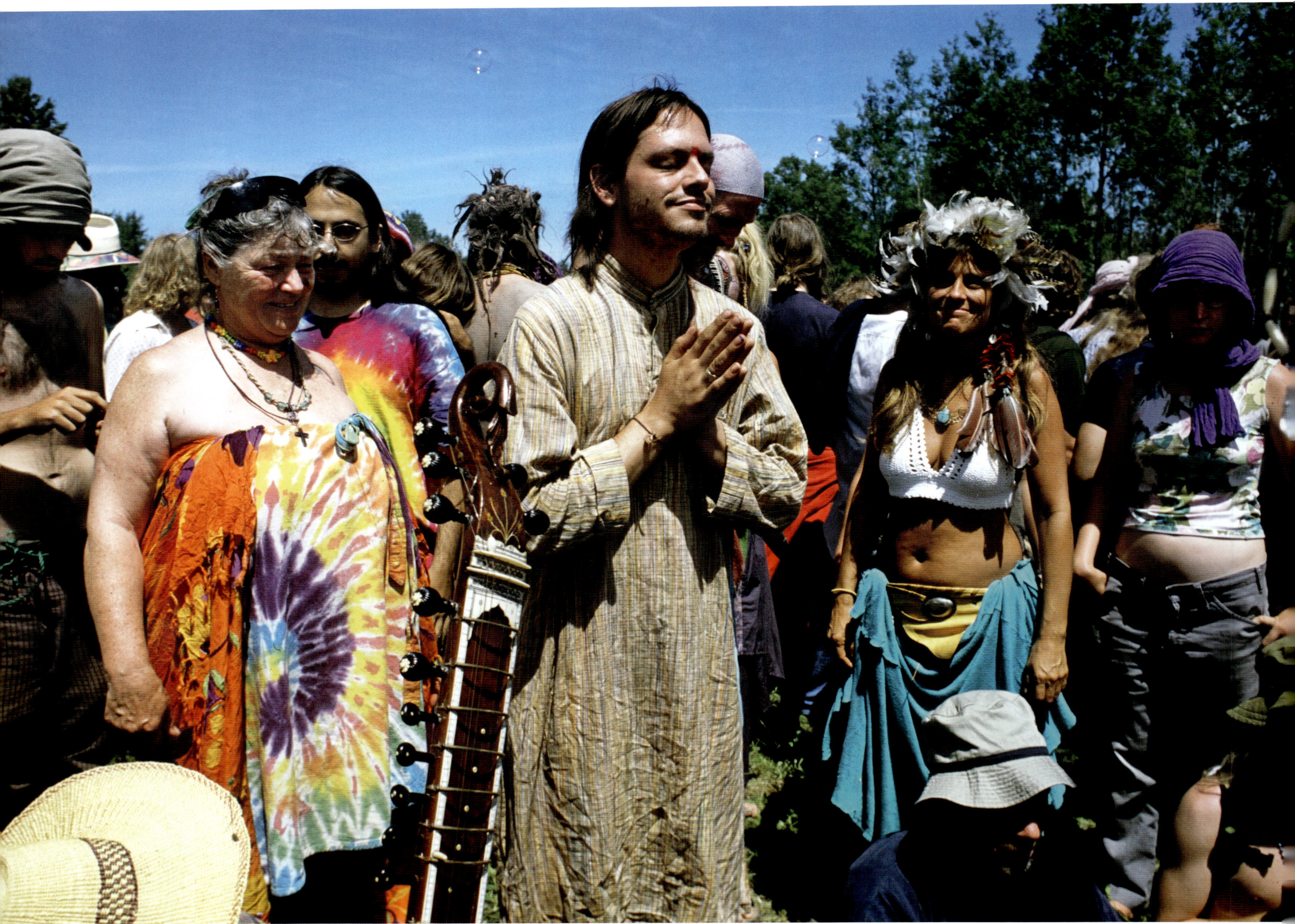

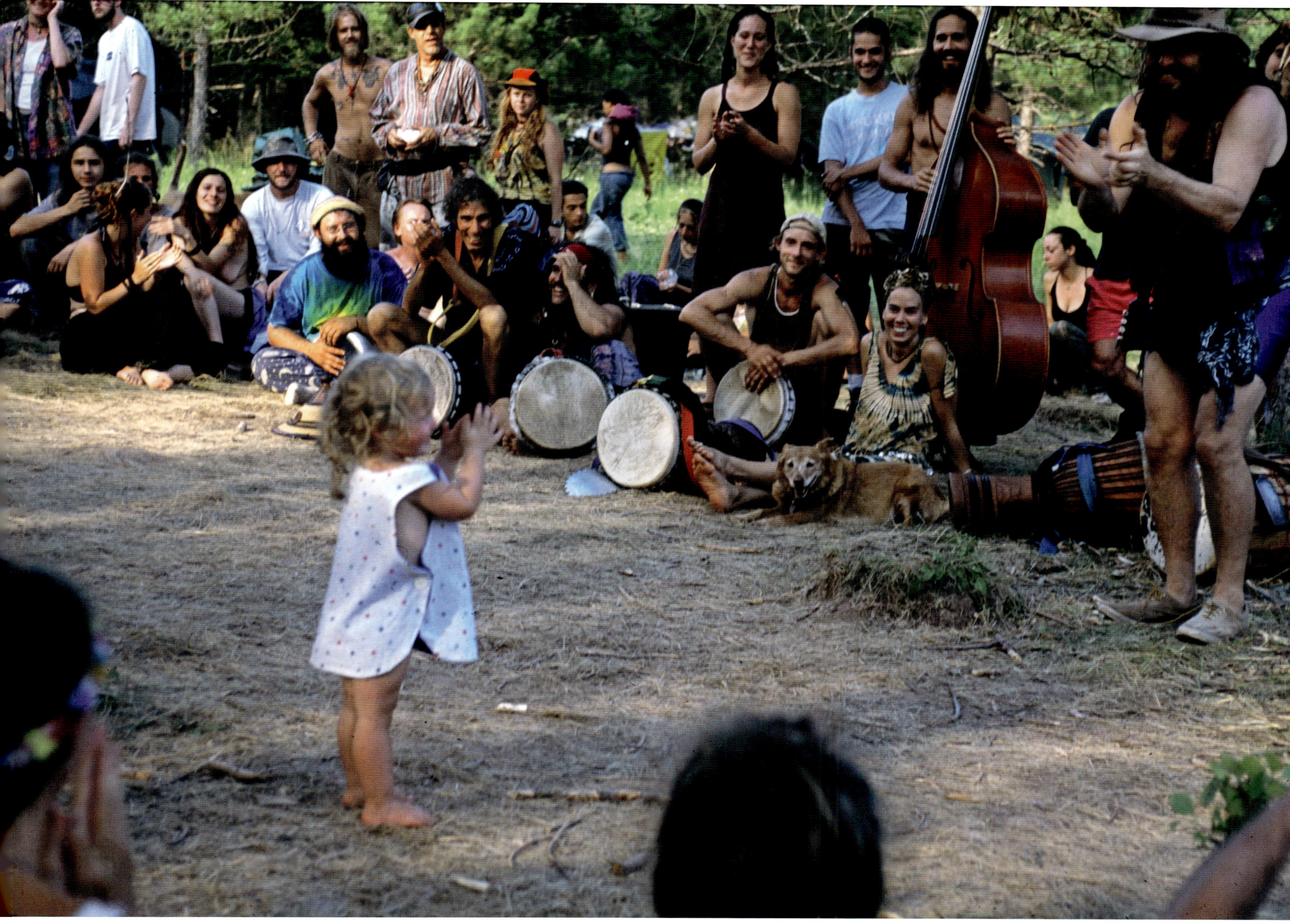

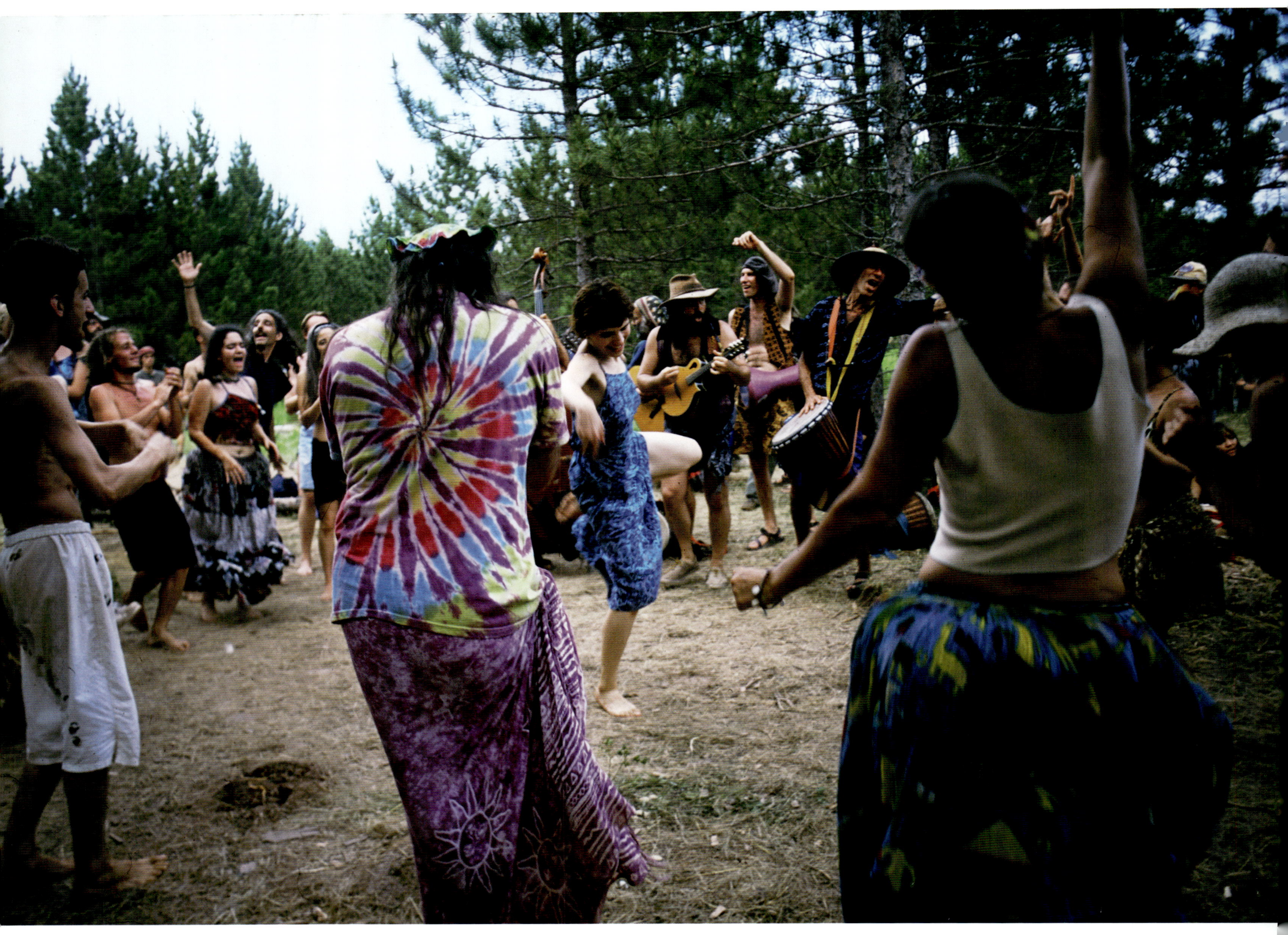

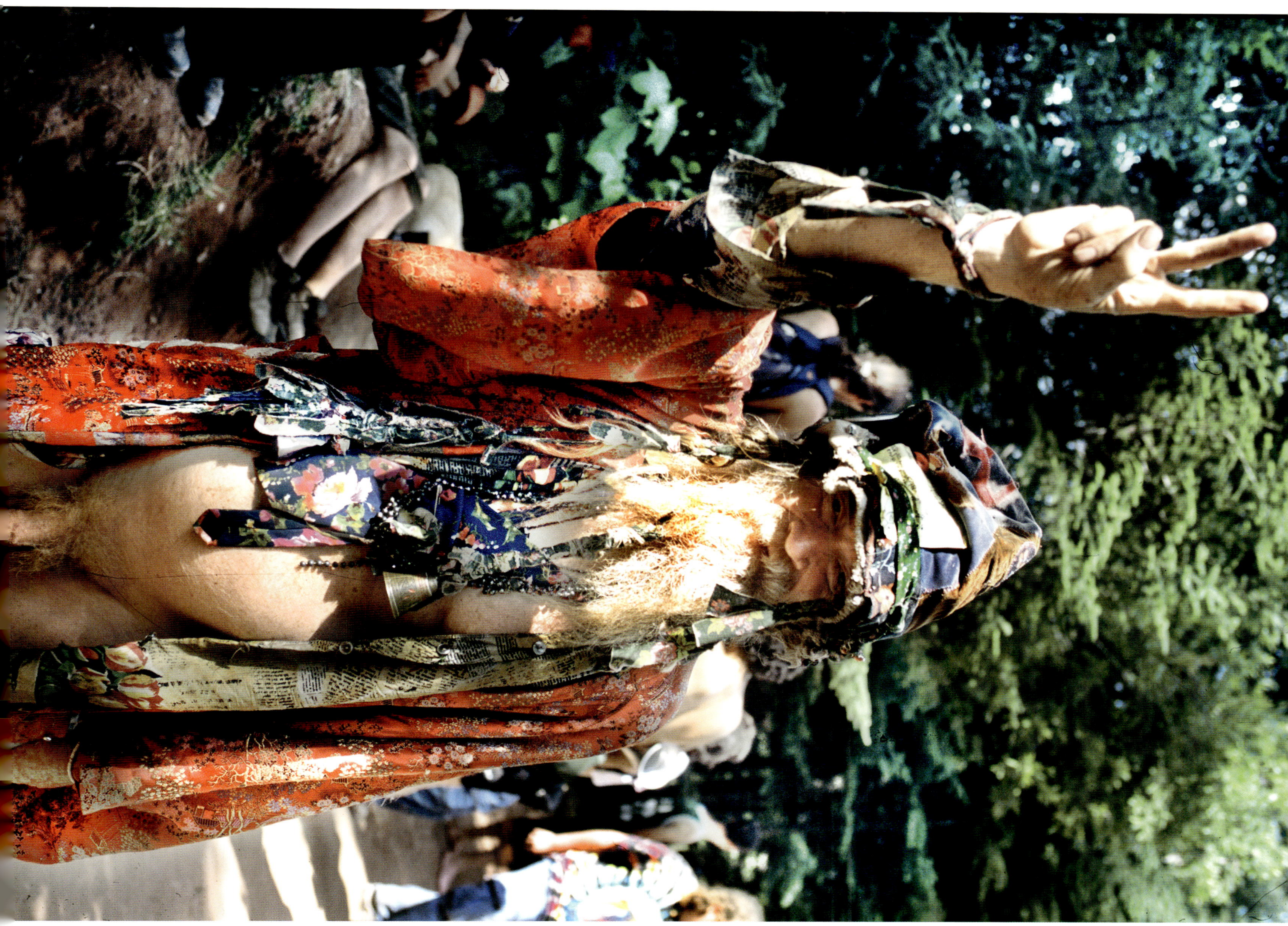

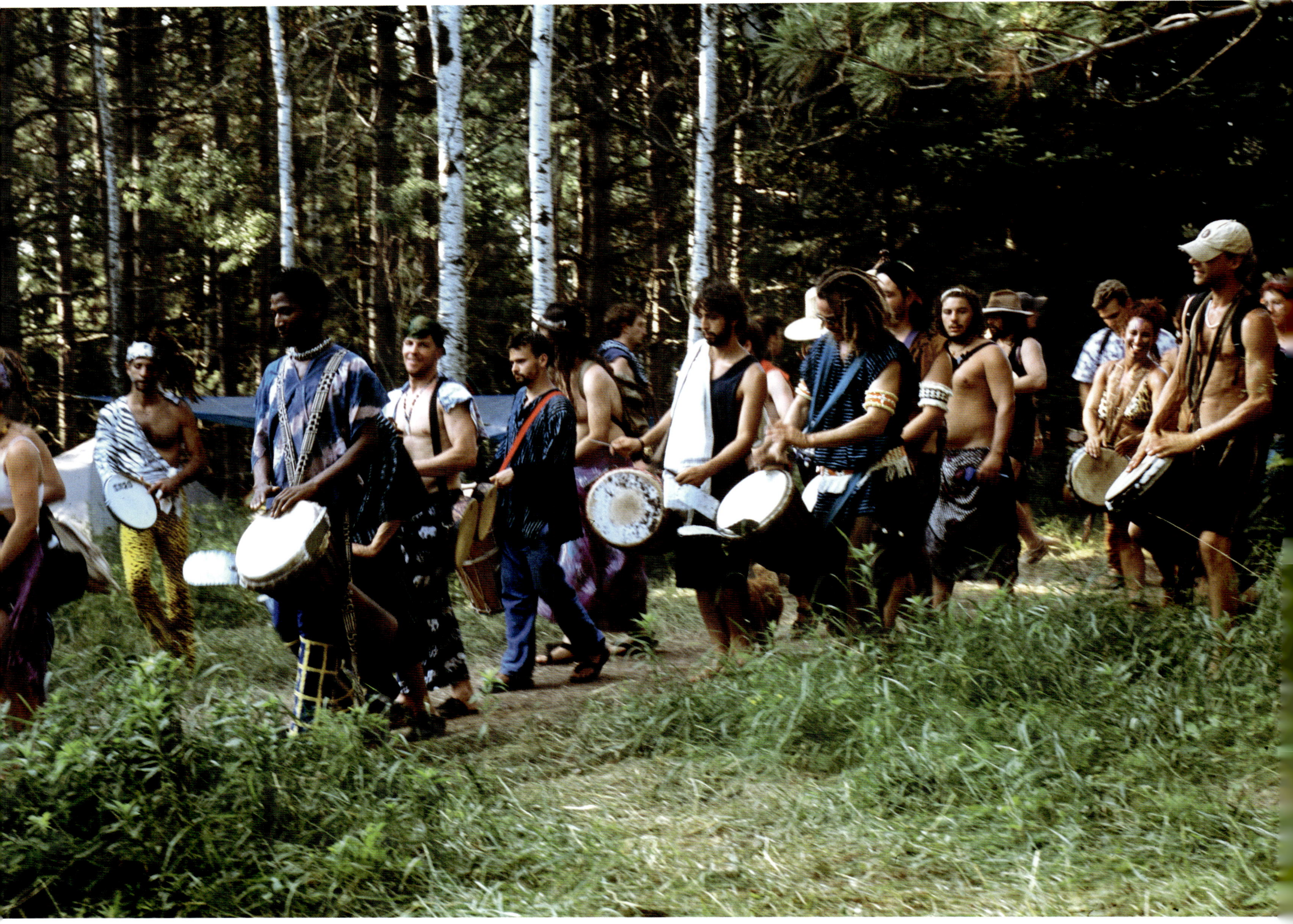

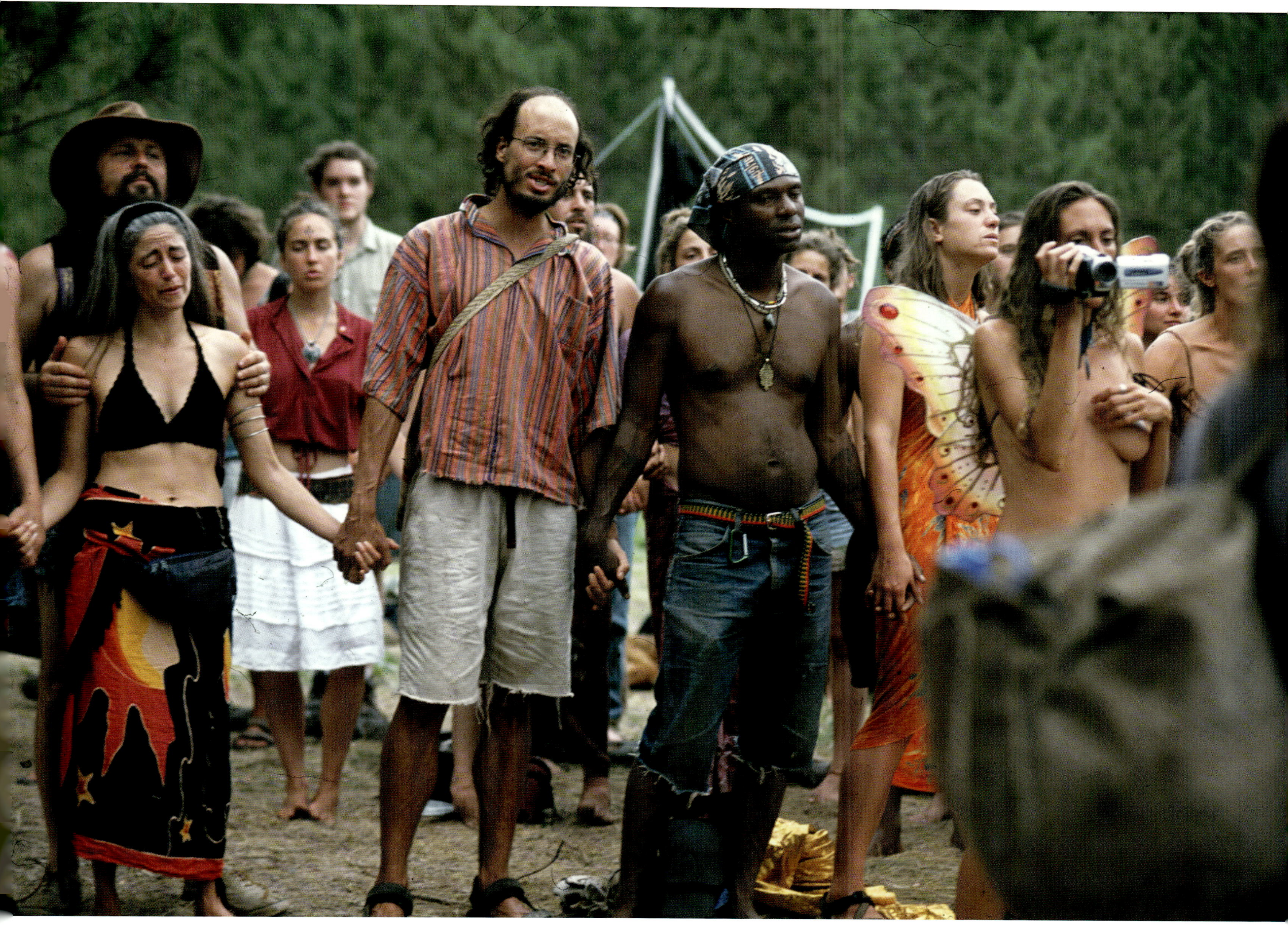

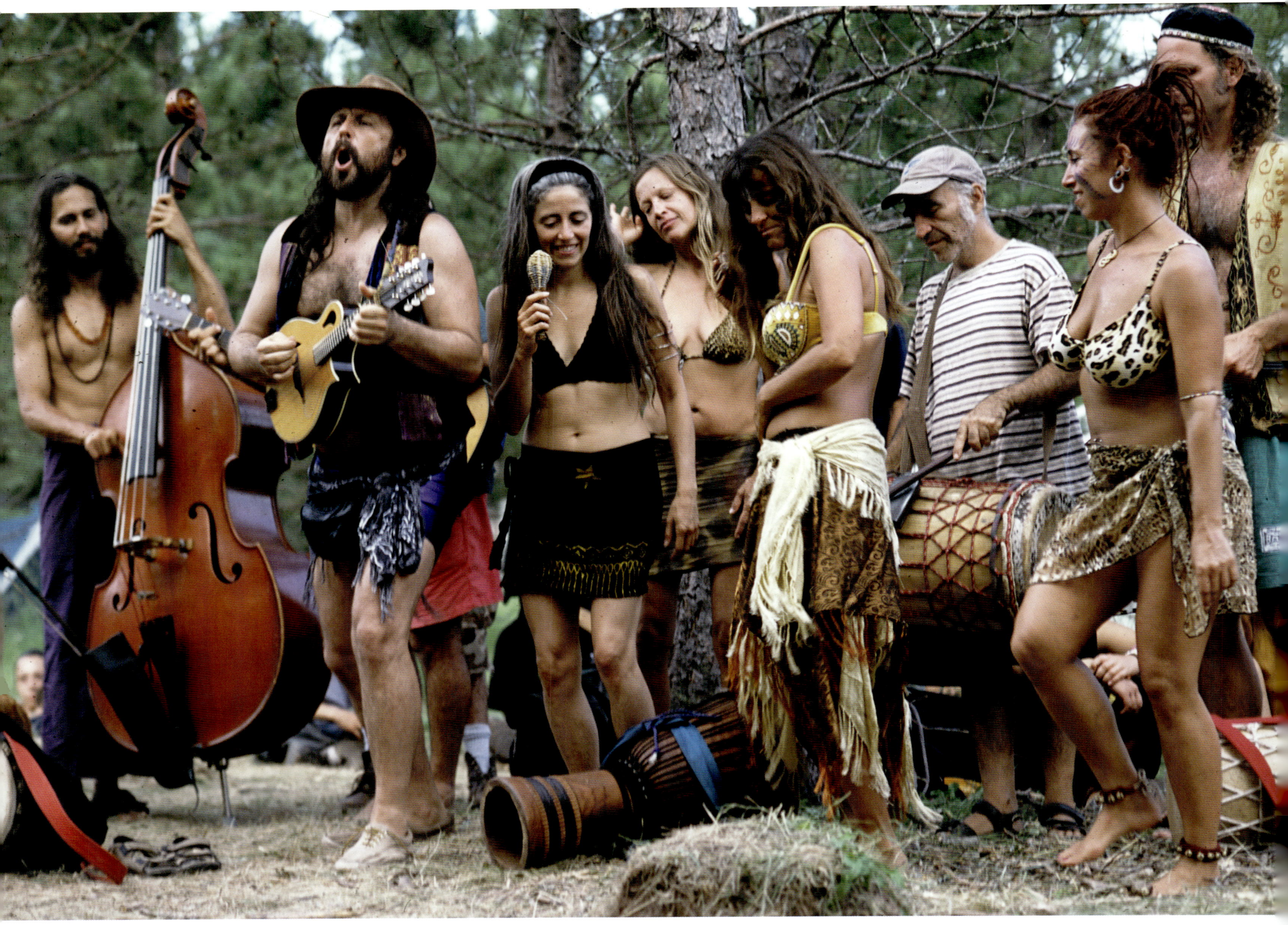

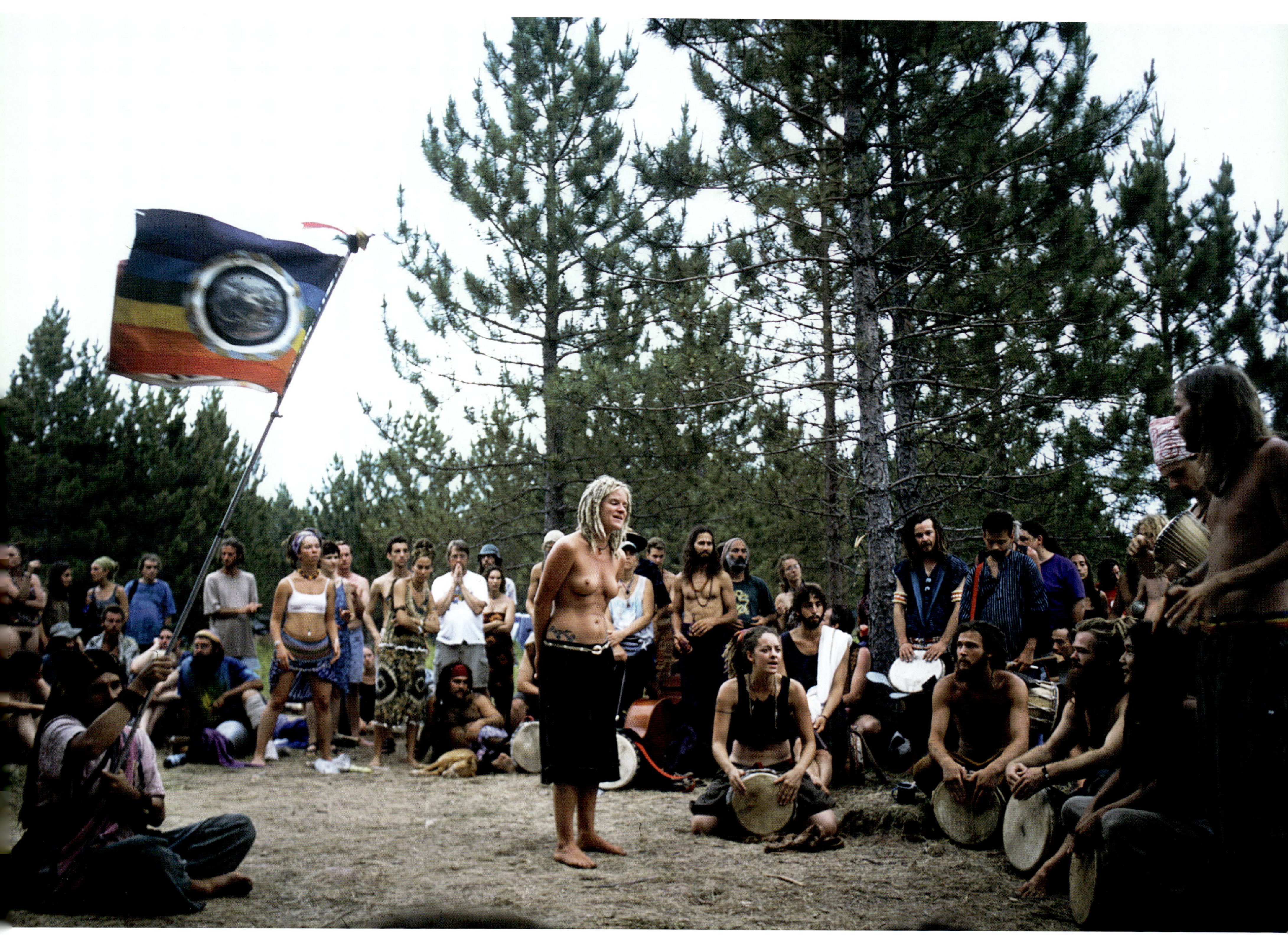

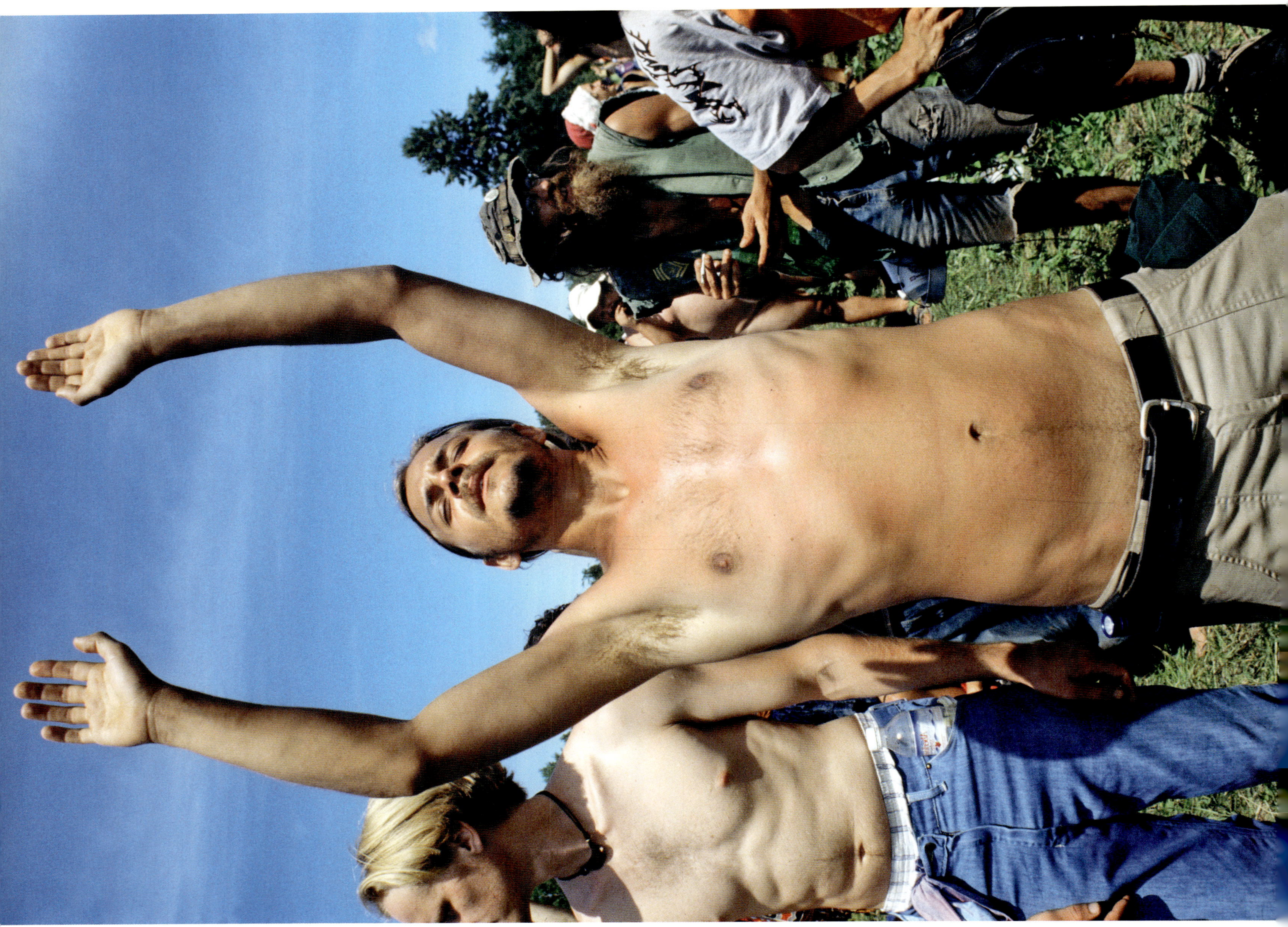

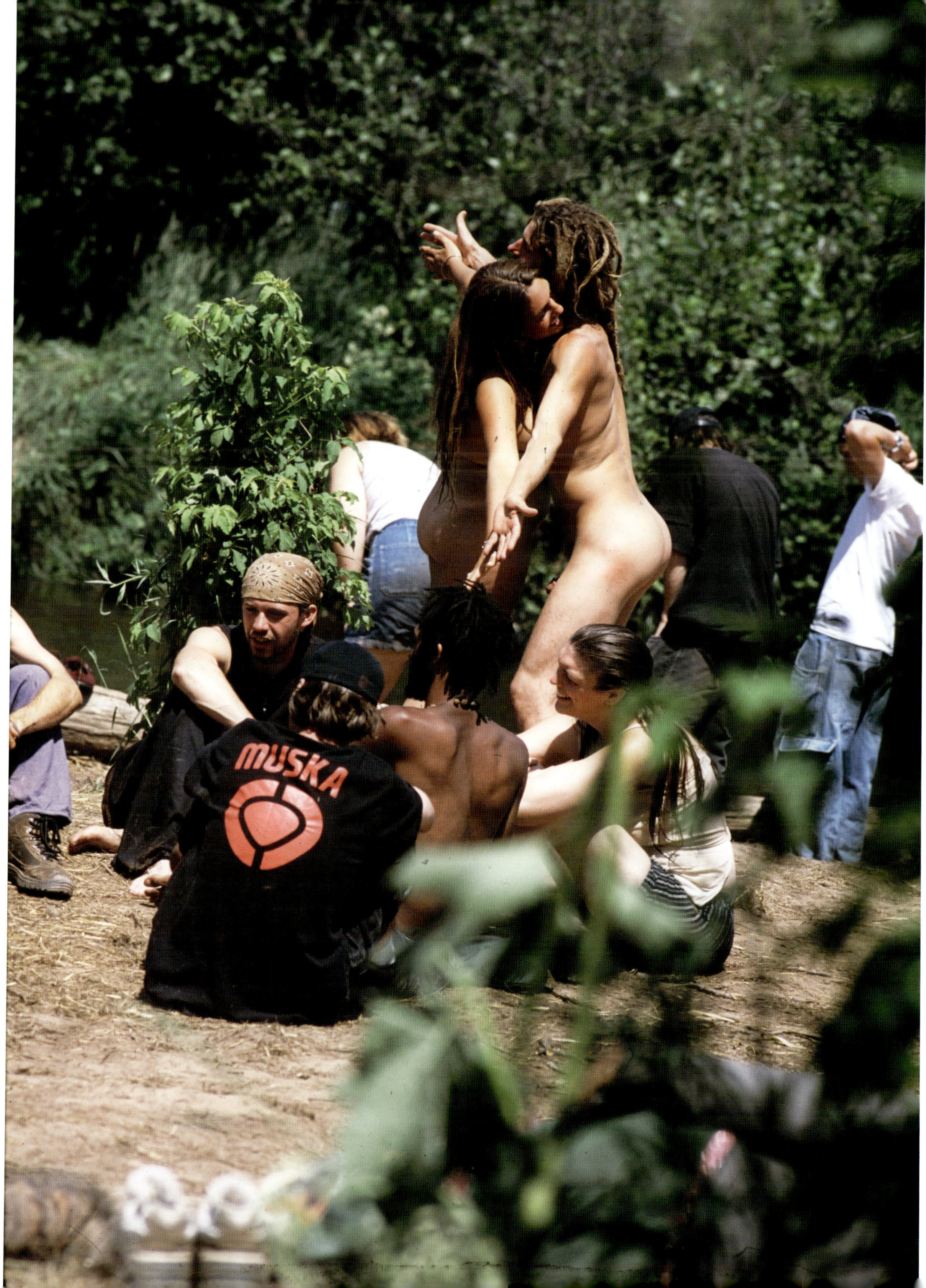

MUSKA

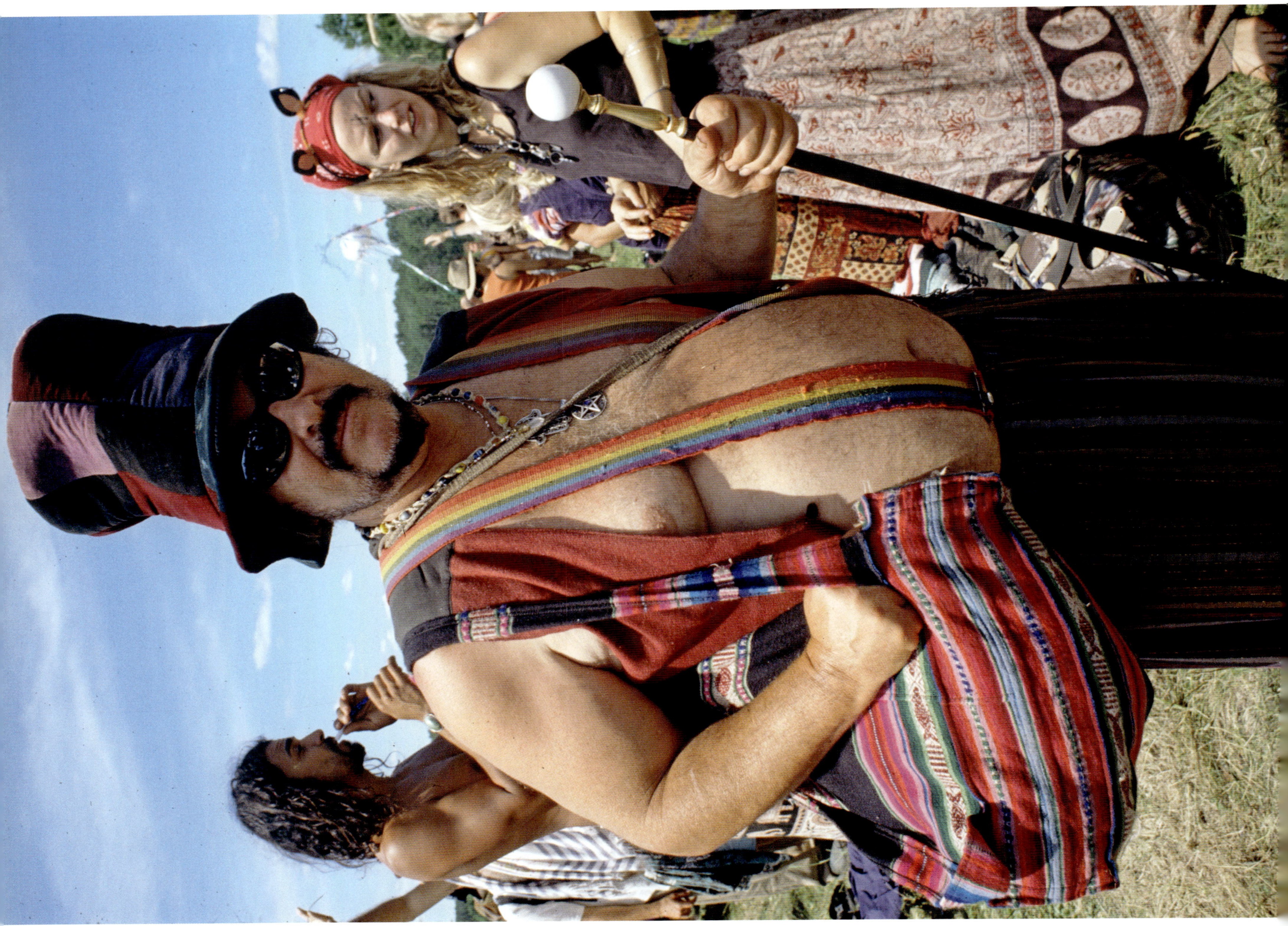

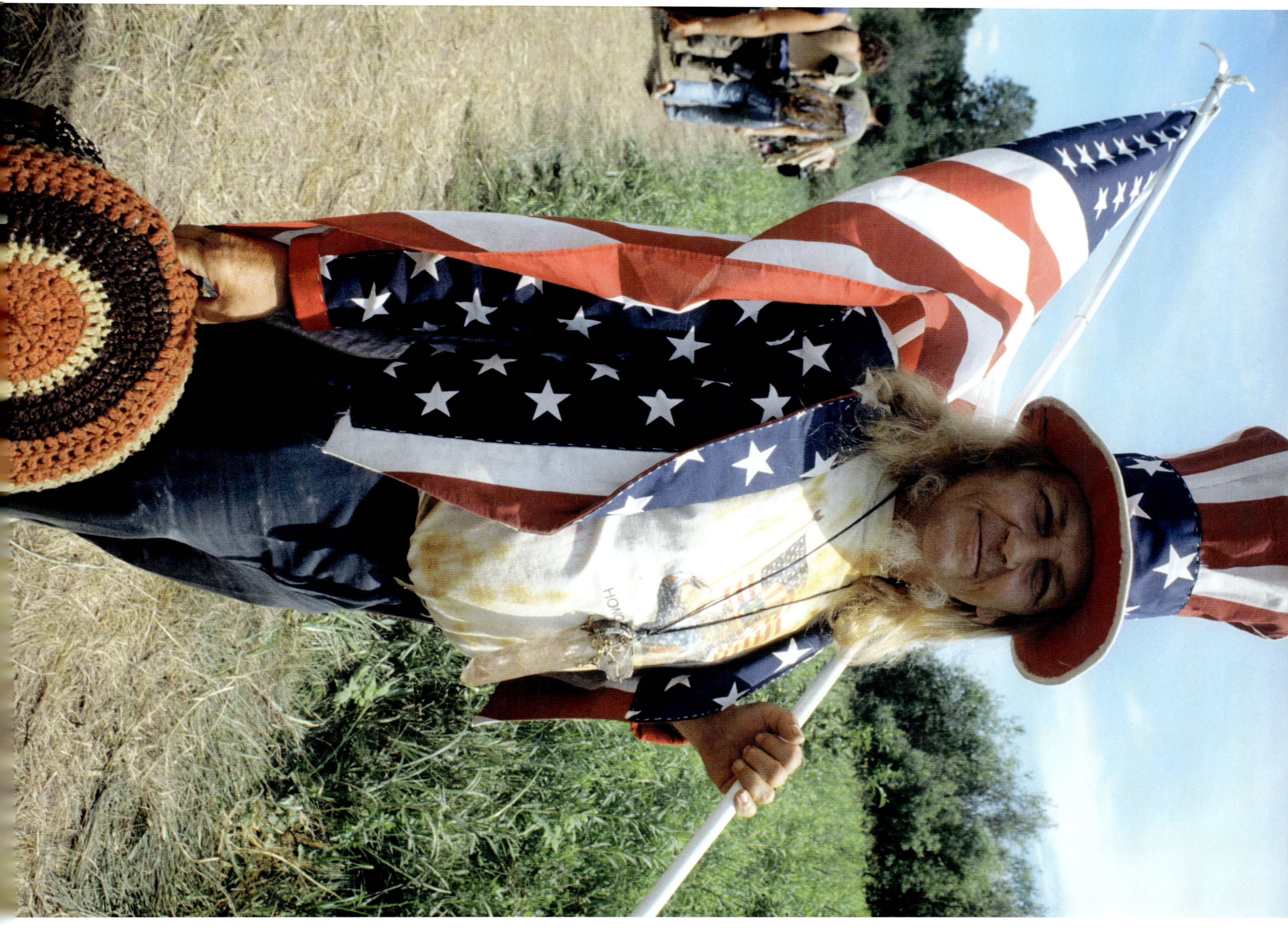

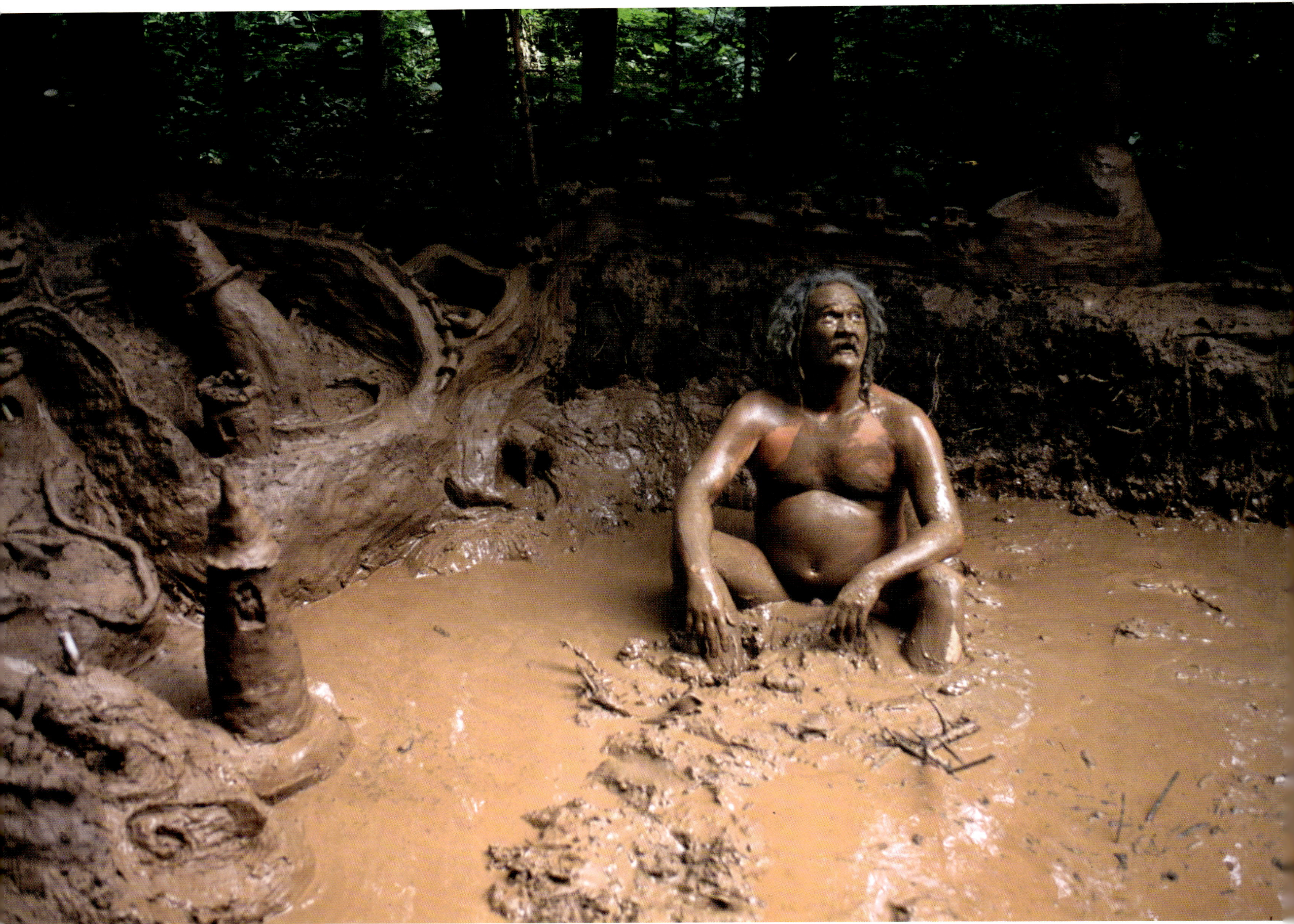

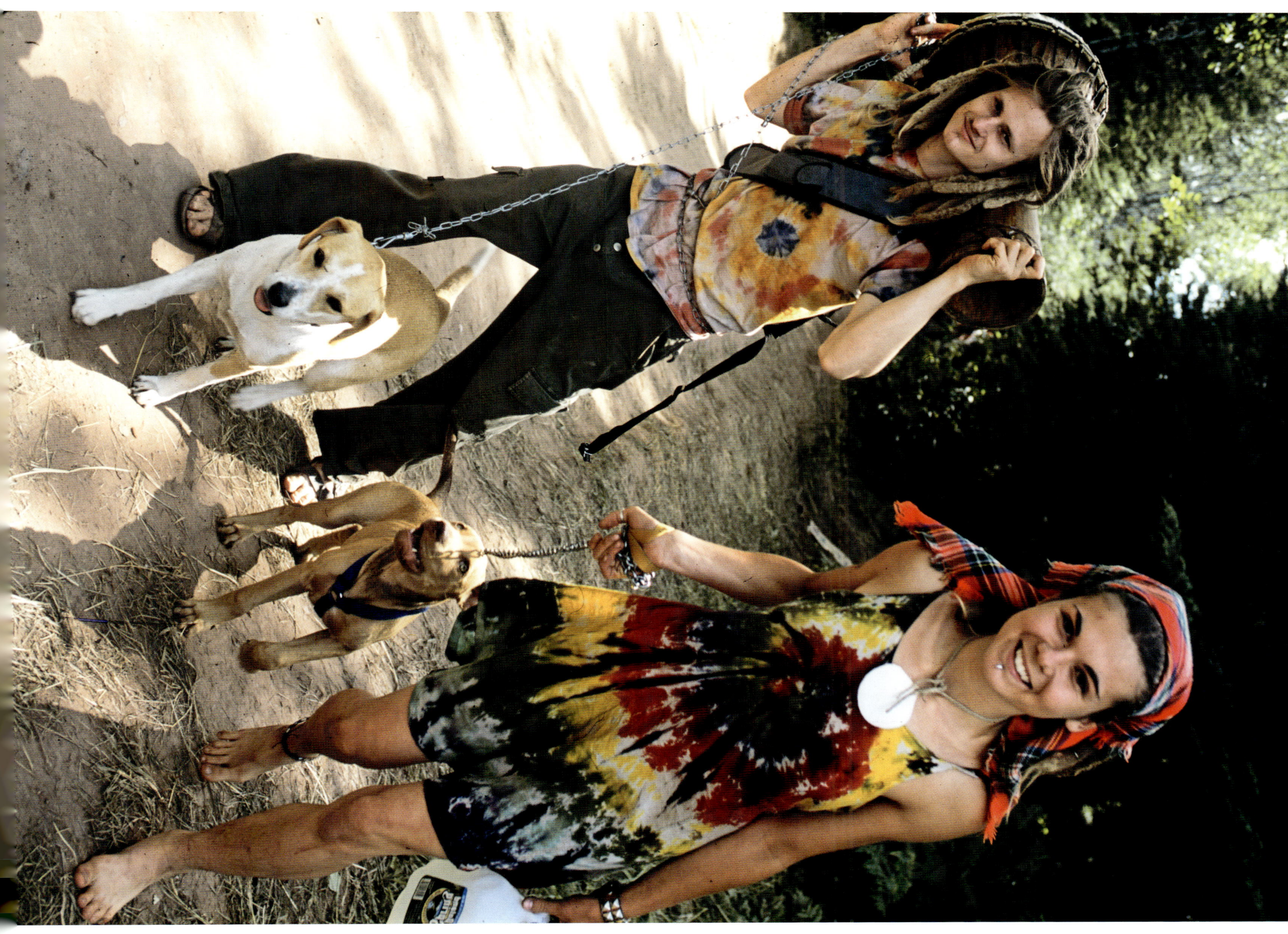

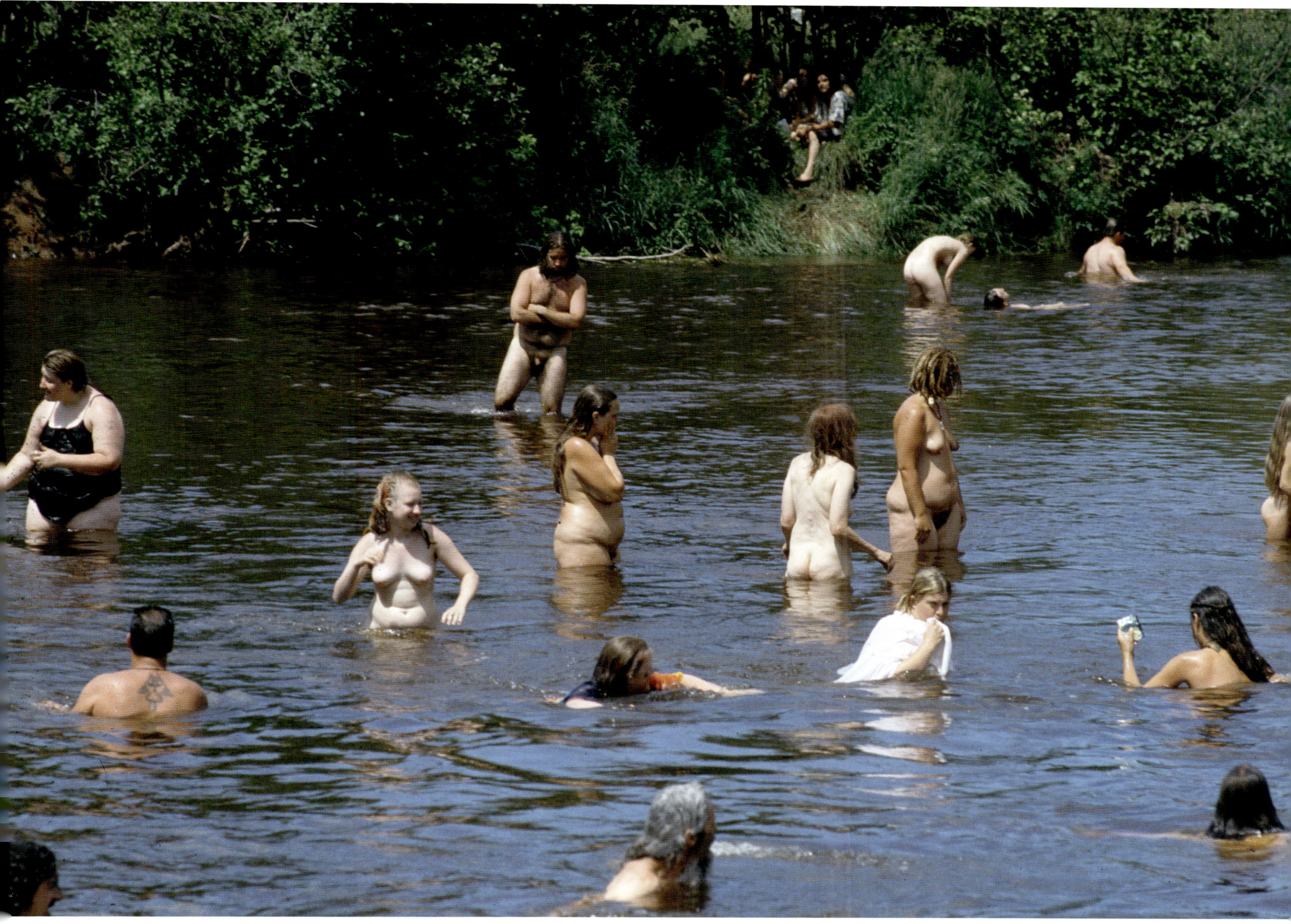

Mt. Shasta, California

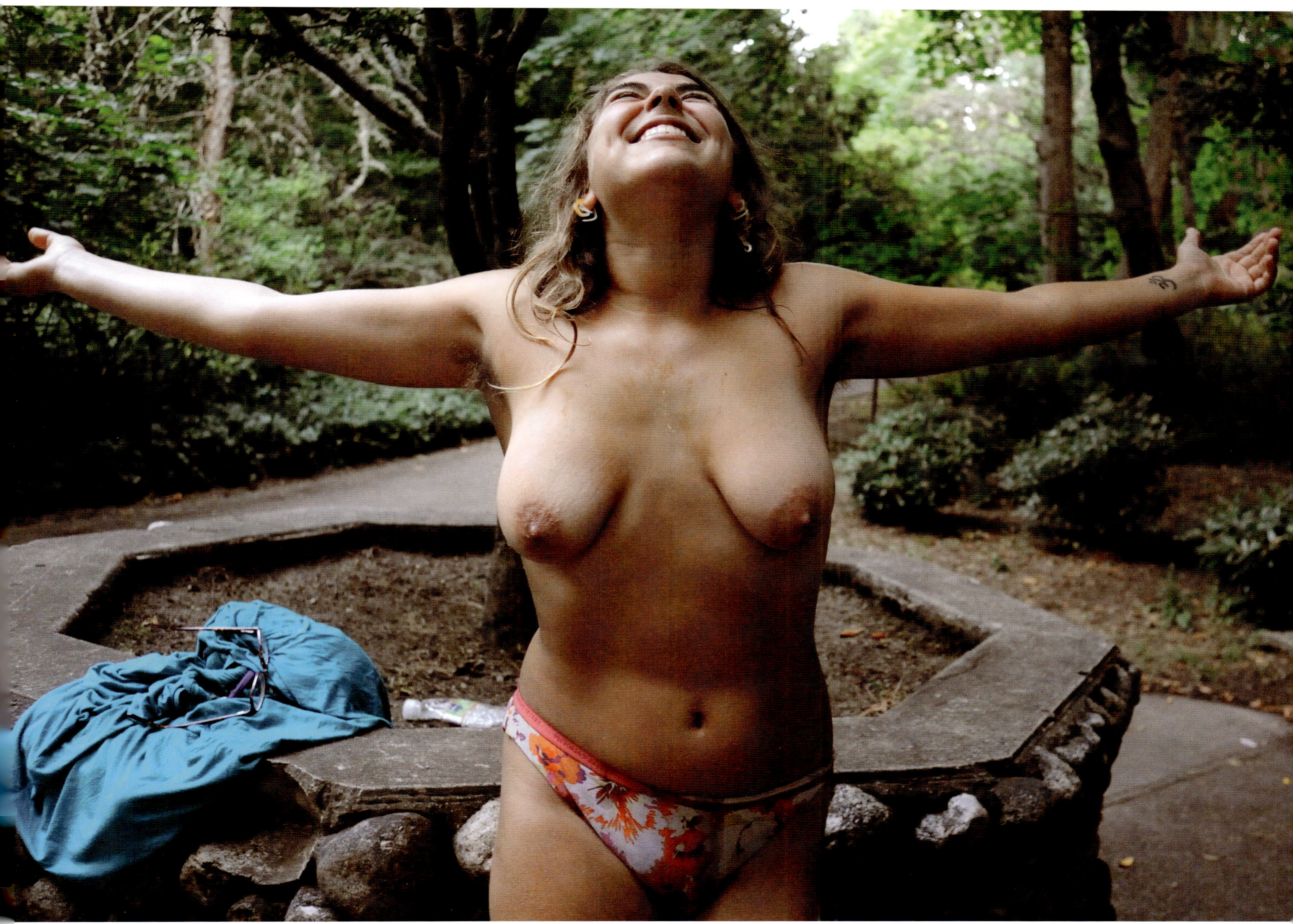

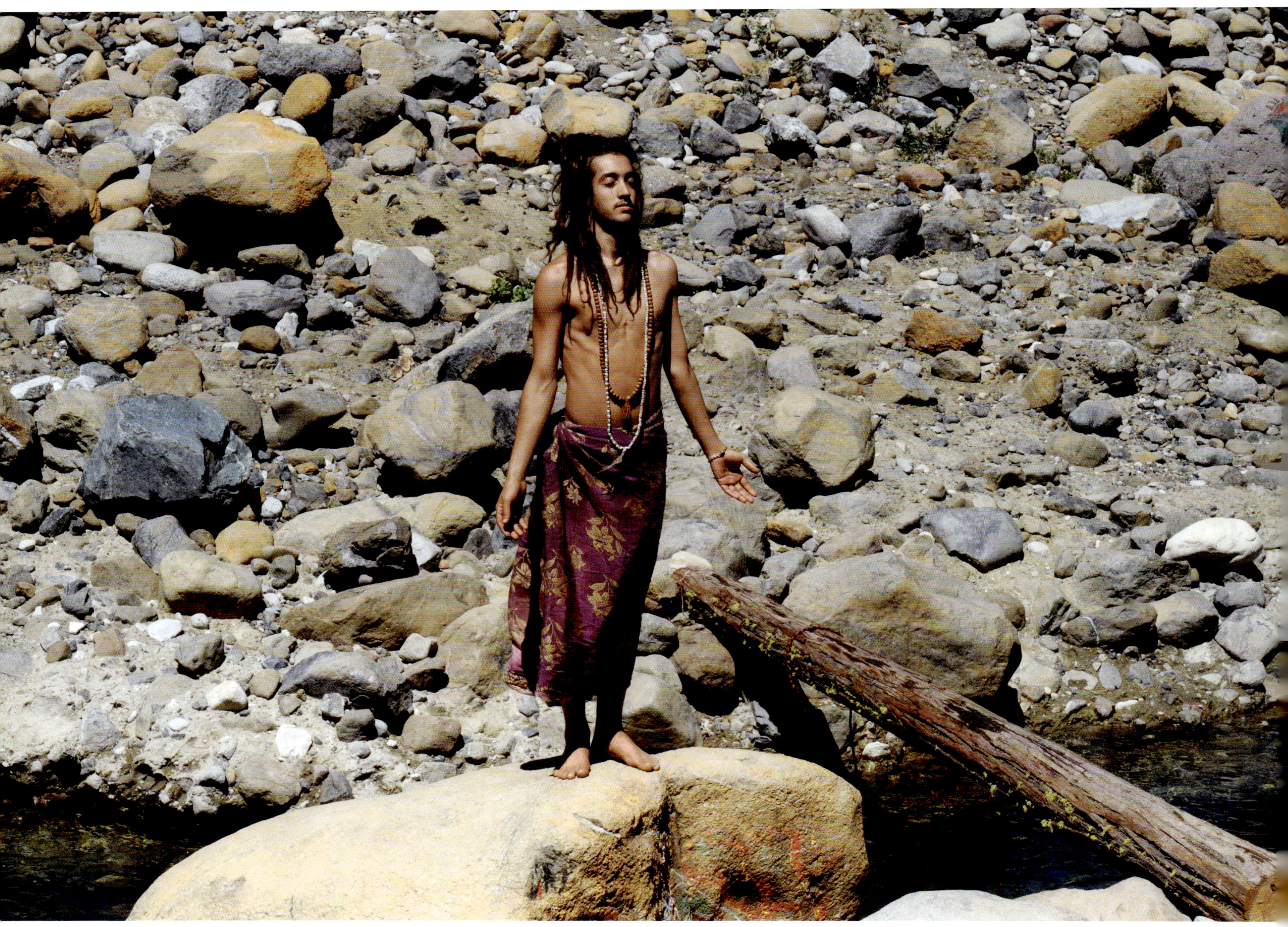

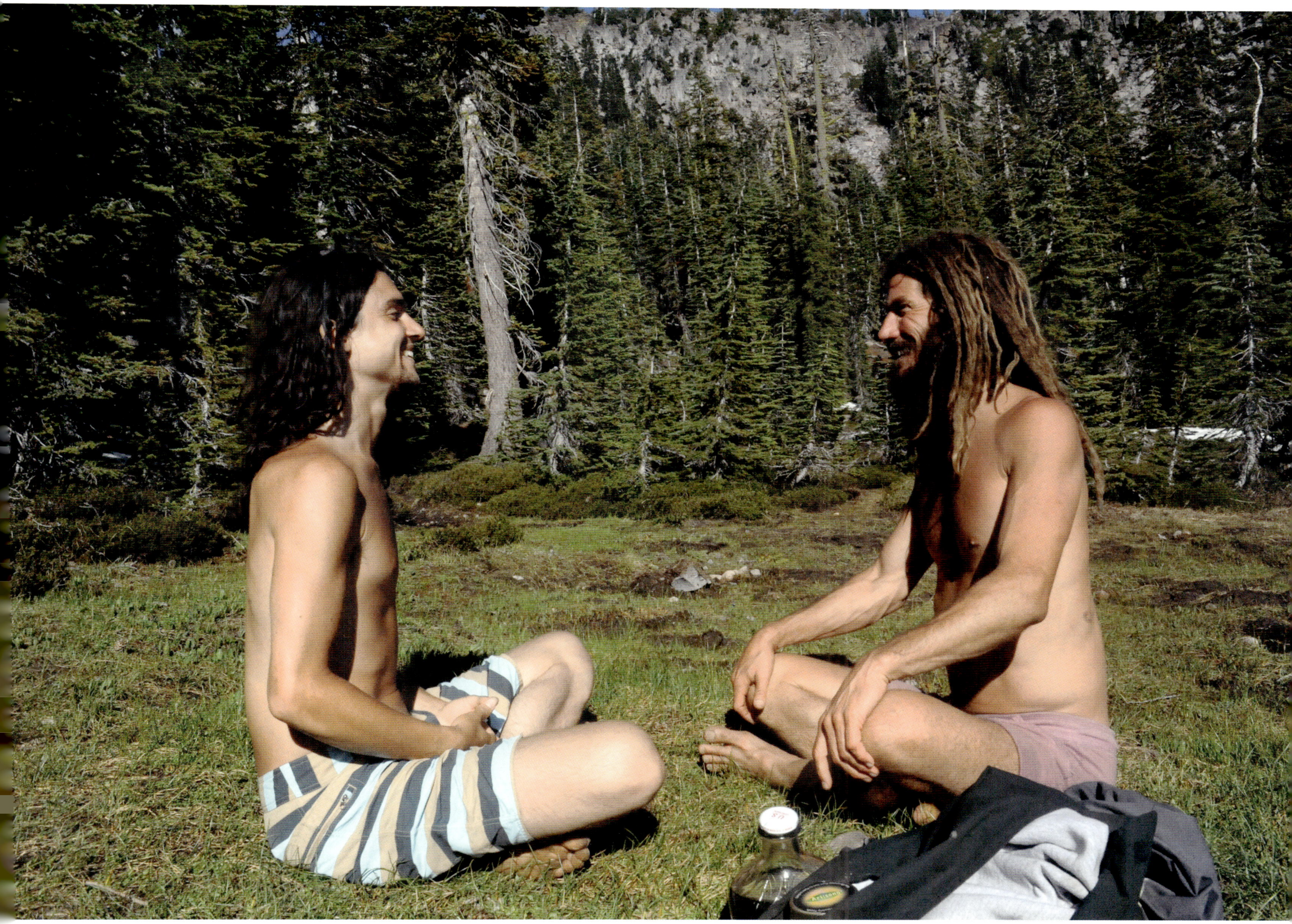

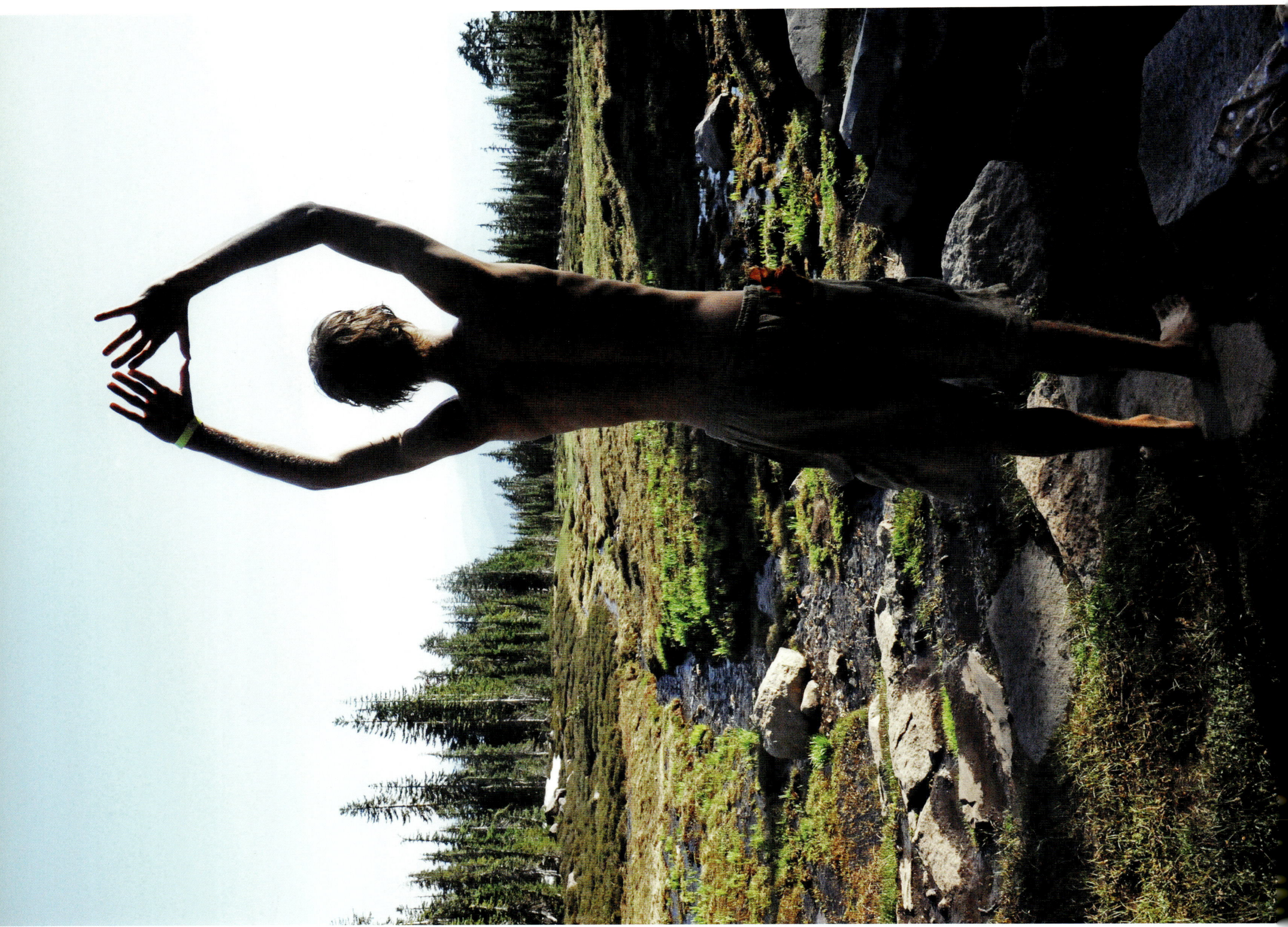

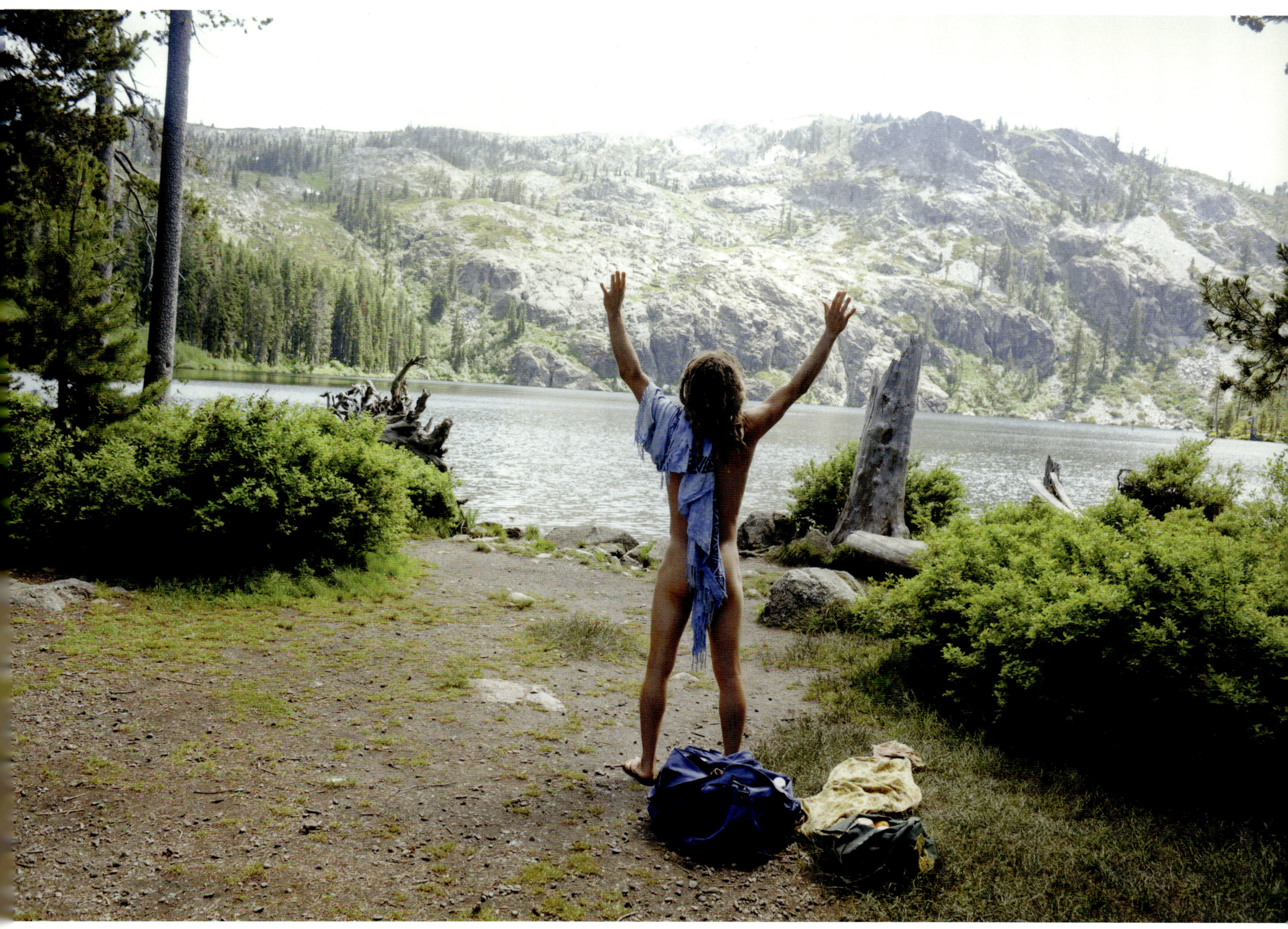

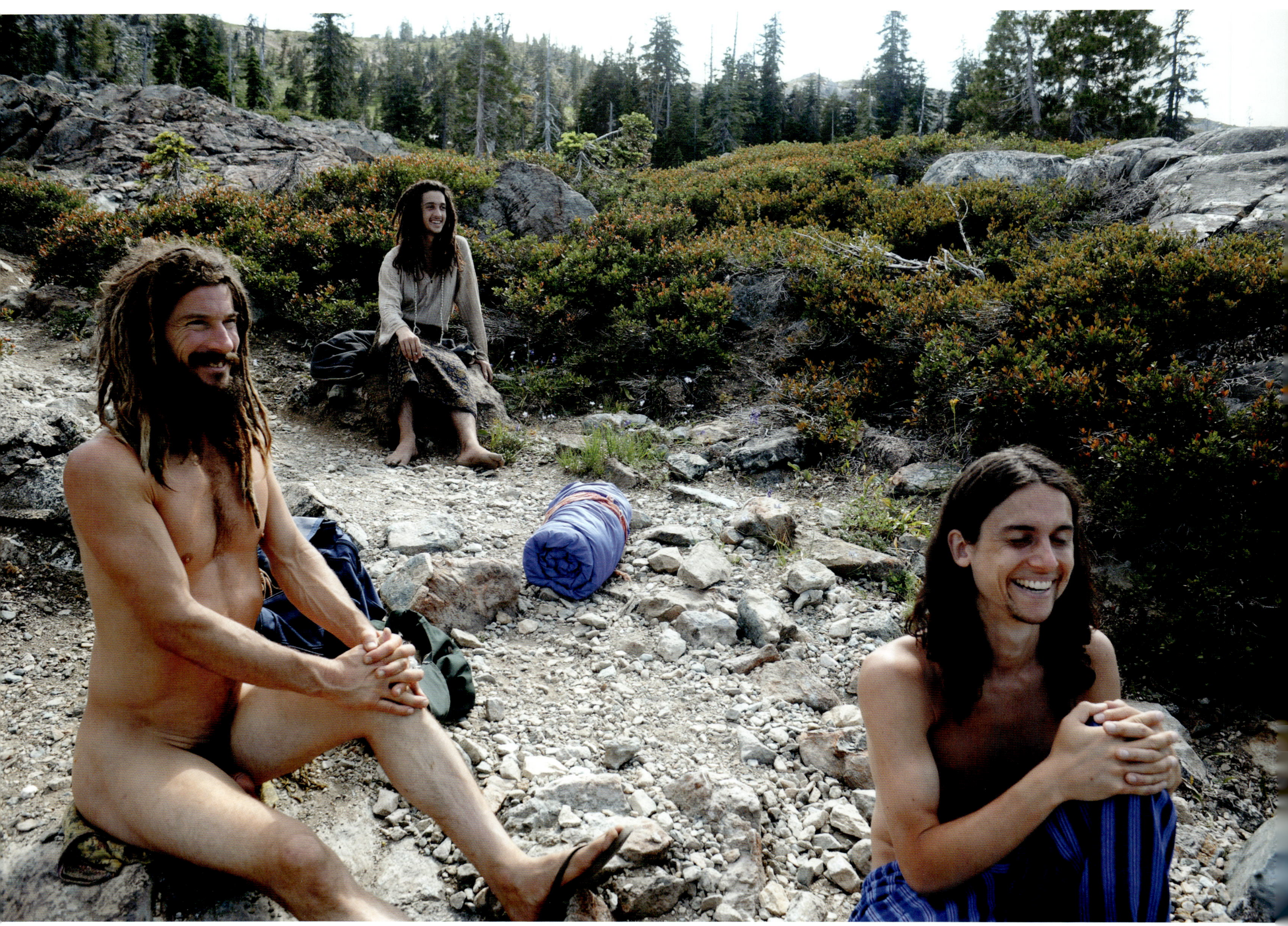

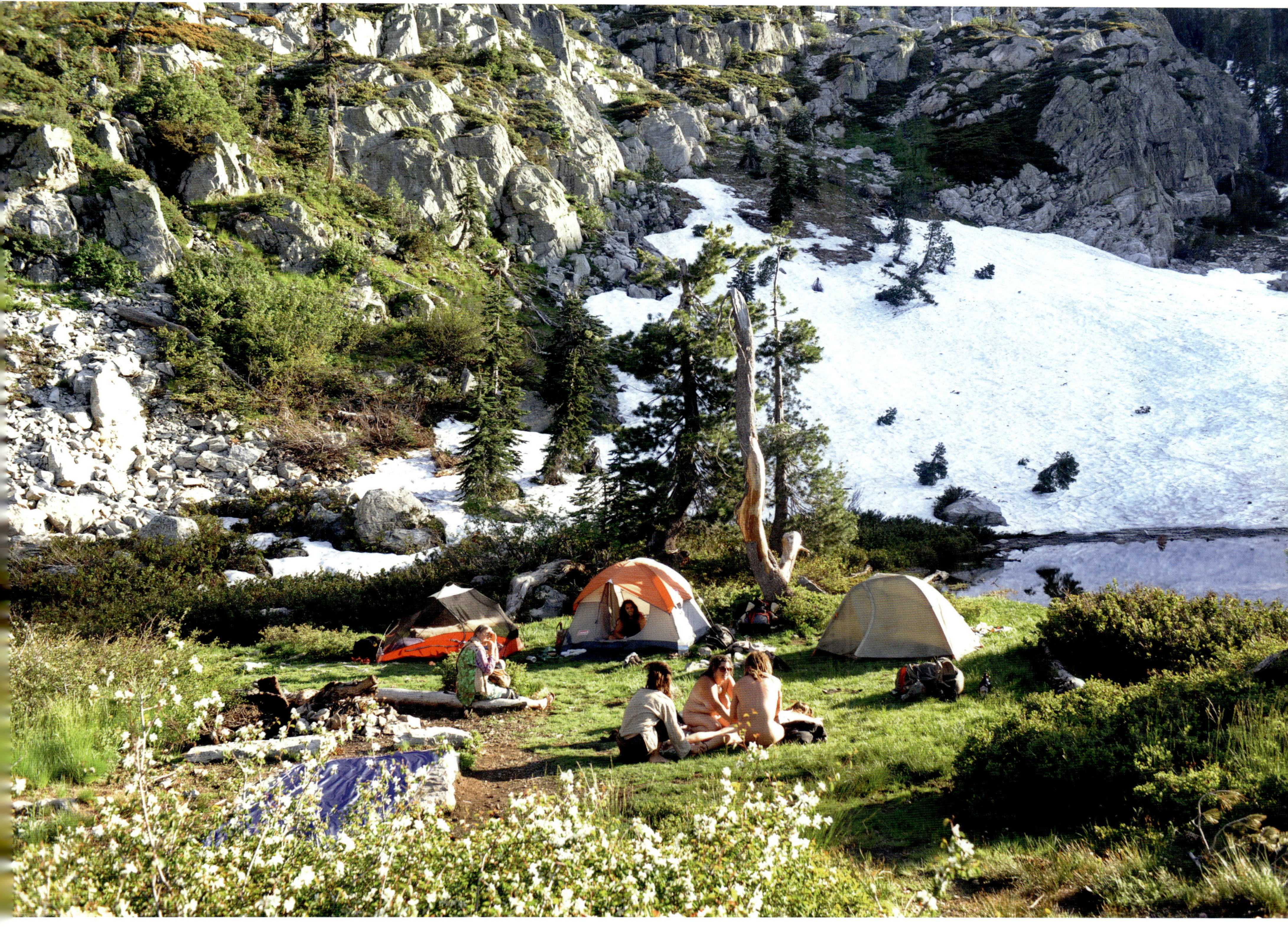

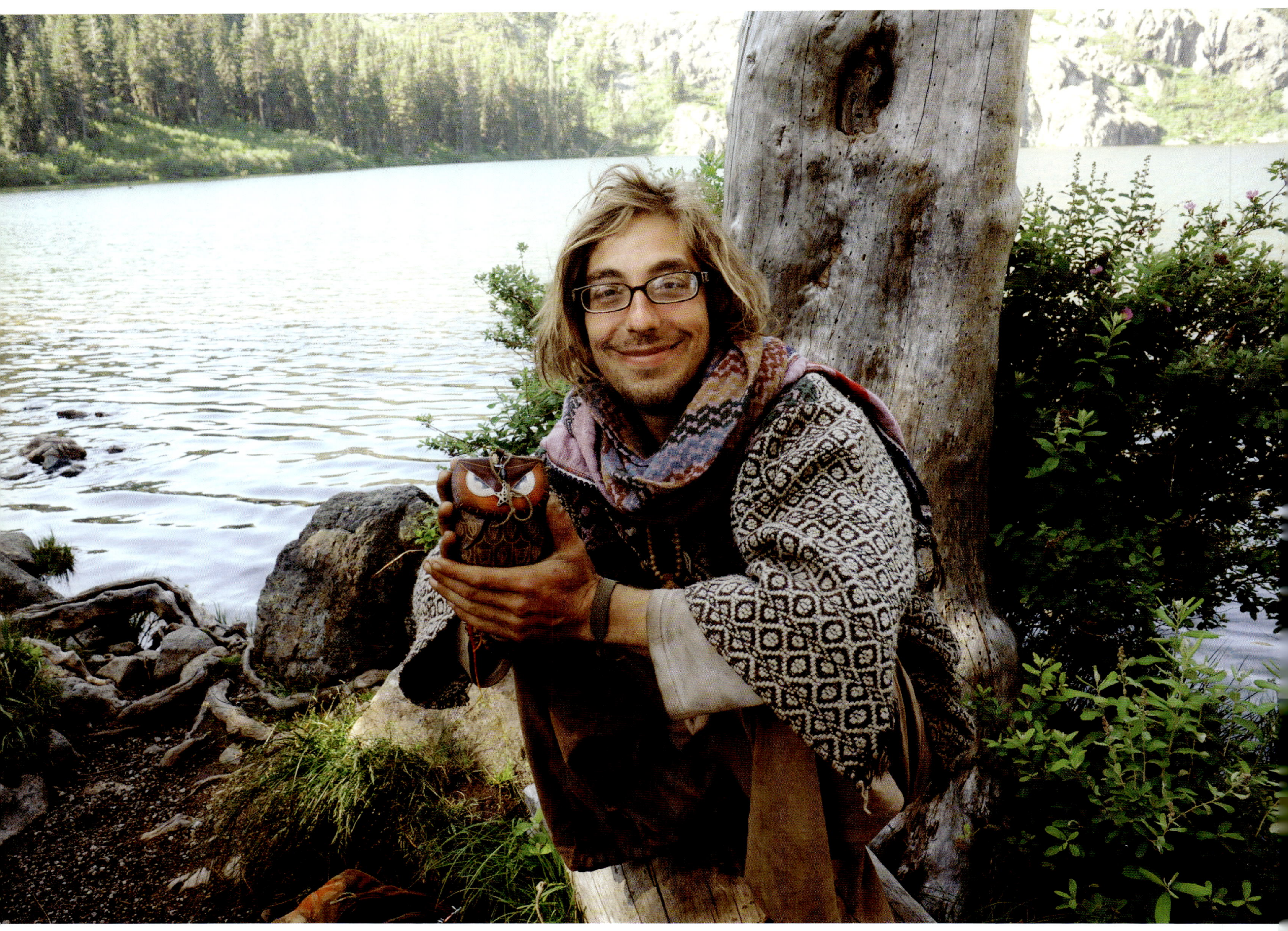

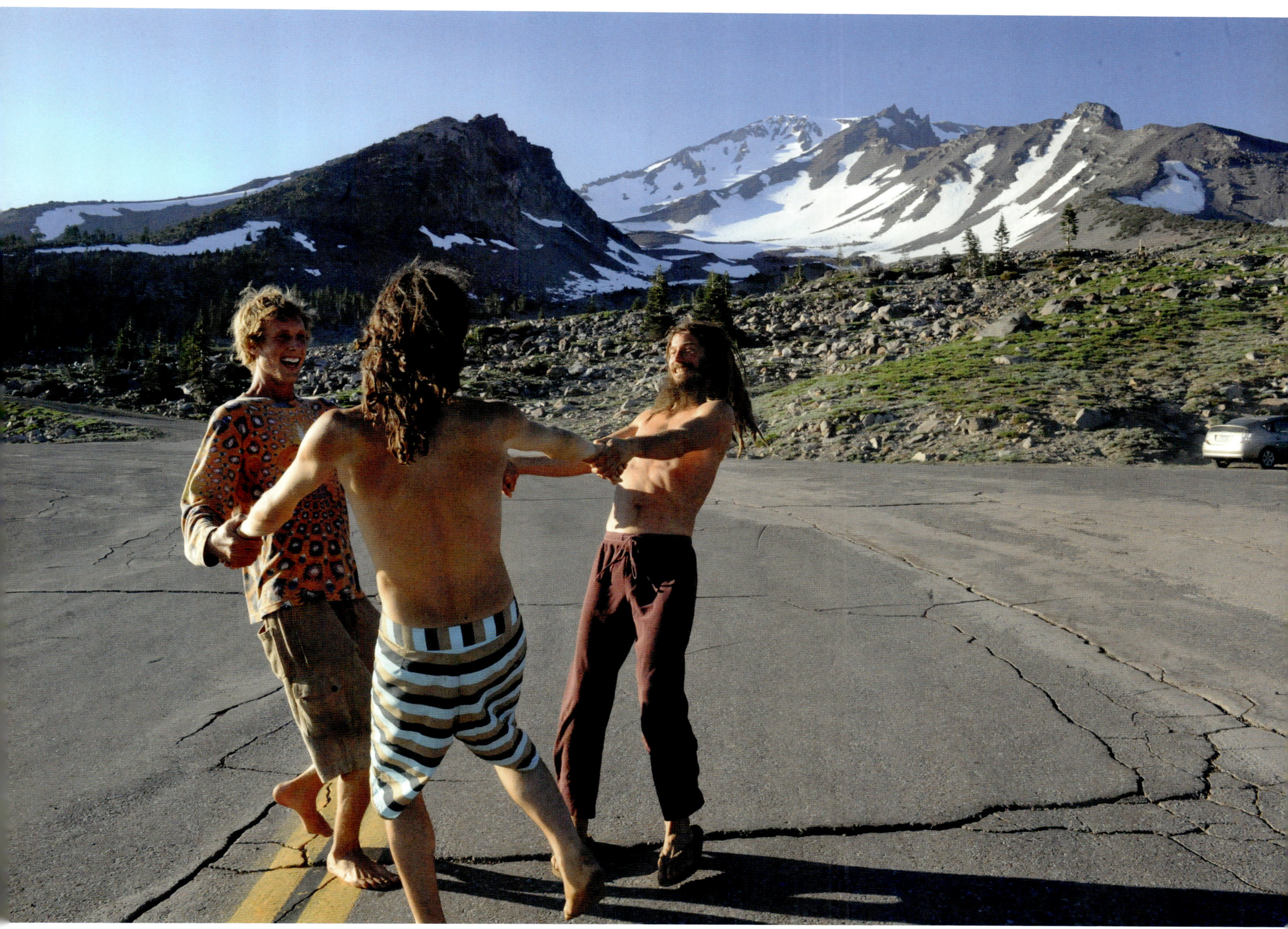

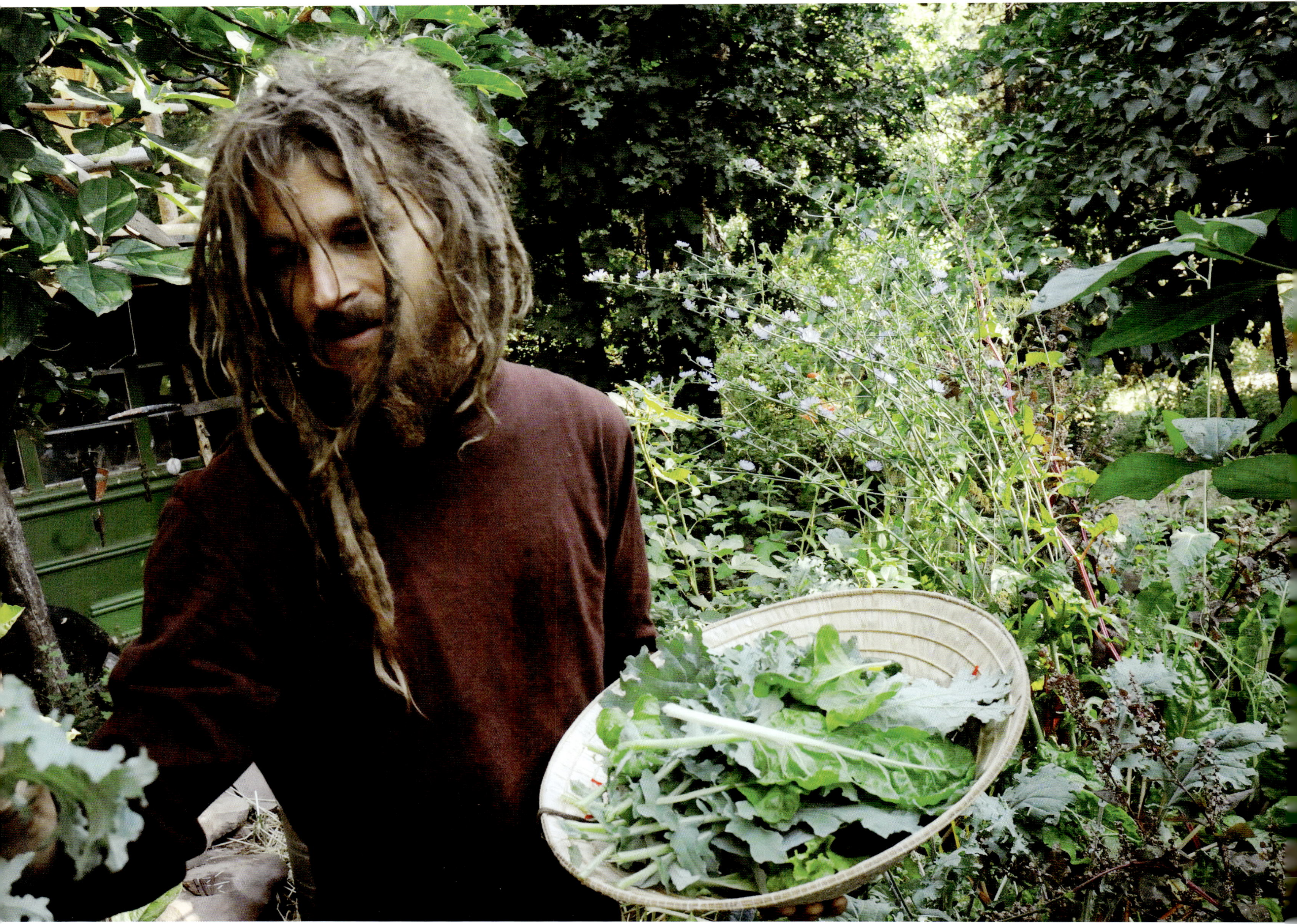

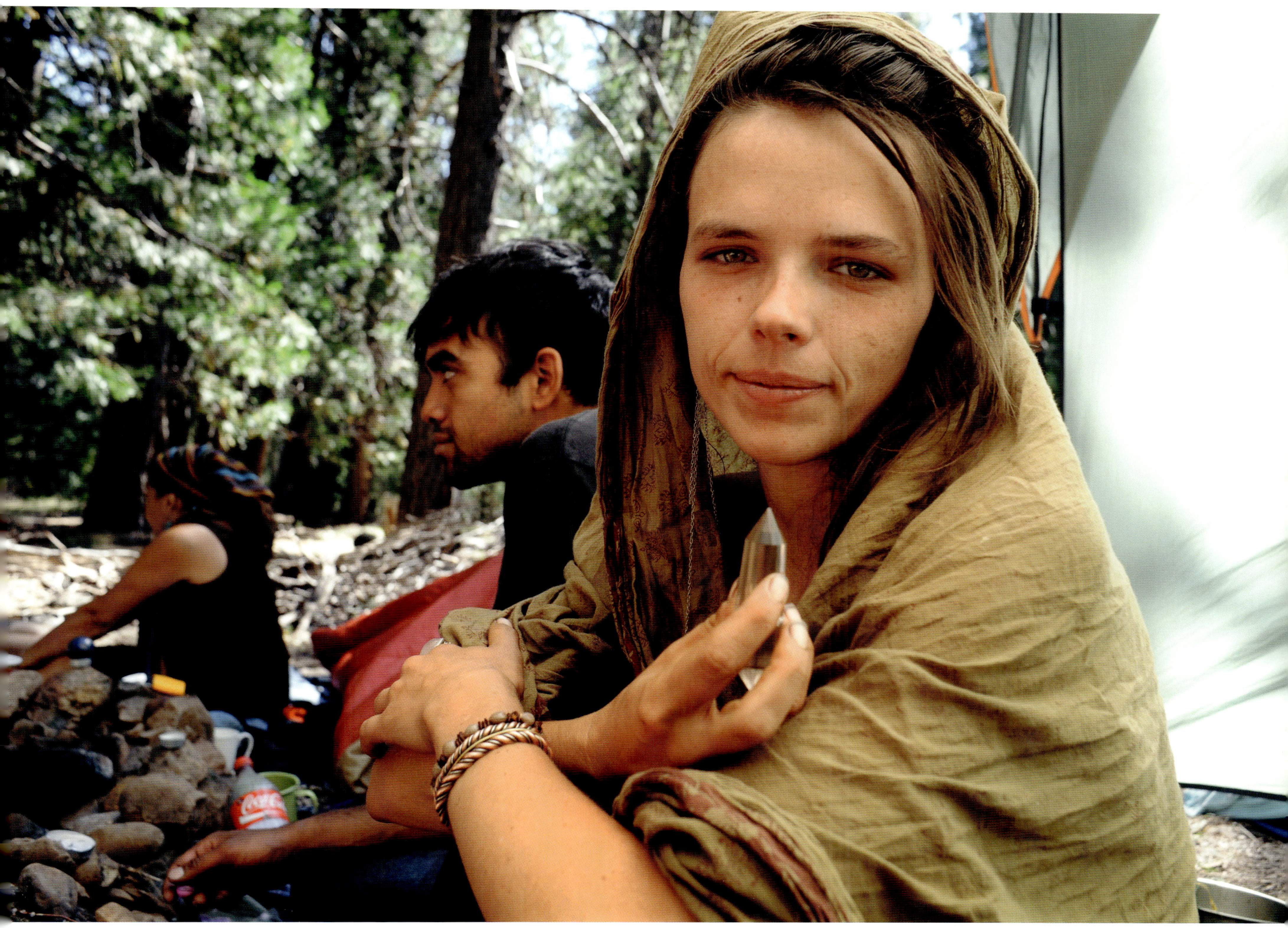

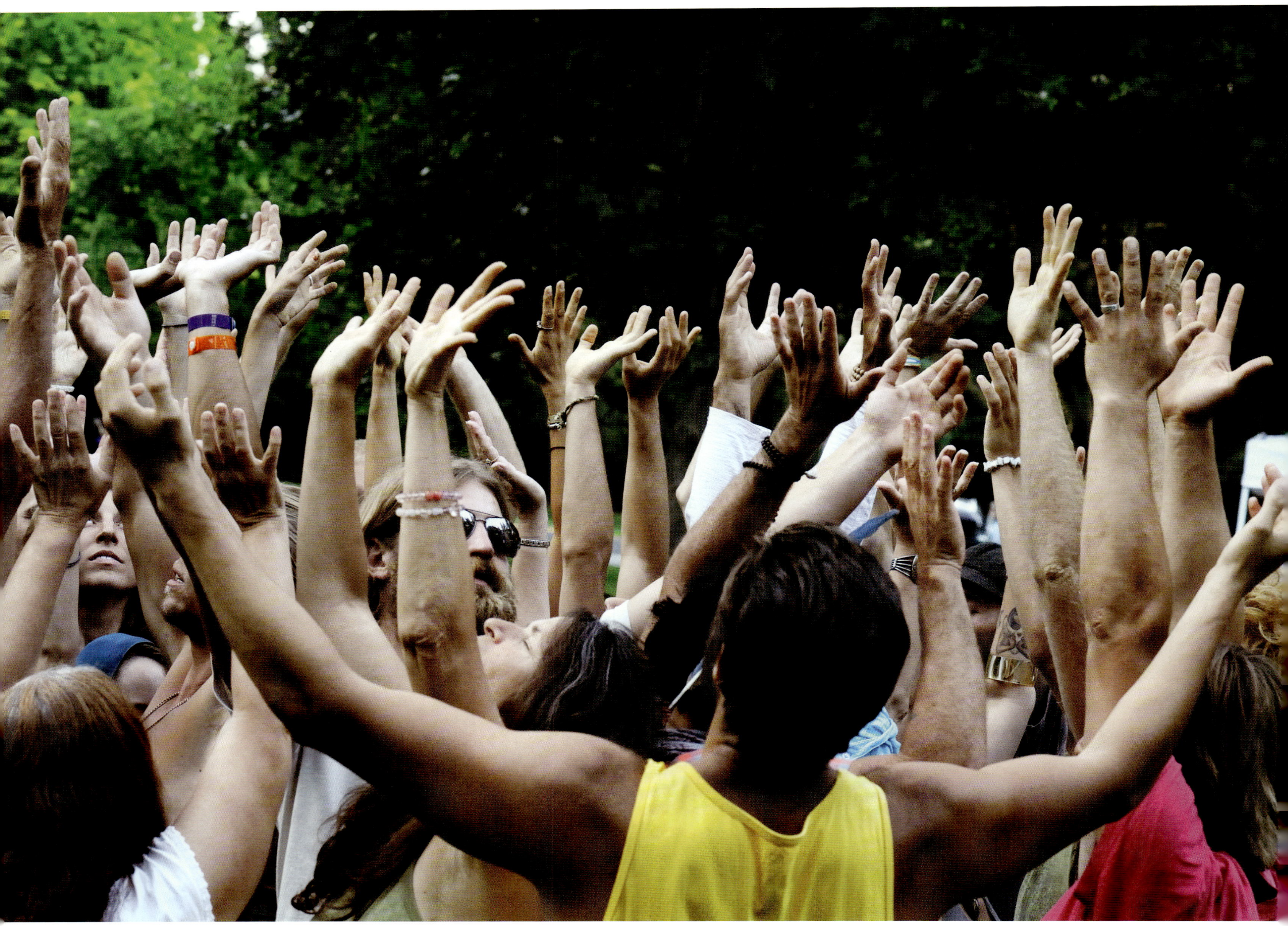

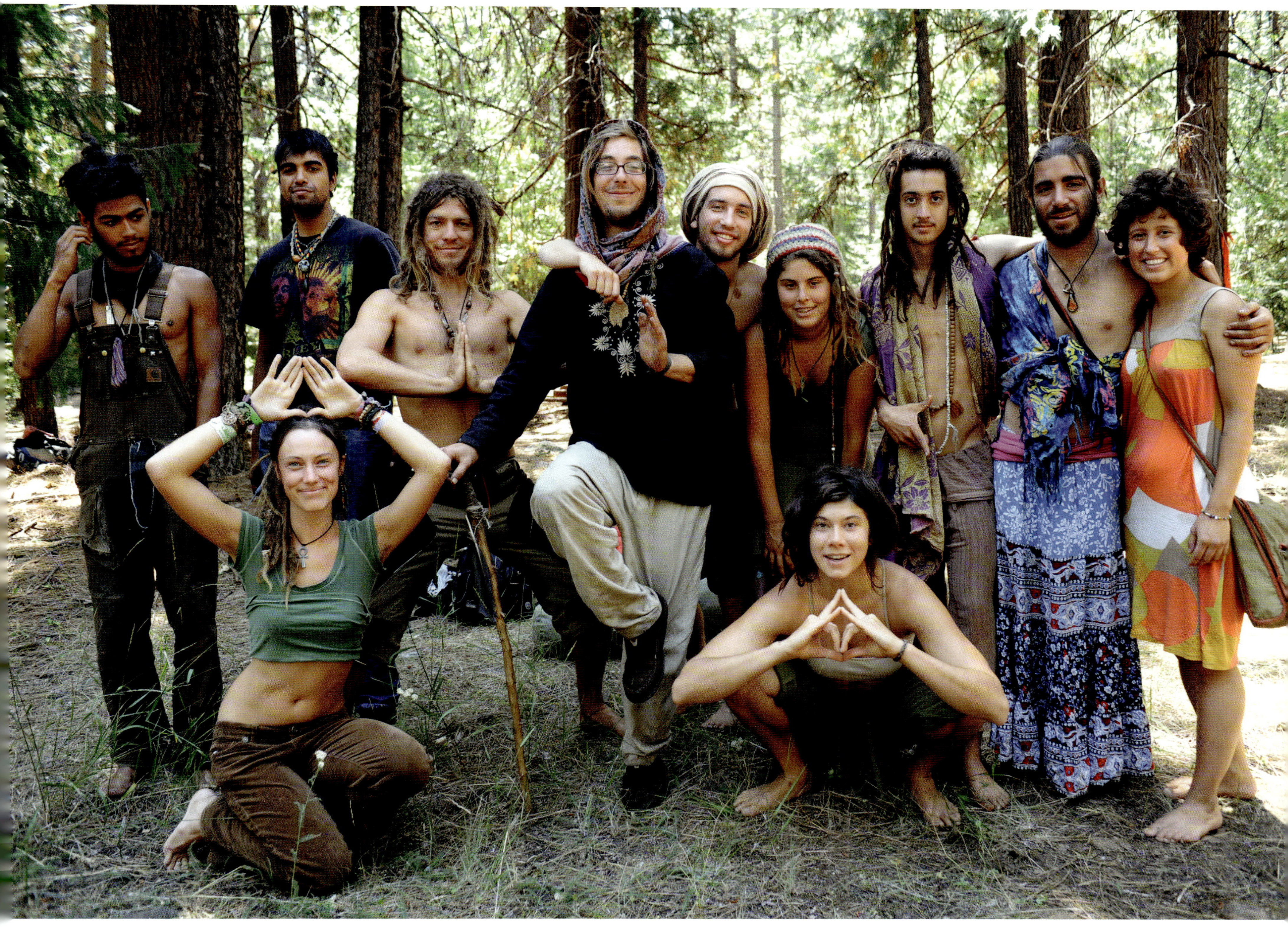

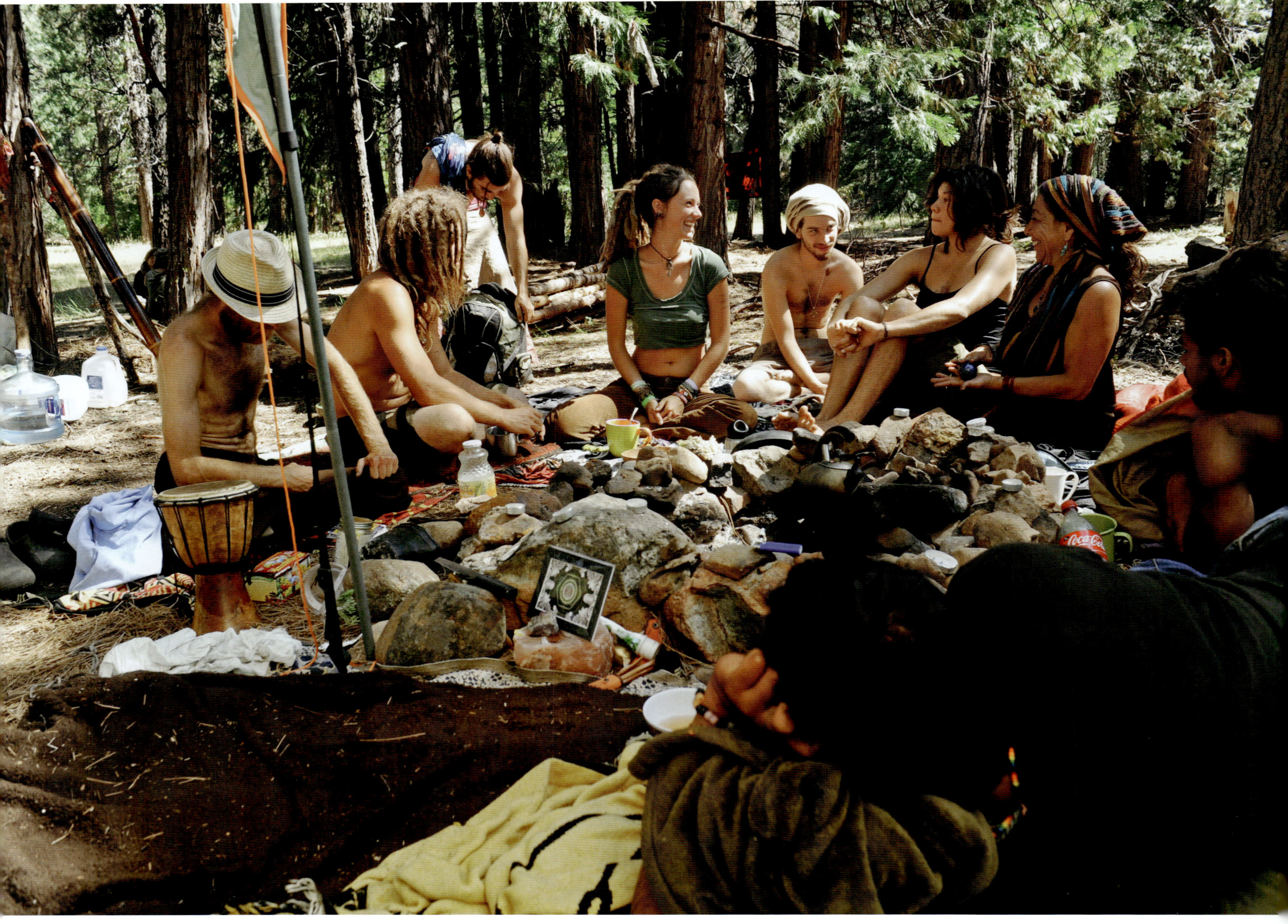

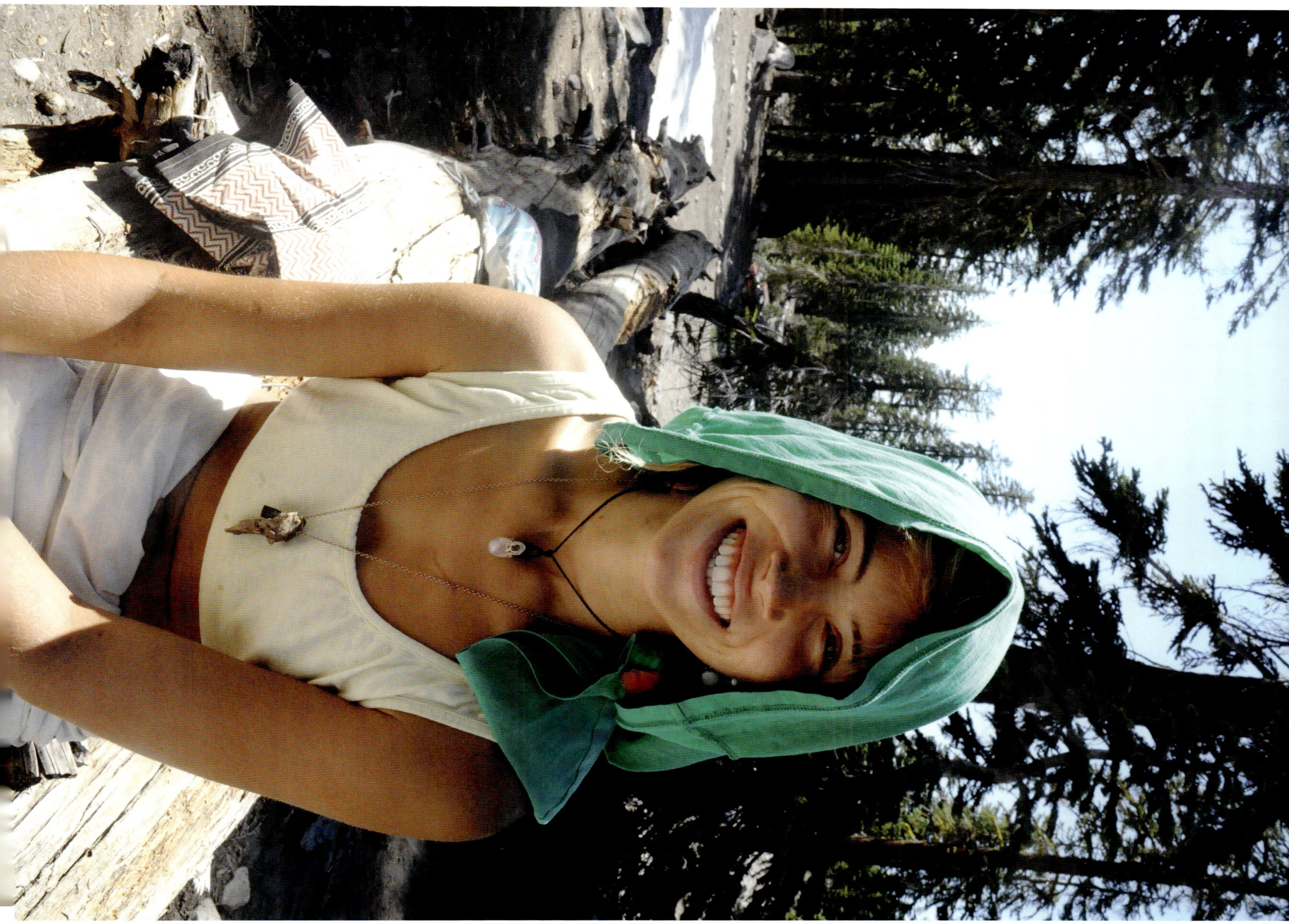

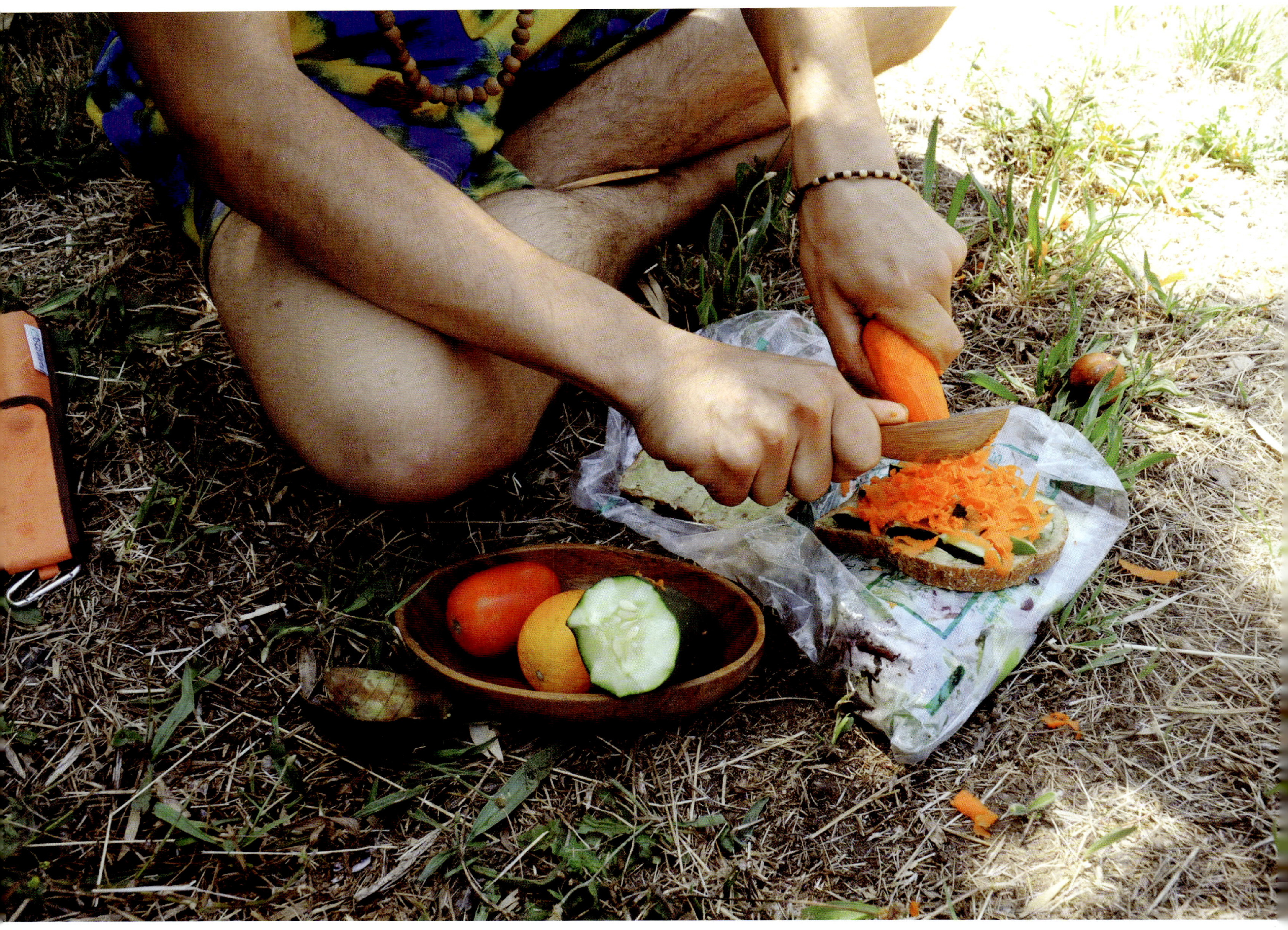

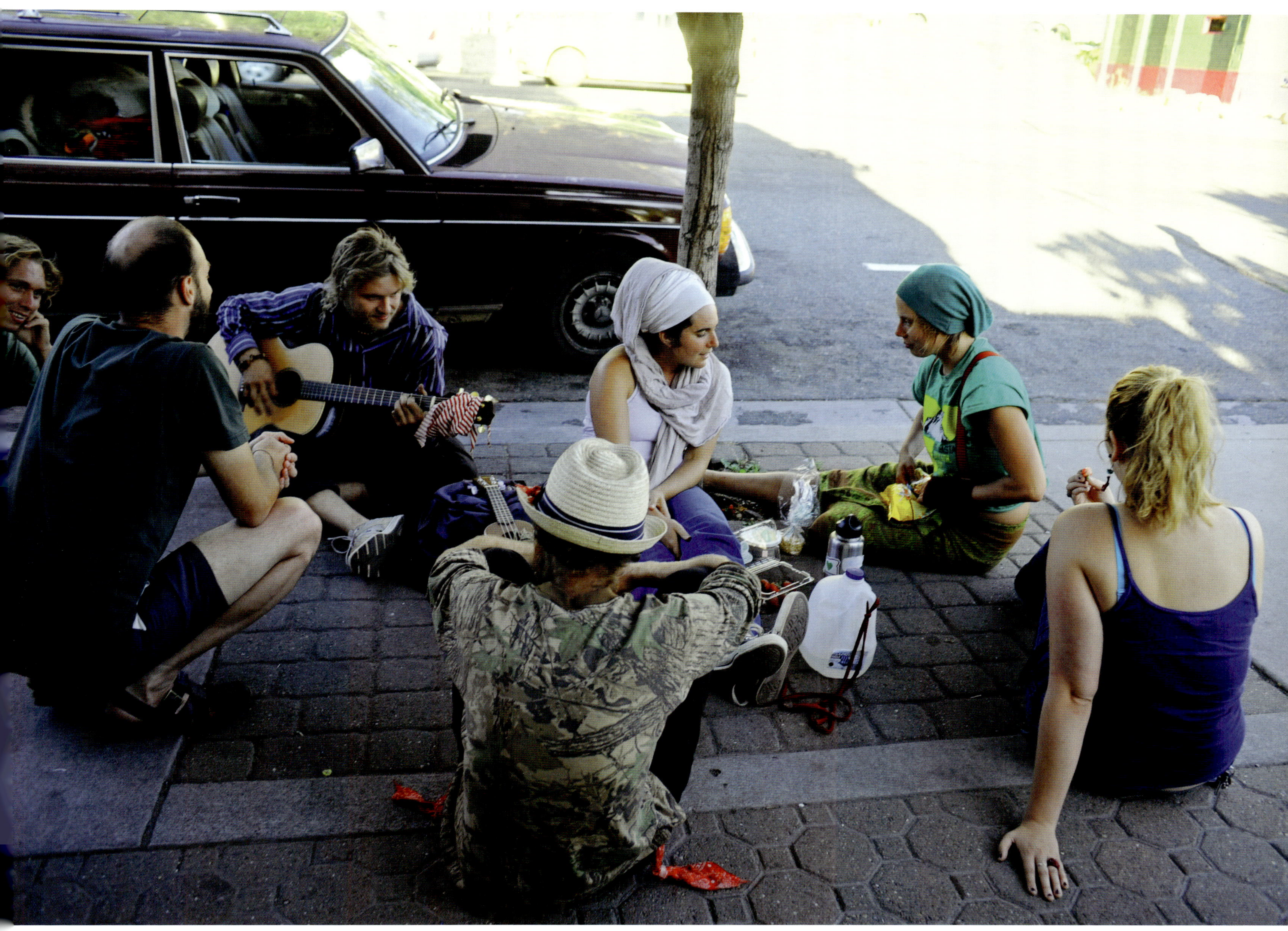

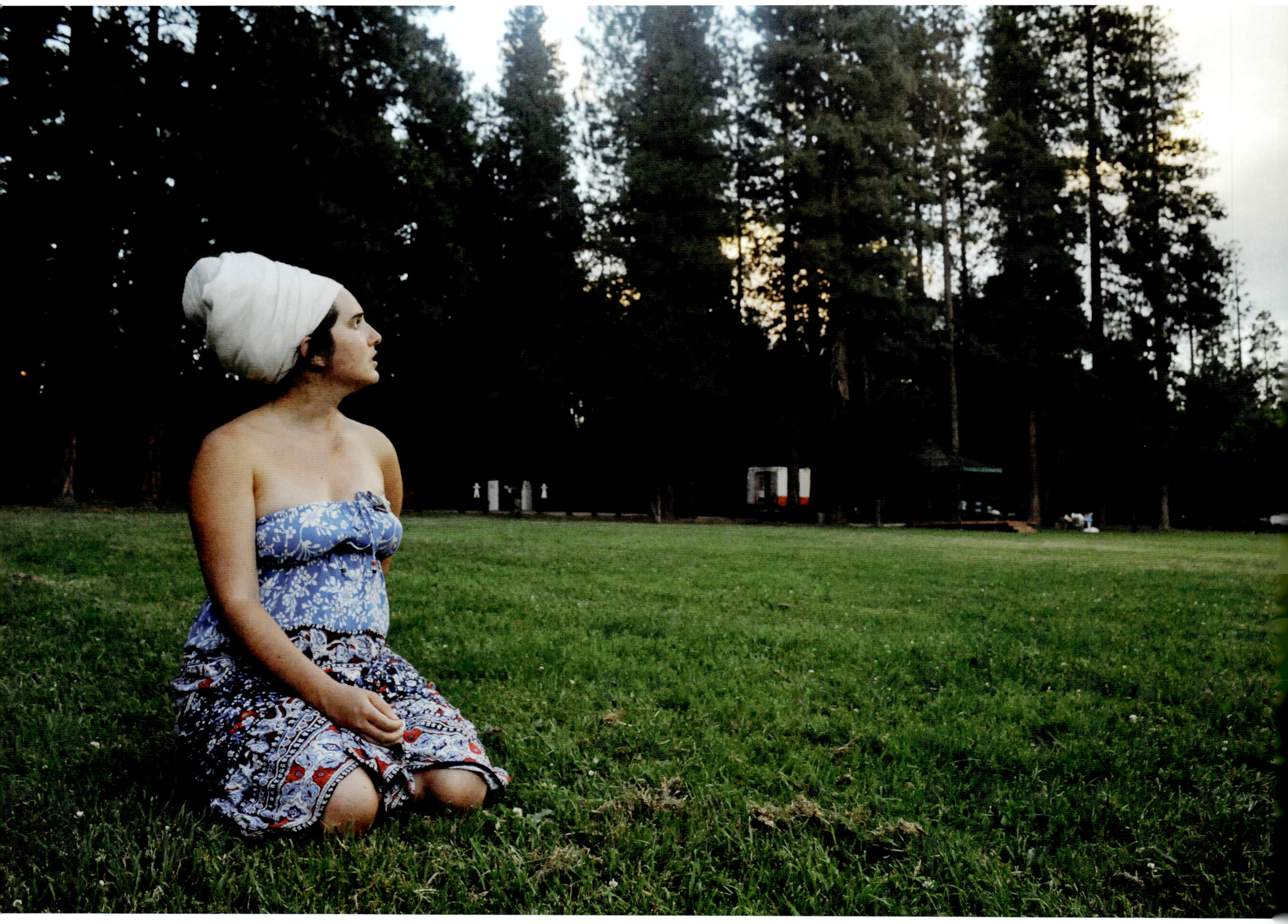

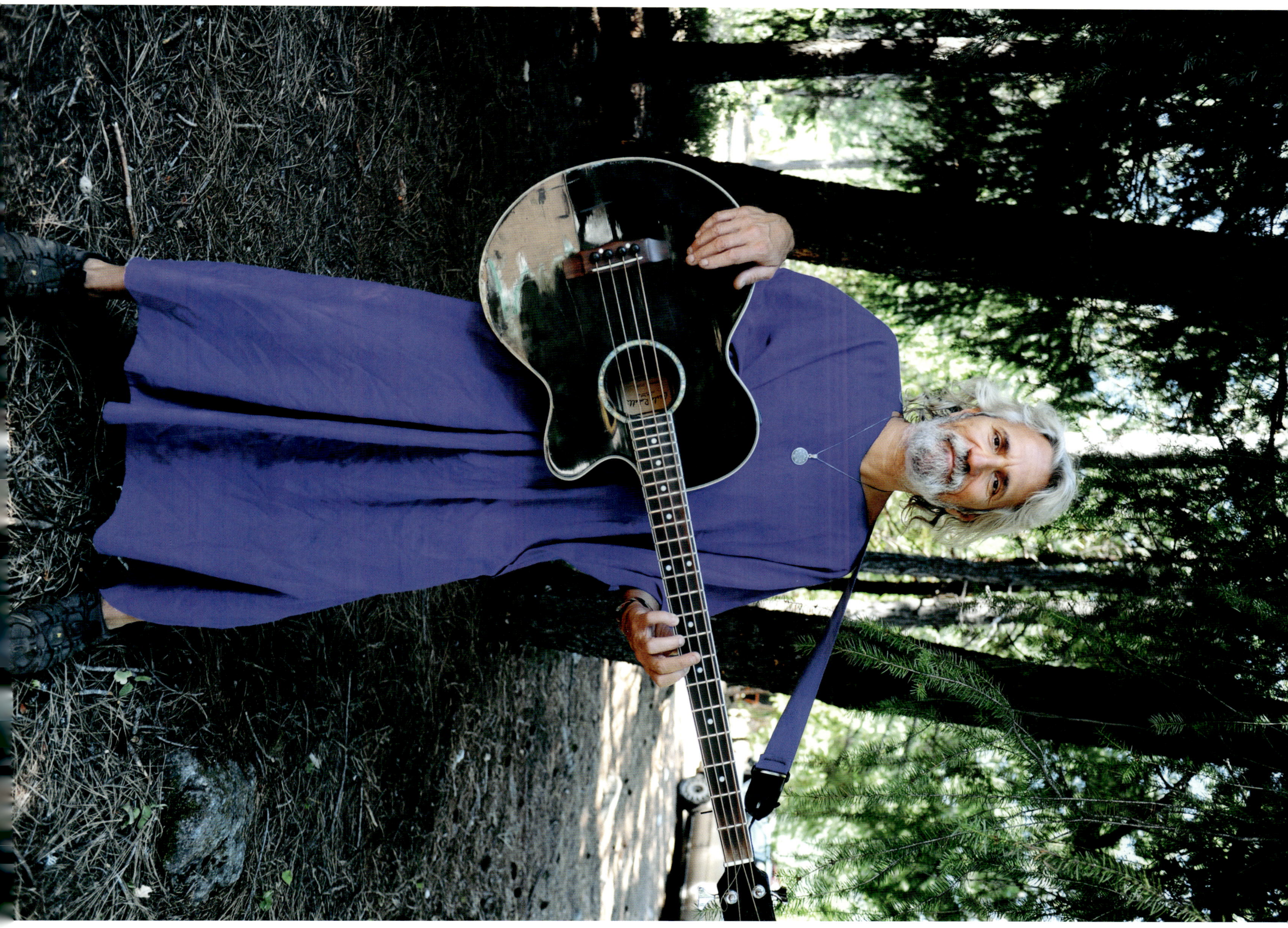

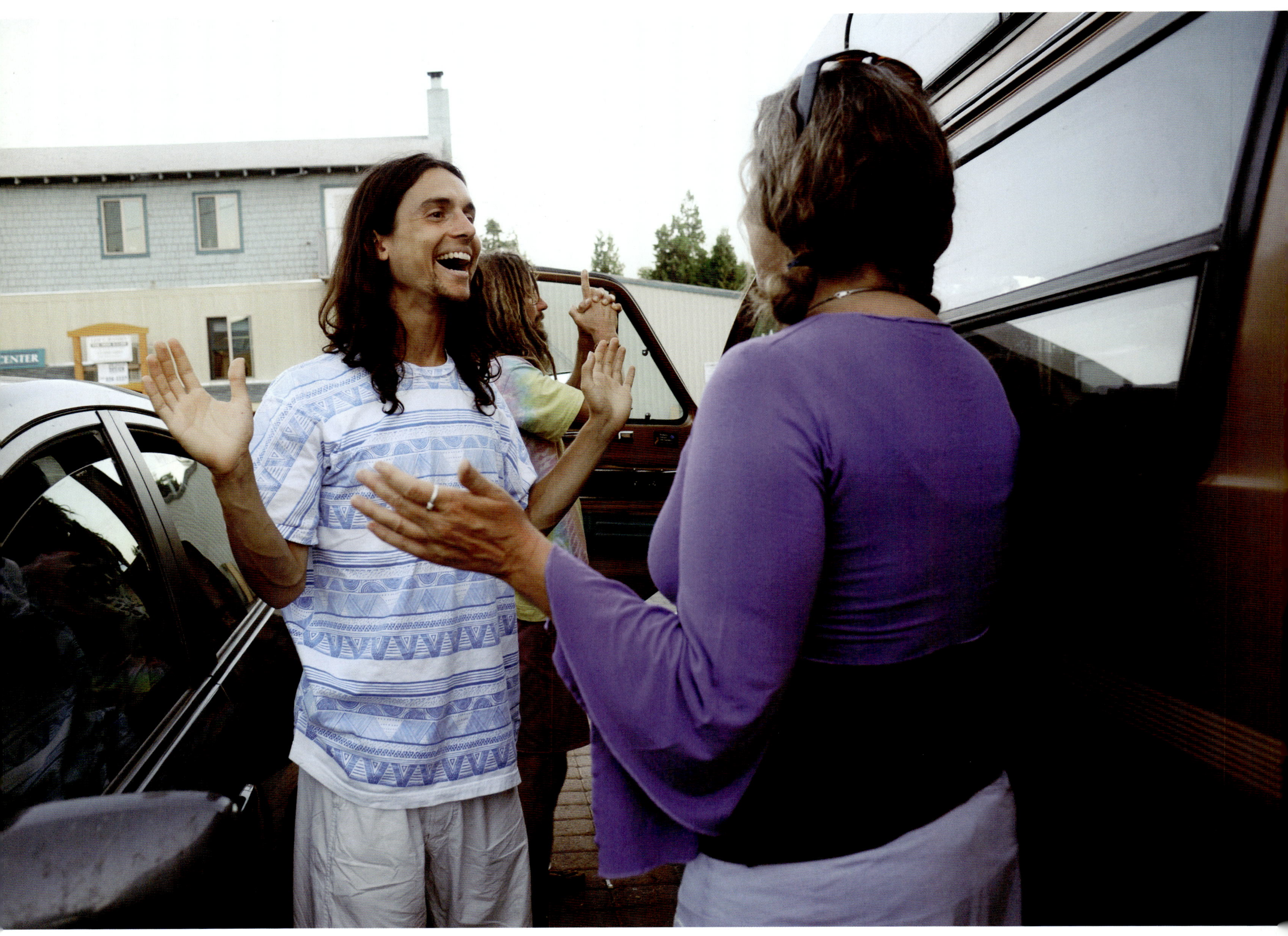

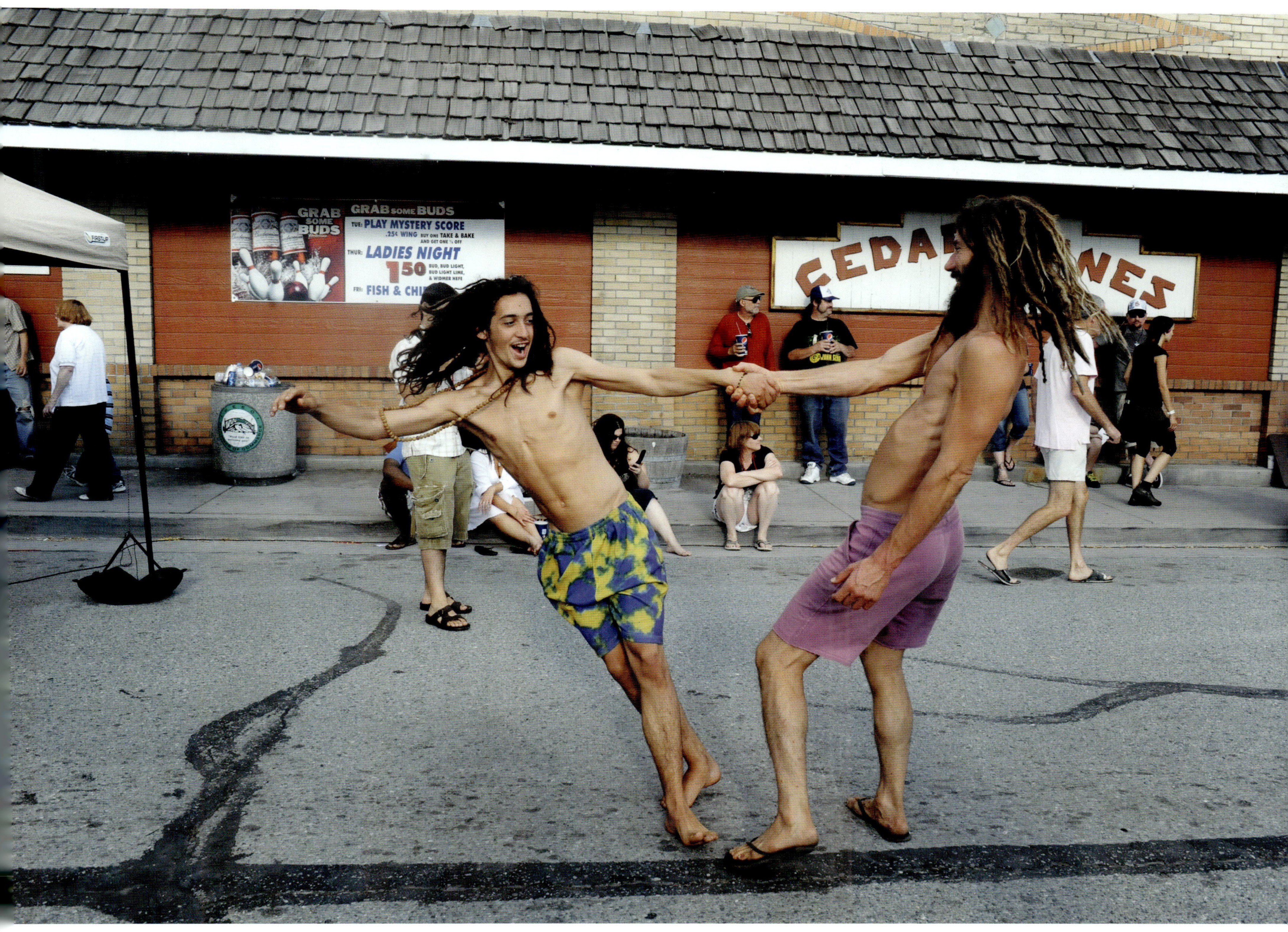

GRAB SOME BUDS
GRAB SOME BUDS
TUE: PLAY MYSTERY SCORE
.25¢ WING BUY ONE TAKE & BAKE
AND GET ONE ½ OFF
THUR: LADIES NIGHT
150 BUD, BUD LIGHT,
BUD LIGHT LIME,
& WIDMER HEFE
FRI: FISH & CHI
CEDAR LANES

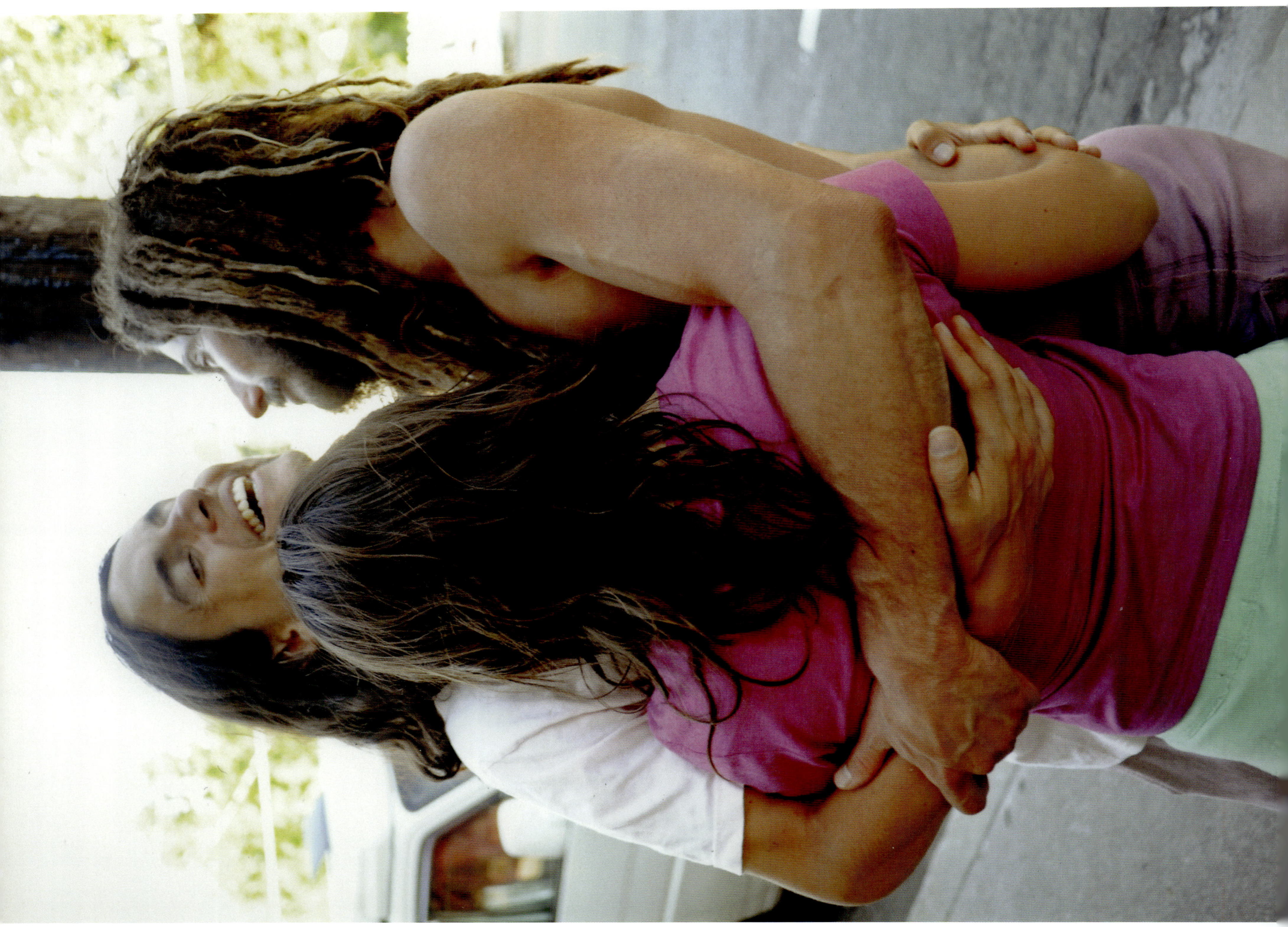

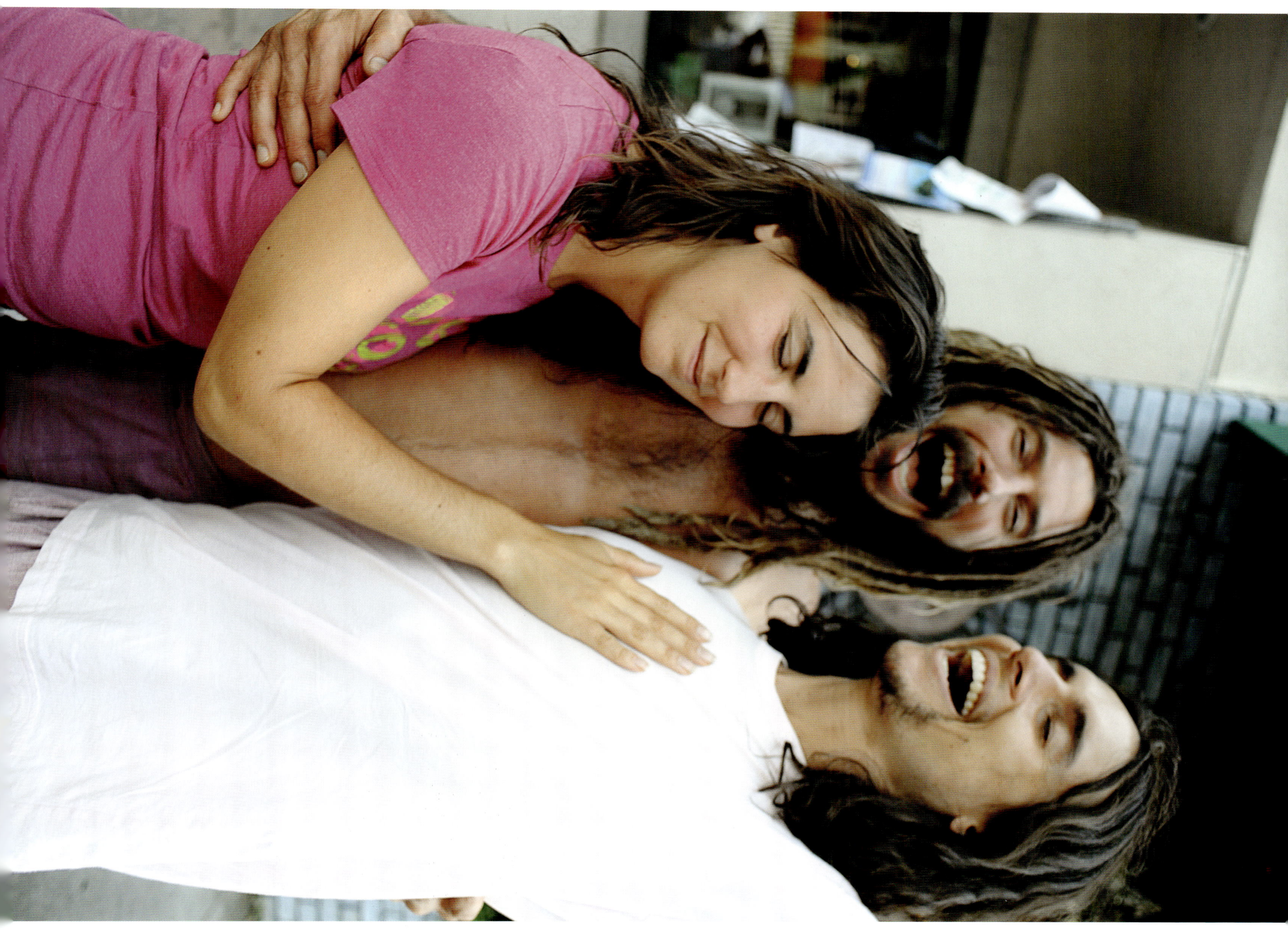

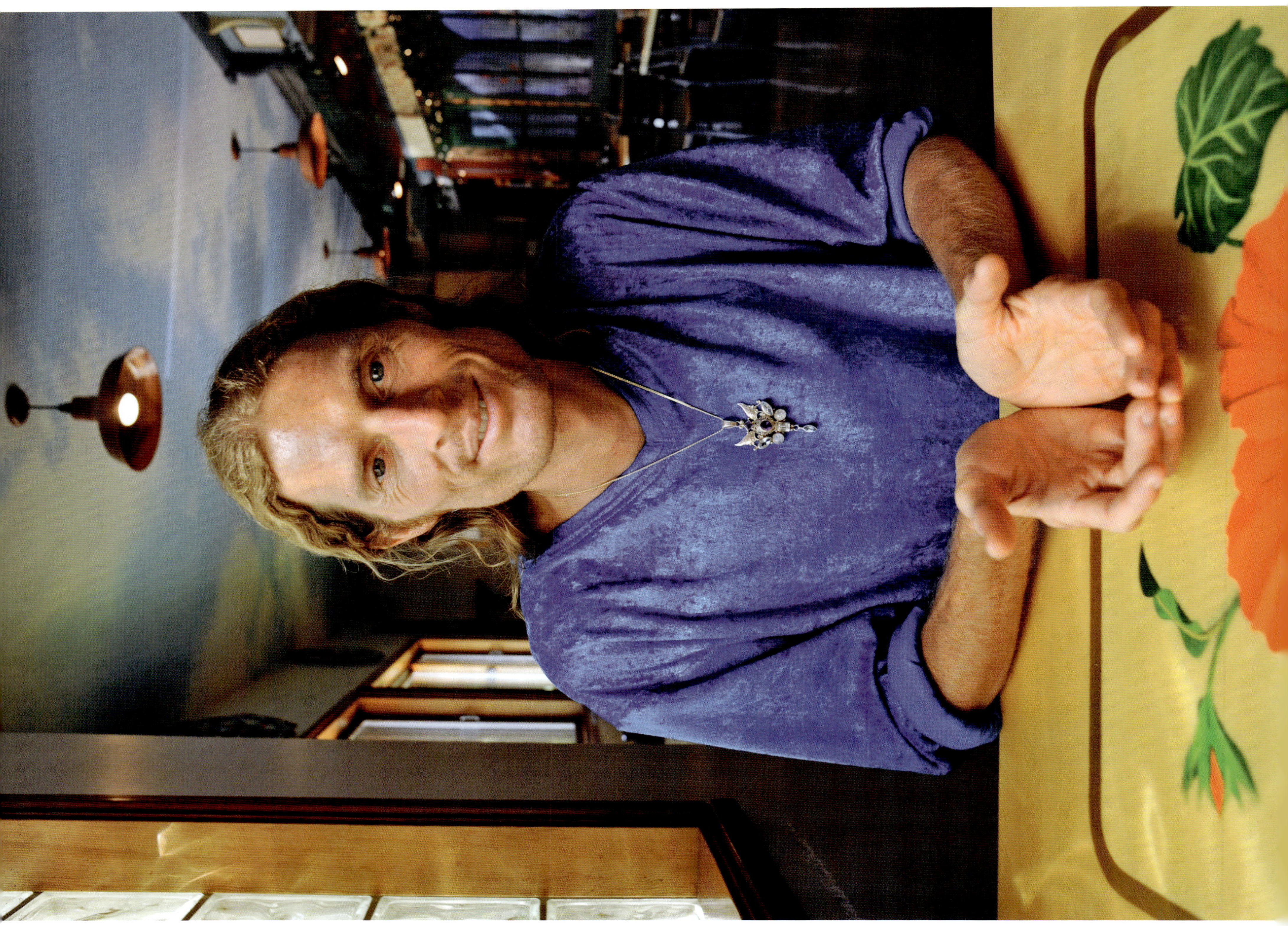

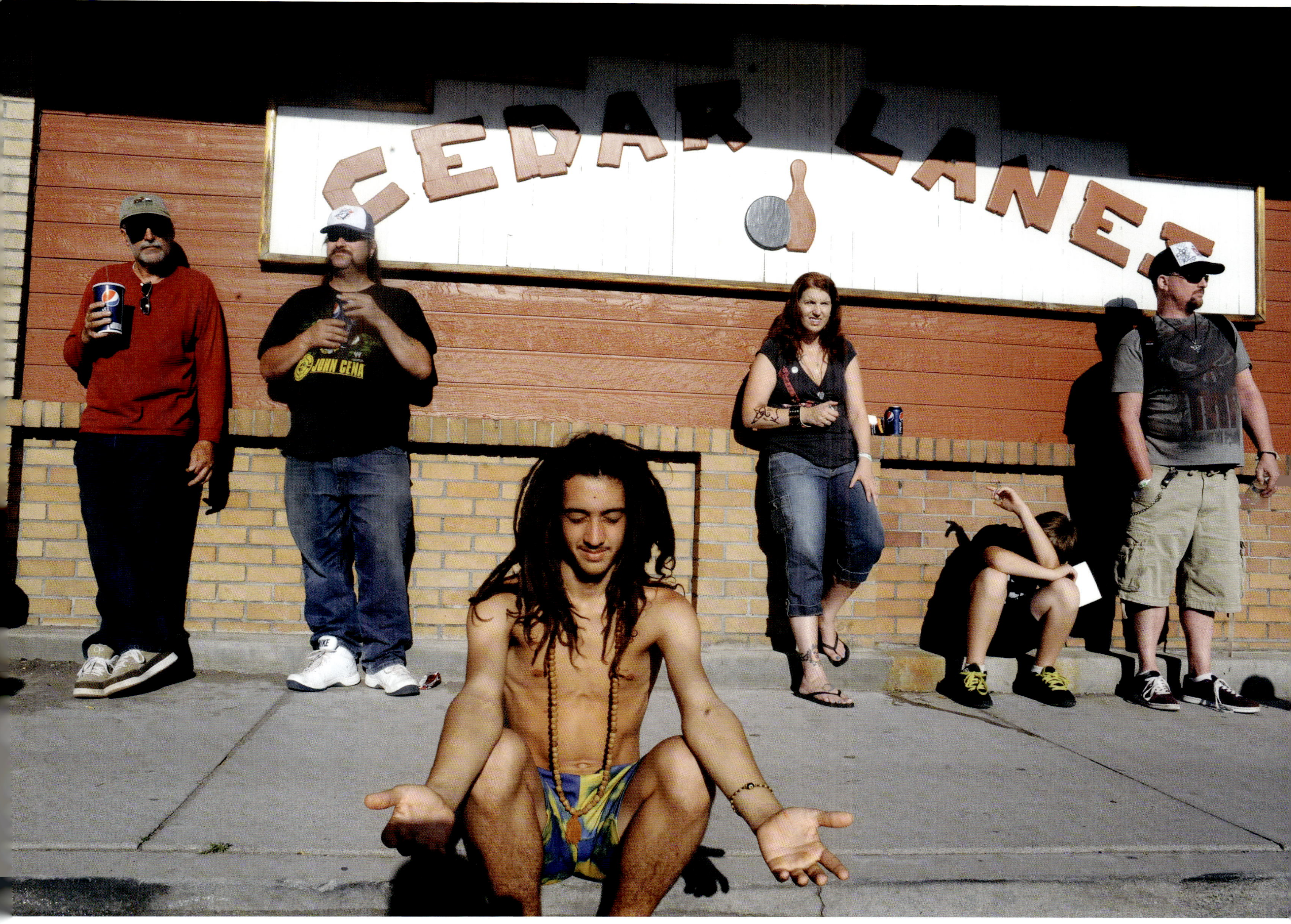

CEDAR LANES
JOHN CENA

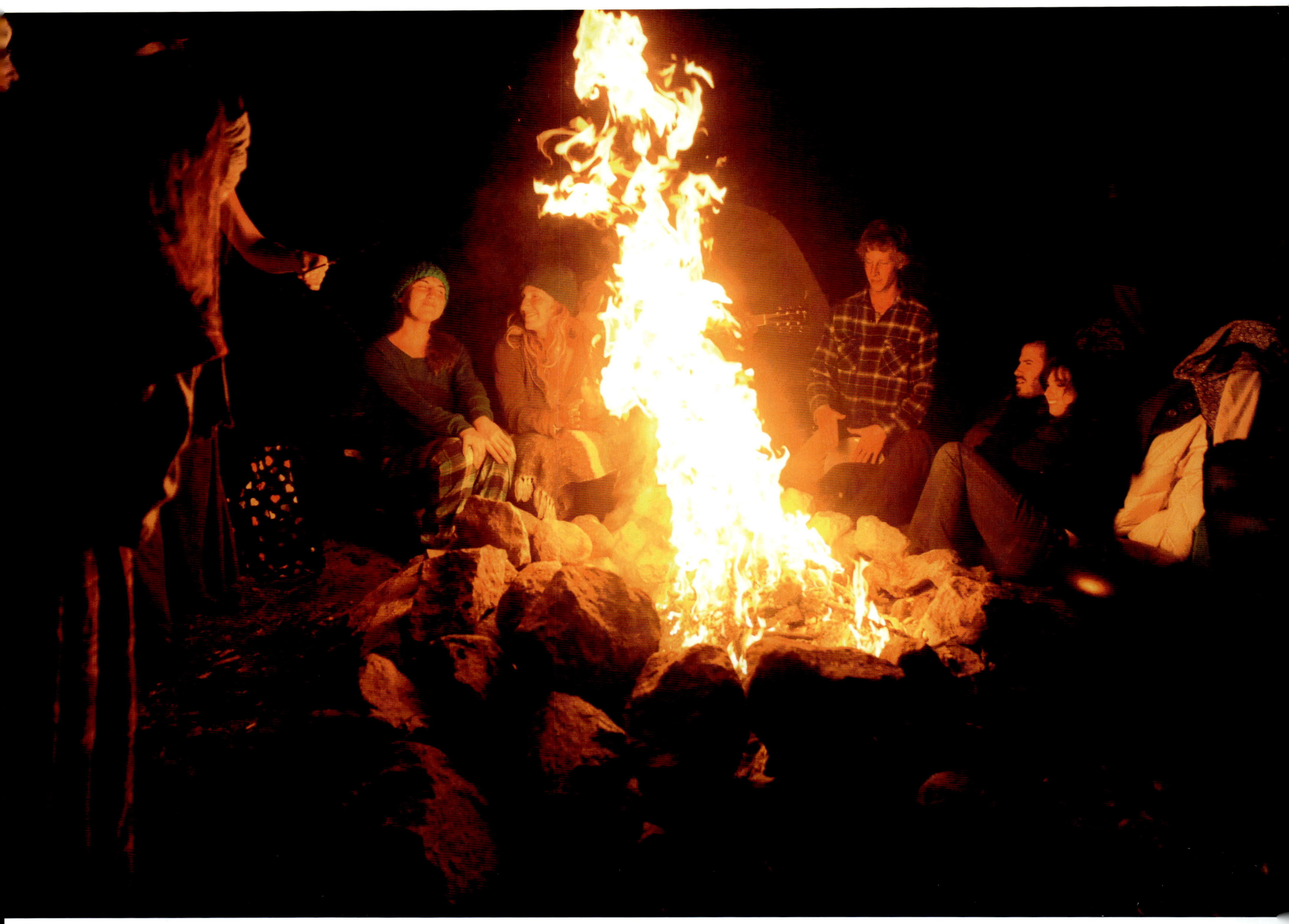

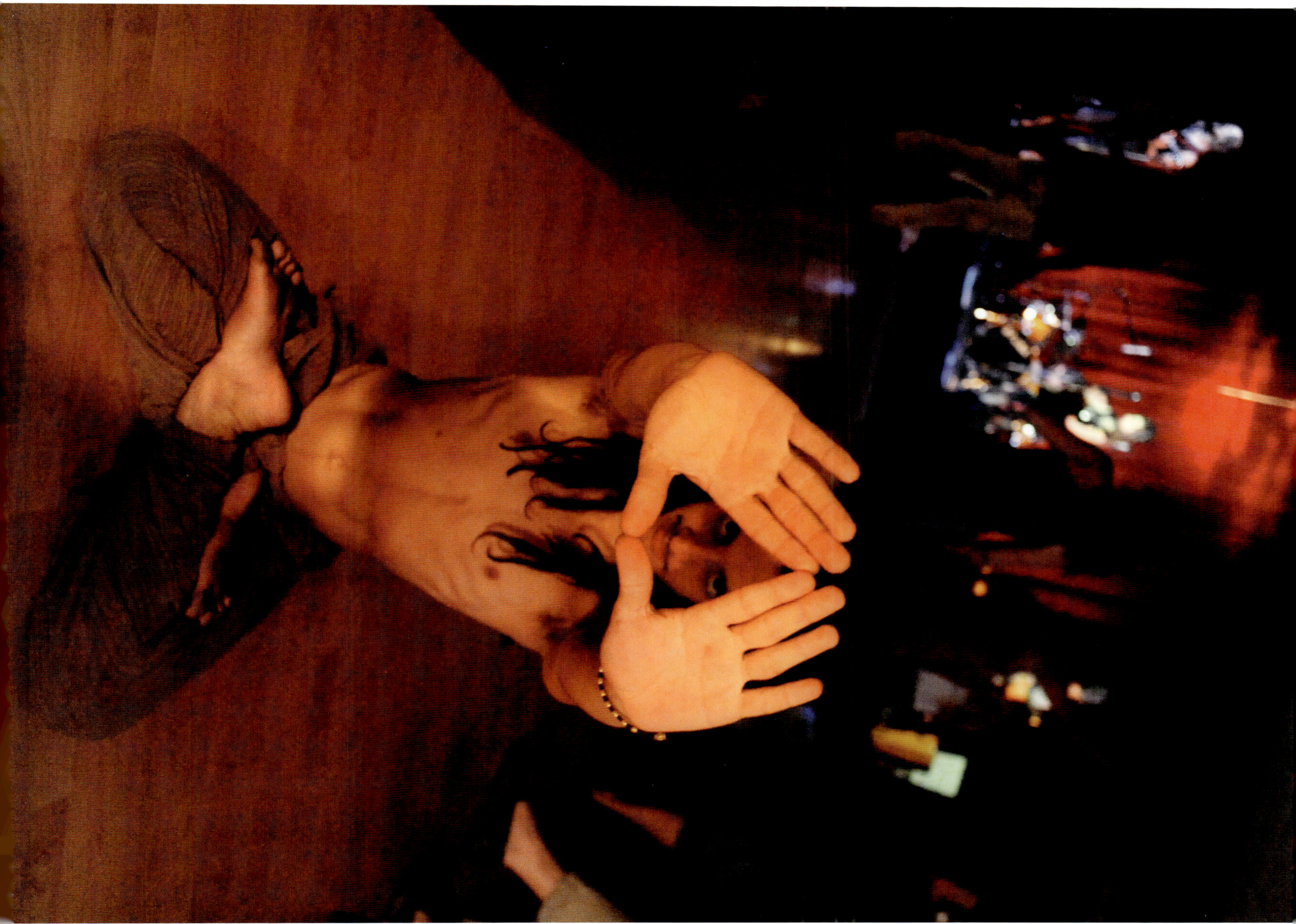

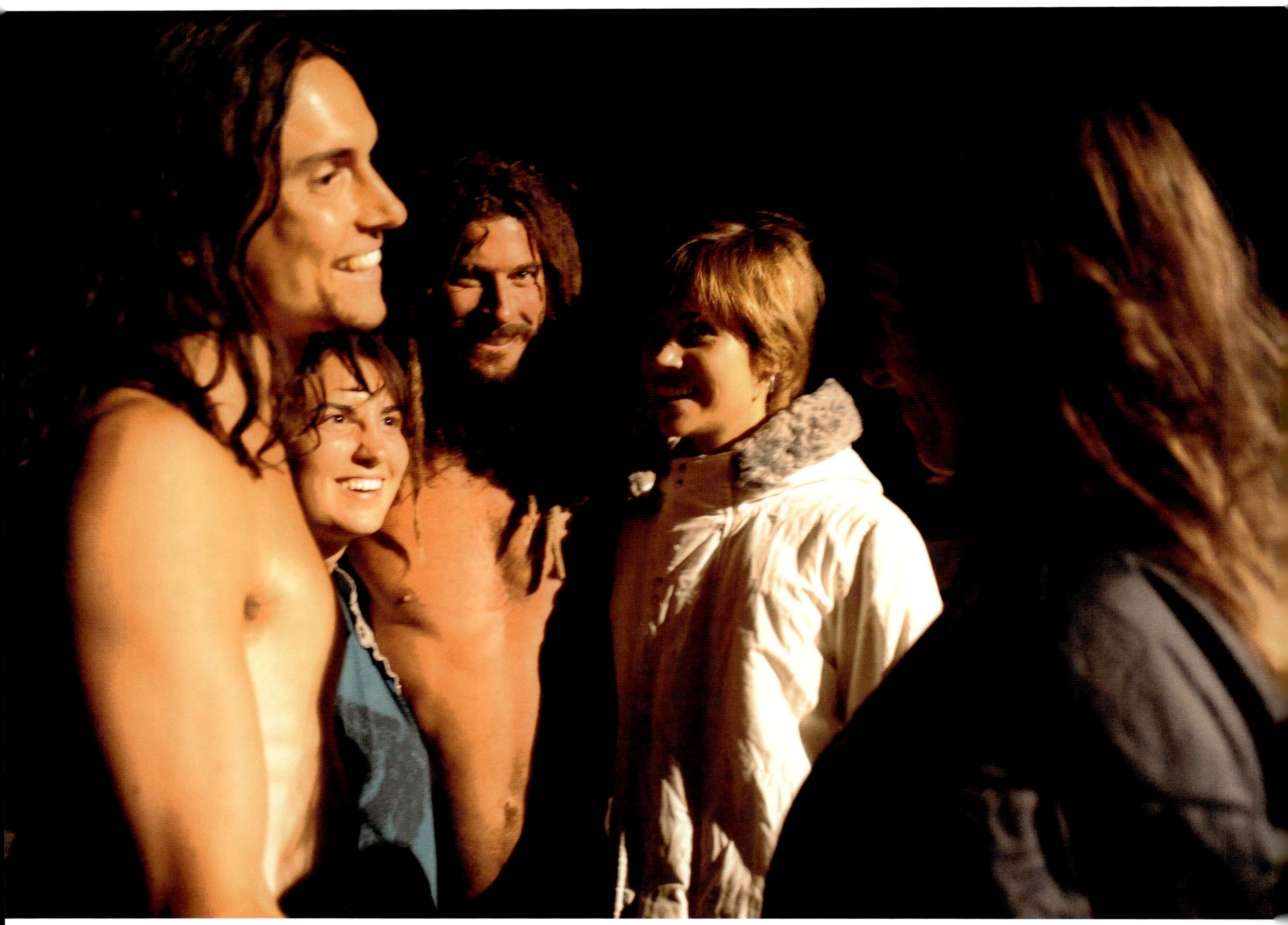

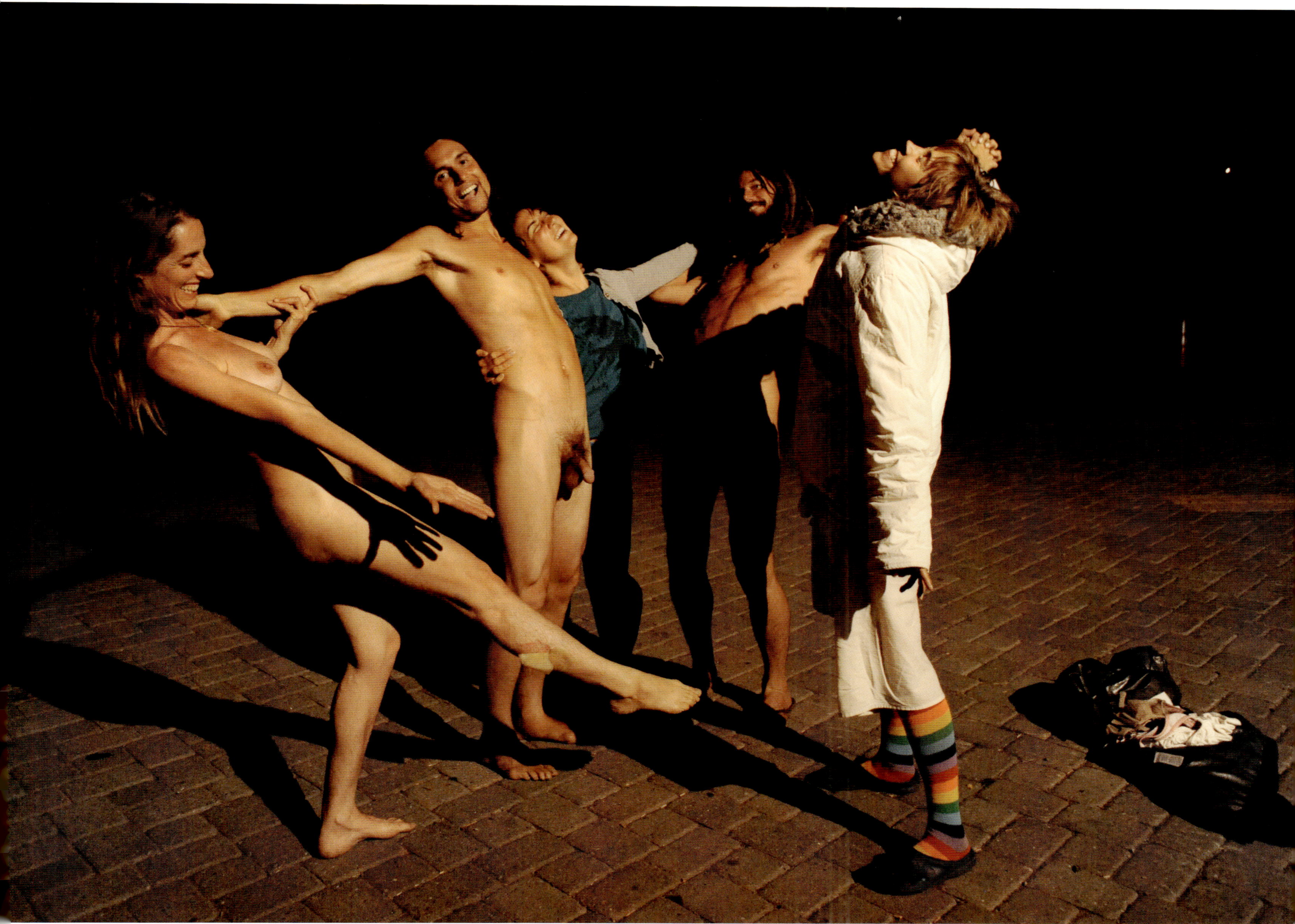

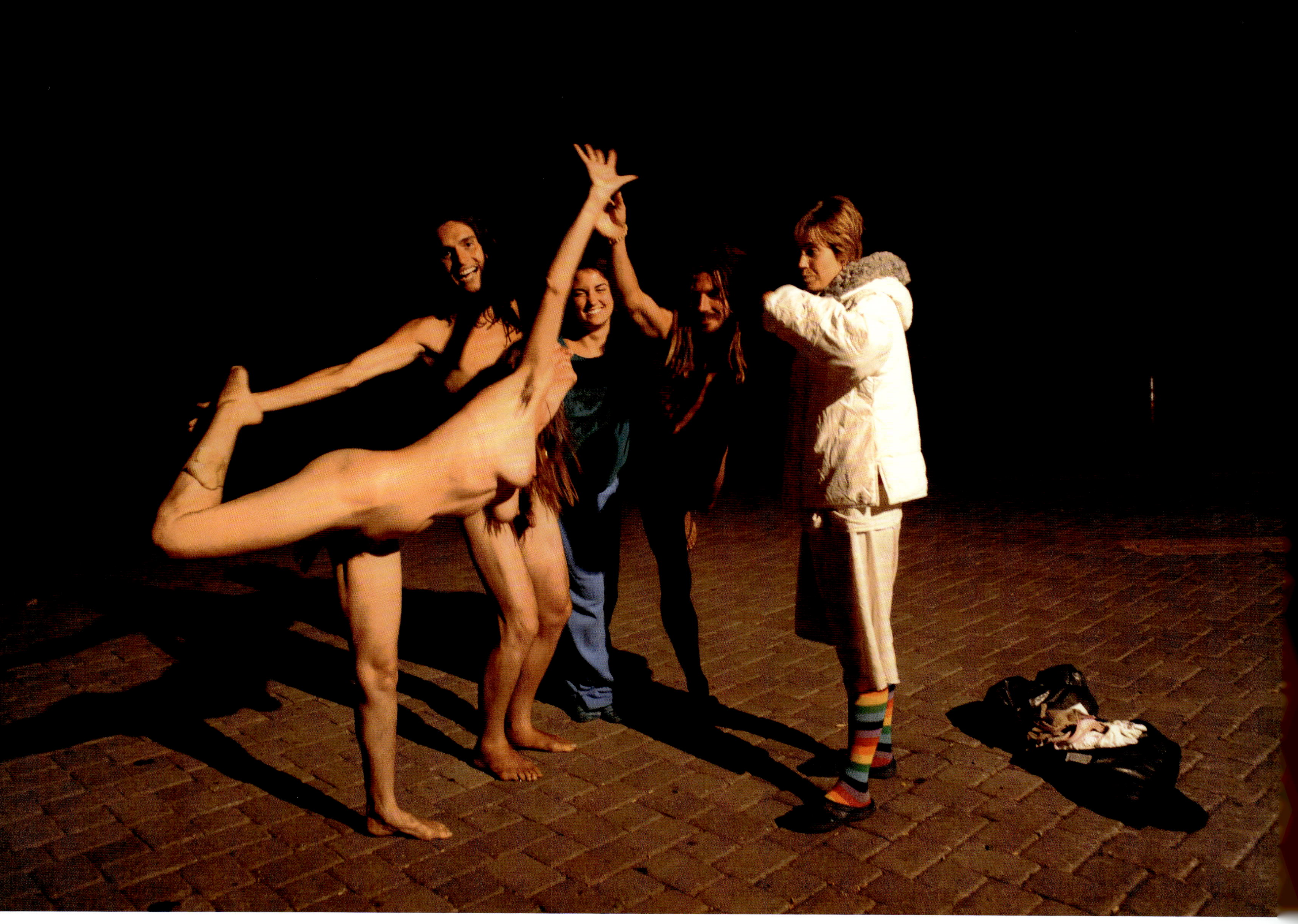

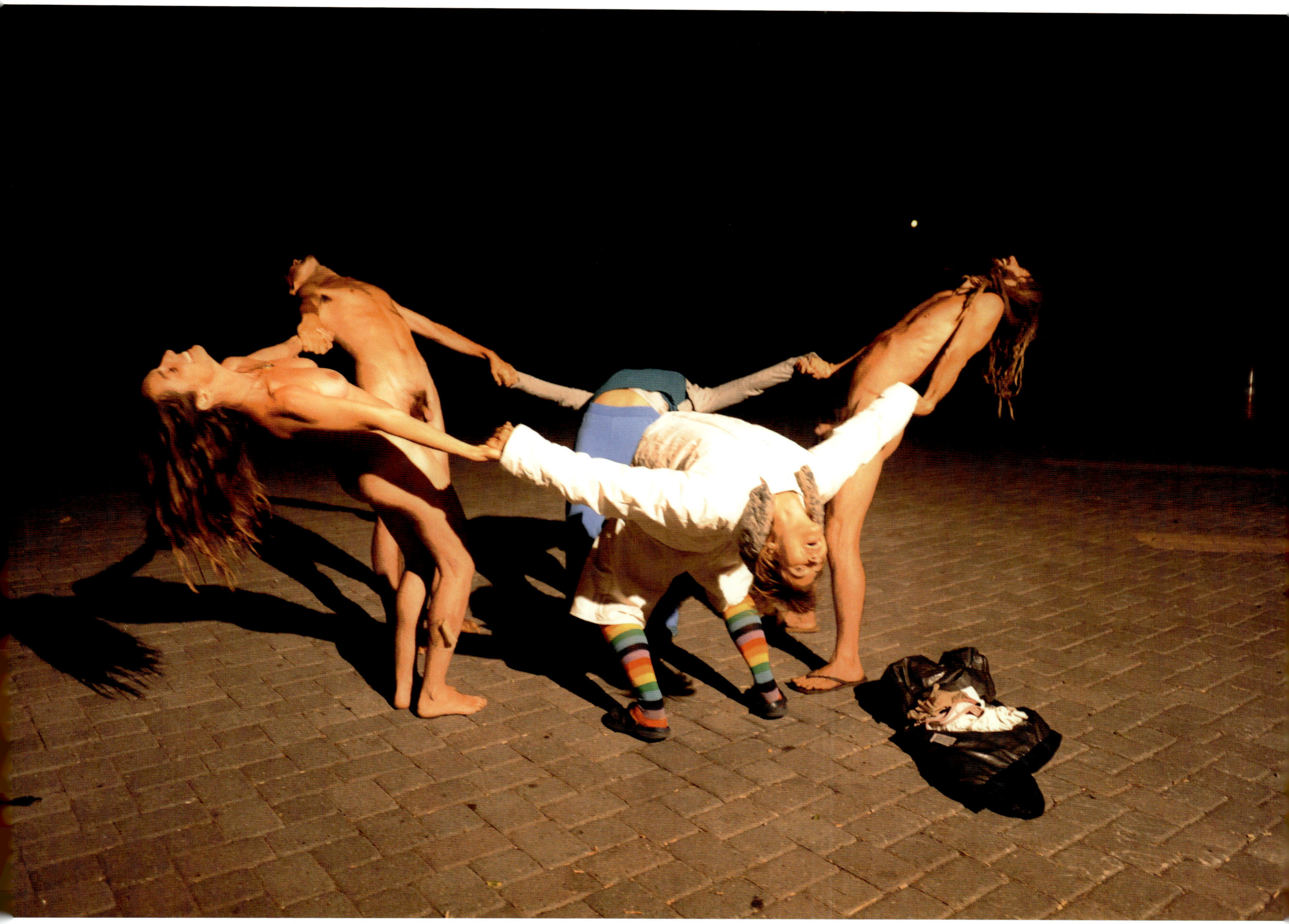

Beloved, Oregon

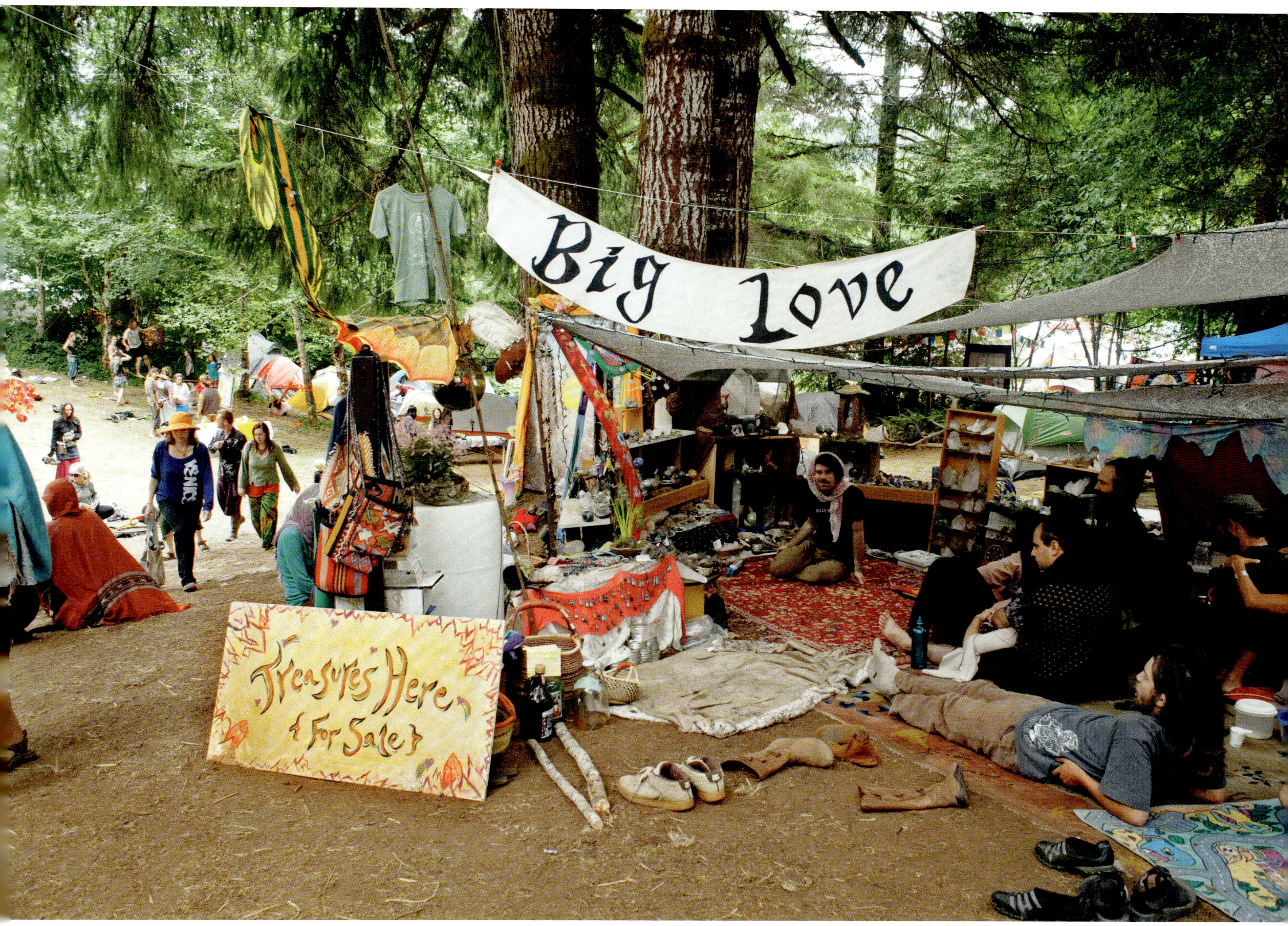

Big love
Treasures Here
For Sale

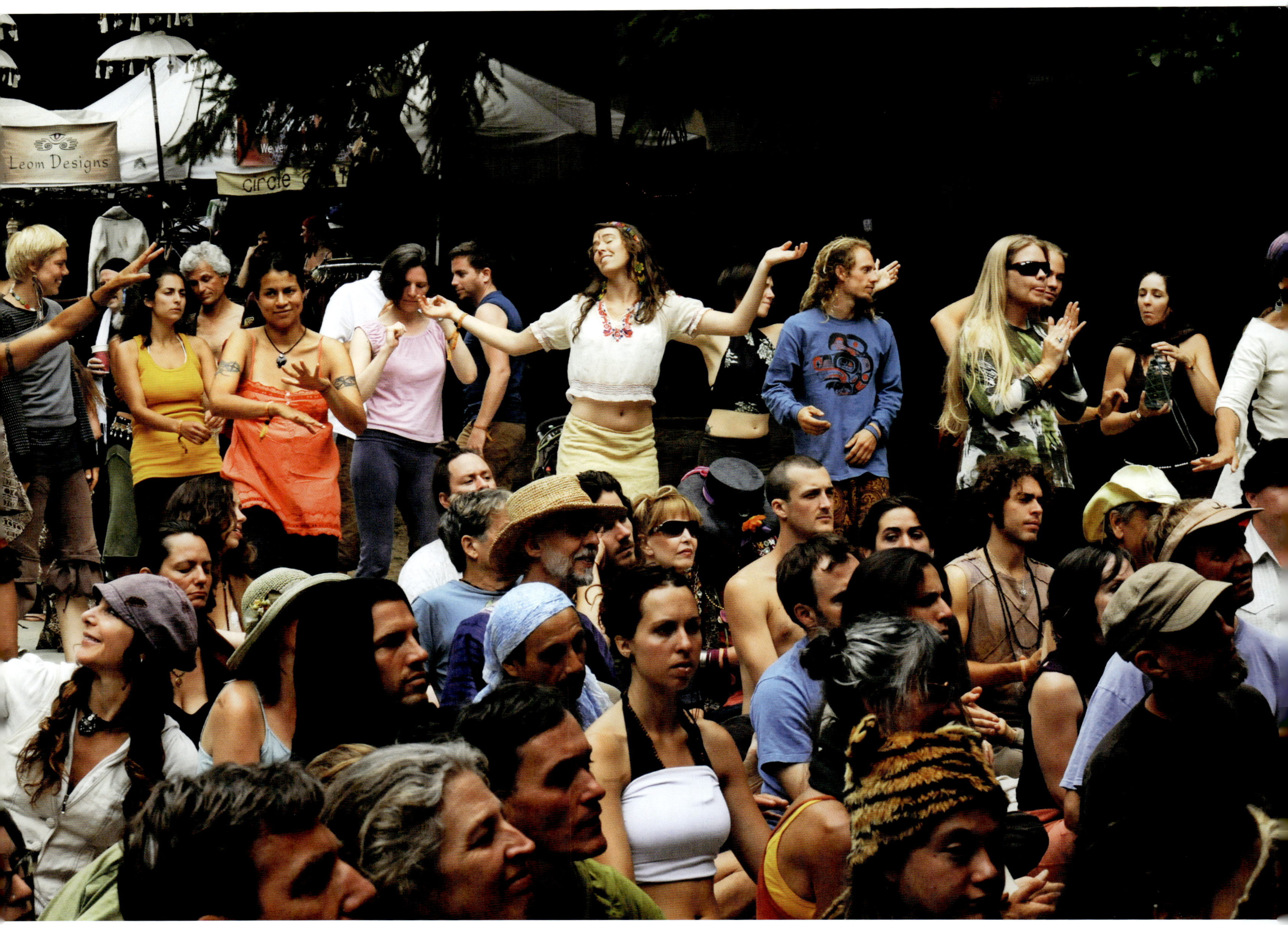

Leom Designs
We ve
circle

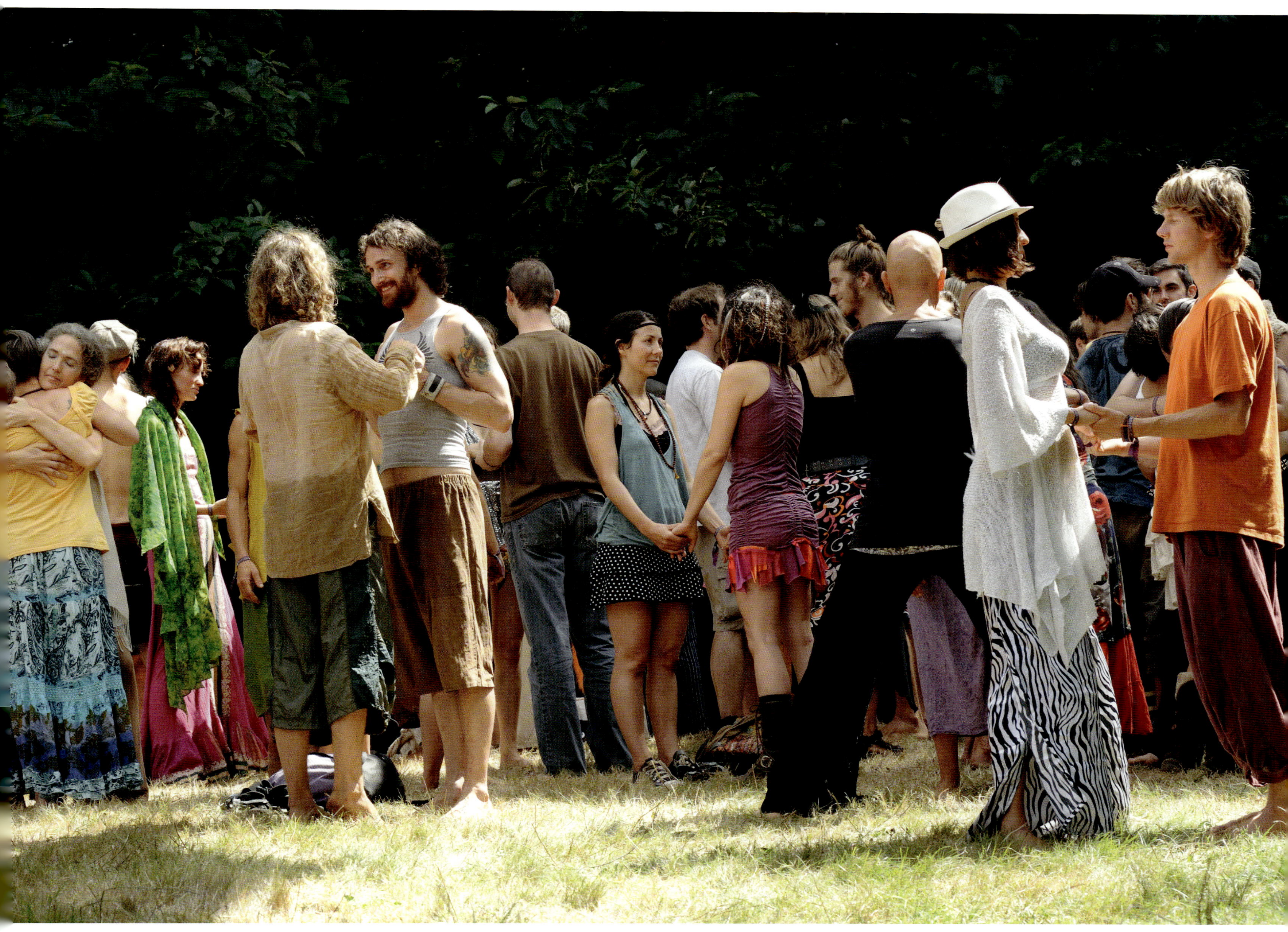

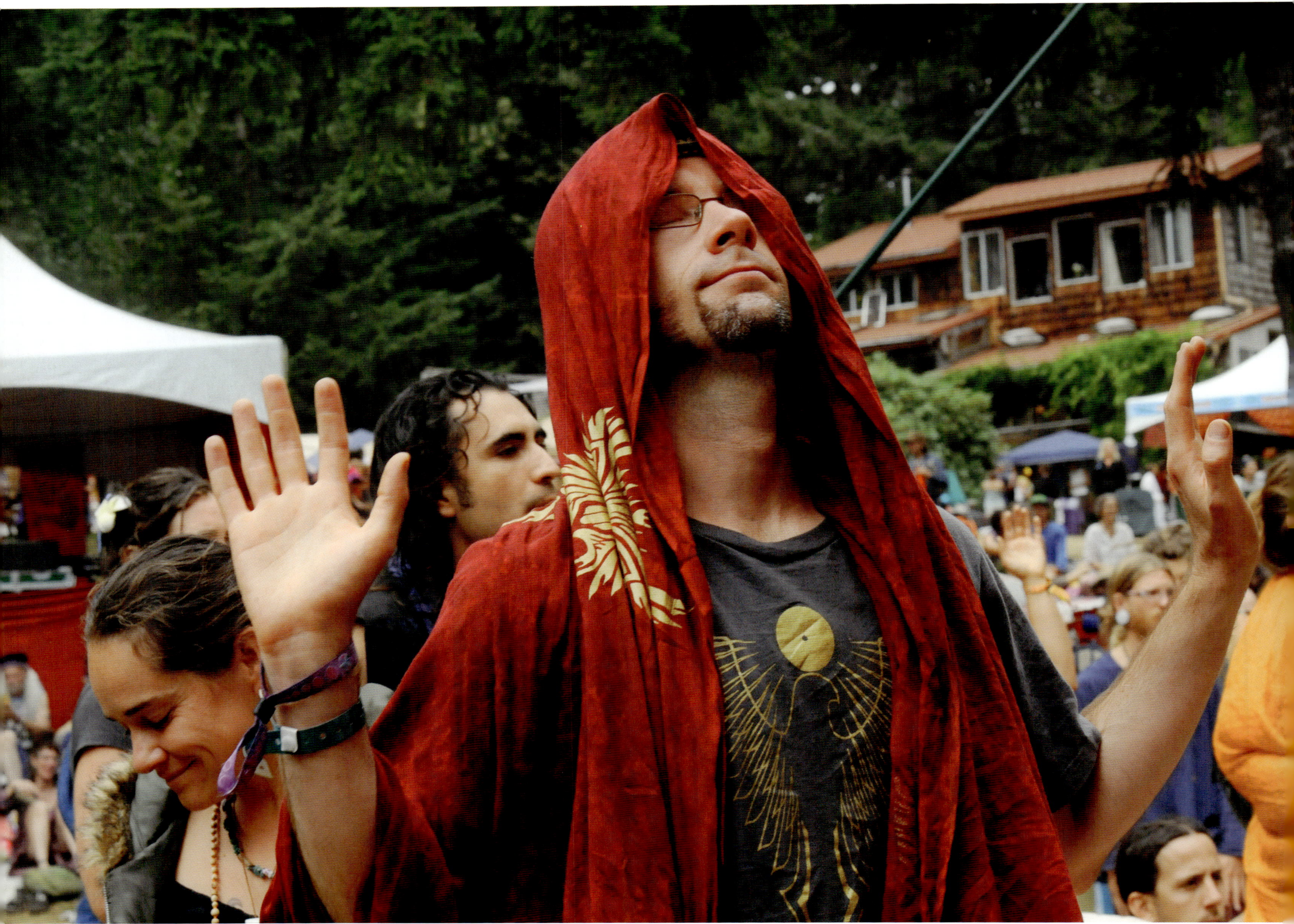

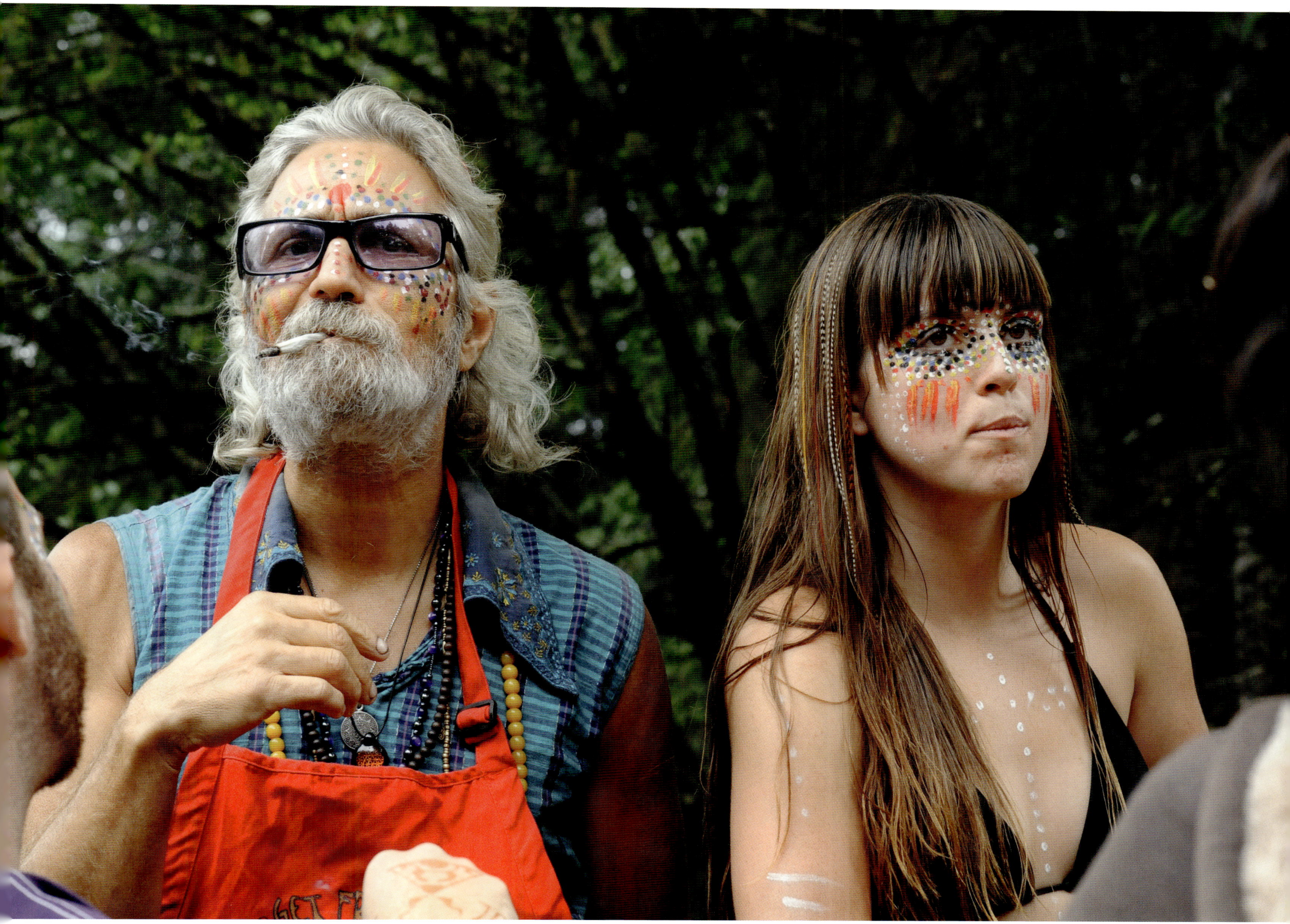

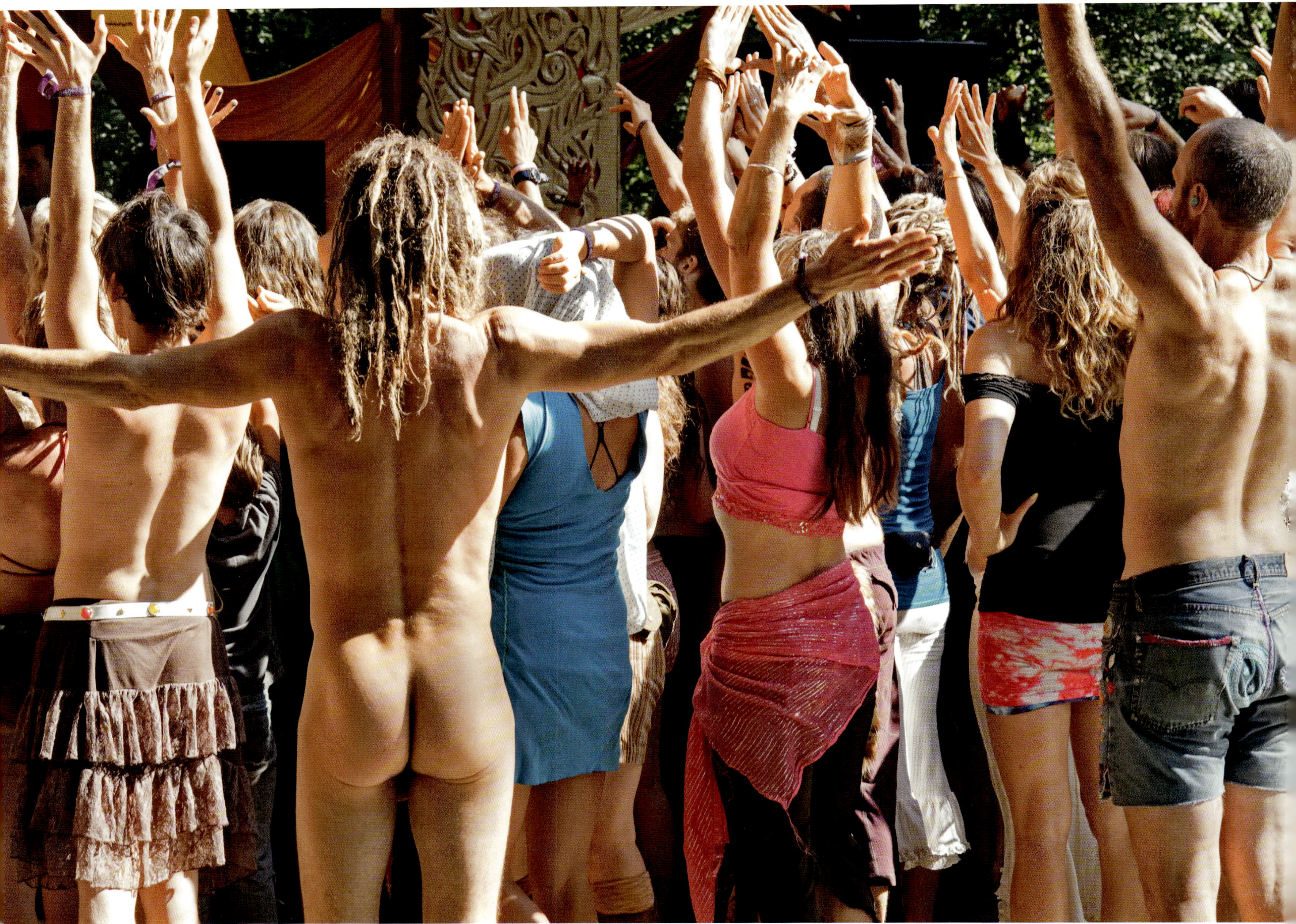

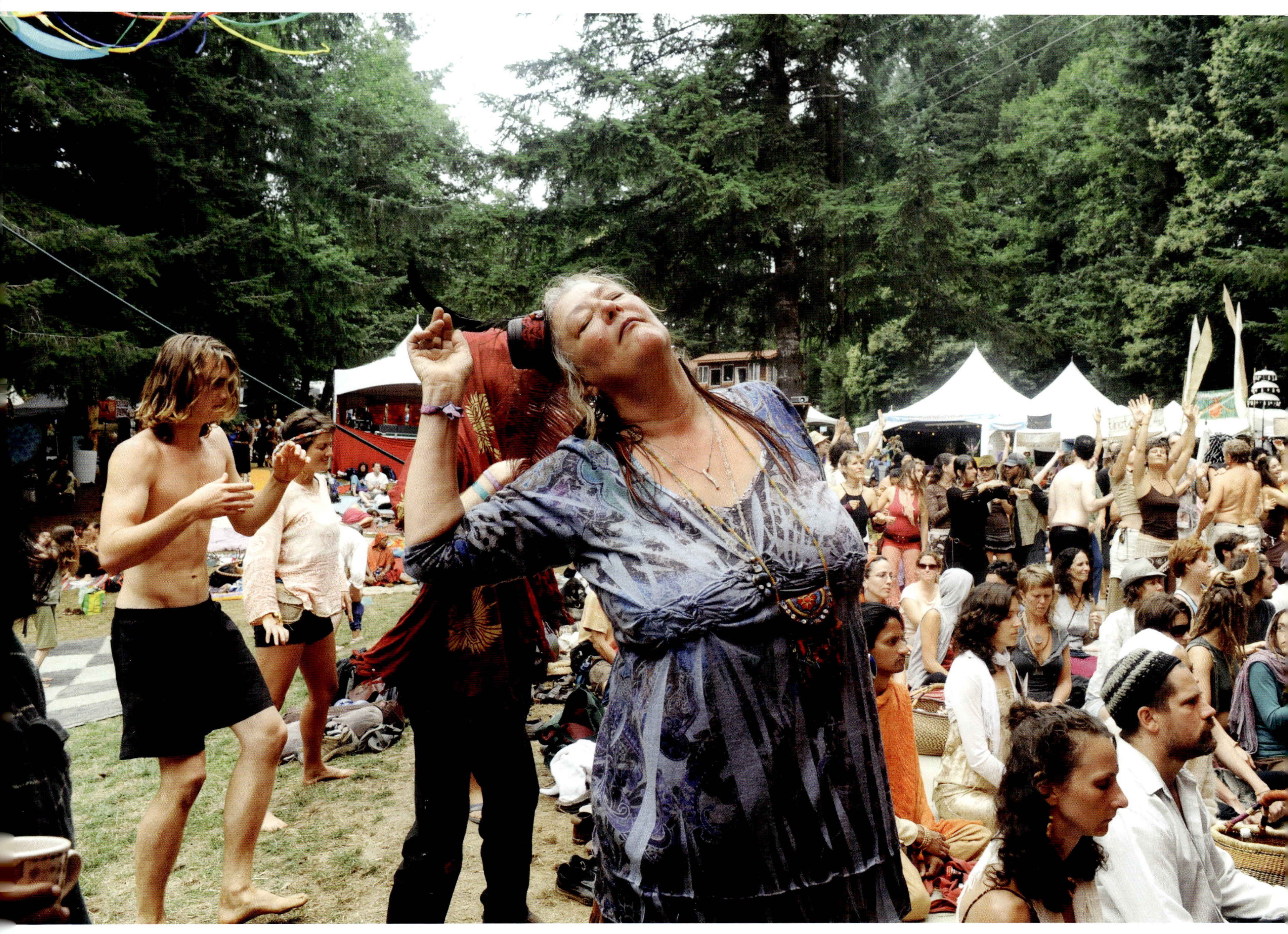

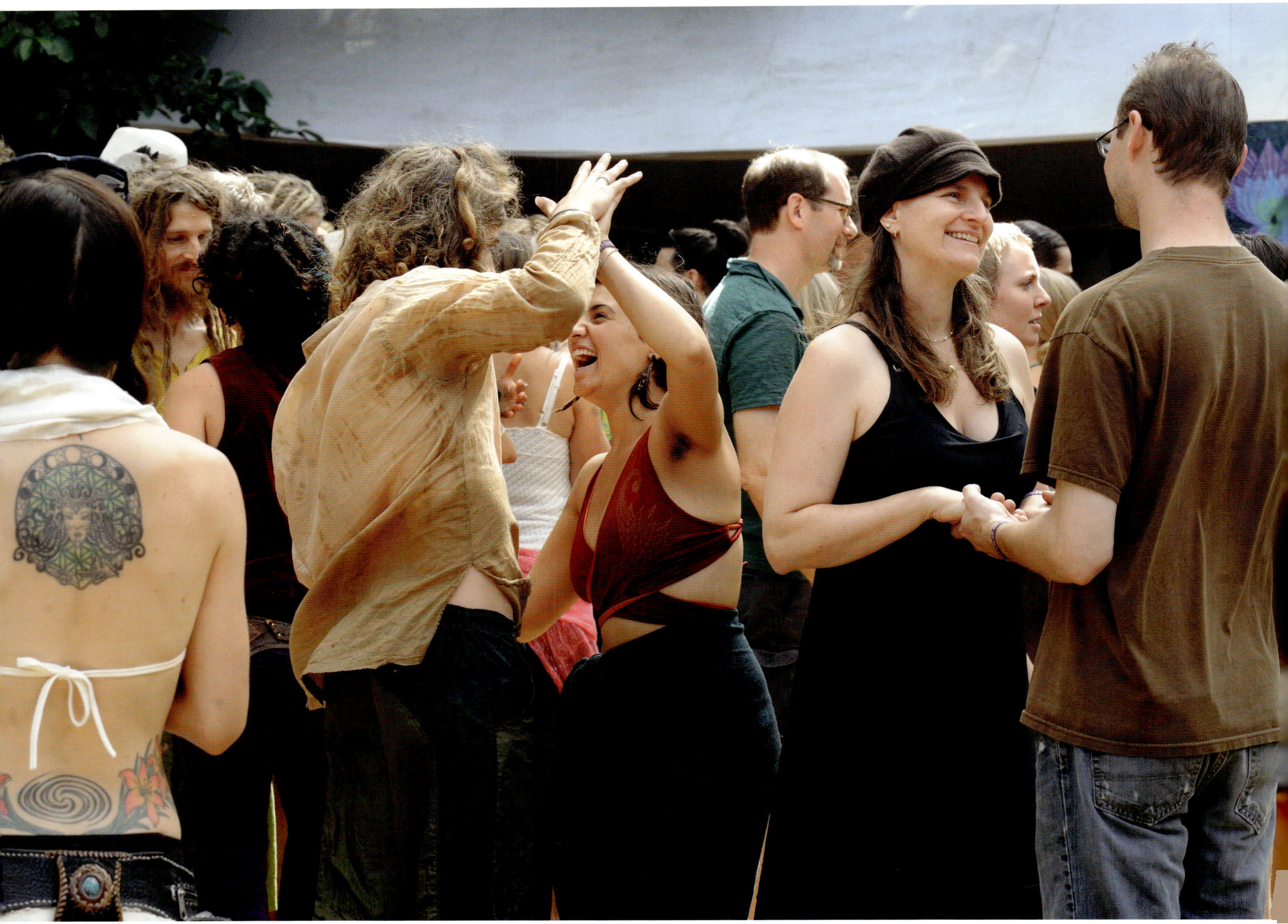

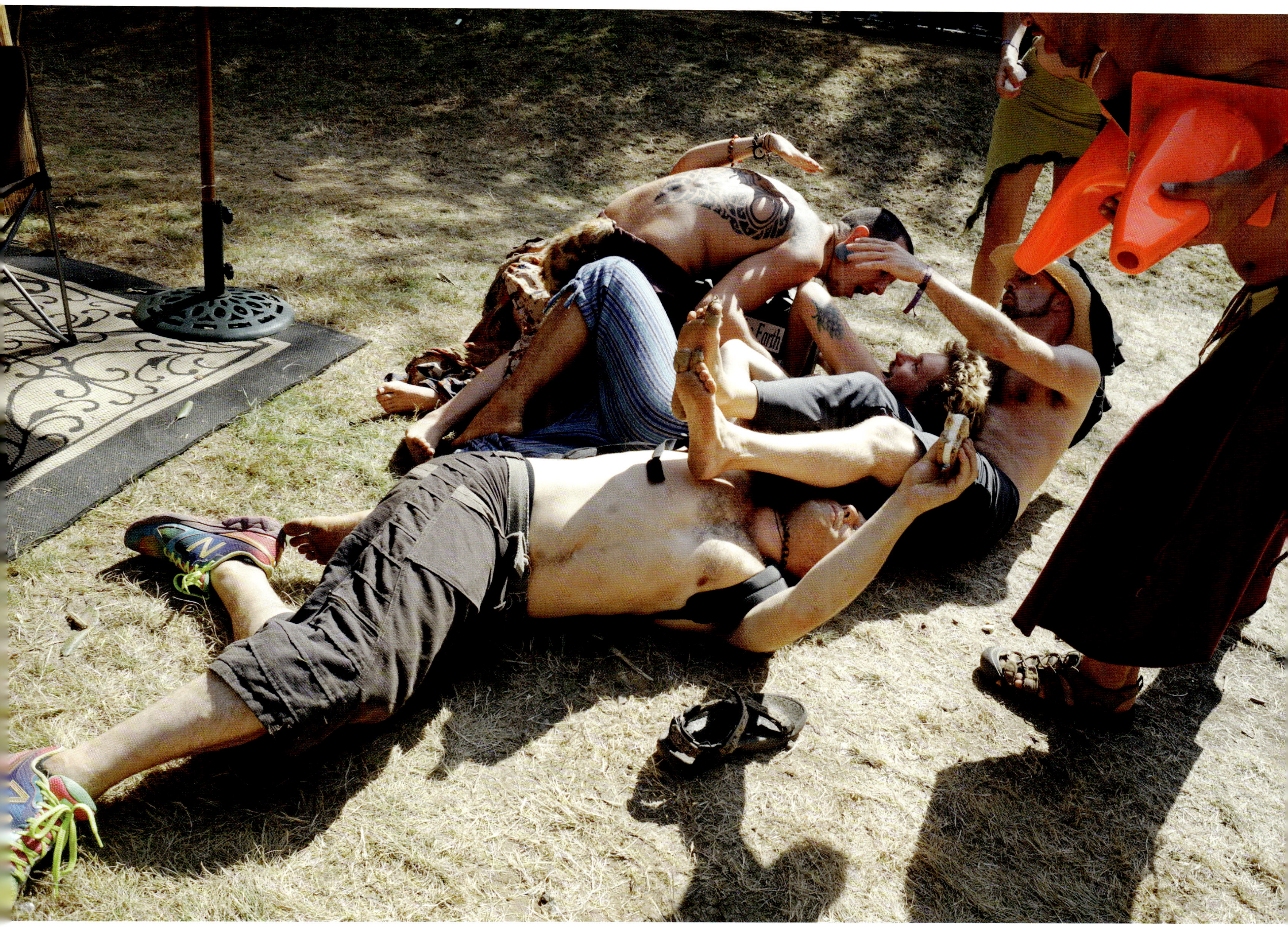

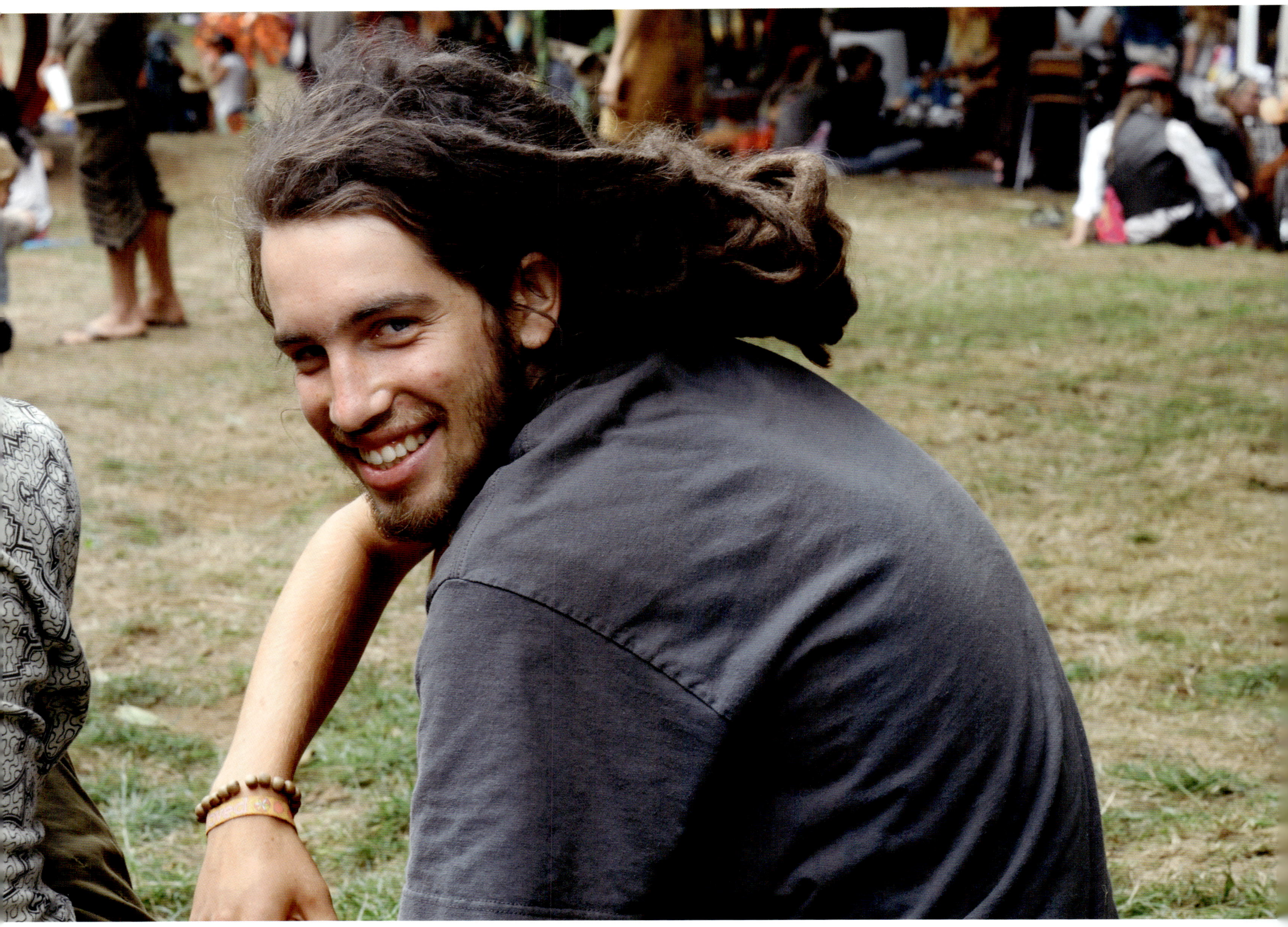

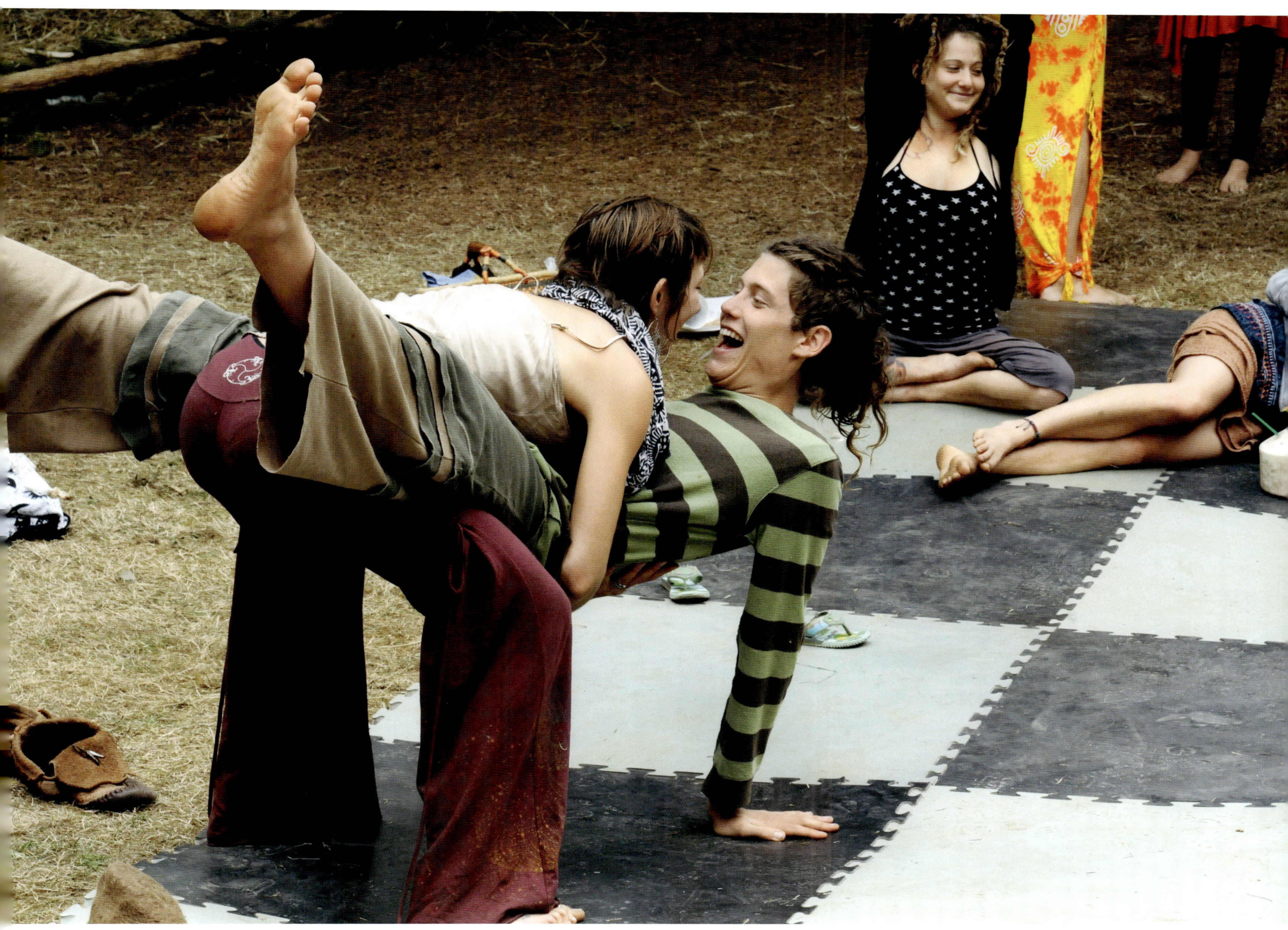

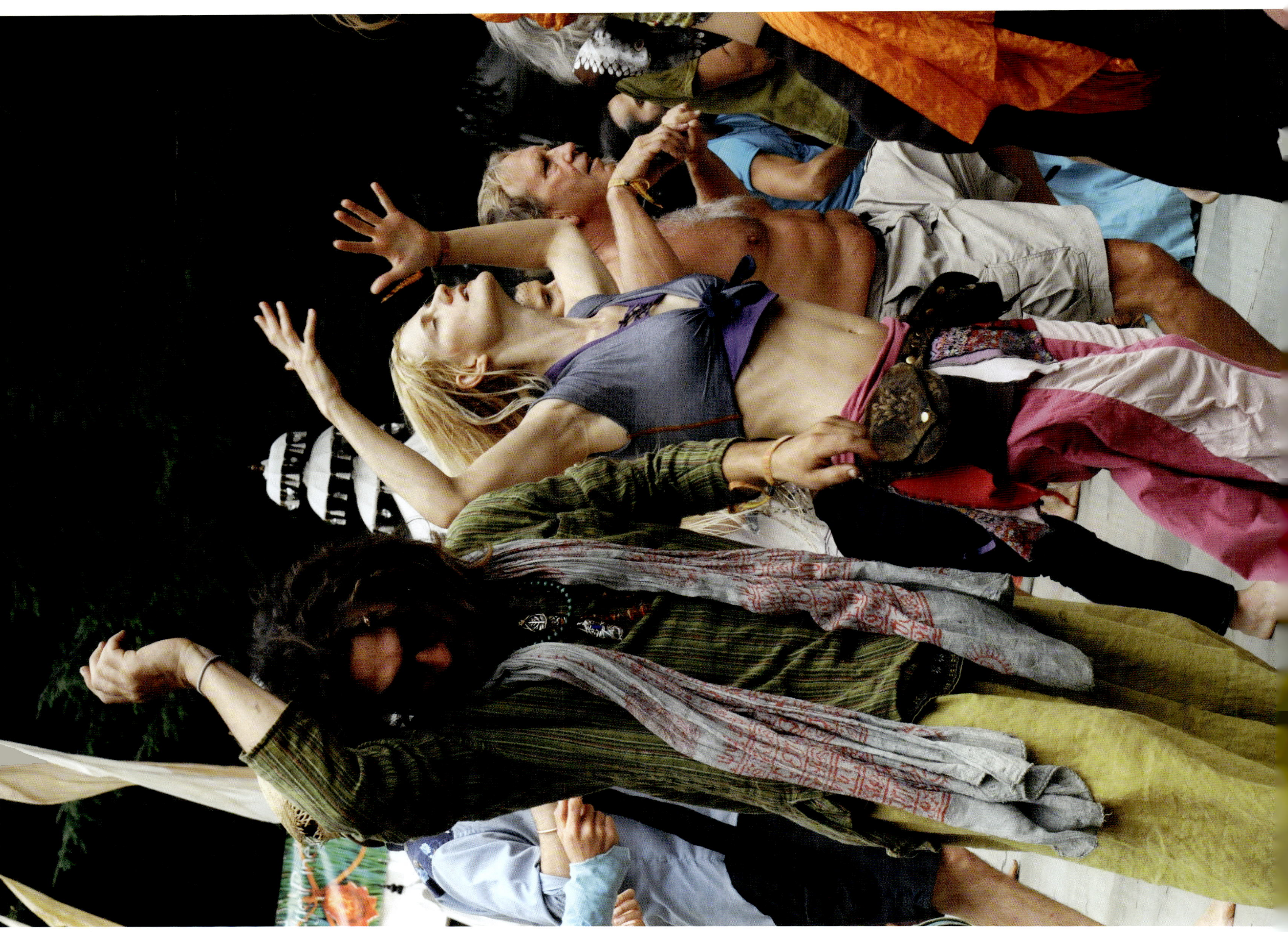

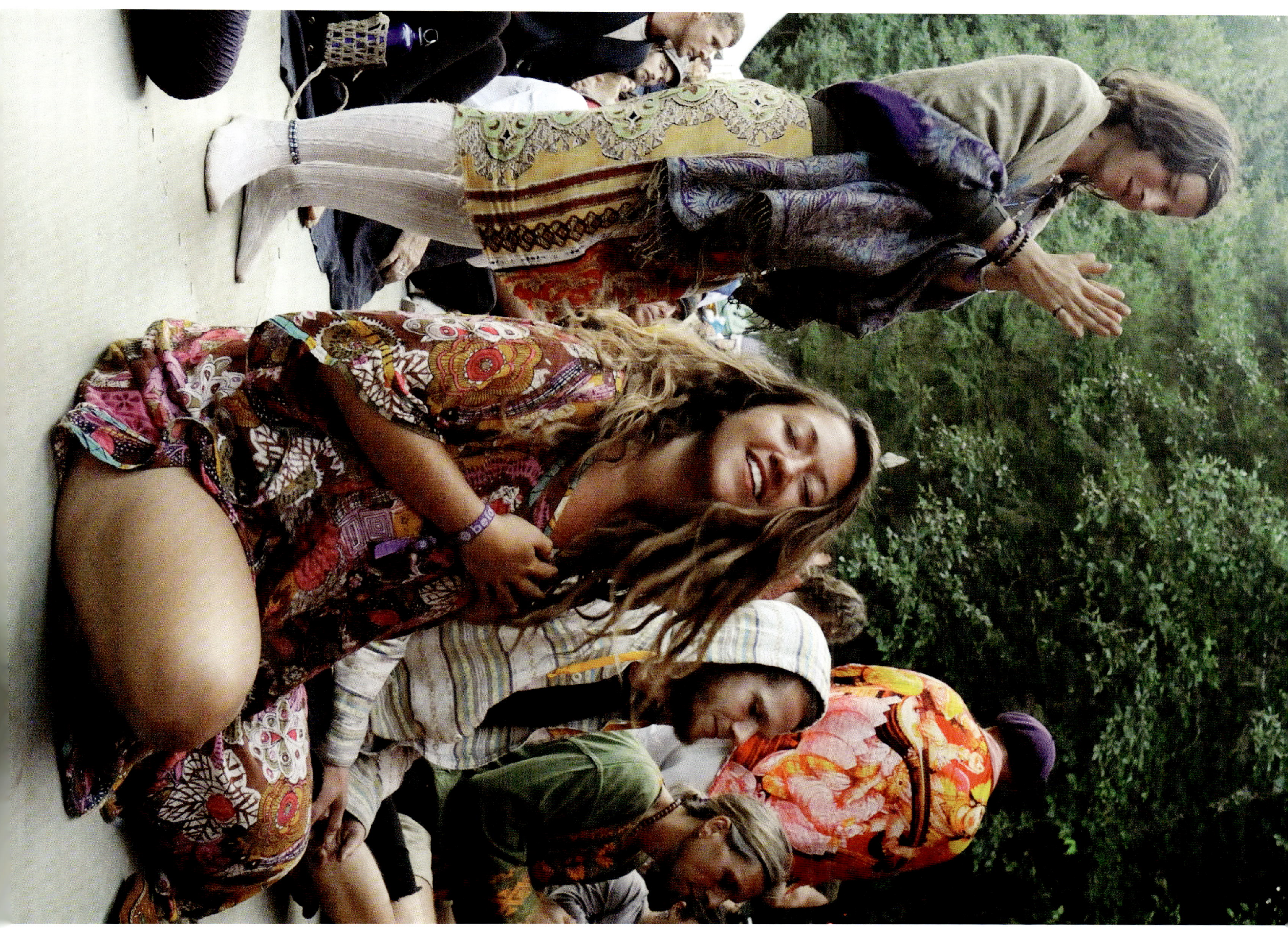

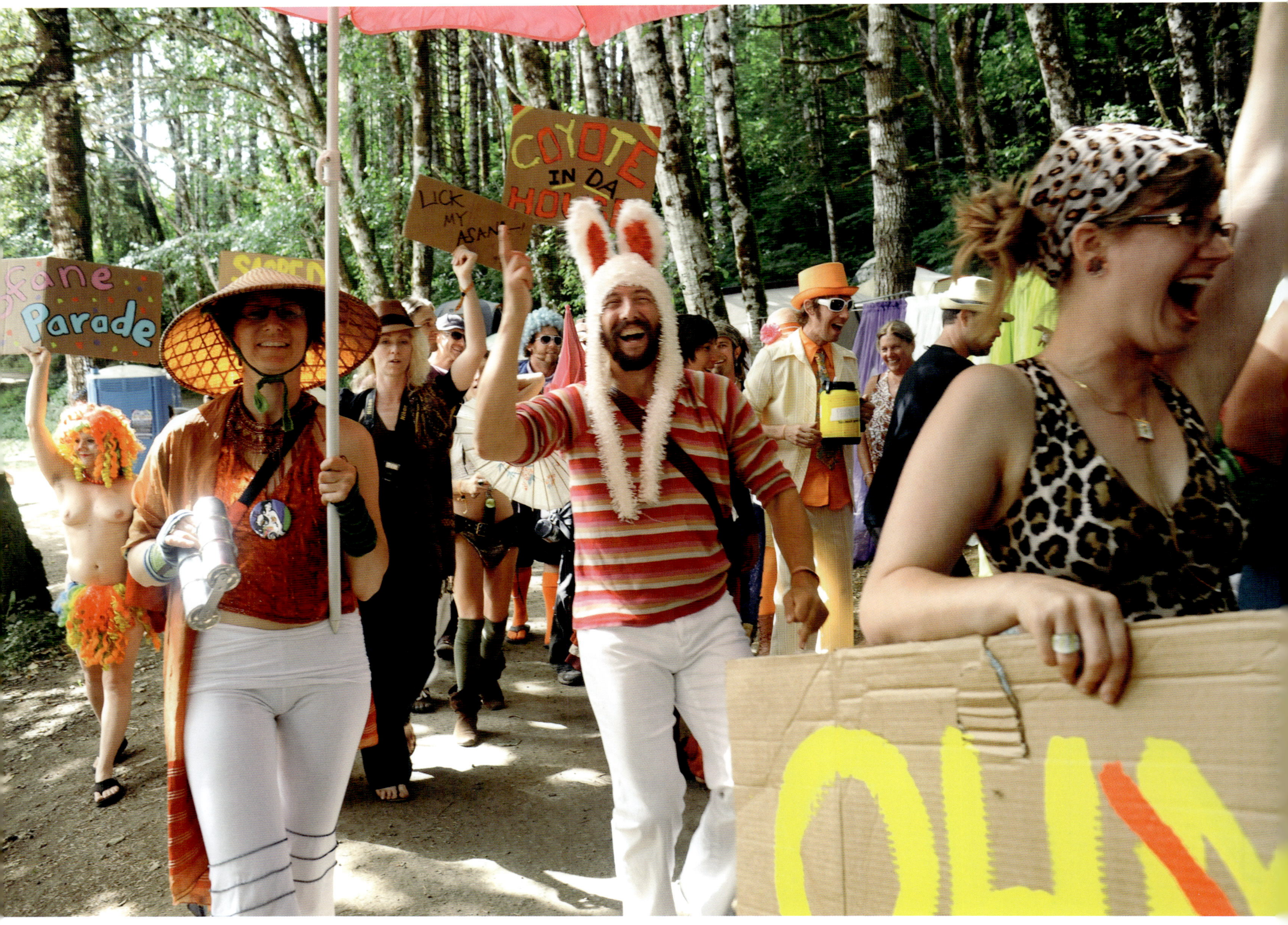
COYOTE
IN DA
HOUSE
LICK
MY
ASANA
Parade
fane
SACRED

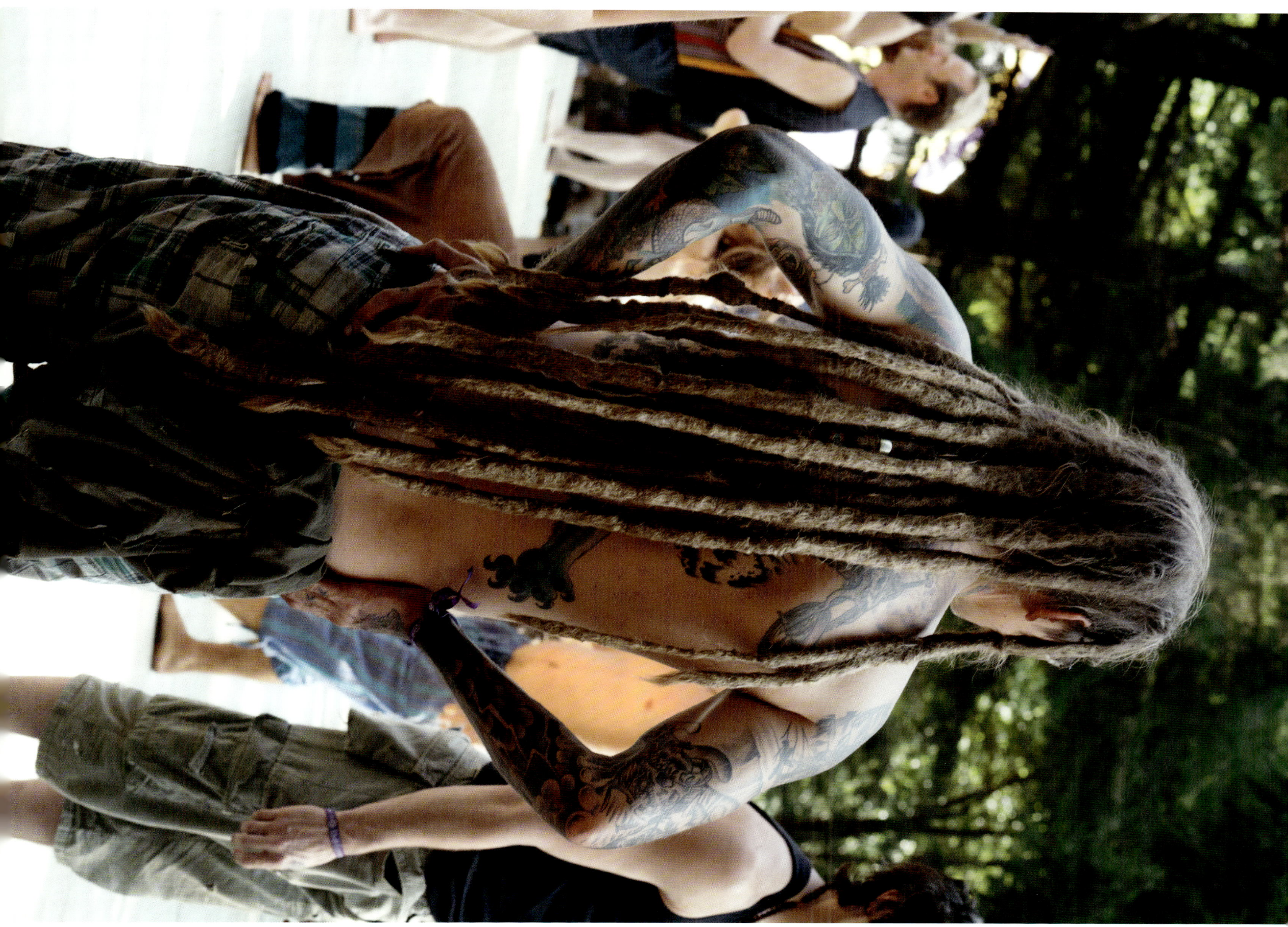

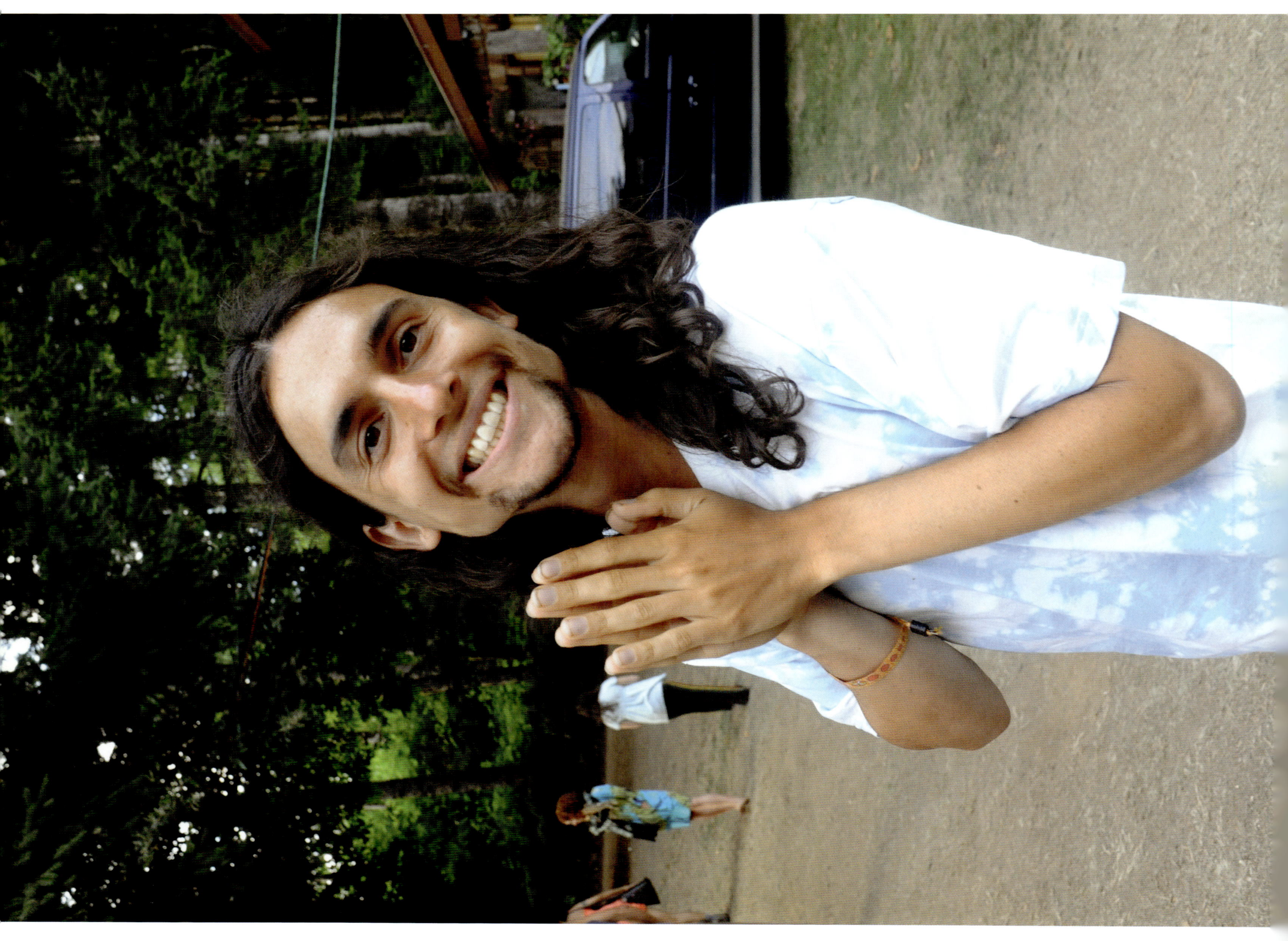

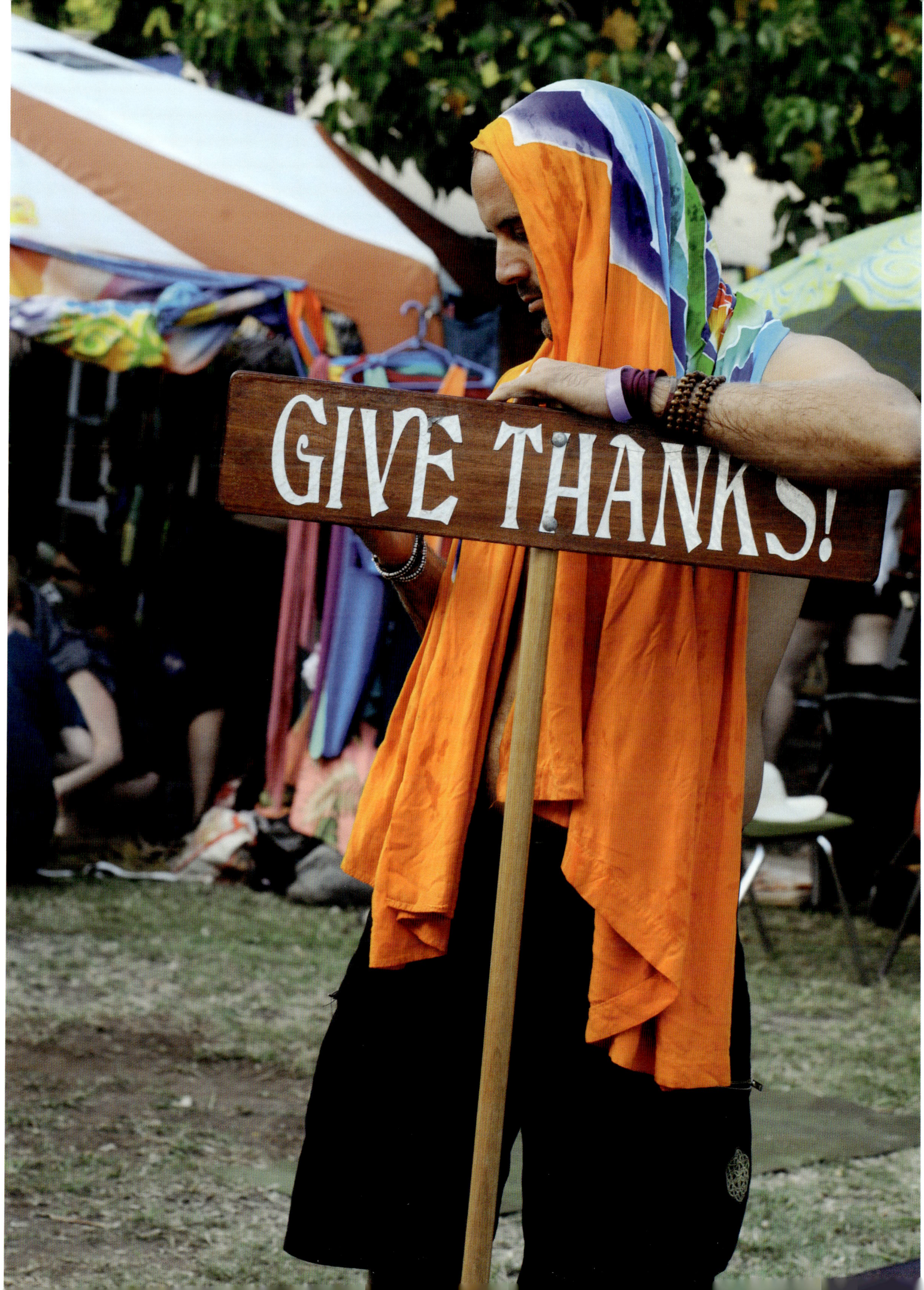

GIVE THANKS!

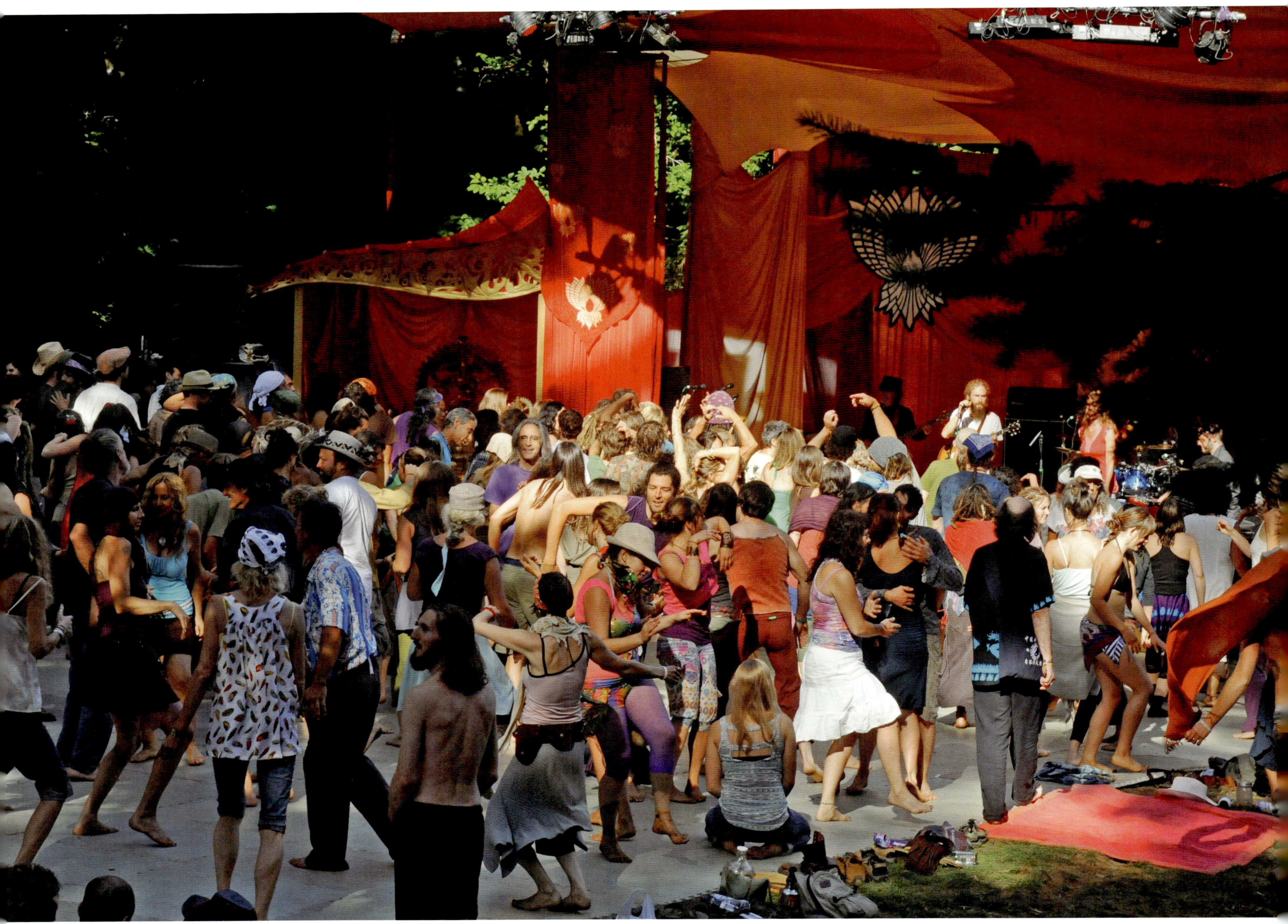

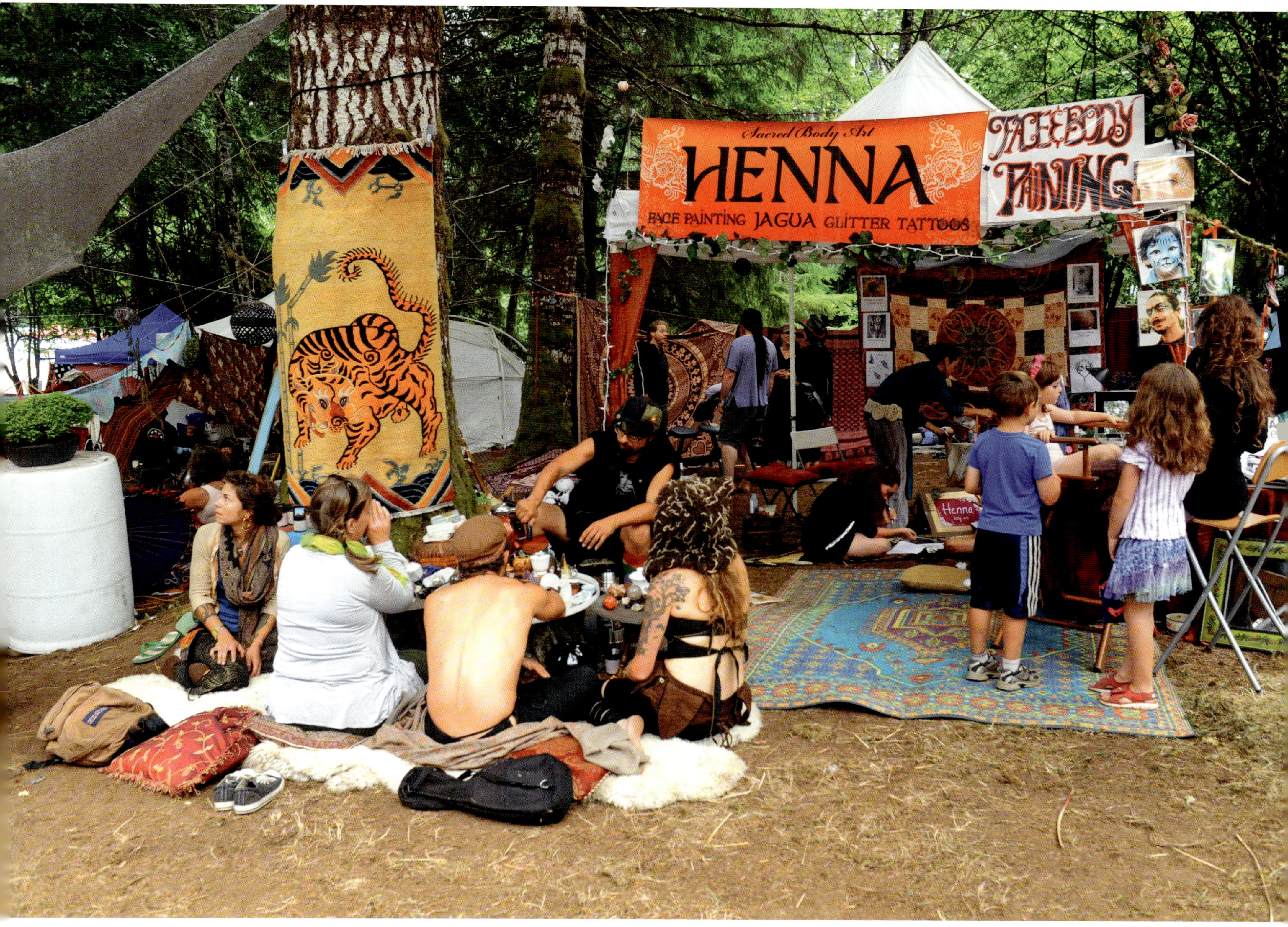

Sacred Body Art
HENNA
FACE PAINTING JAGUA GLITTER TATTOOS
FACE & BODY PAINTING
Henna body art

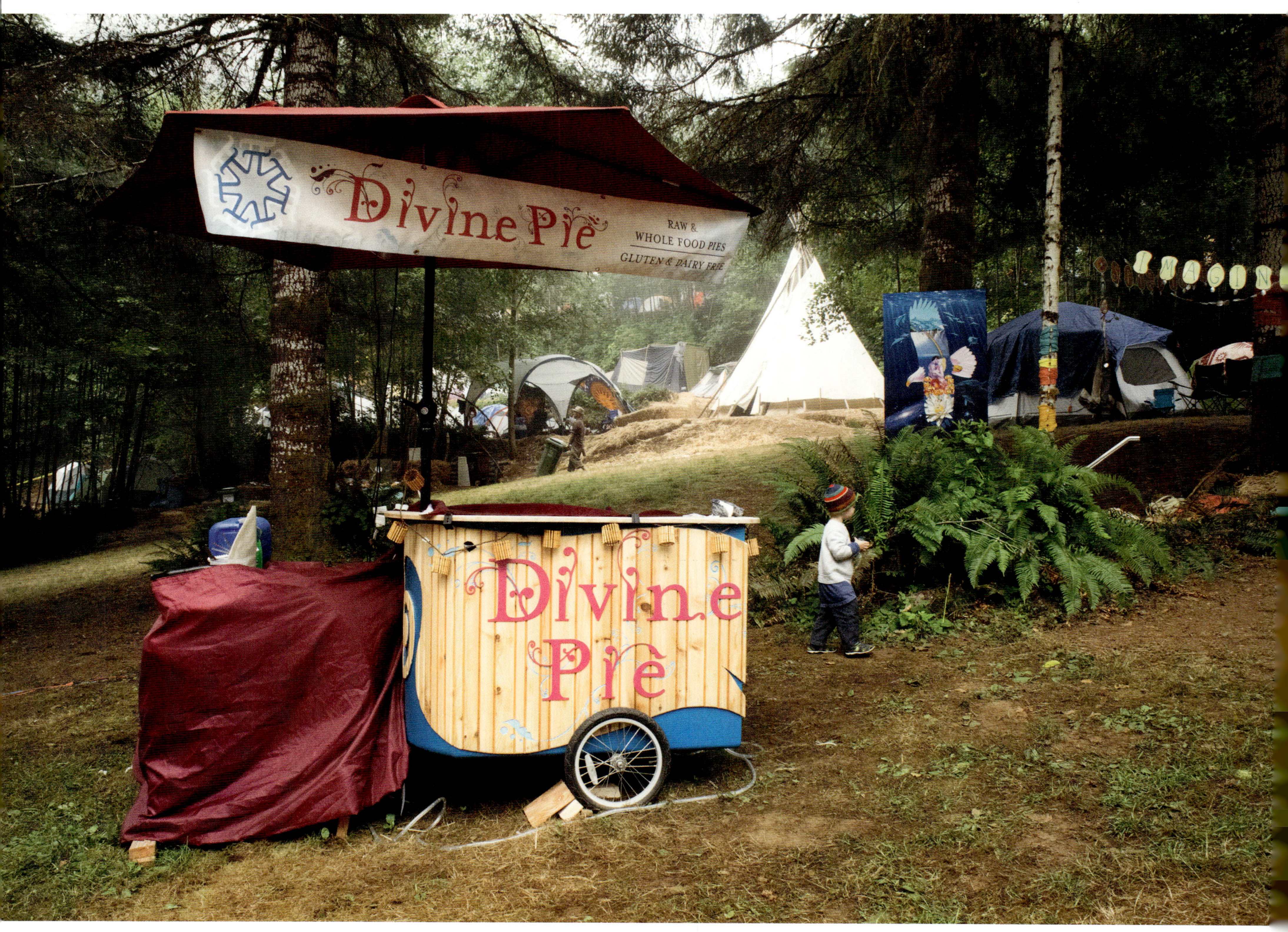
Divine Pie
RAW &
WHOLE FOOD PIES
GLUTEN & DAIRY FREE
Divine
Pie
IMAGIN

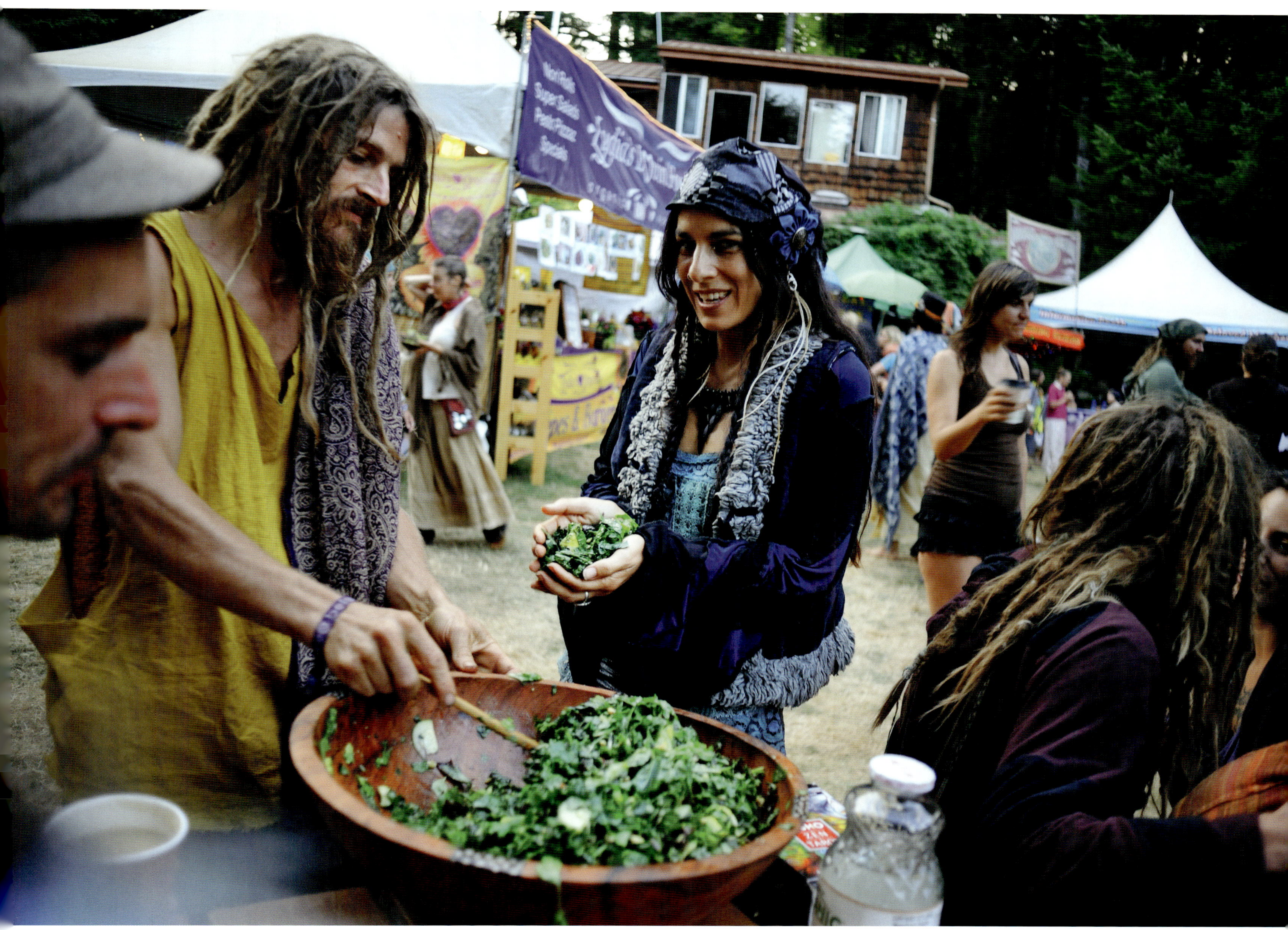

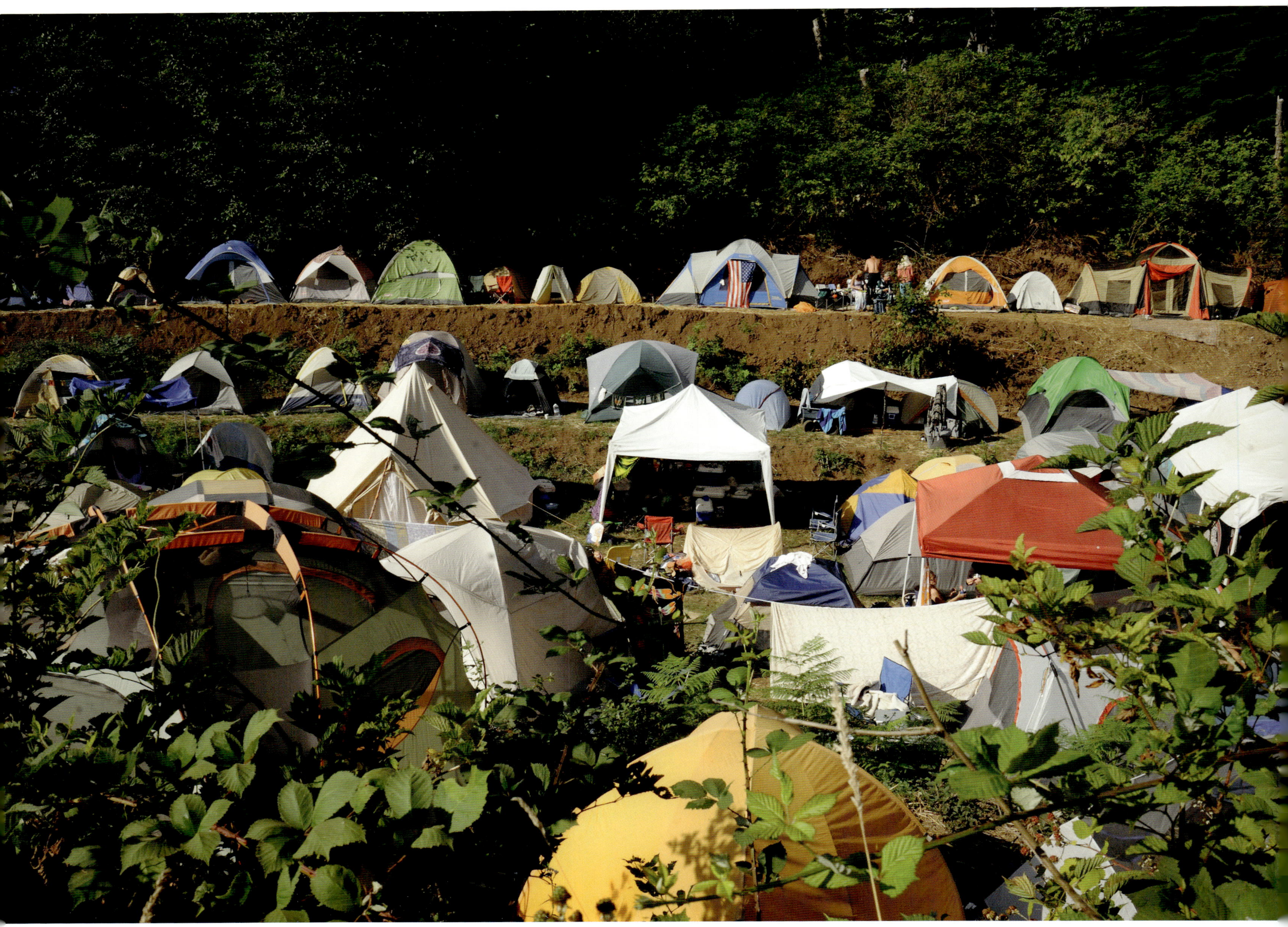

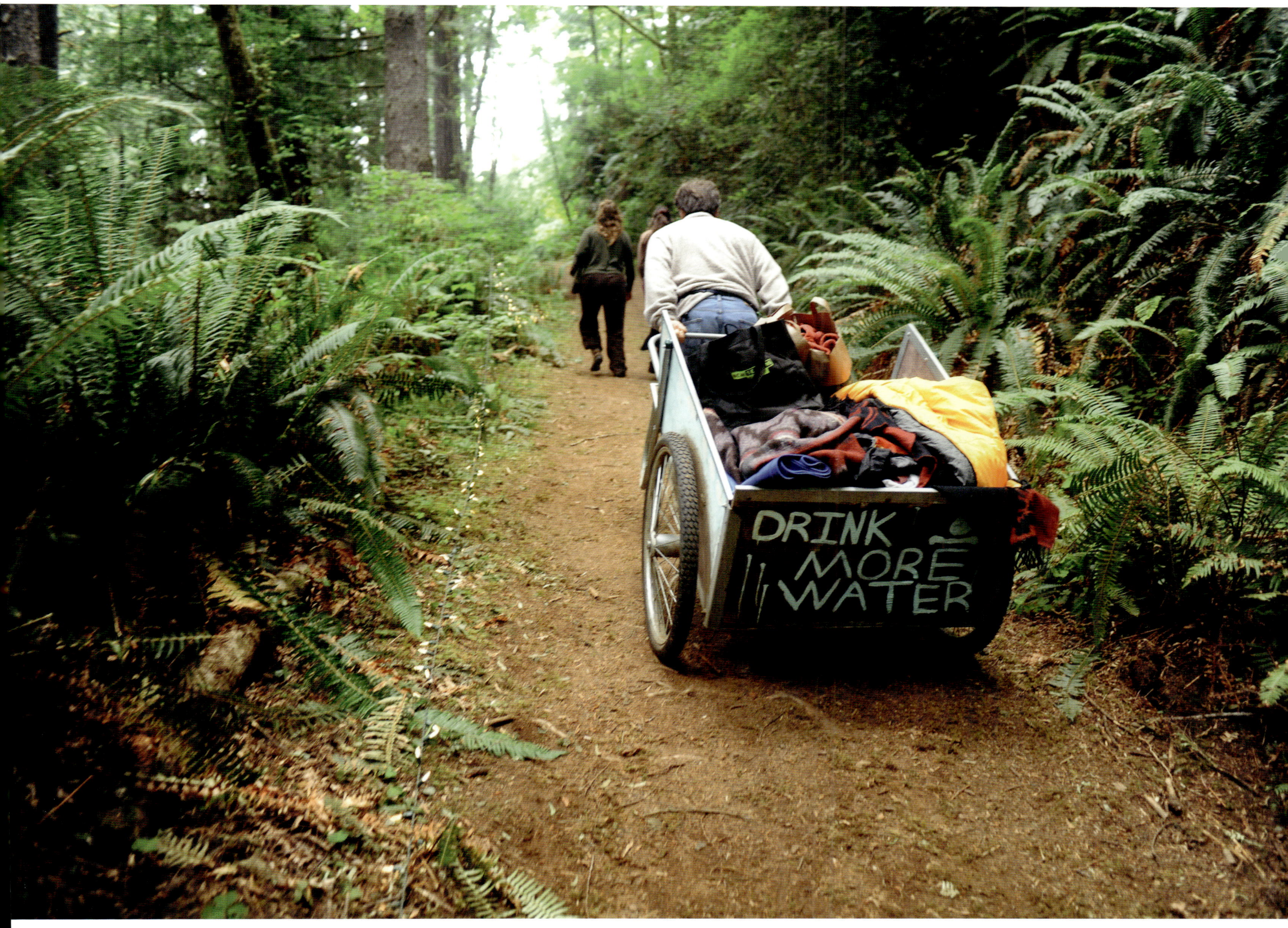
DRINK
MORE
WATER

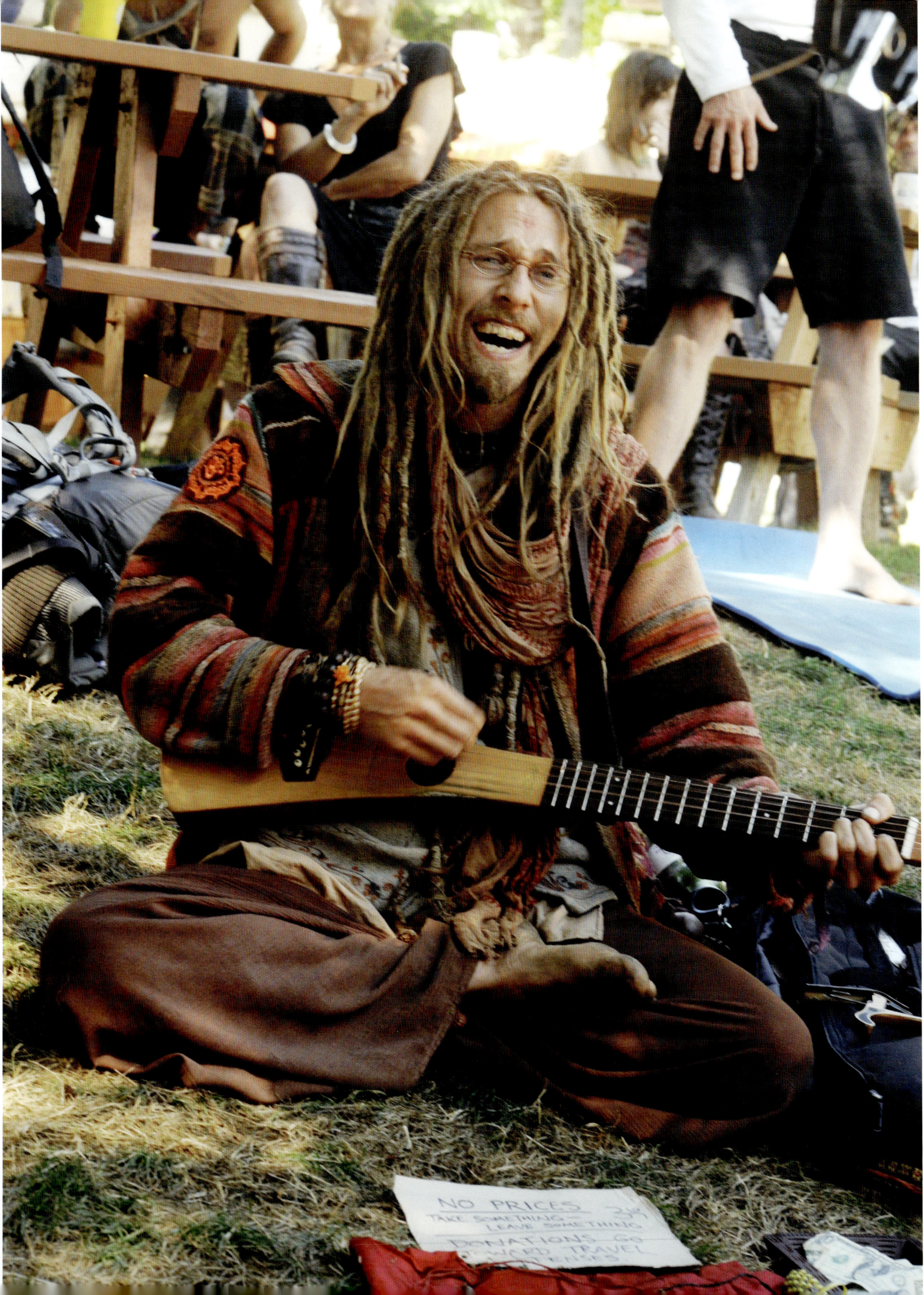

NO PRICES
TAKE SOMETHING — LEAVE SOMETHING
DONATIONS GO
TOWARD TRAVEL
EXPENSES

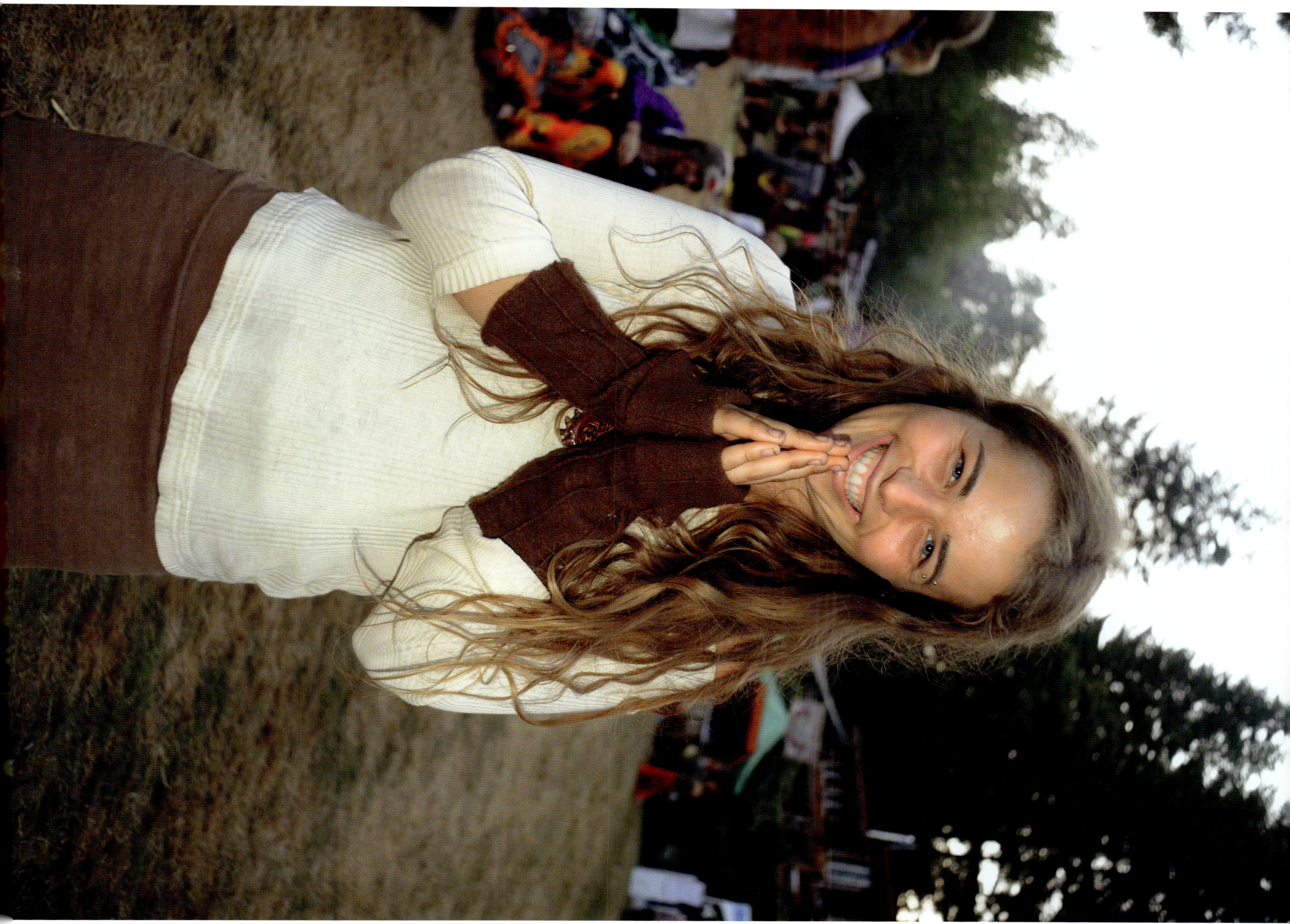

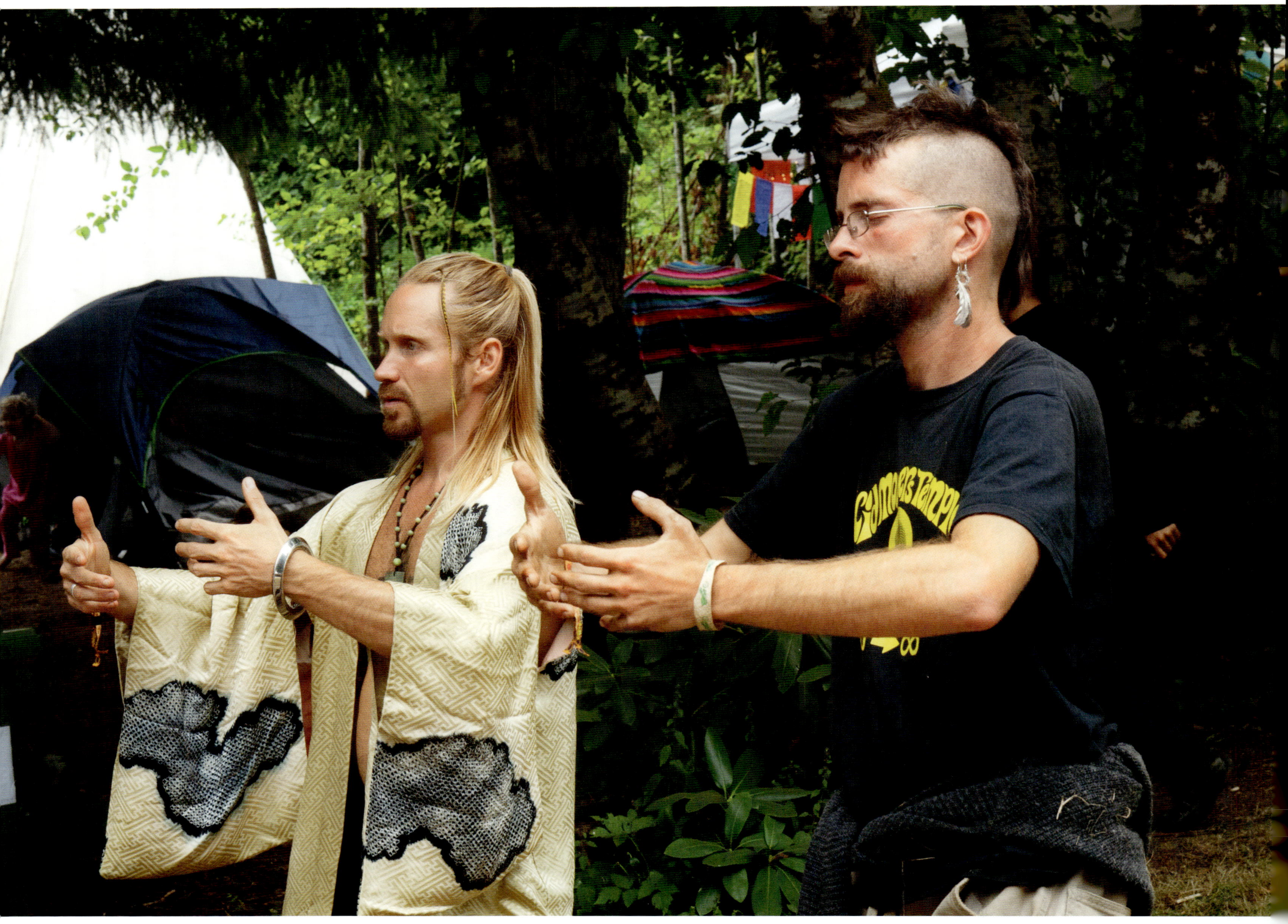

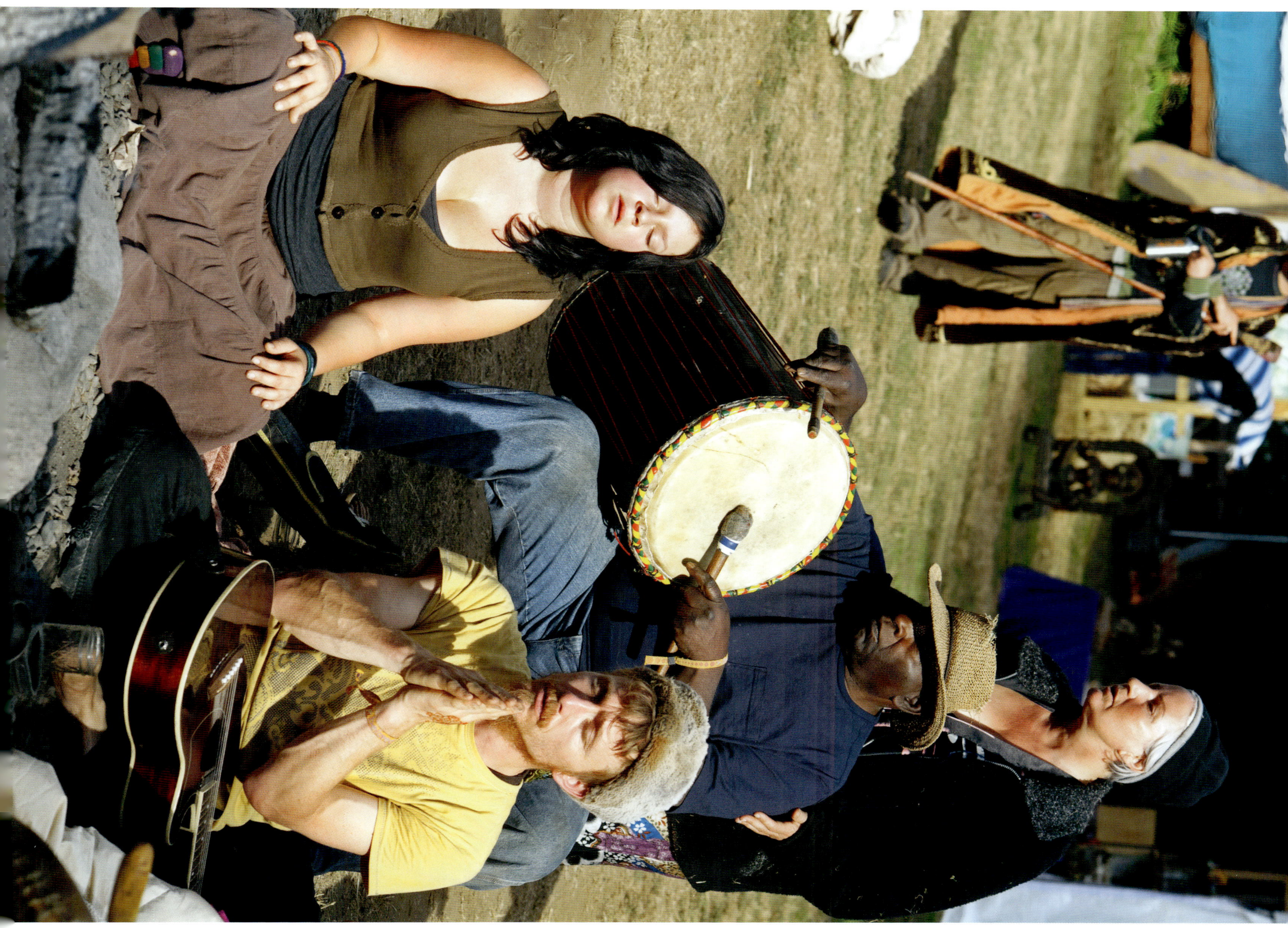

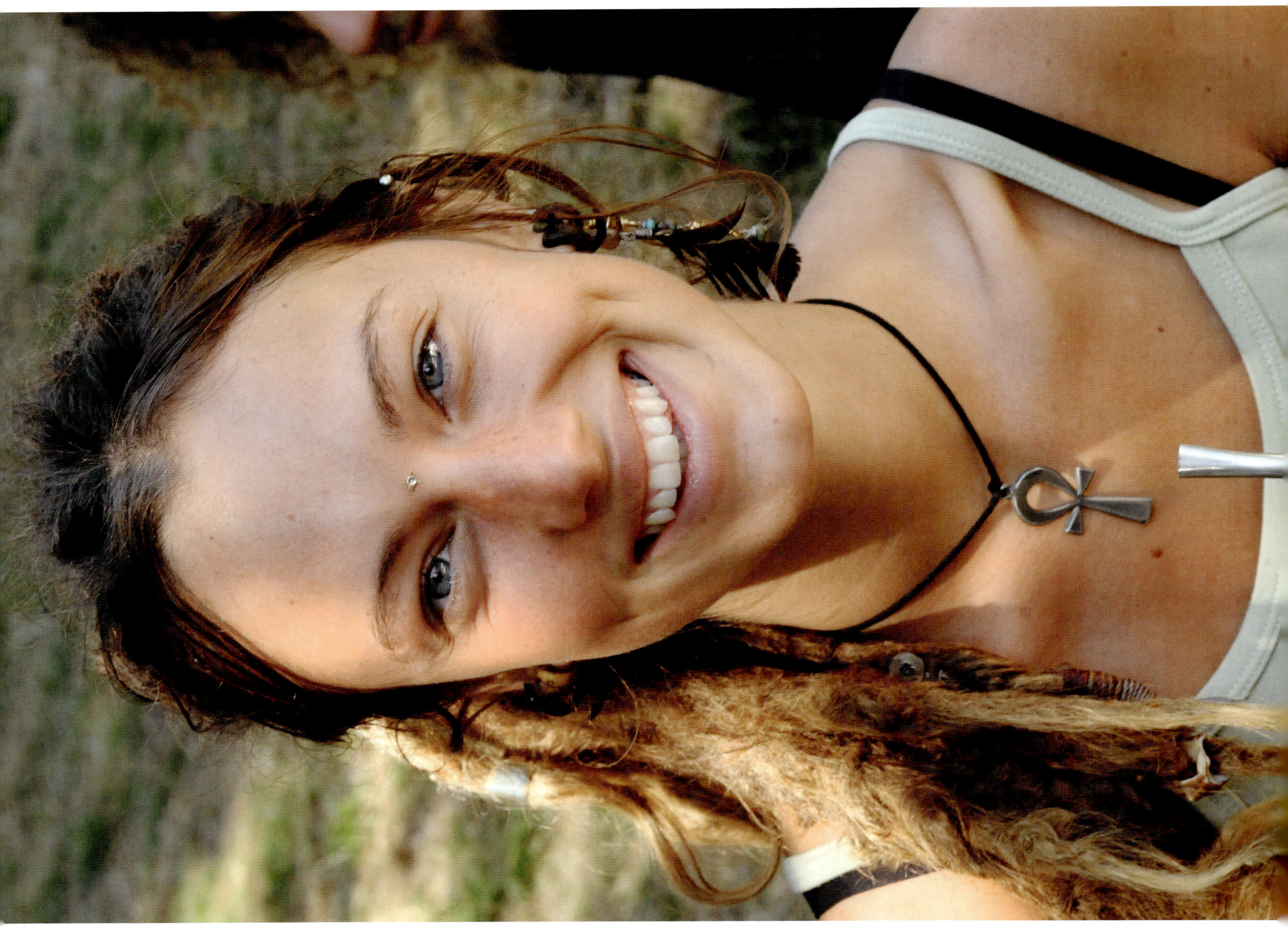

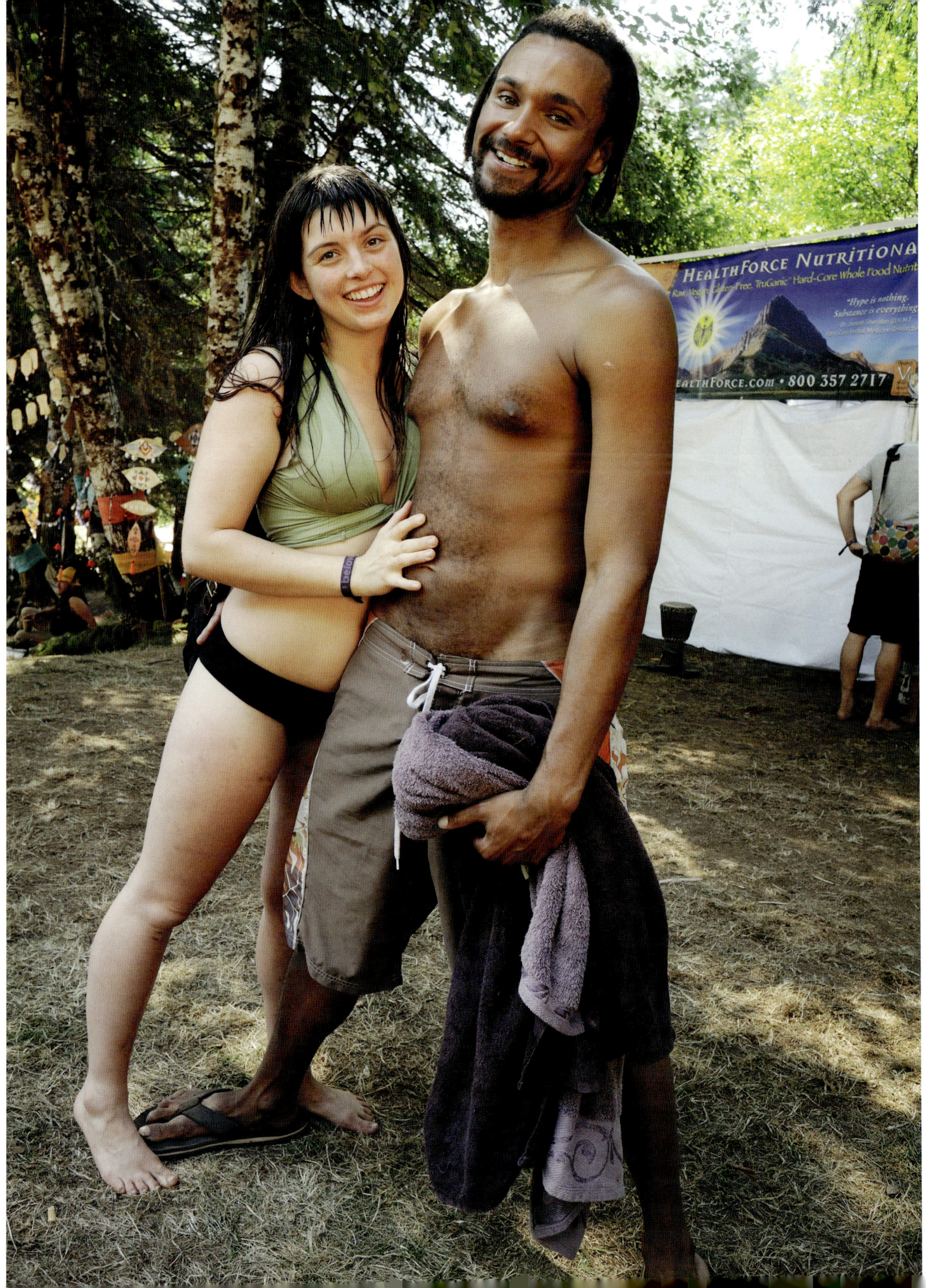

HealthForce Nutritiona
Raw, Vegan, Gluten-Free, TruGanic™ Hard-Core Whole Food Nutri
"Hype is nothing.
Substance is everything."
HealthForce.com • 800 357 2717

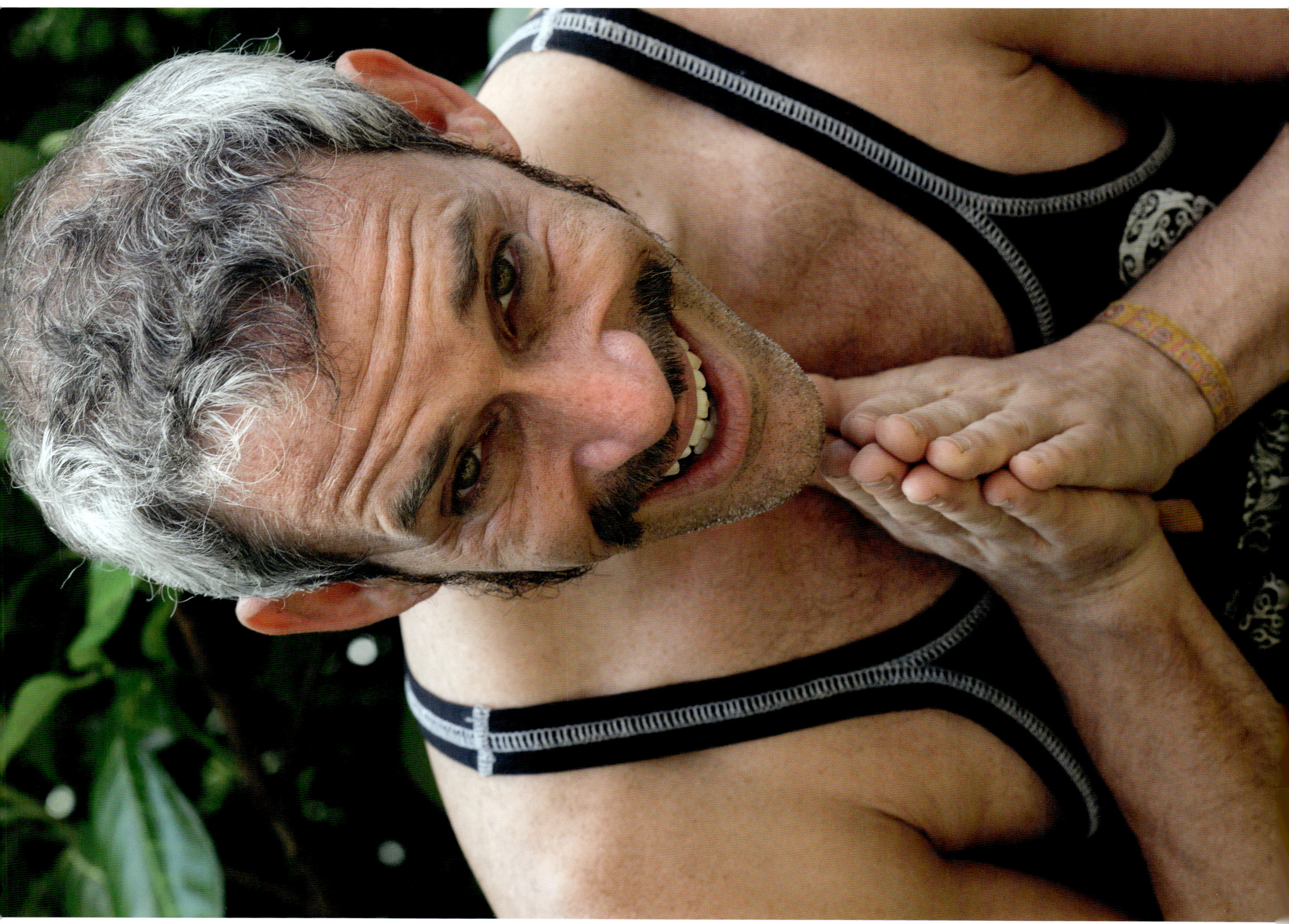

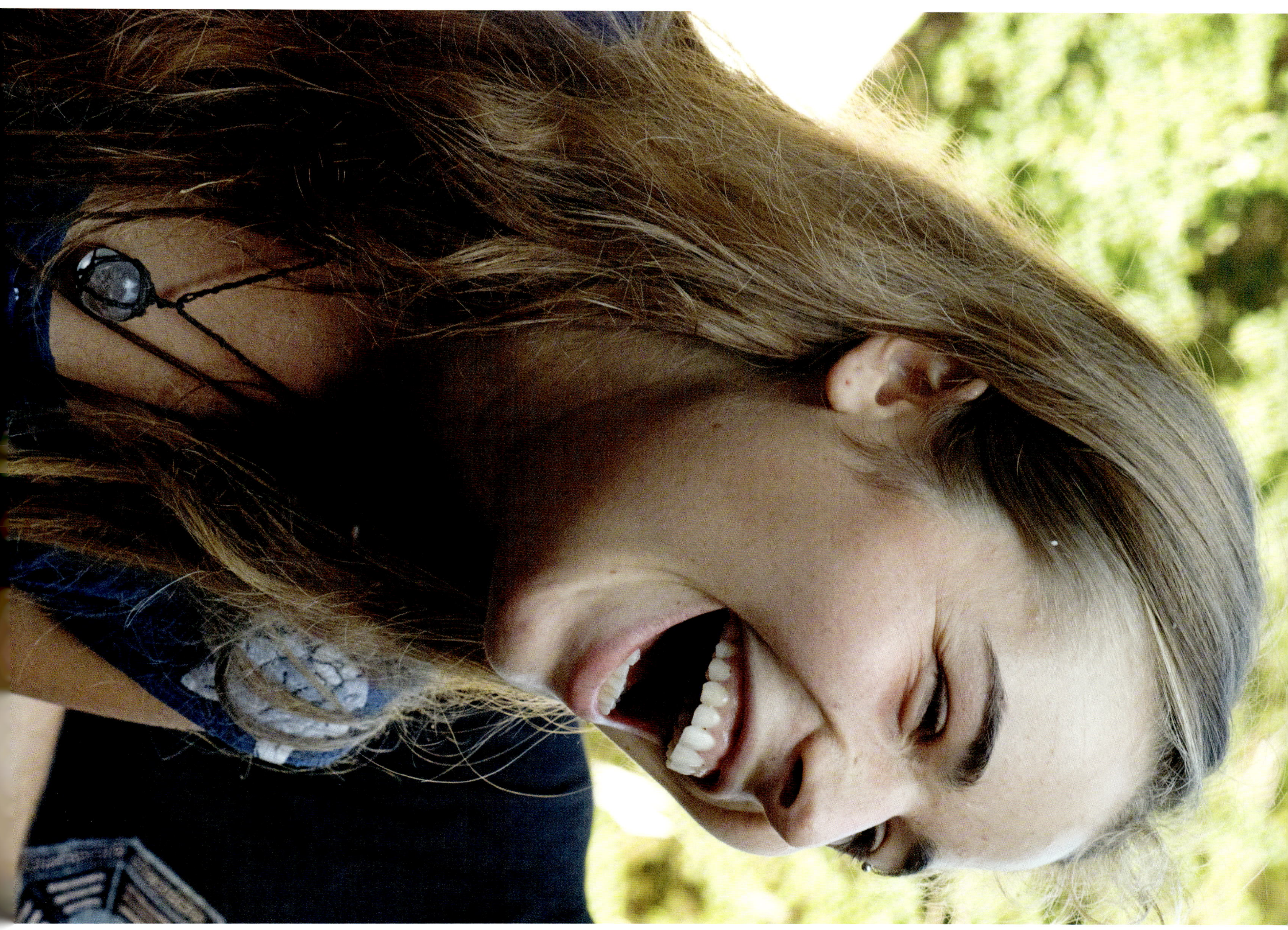

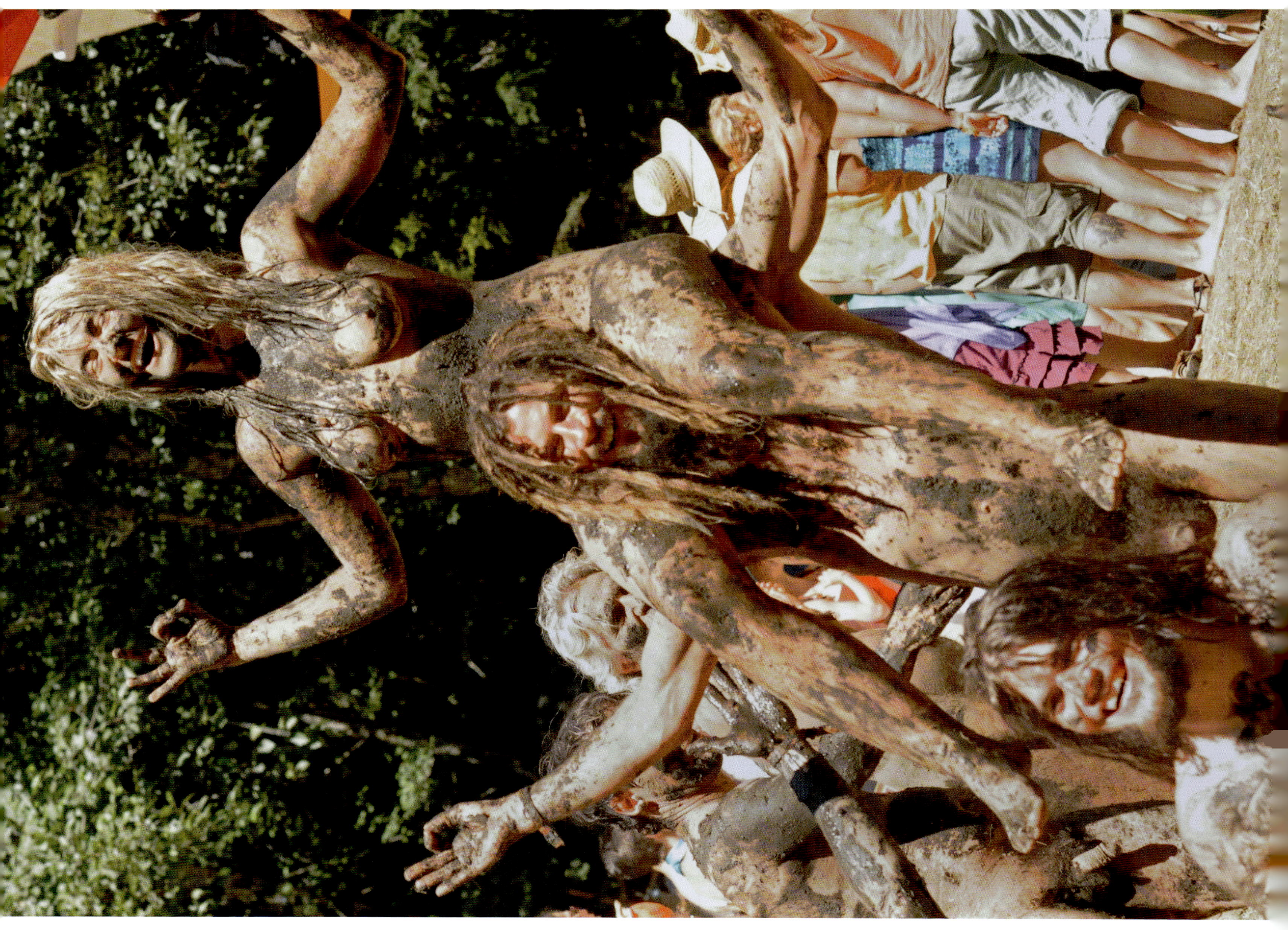

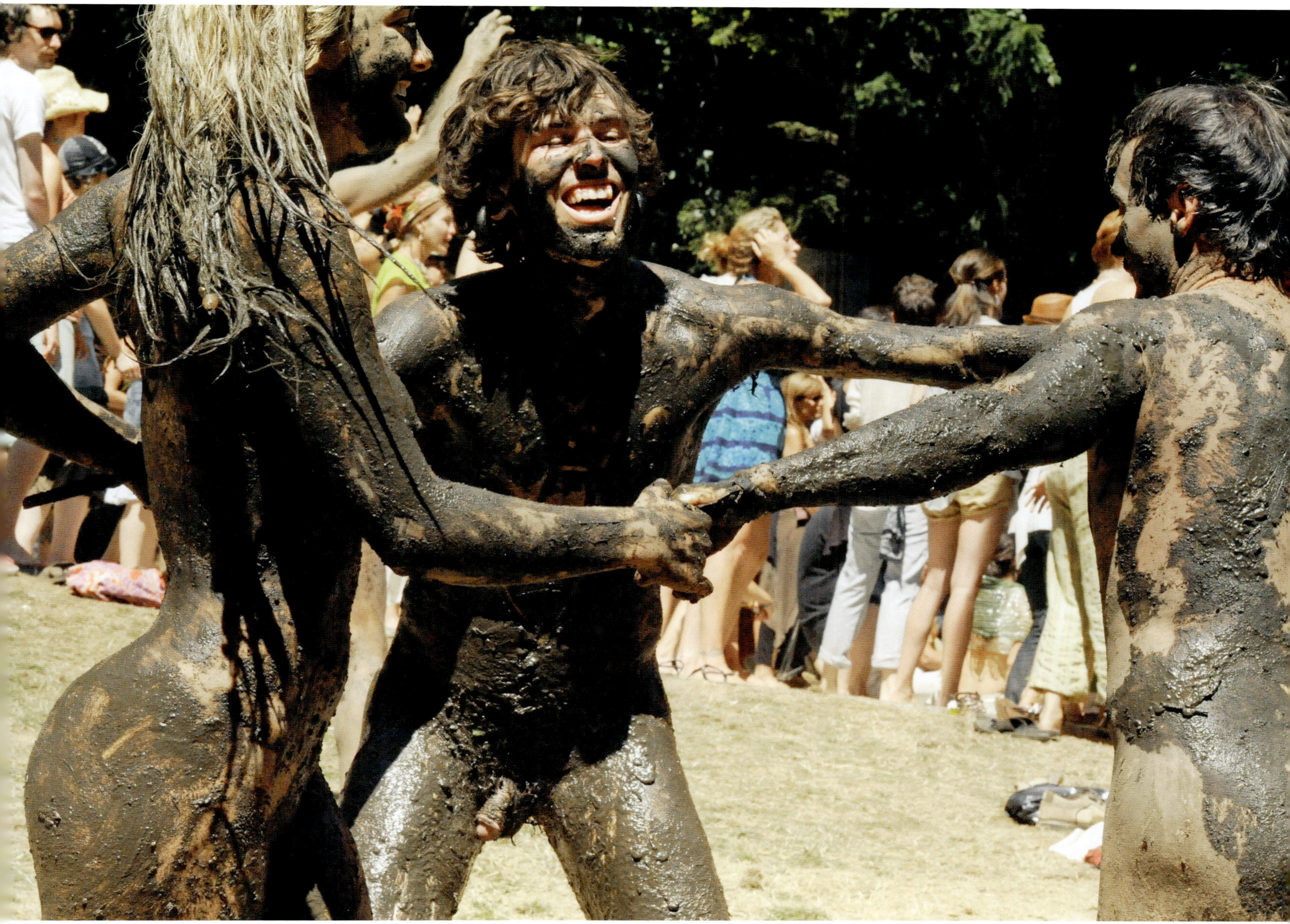

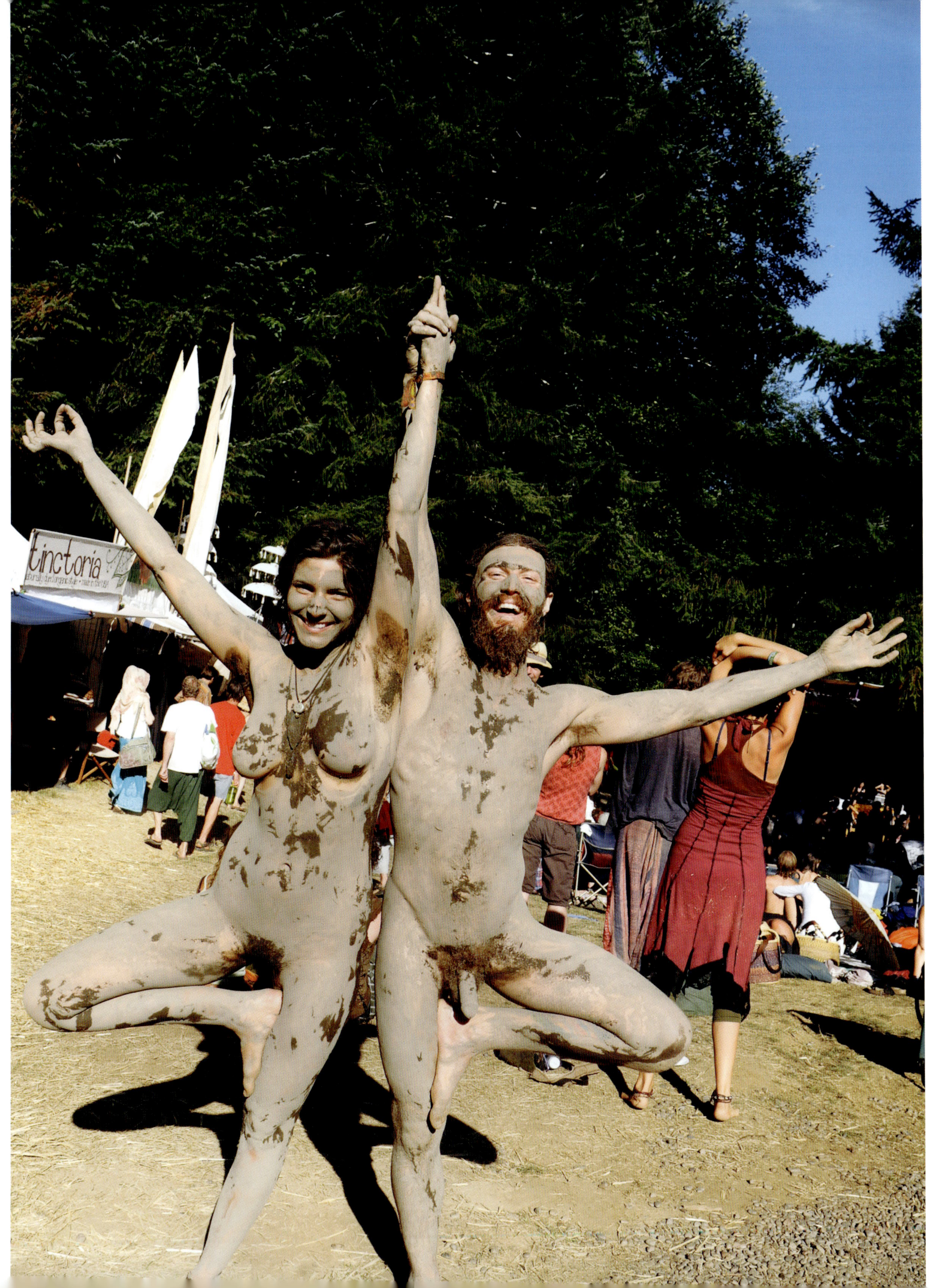
tinctoria

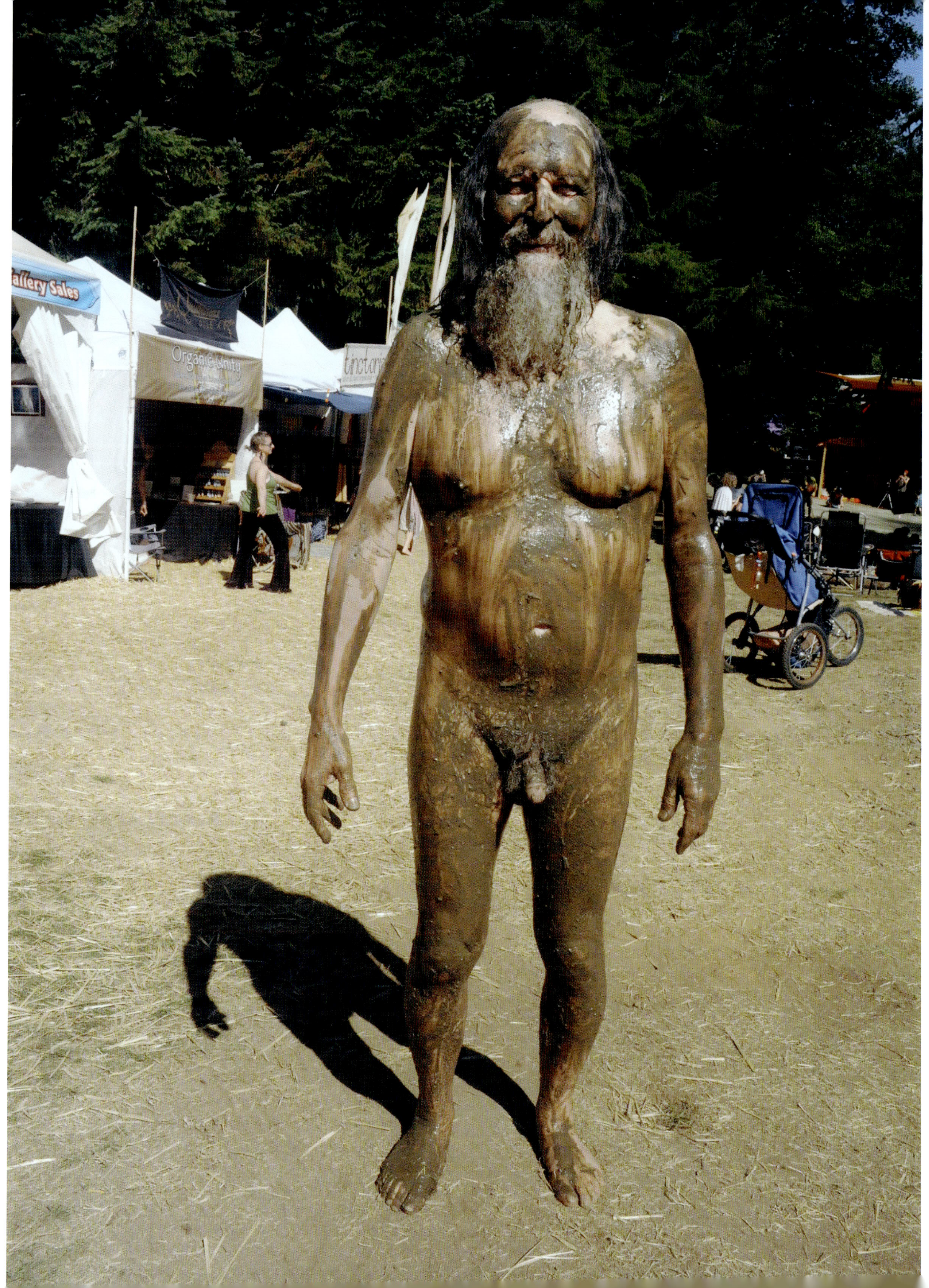
Gallery Sales
Organic Unity
tinctoria

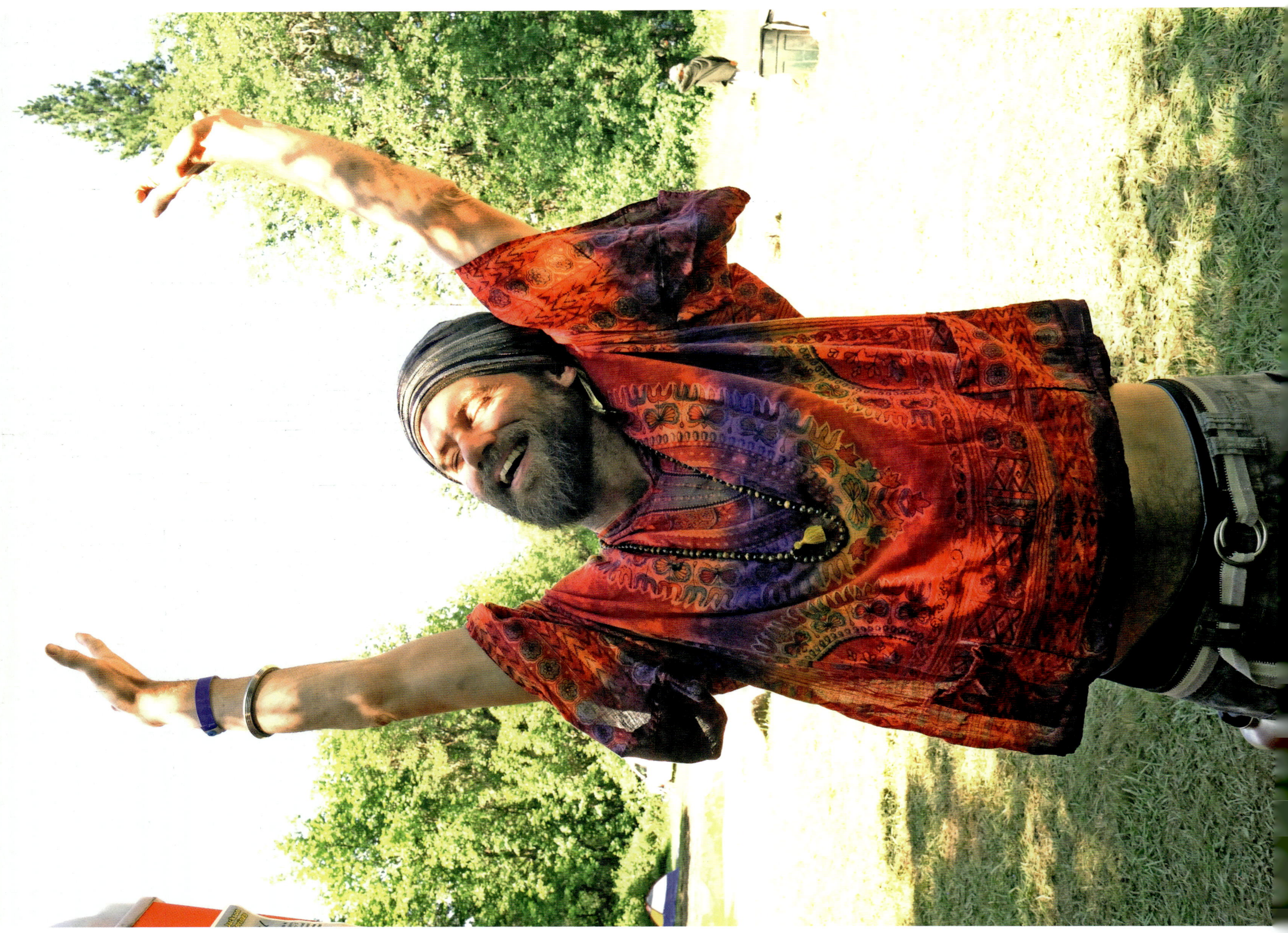

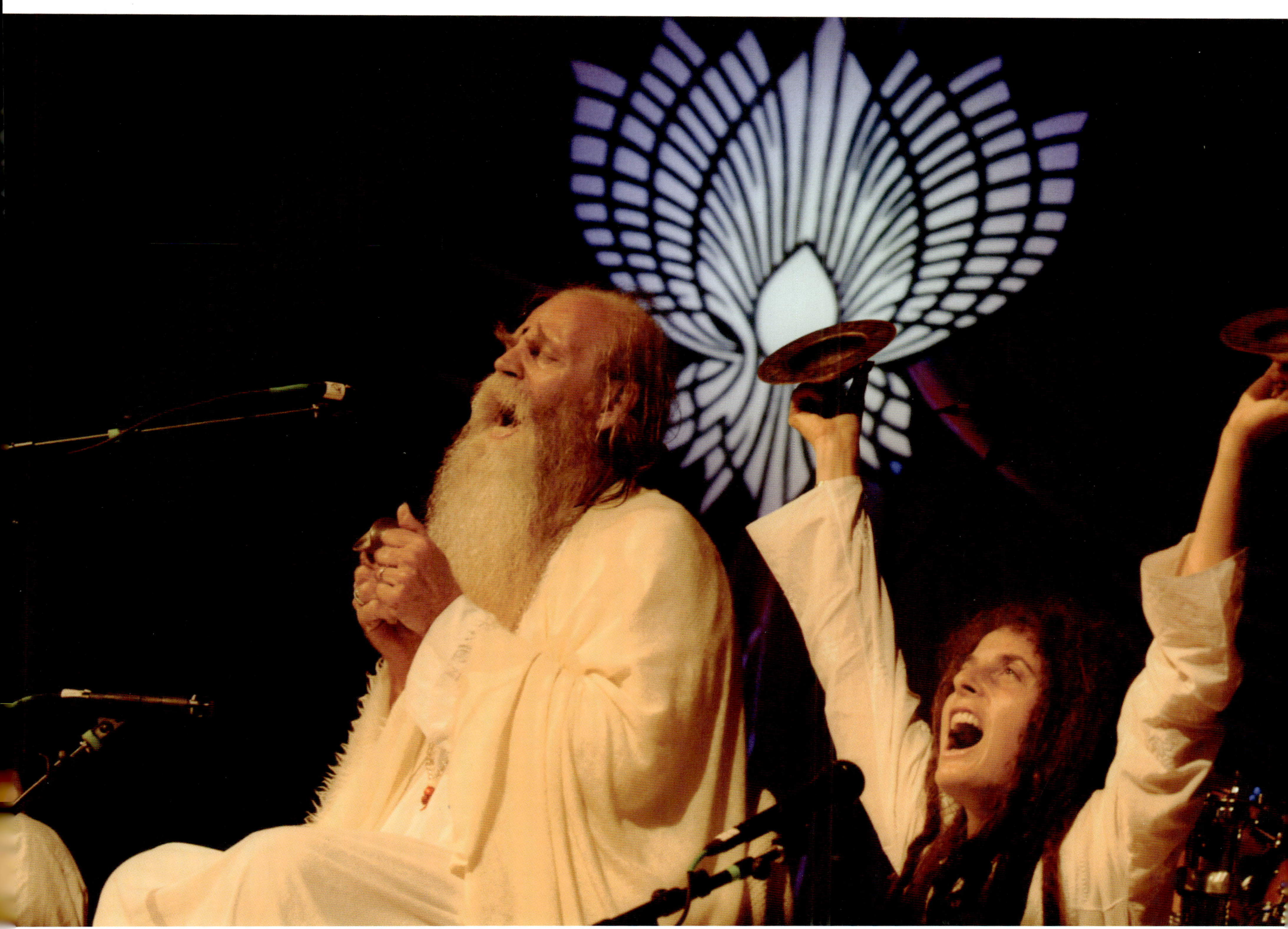

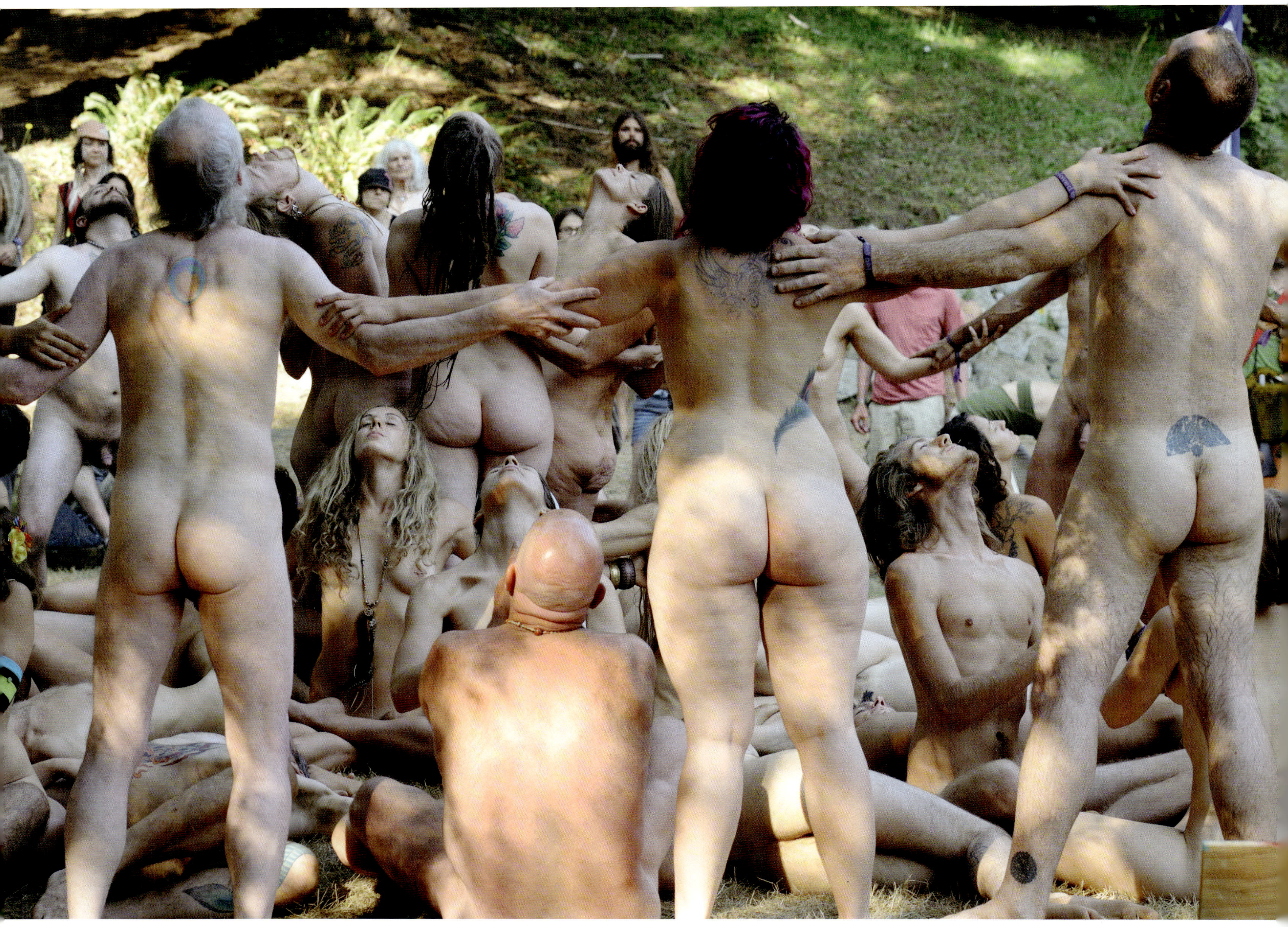

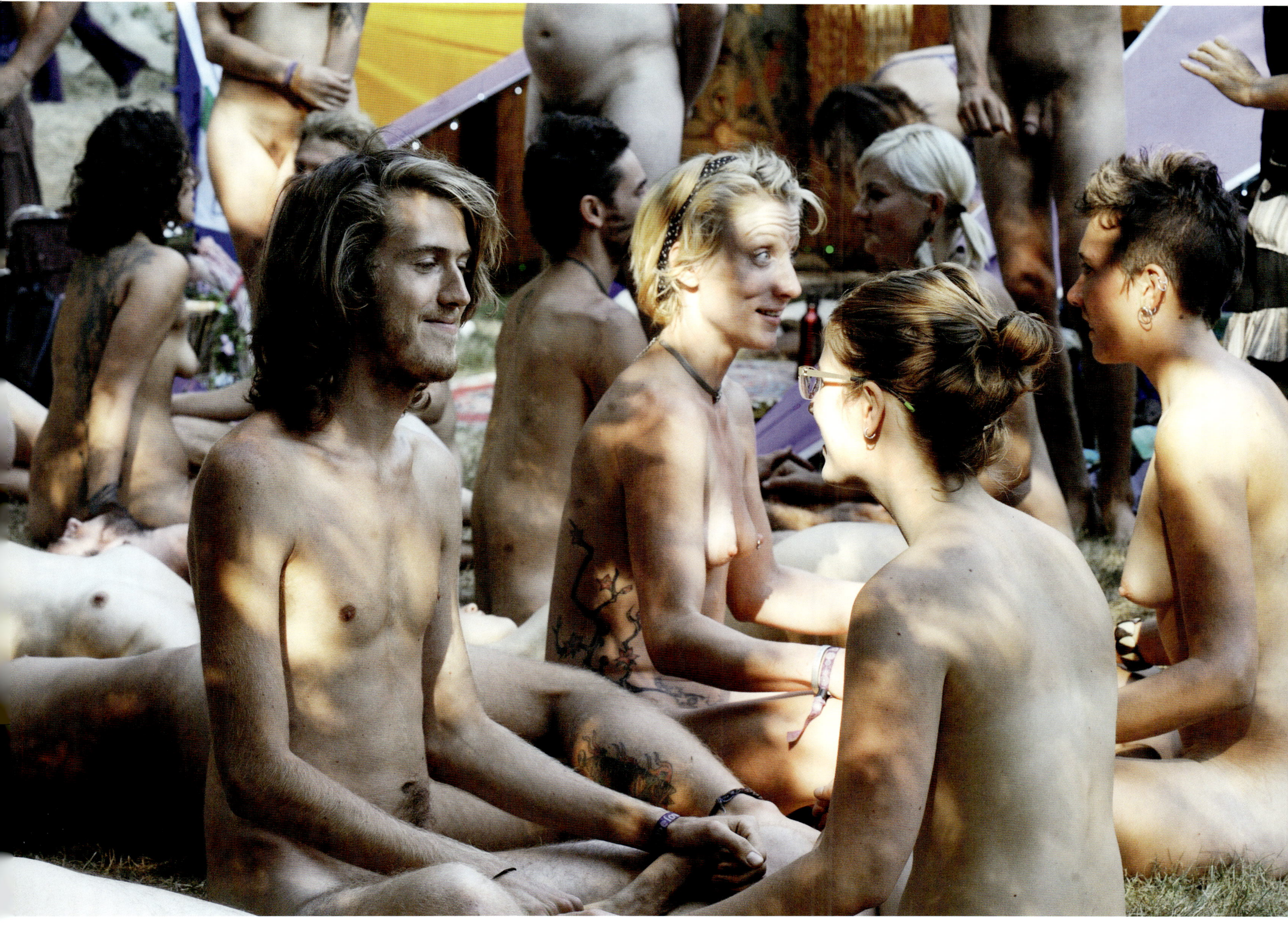

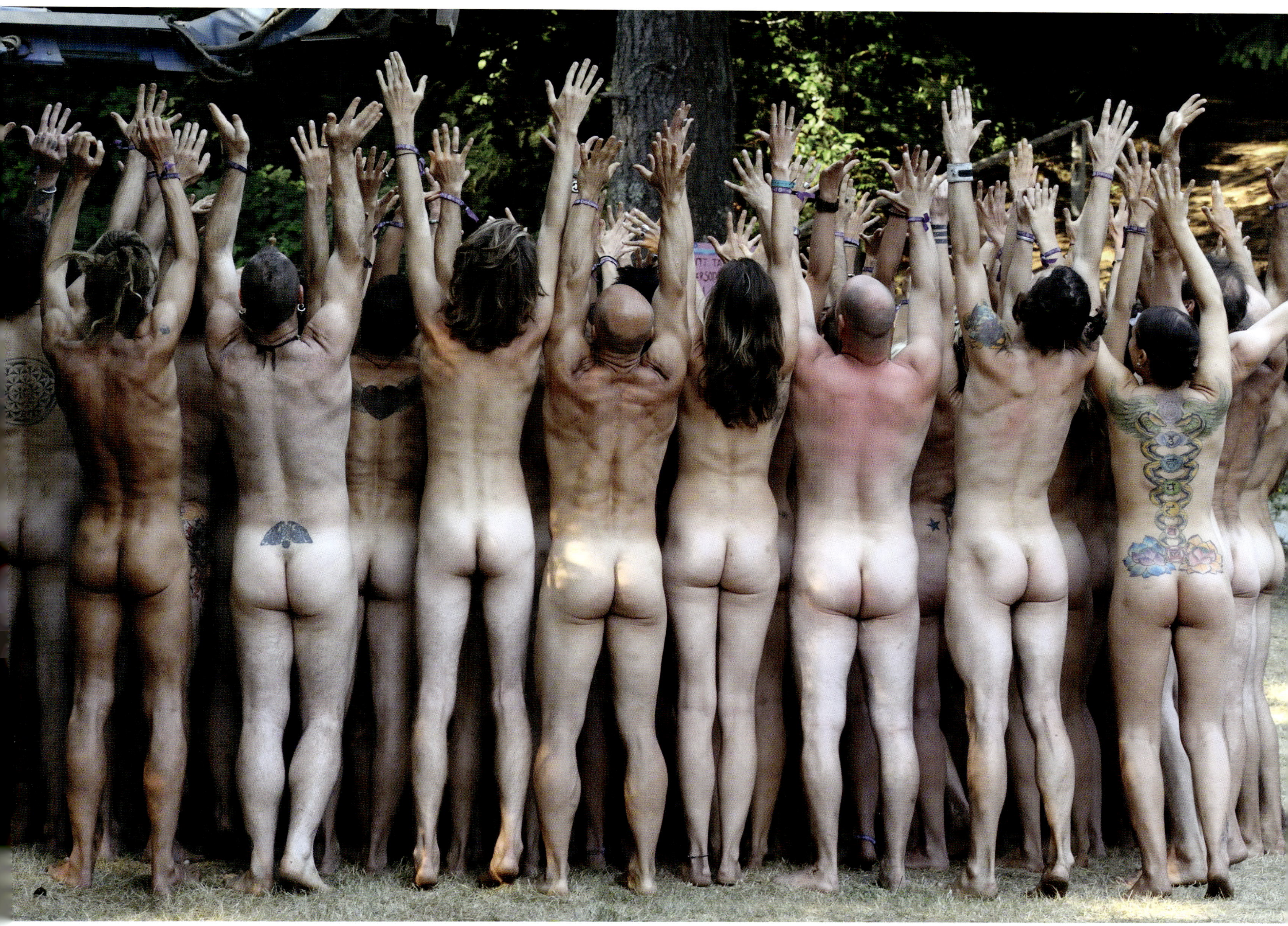

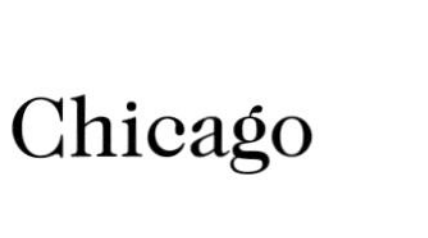

Chicago

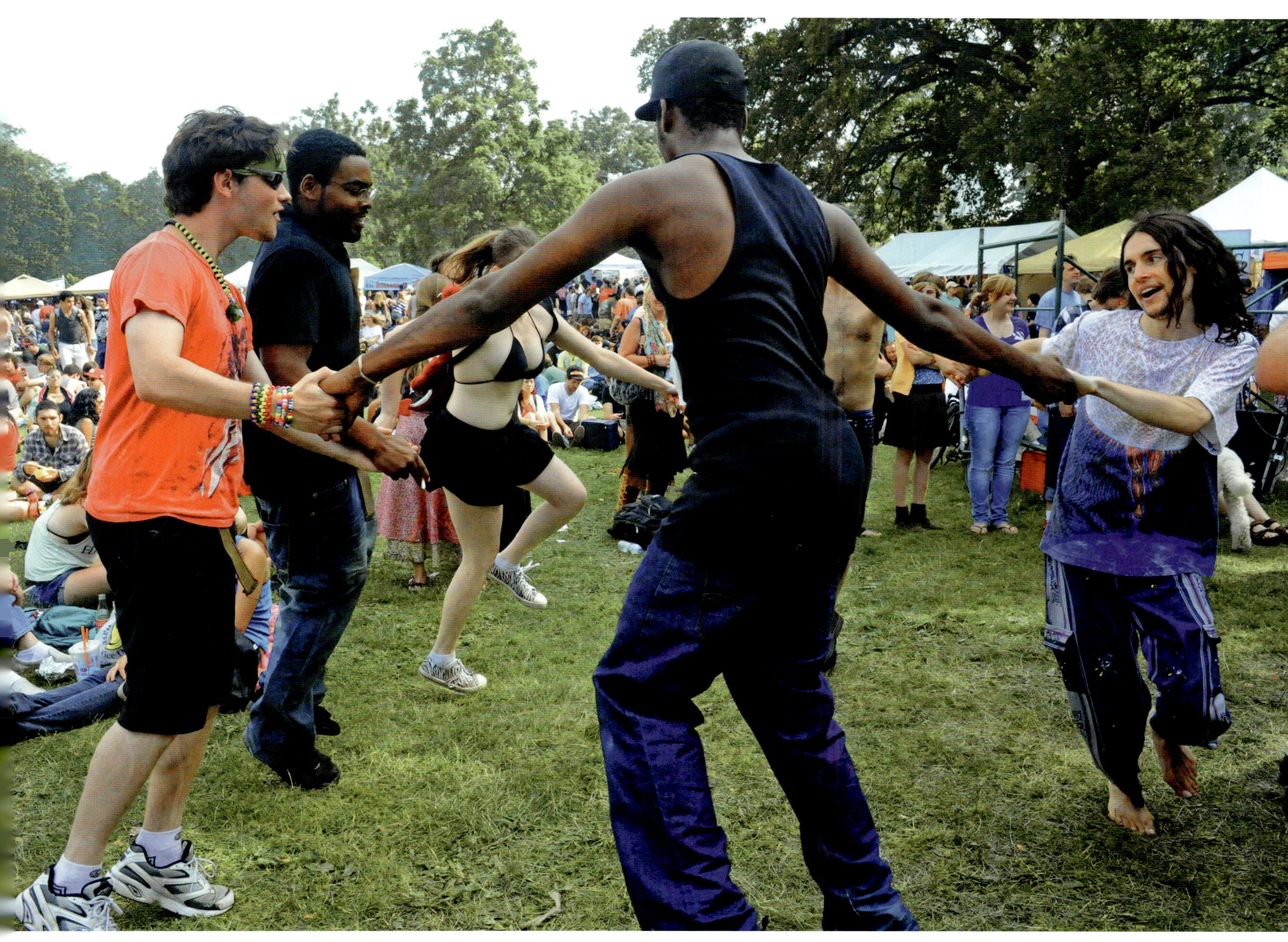

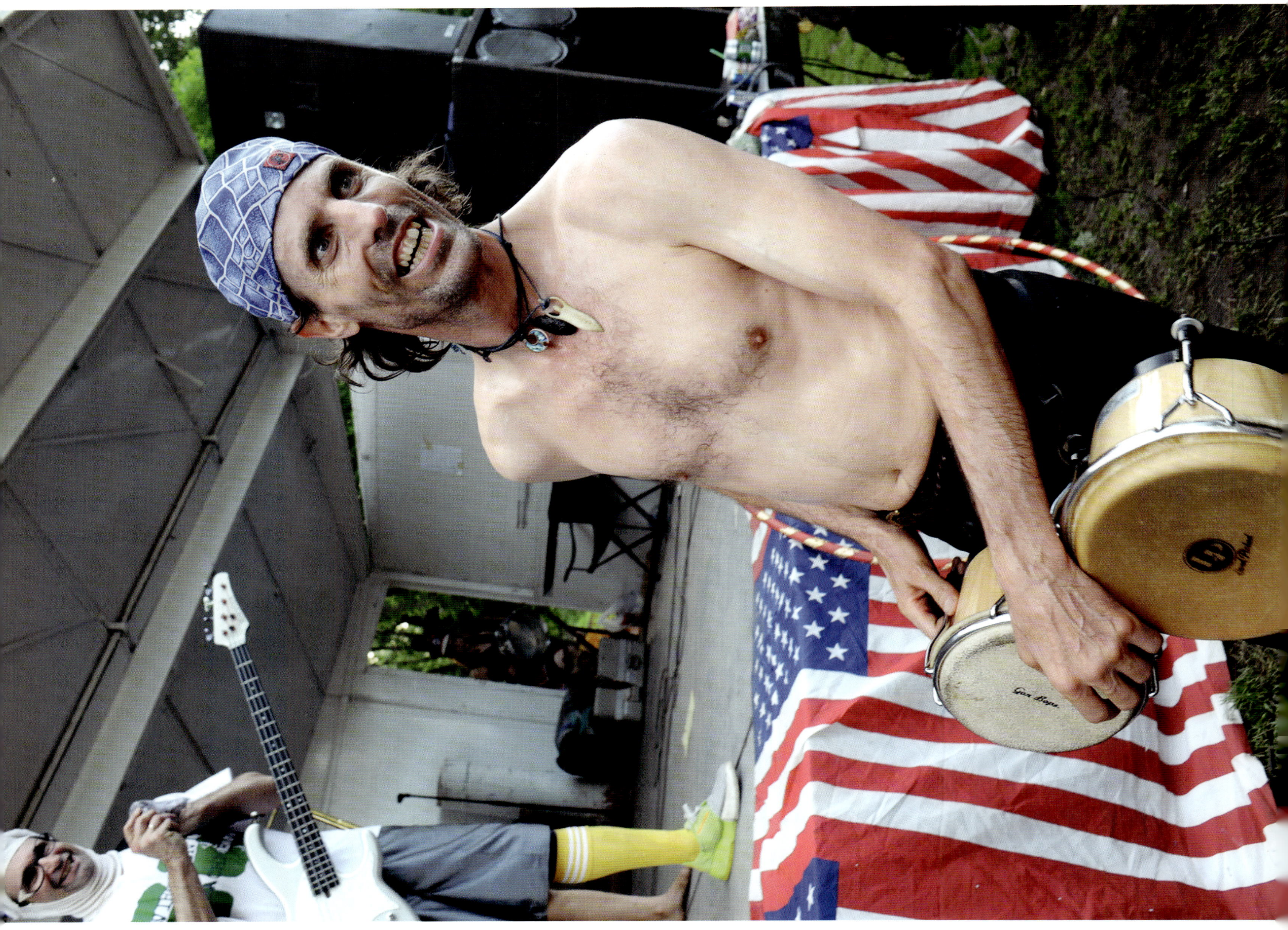

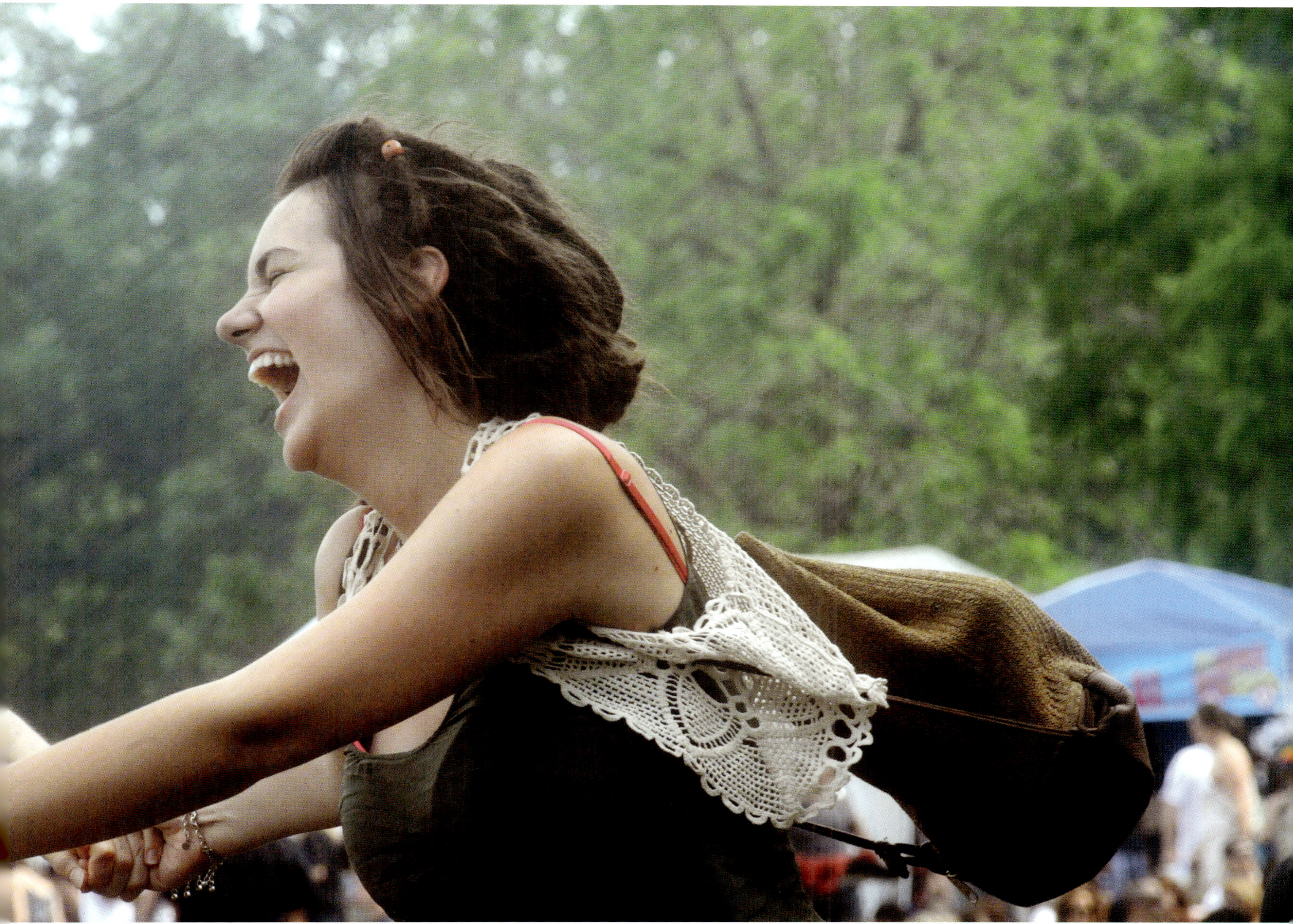

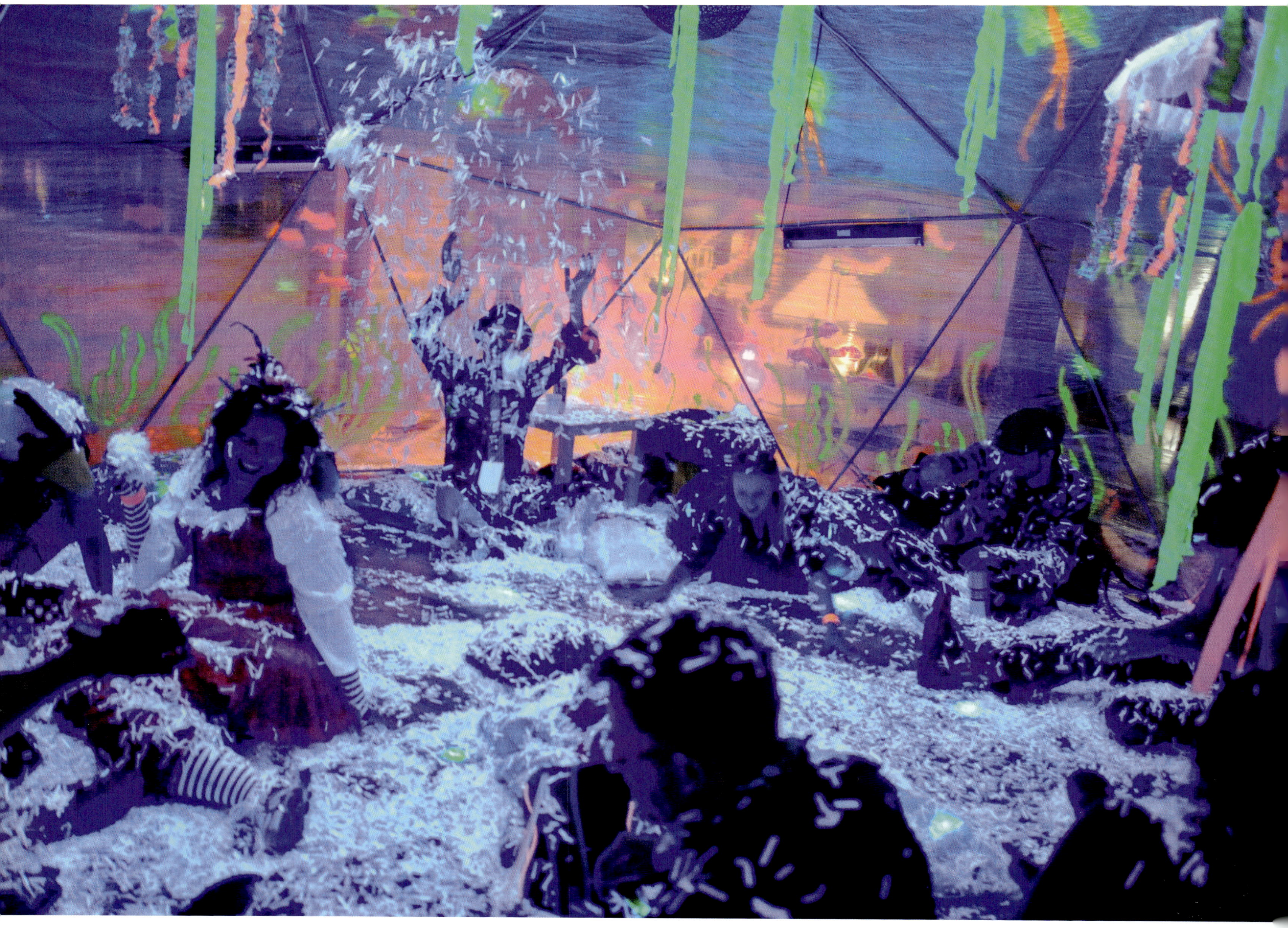

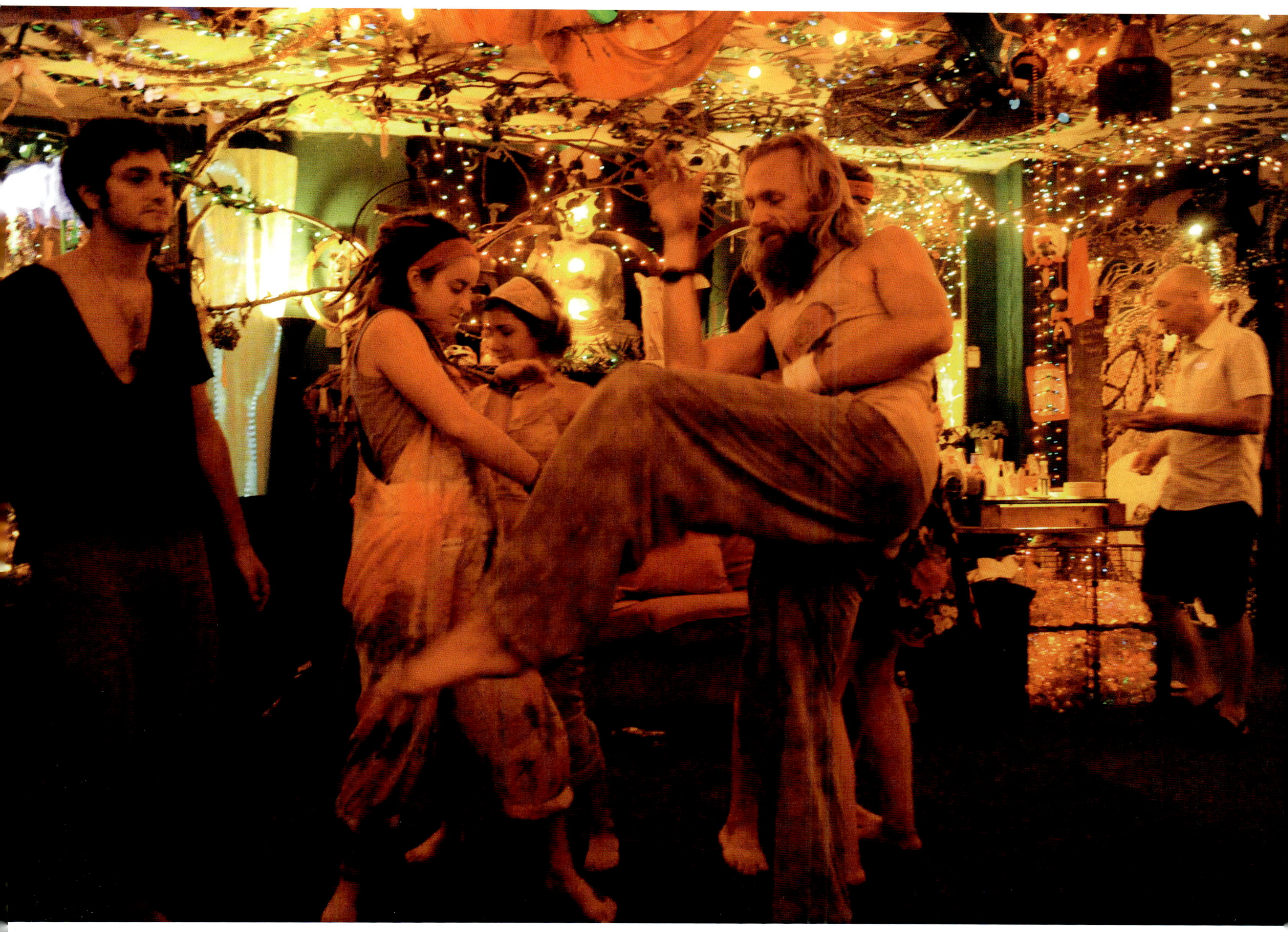

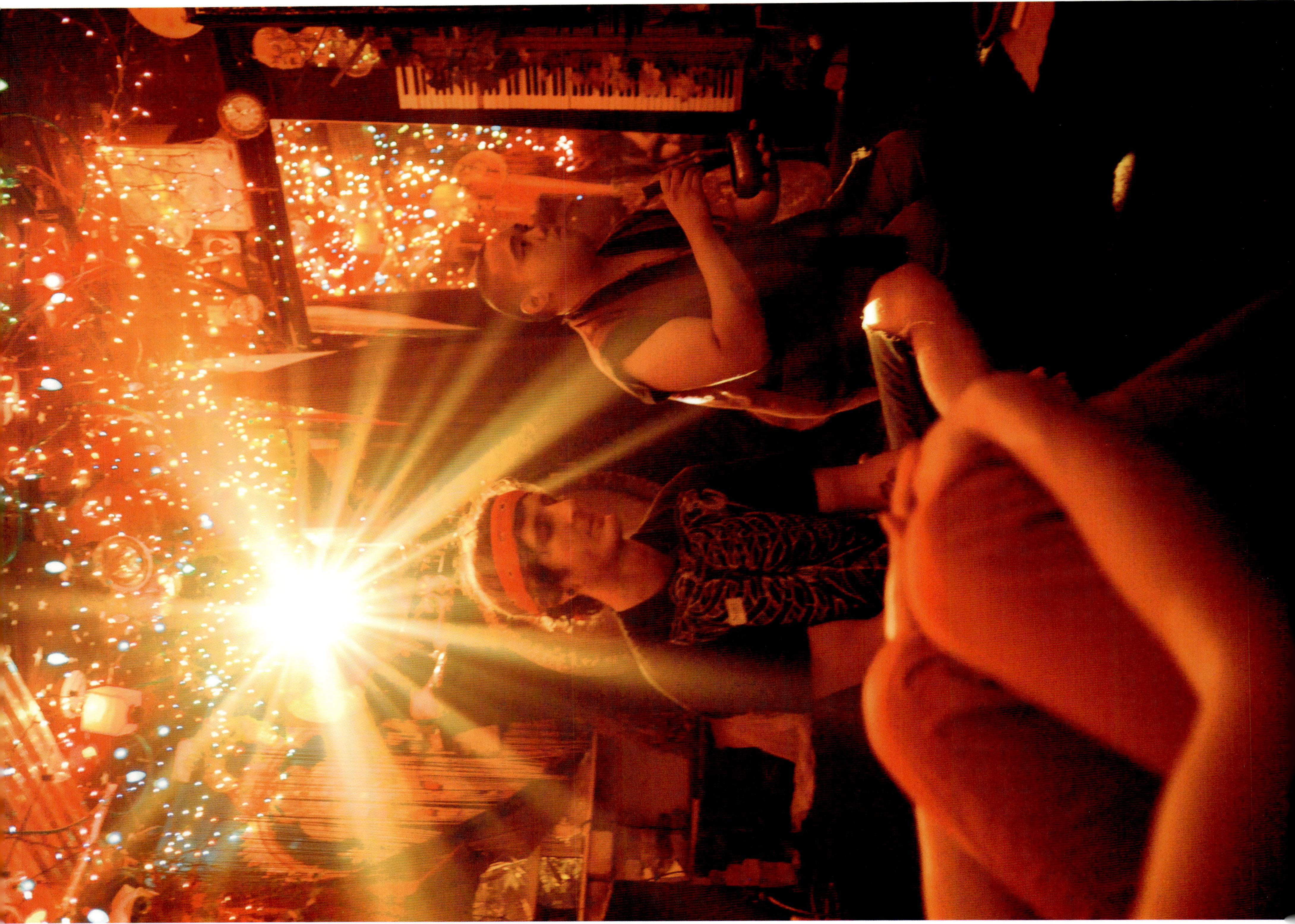

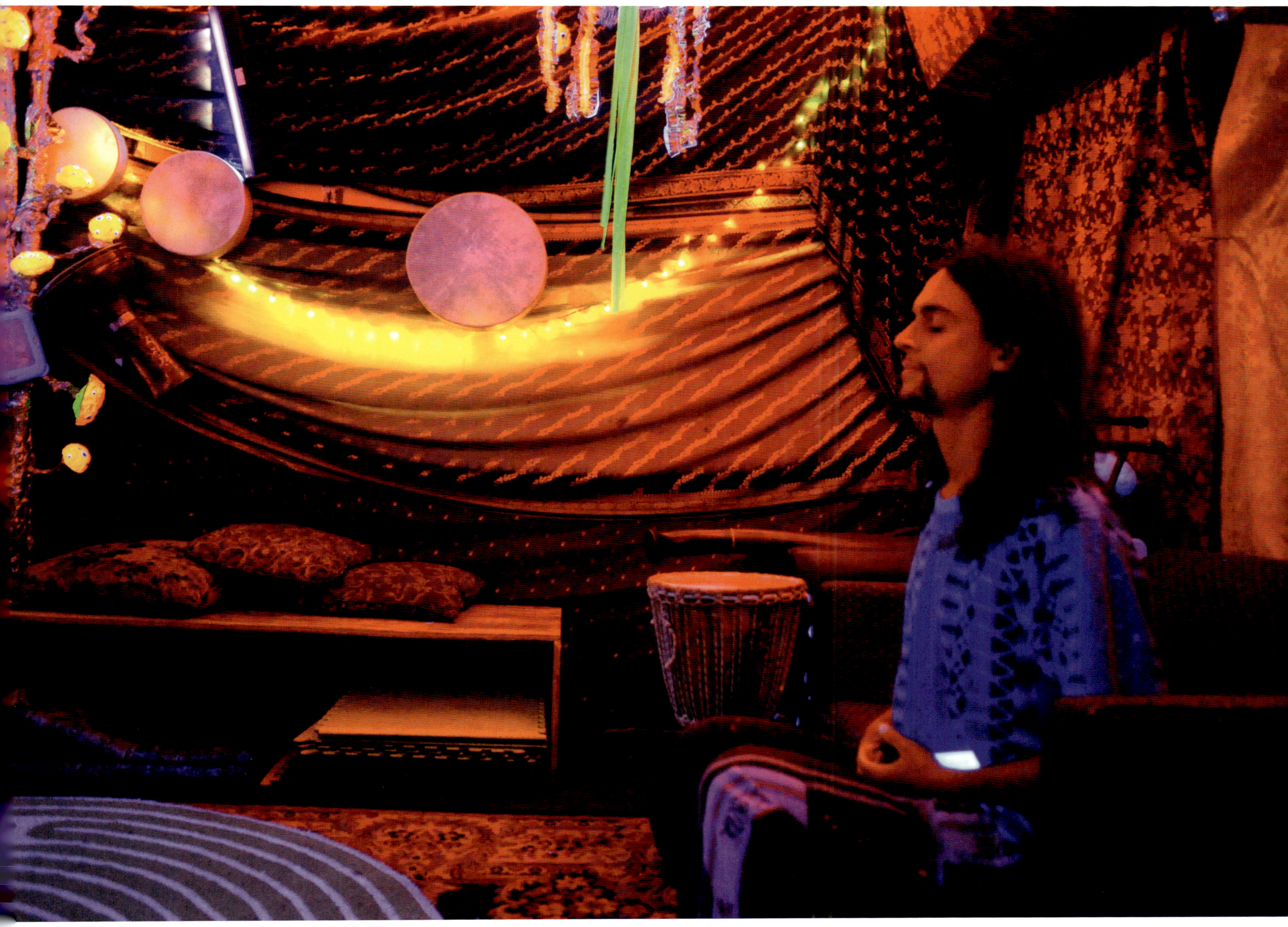

Burning Man, Nevada

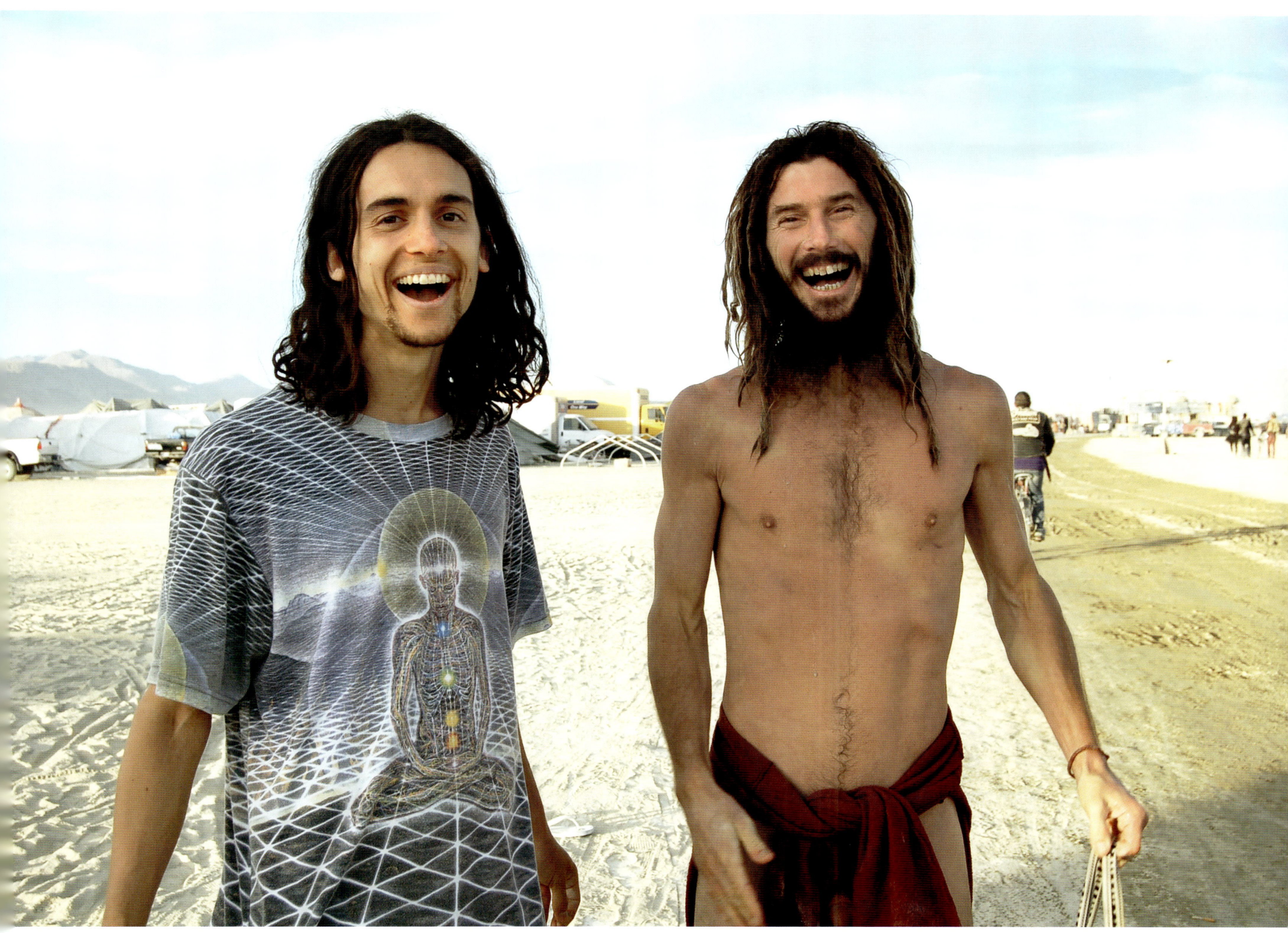

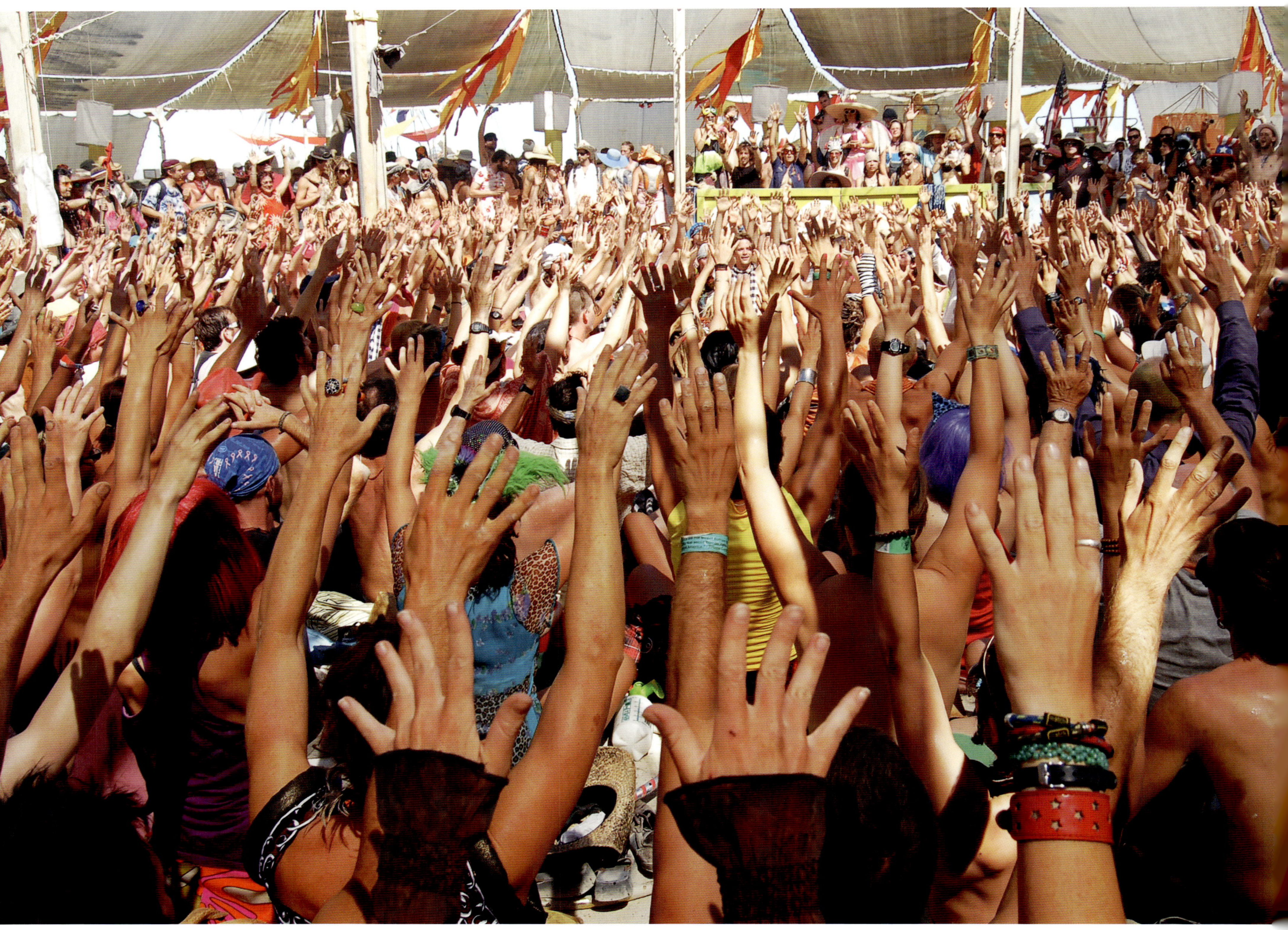

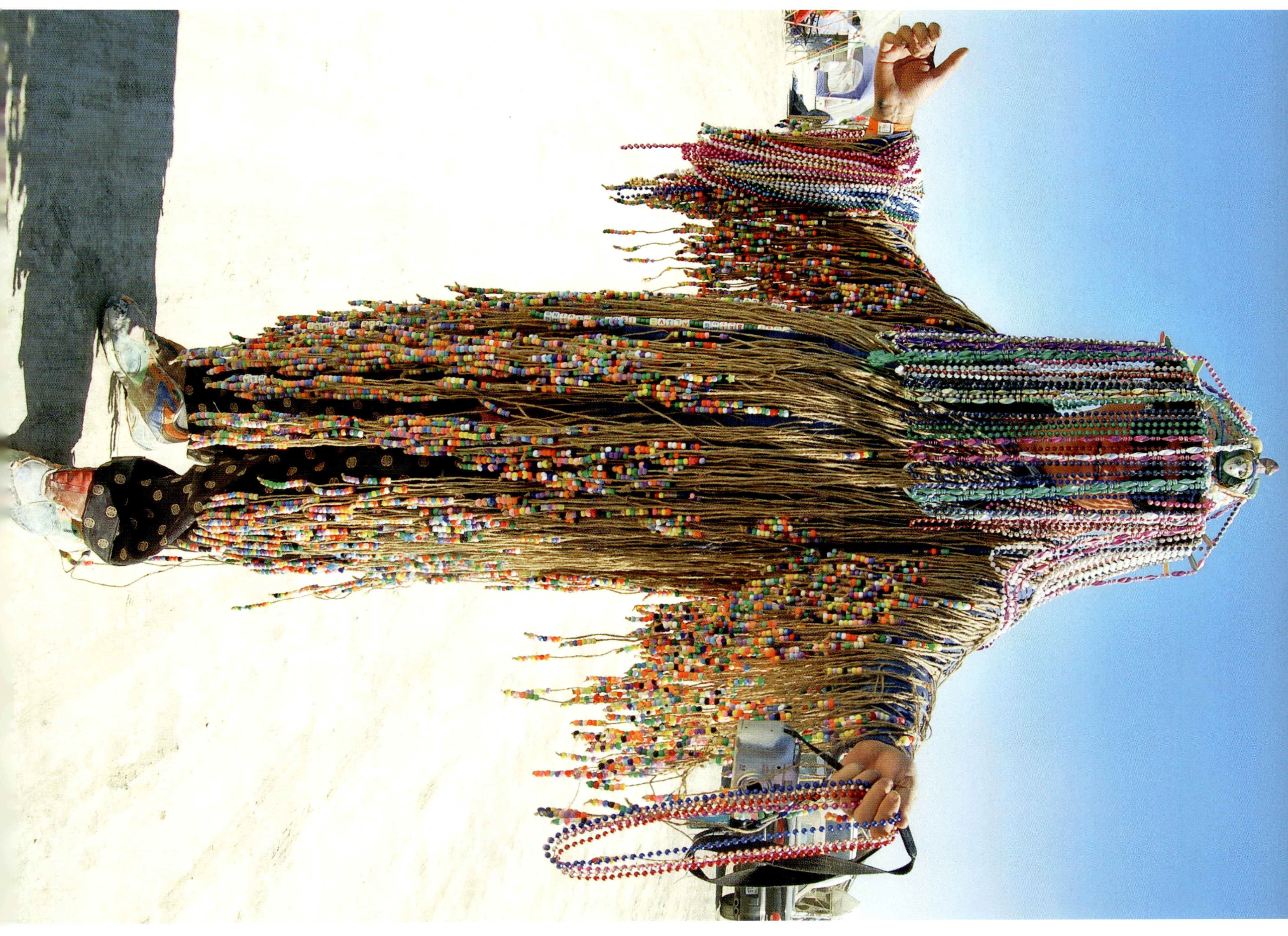

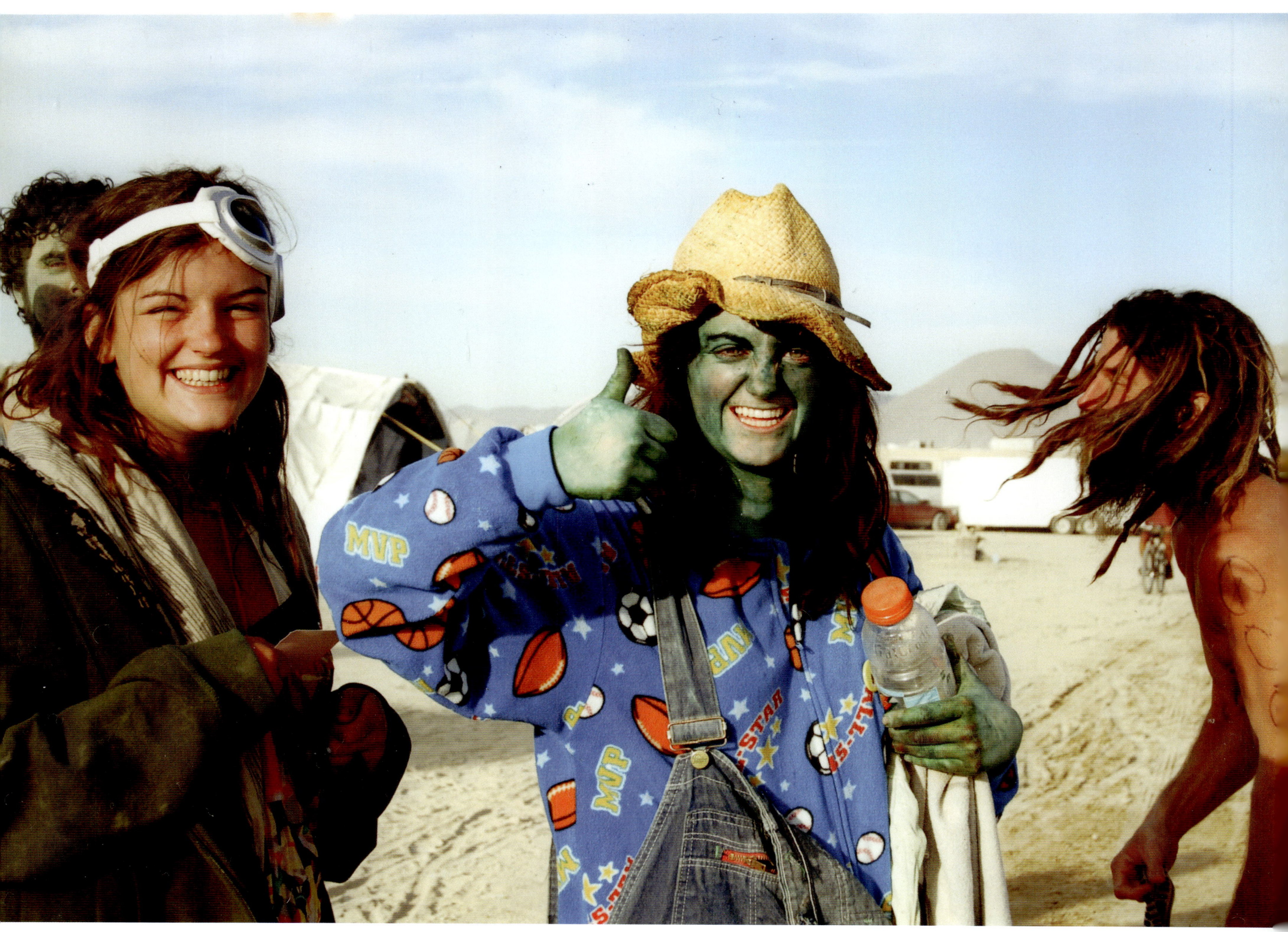

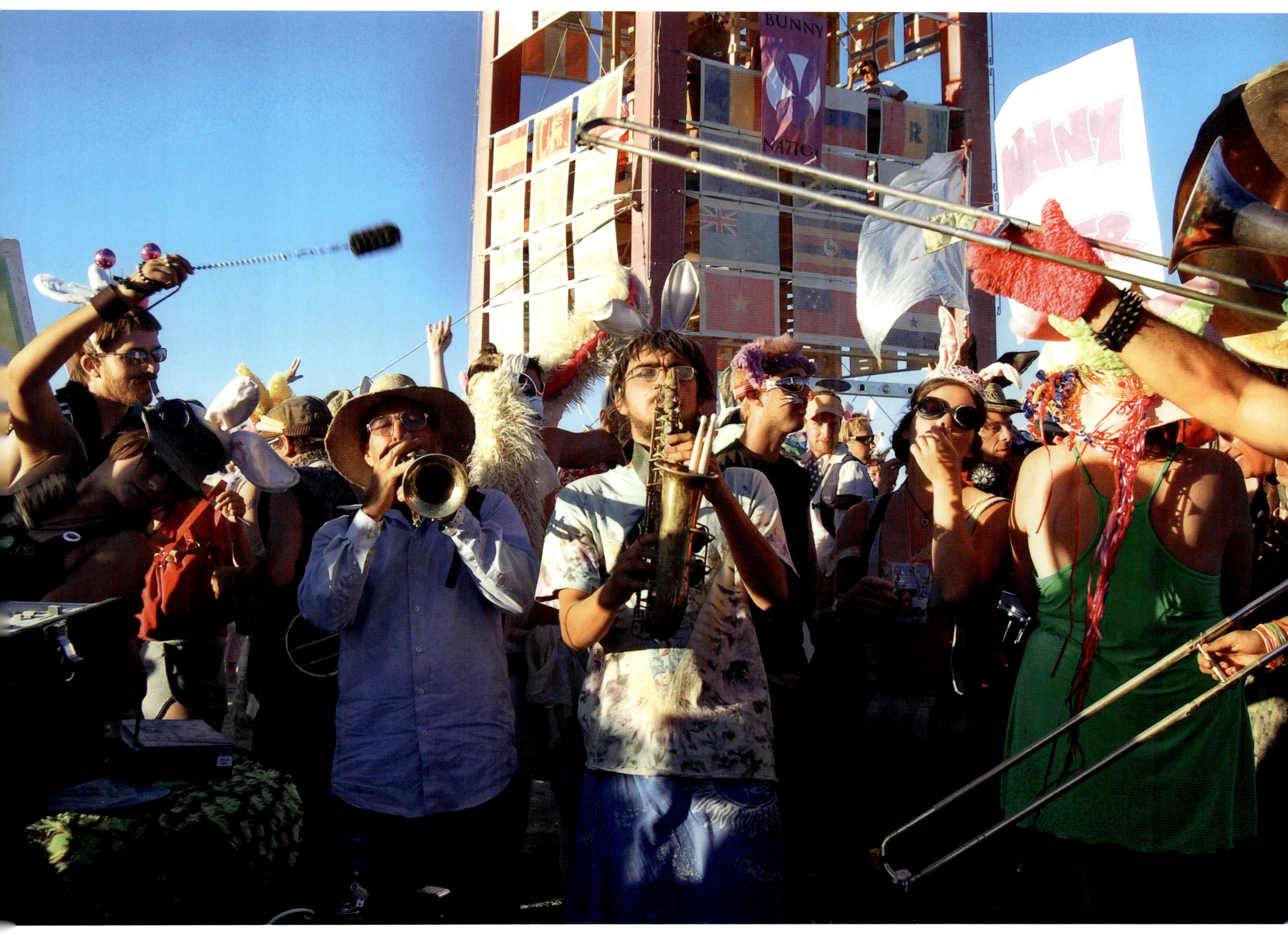

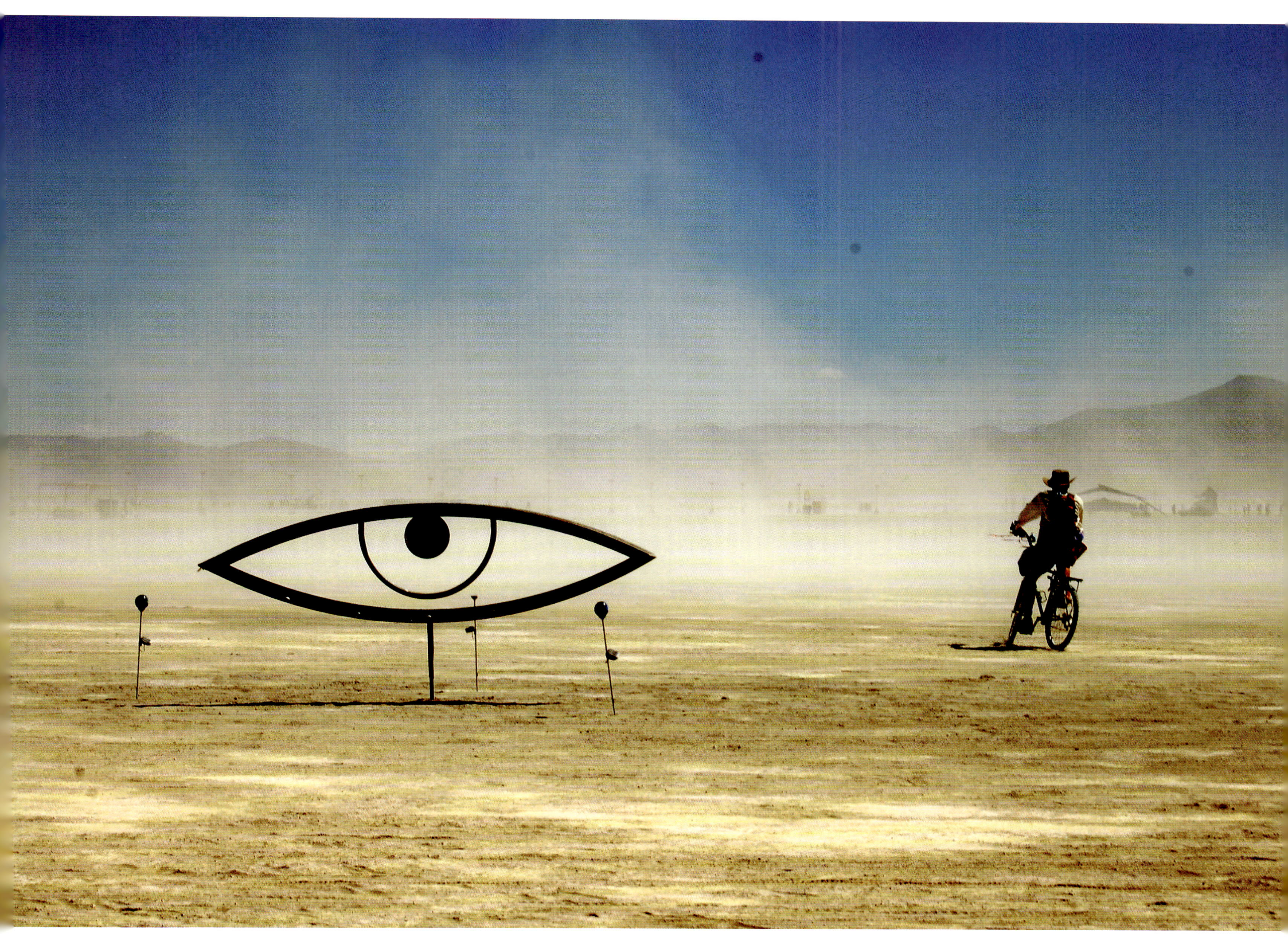

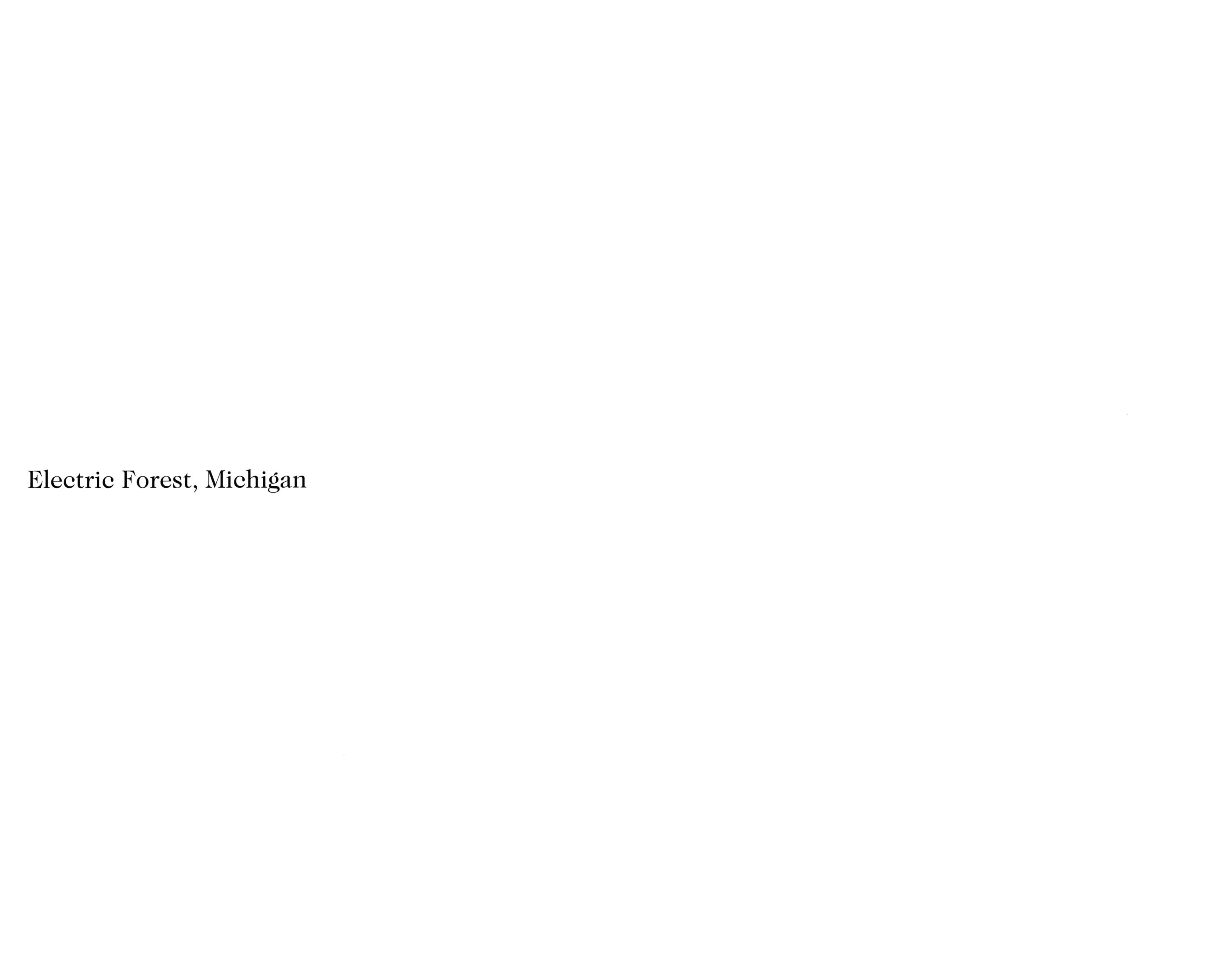

Electric Forest, Michigan

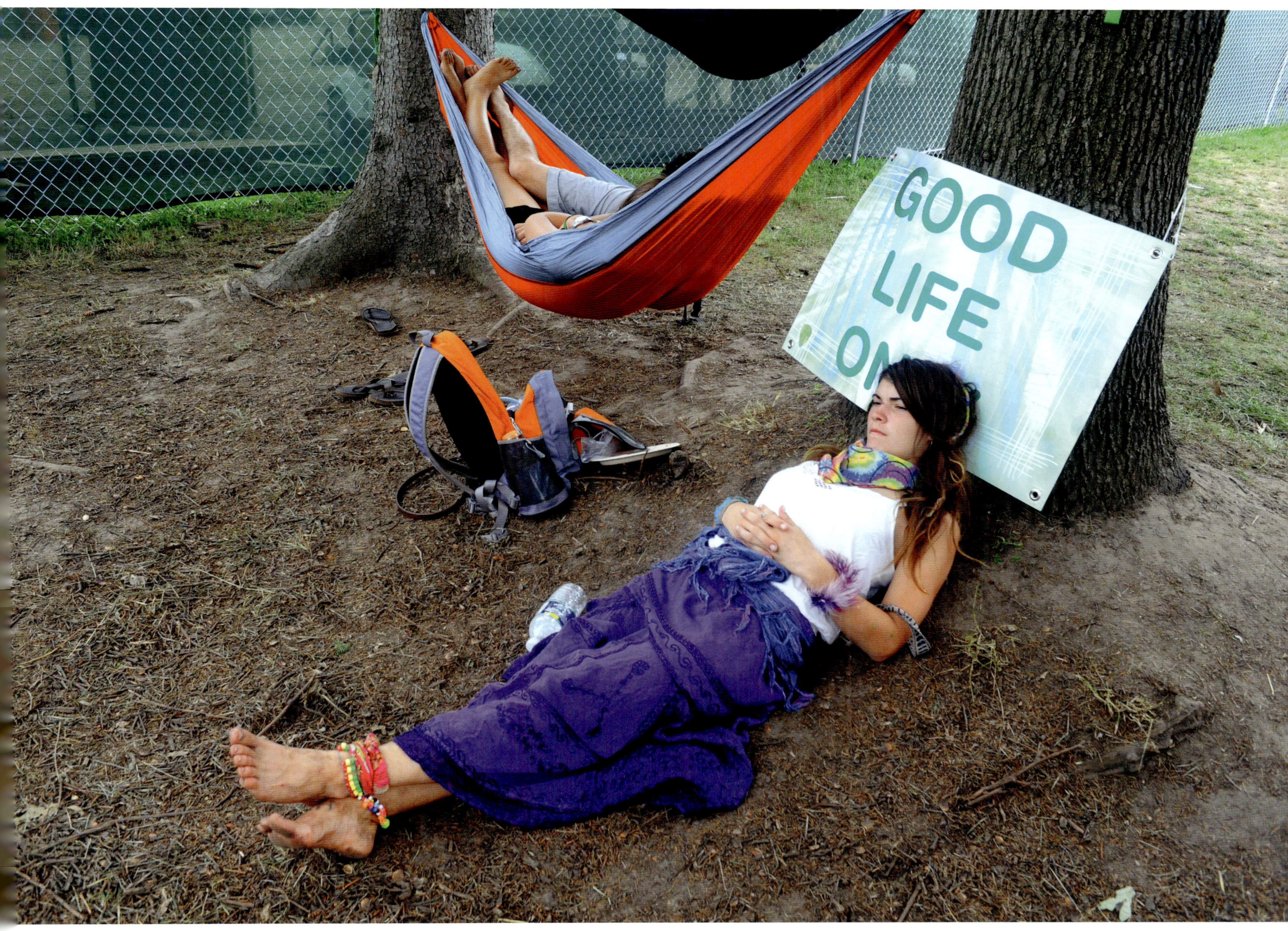
GOOD
LIFE
ON

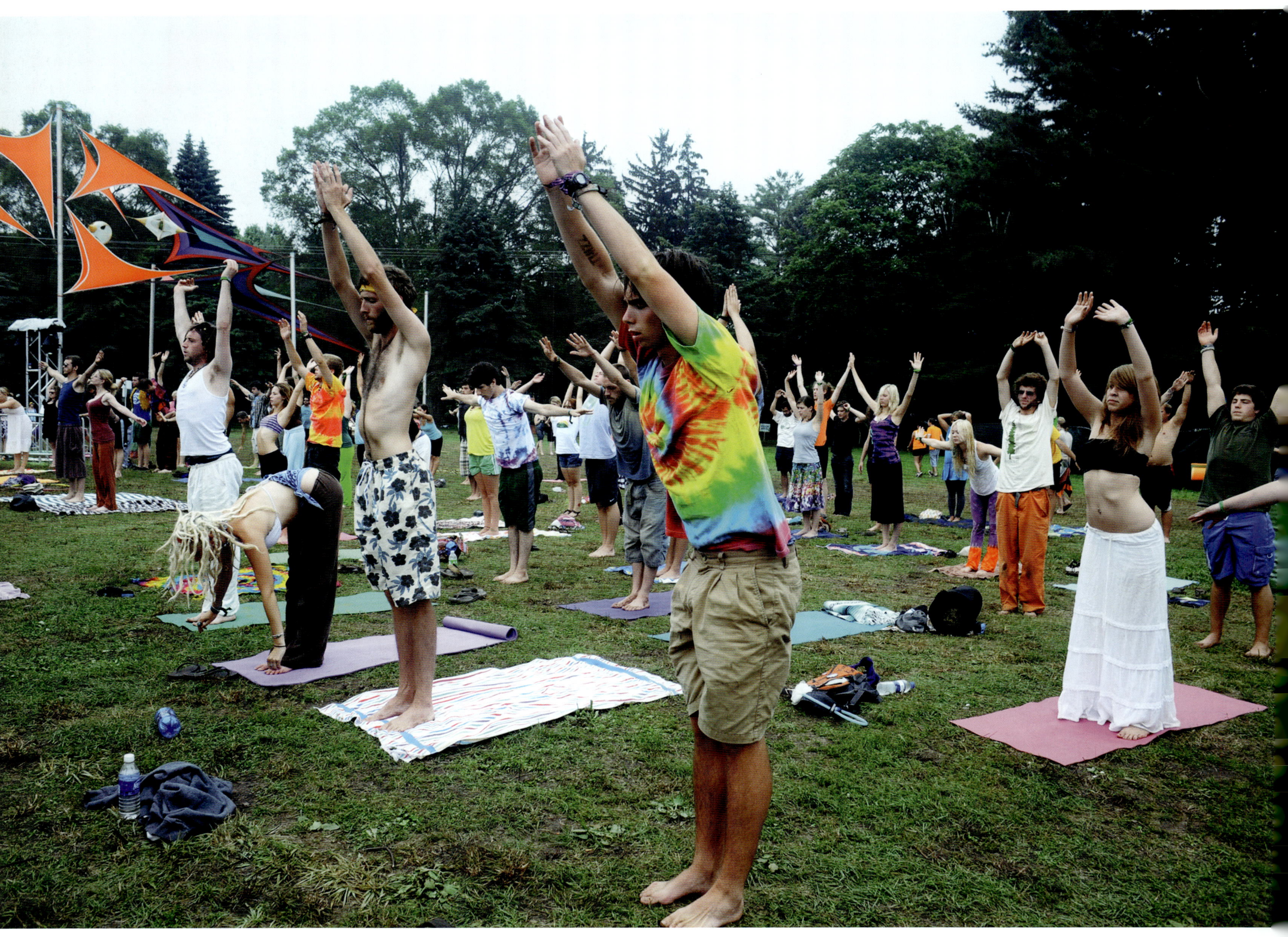

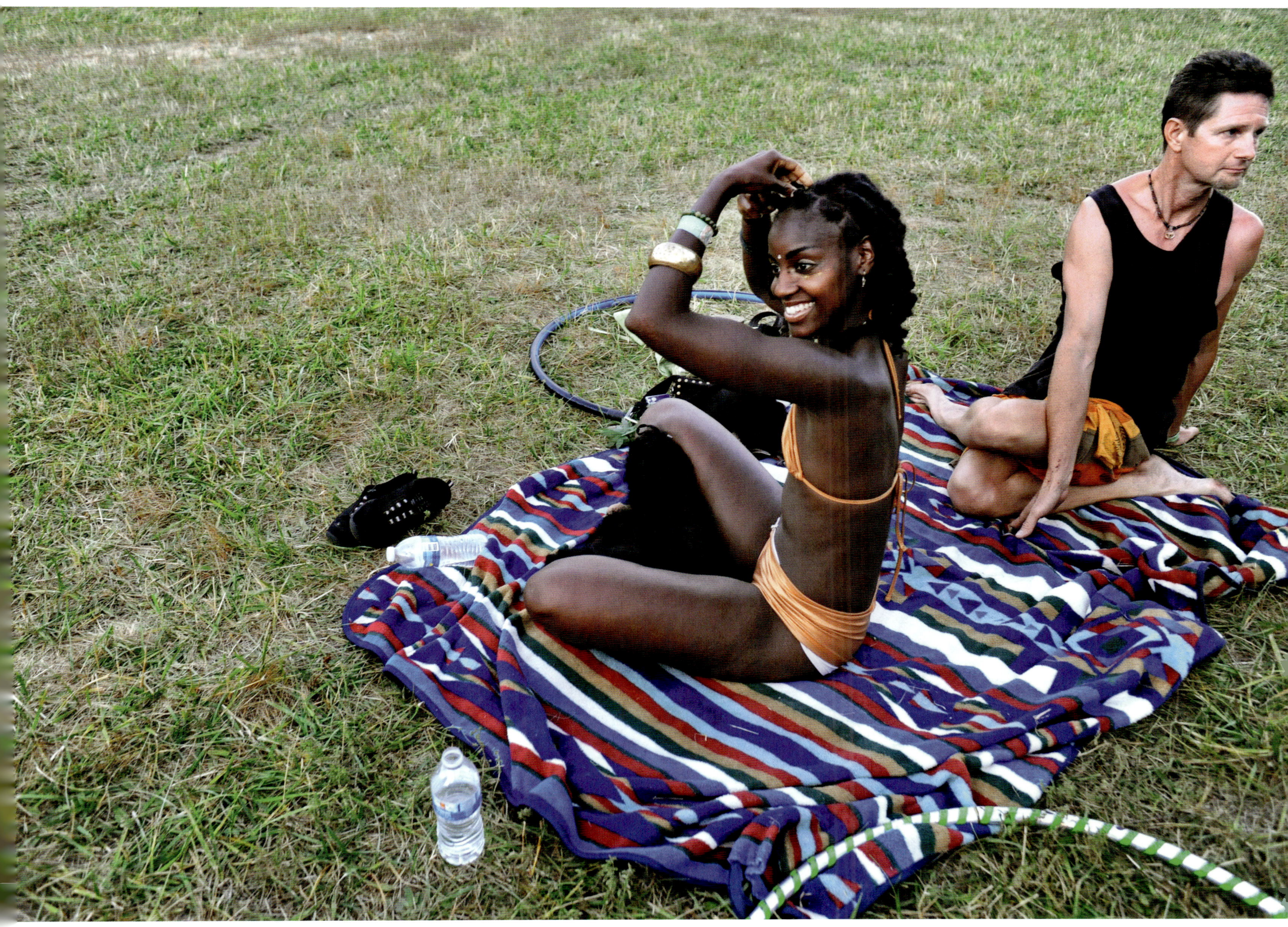

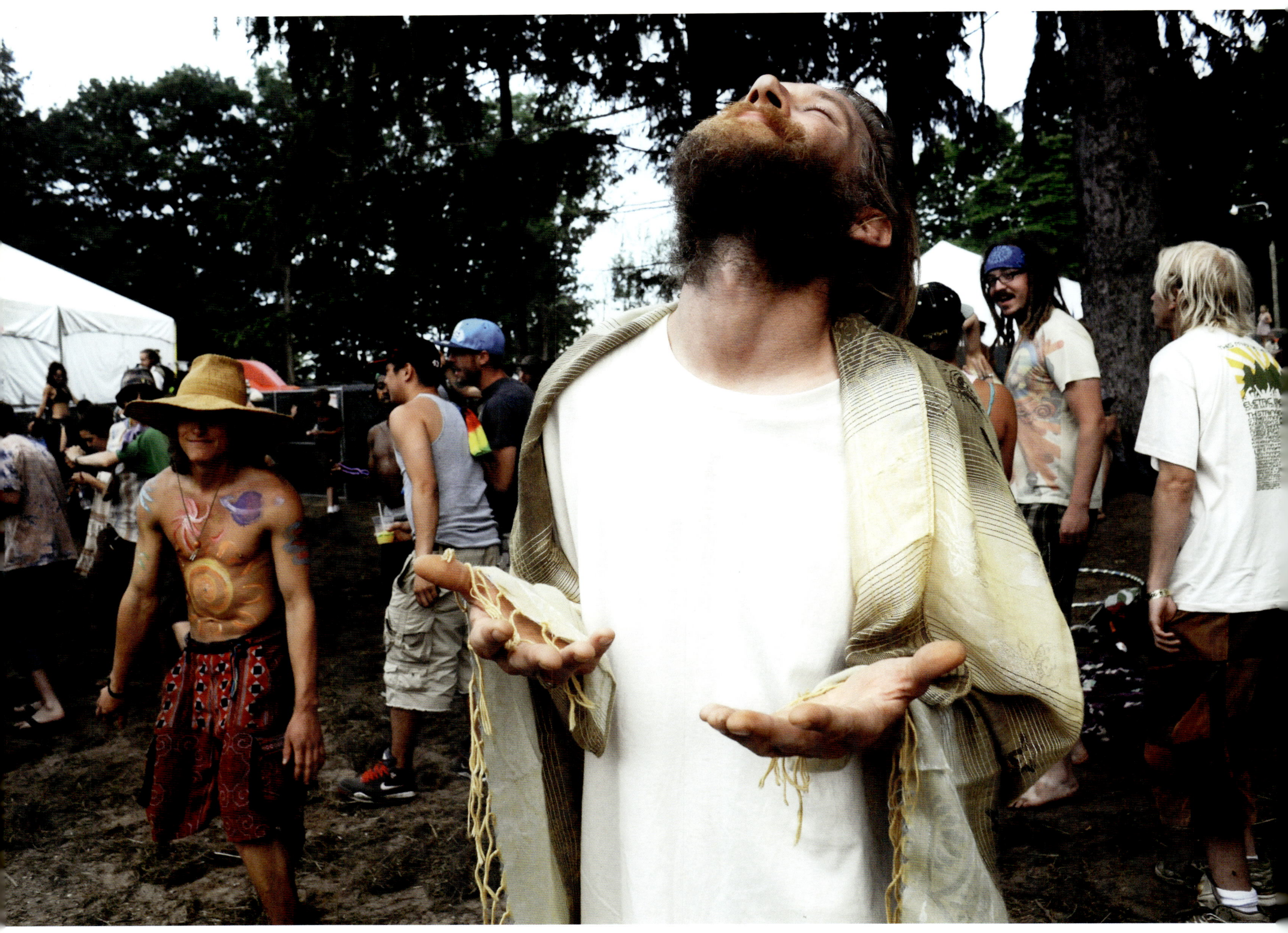

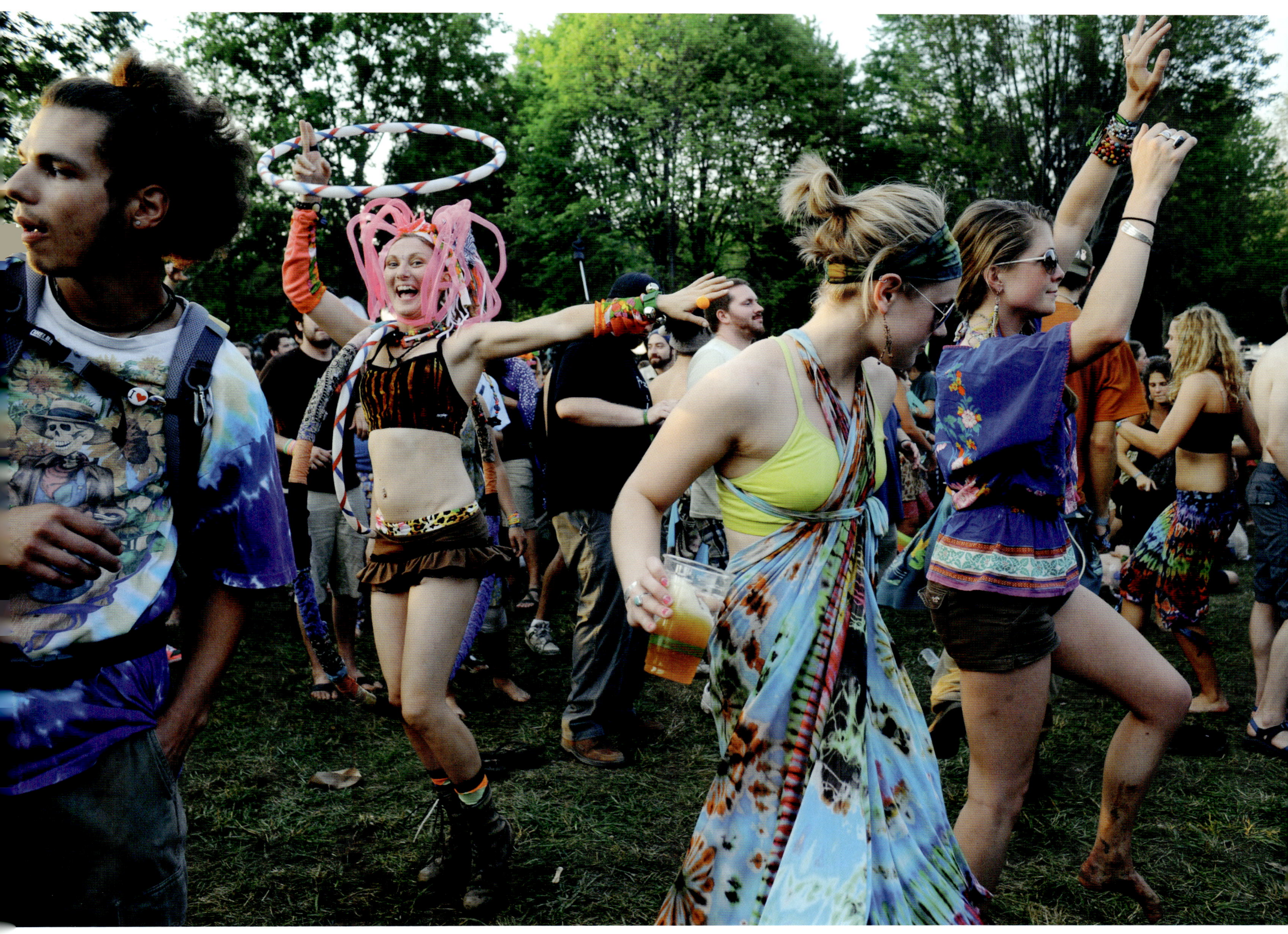

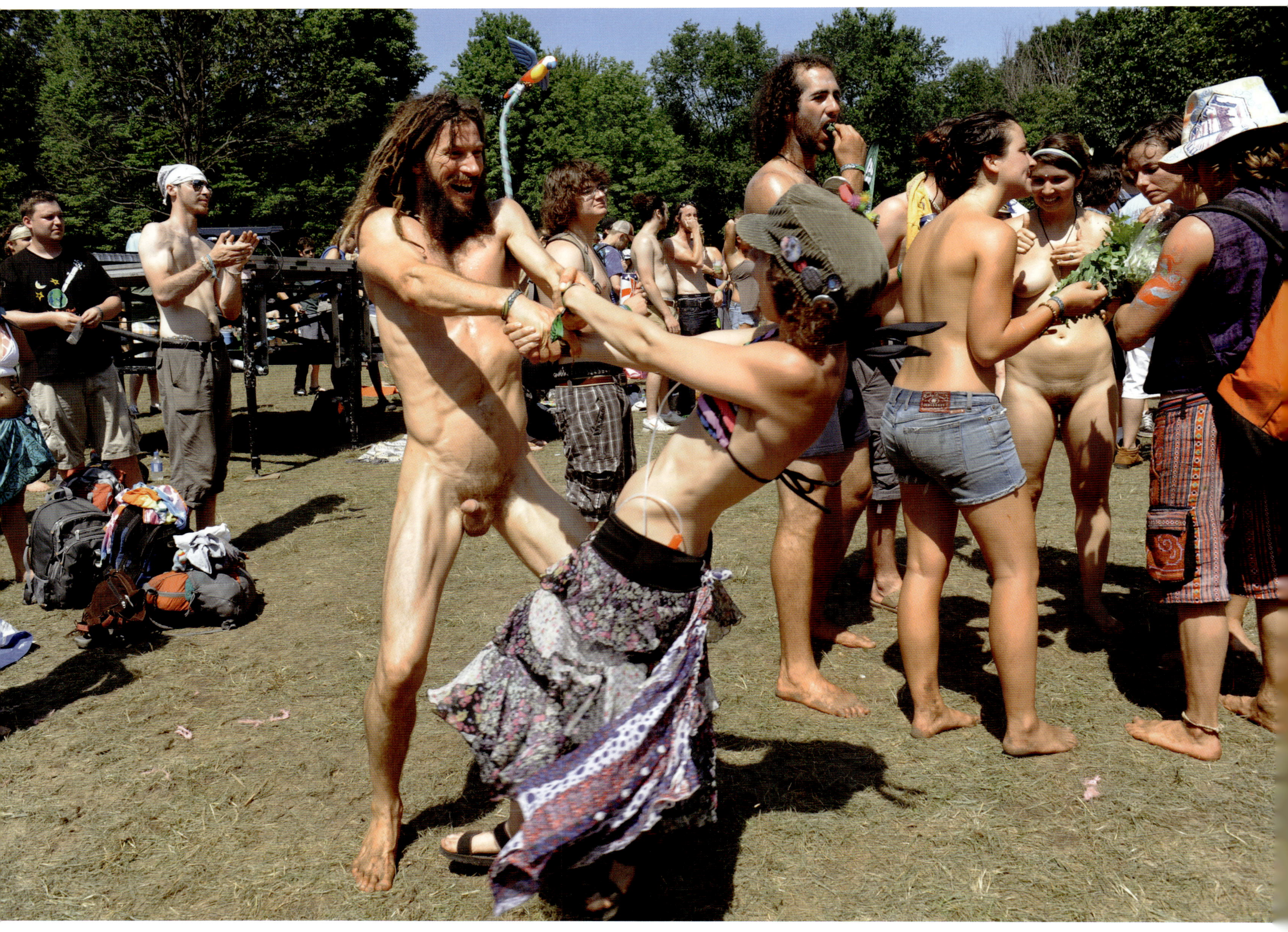

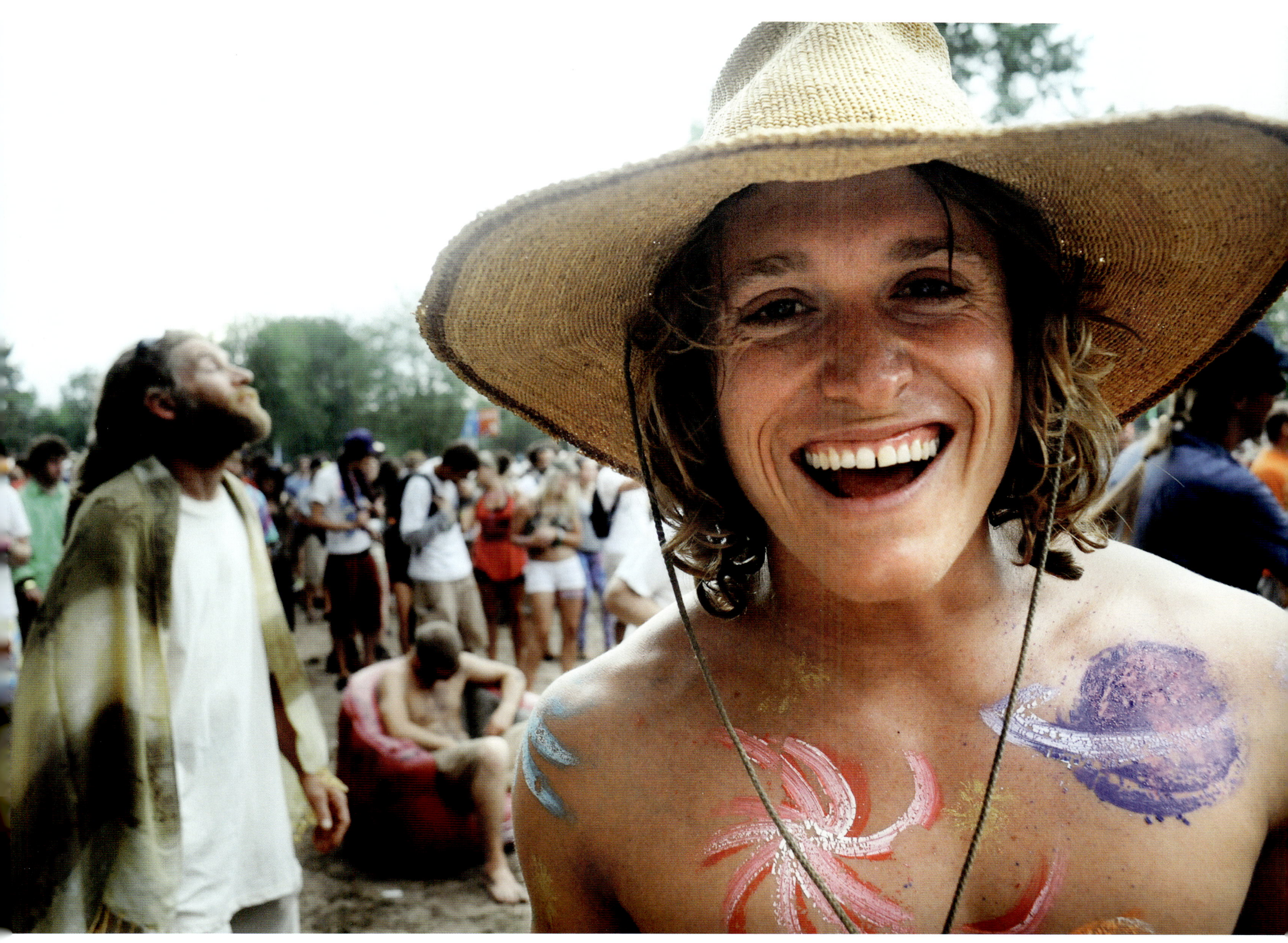

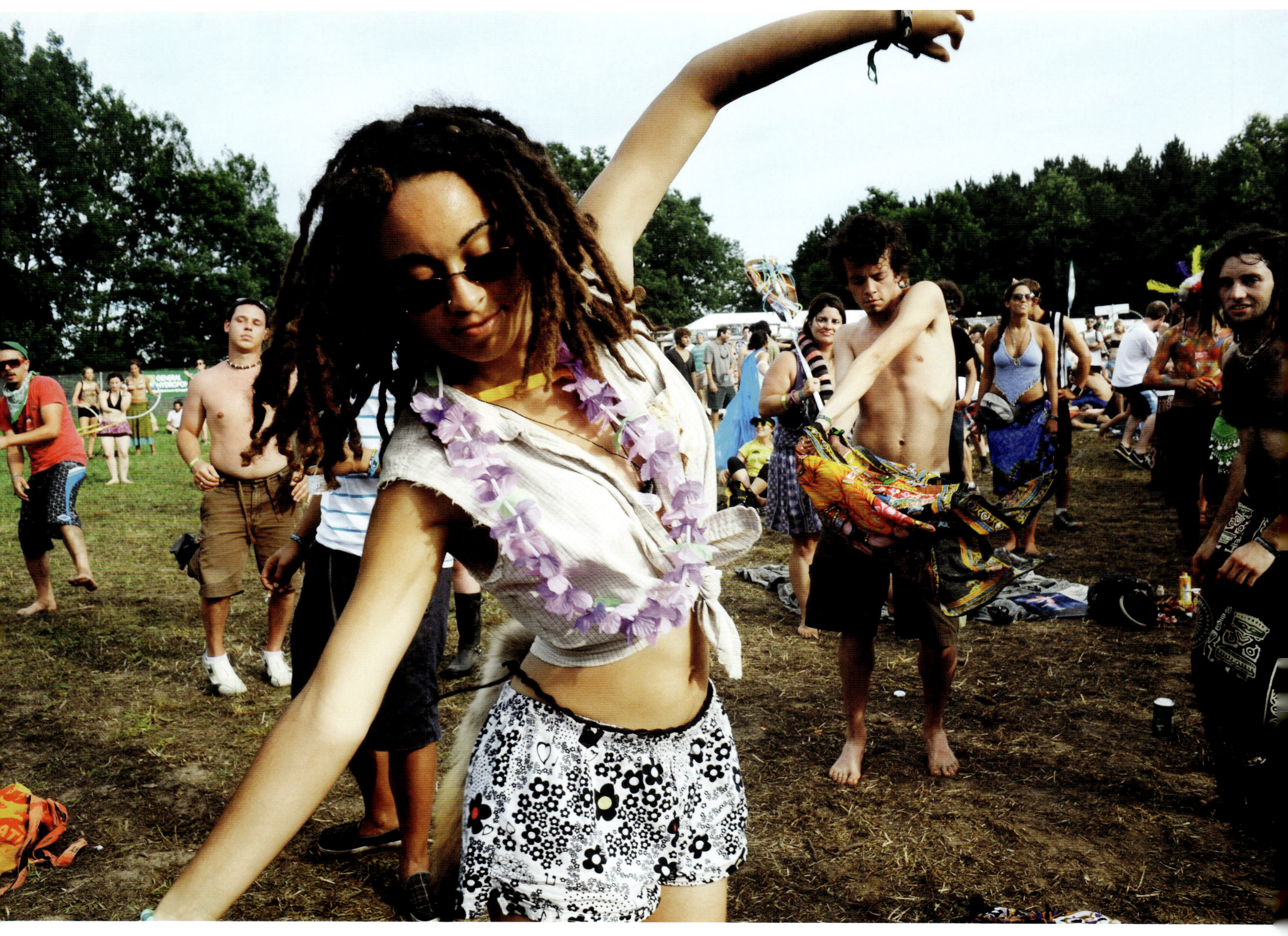

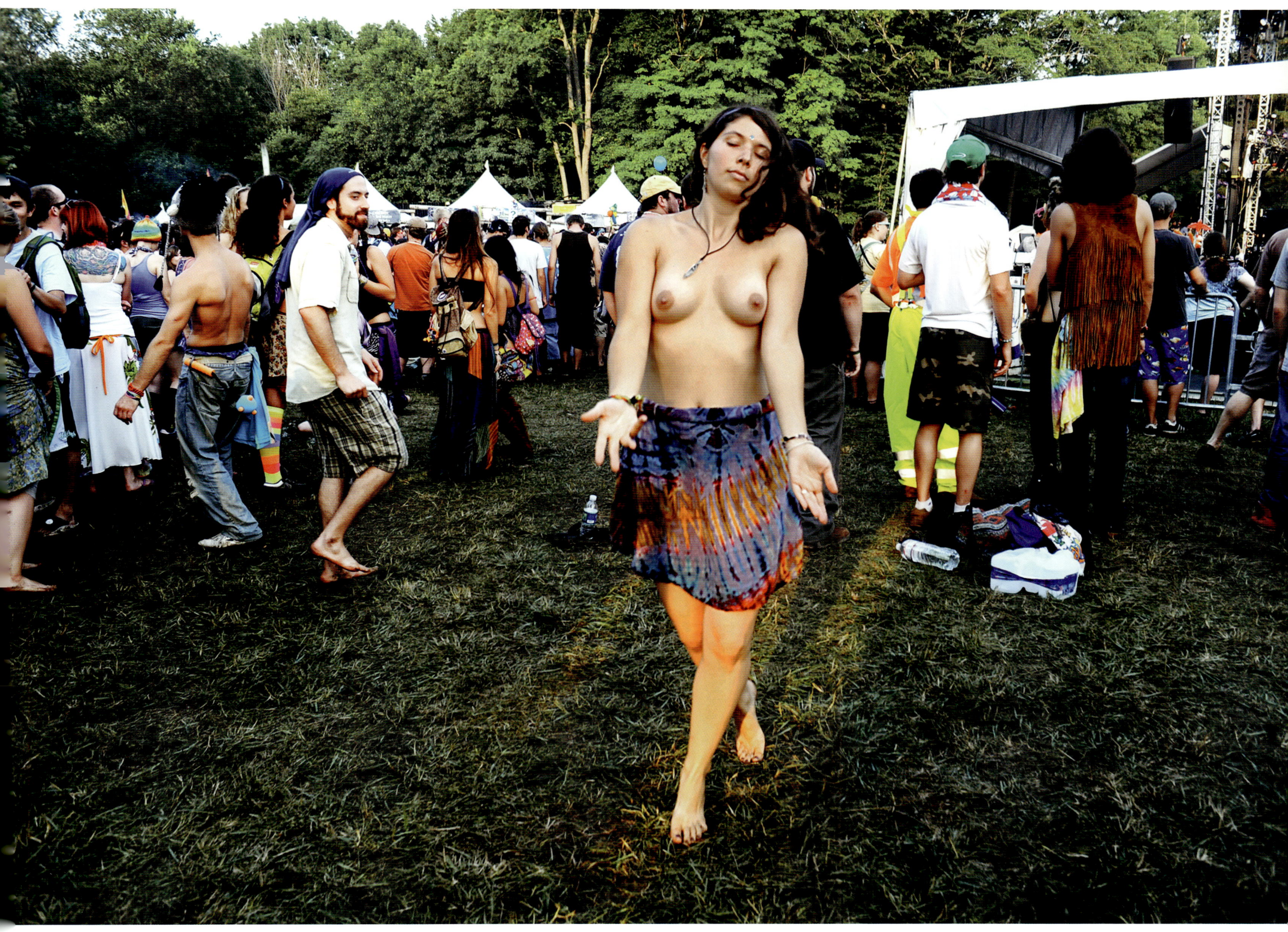

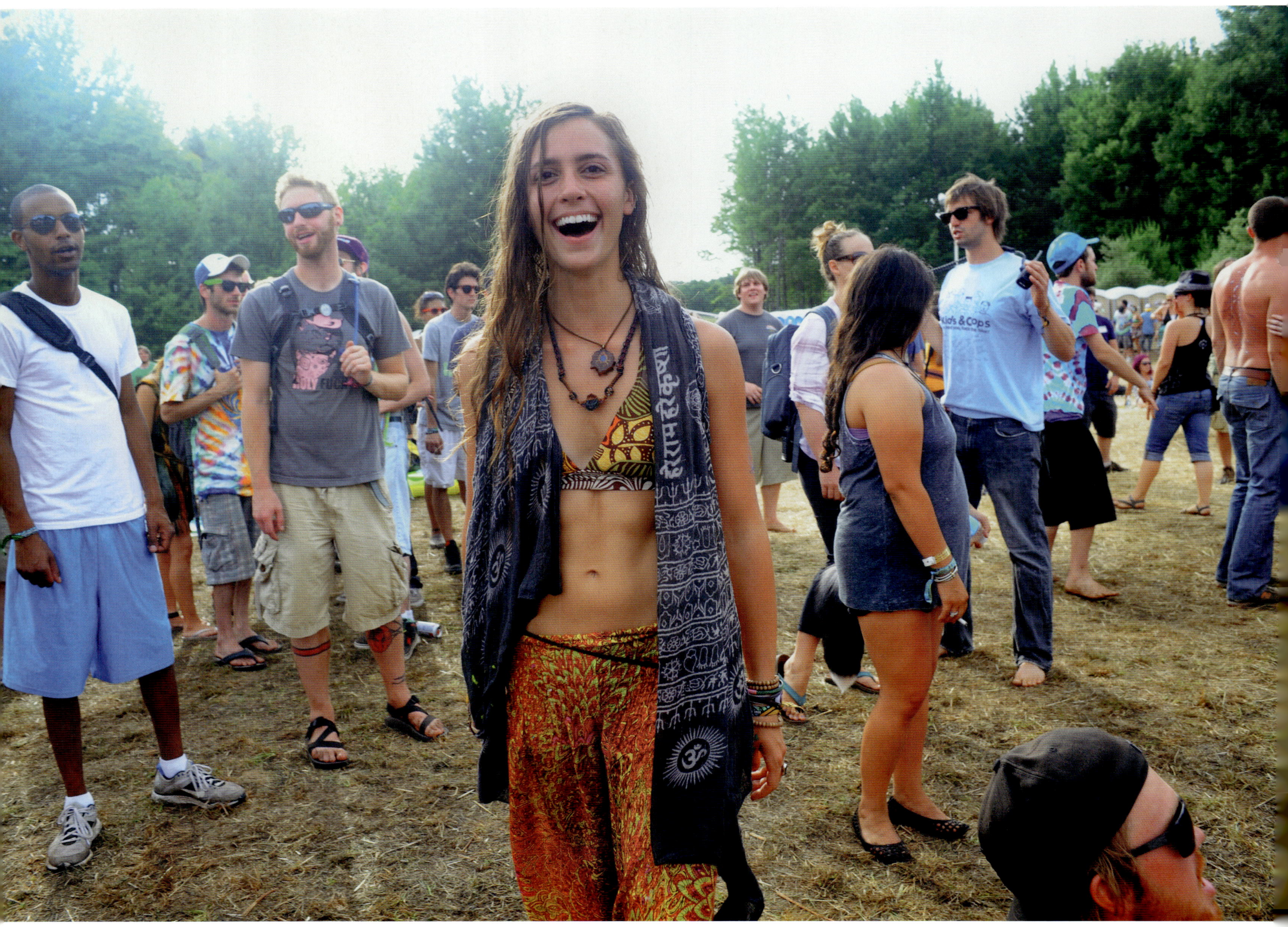

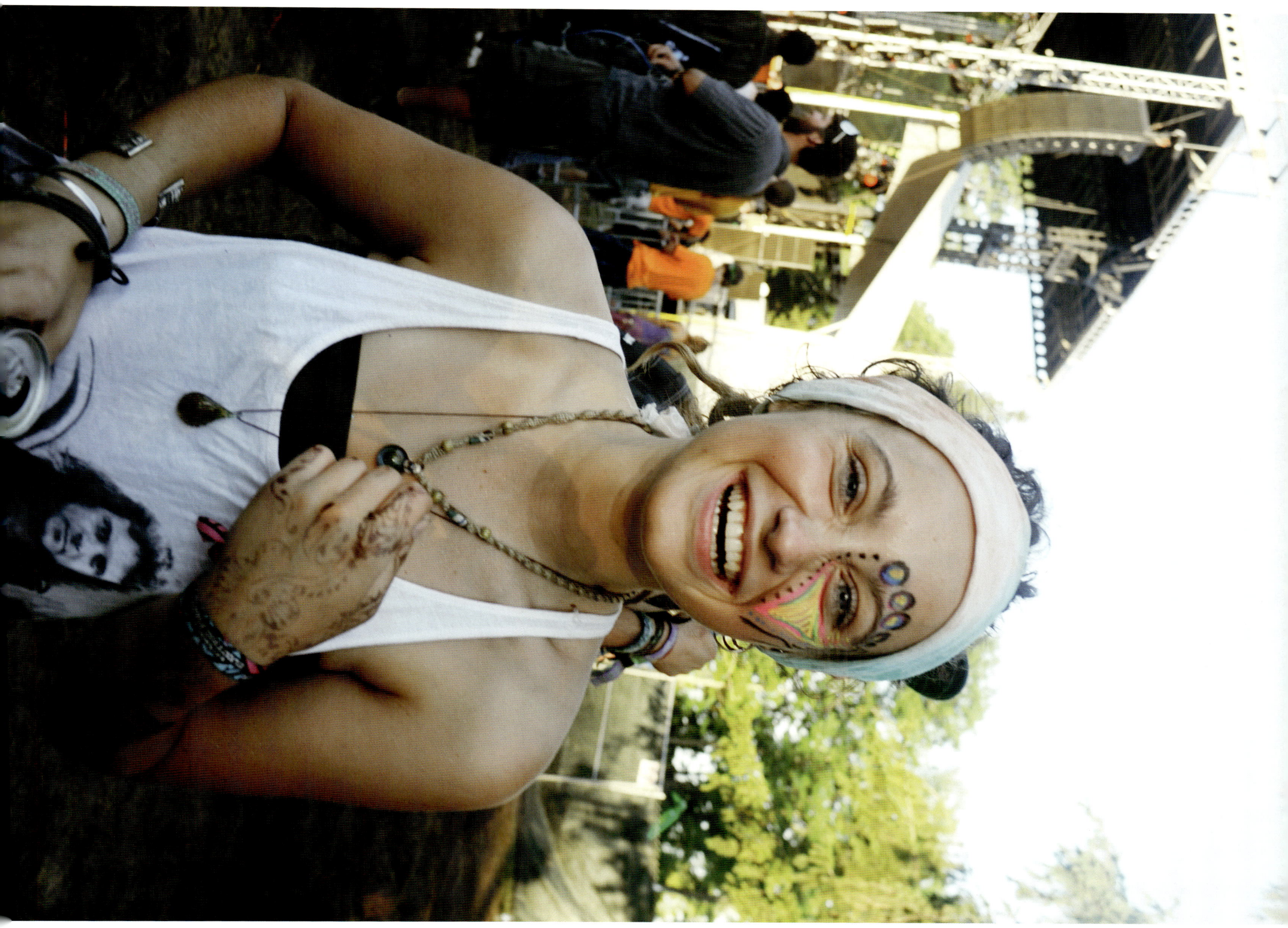

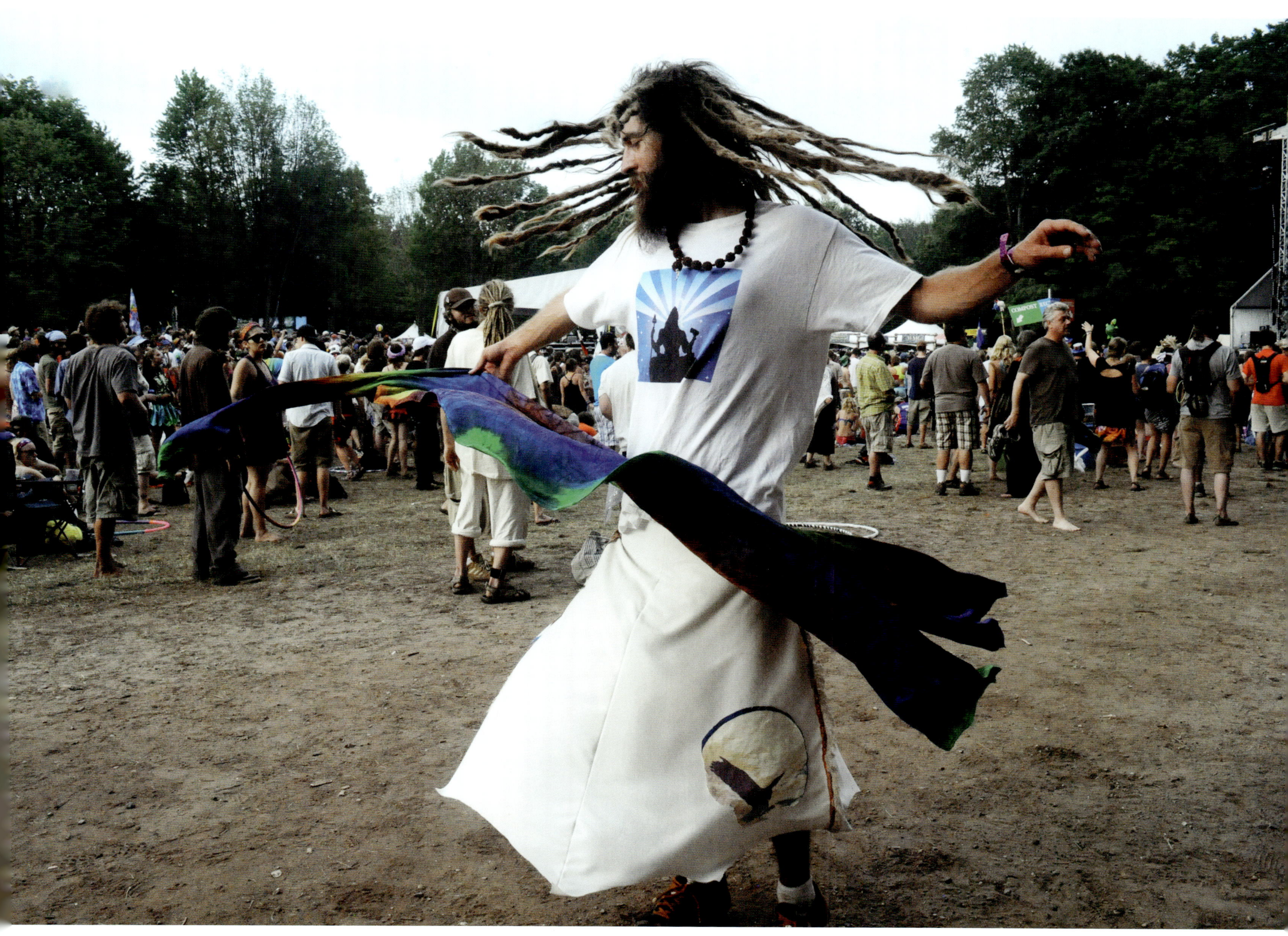

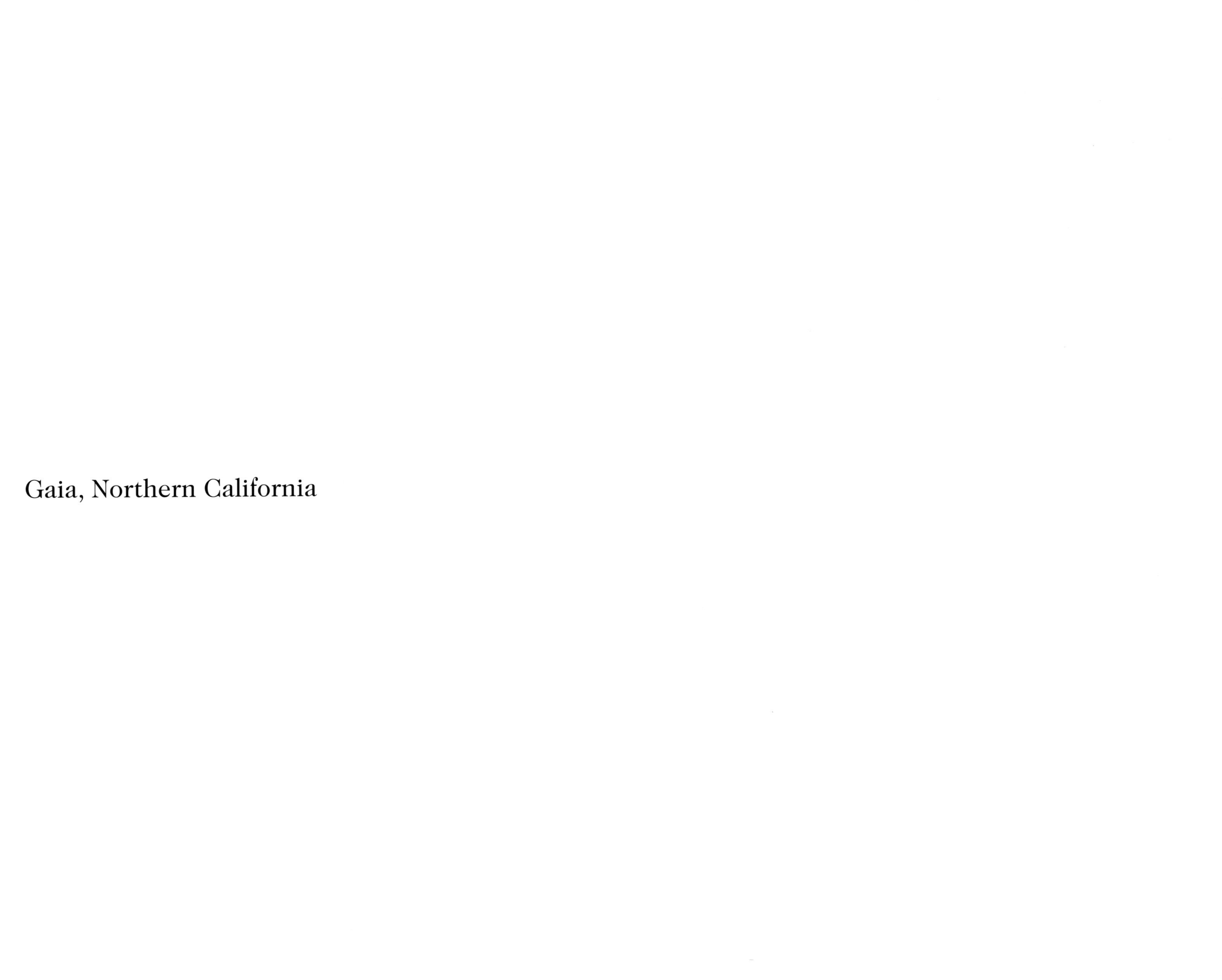

Gaia, Northern California

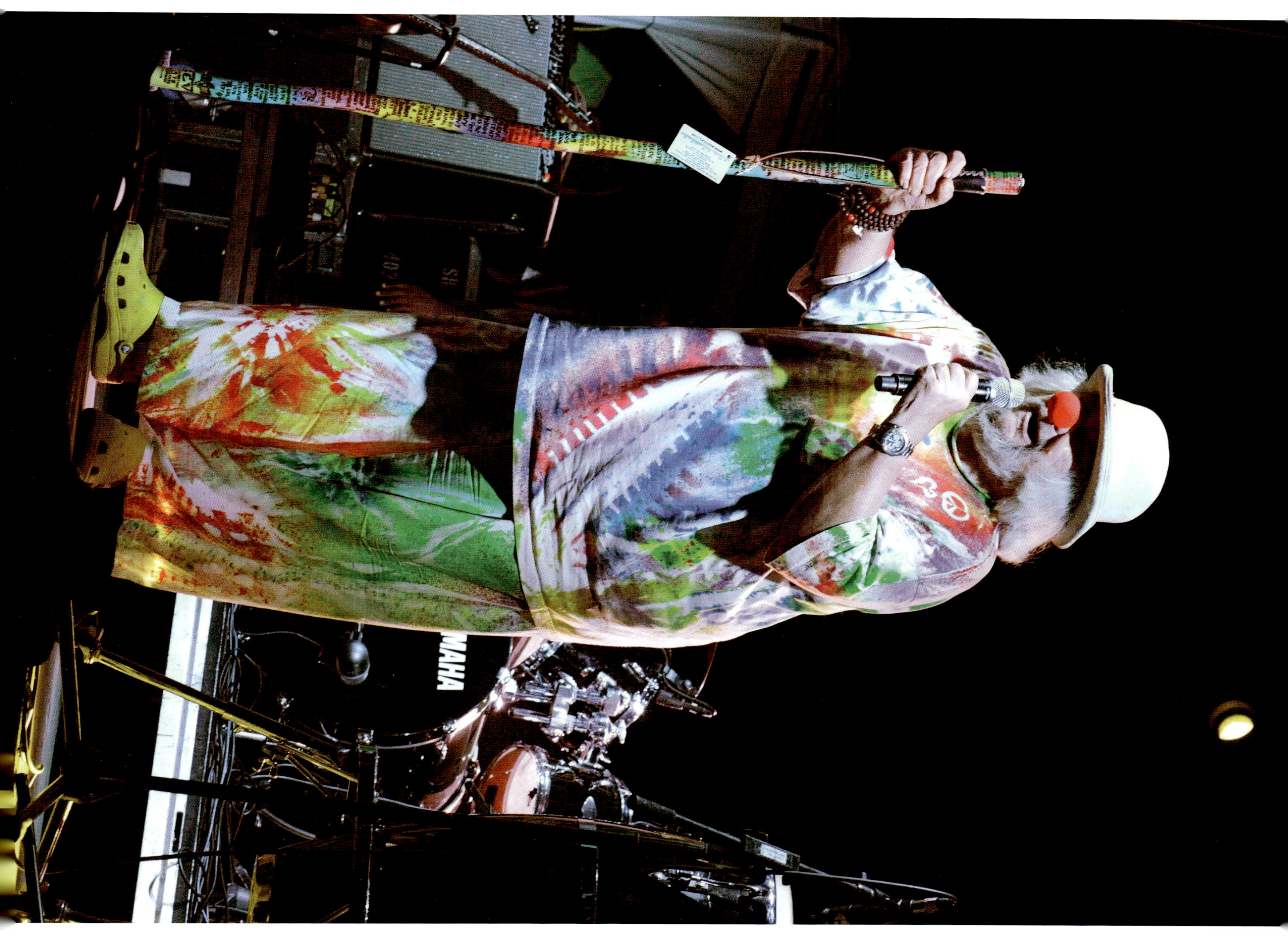

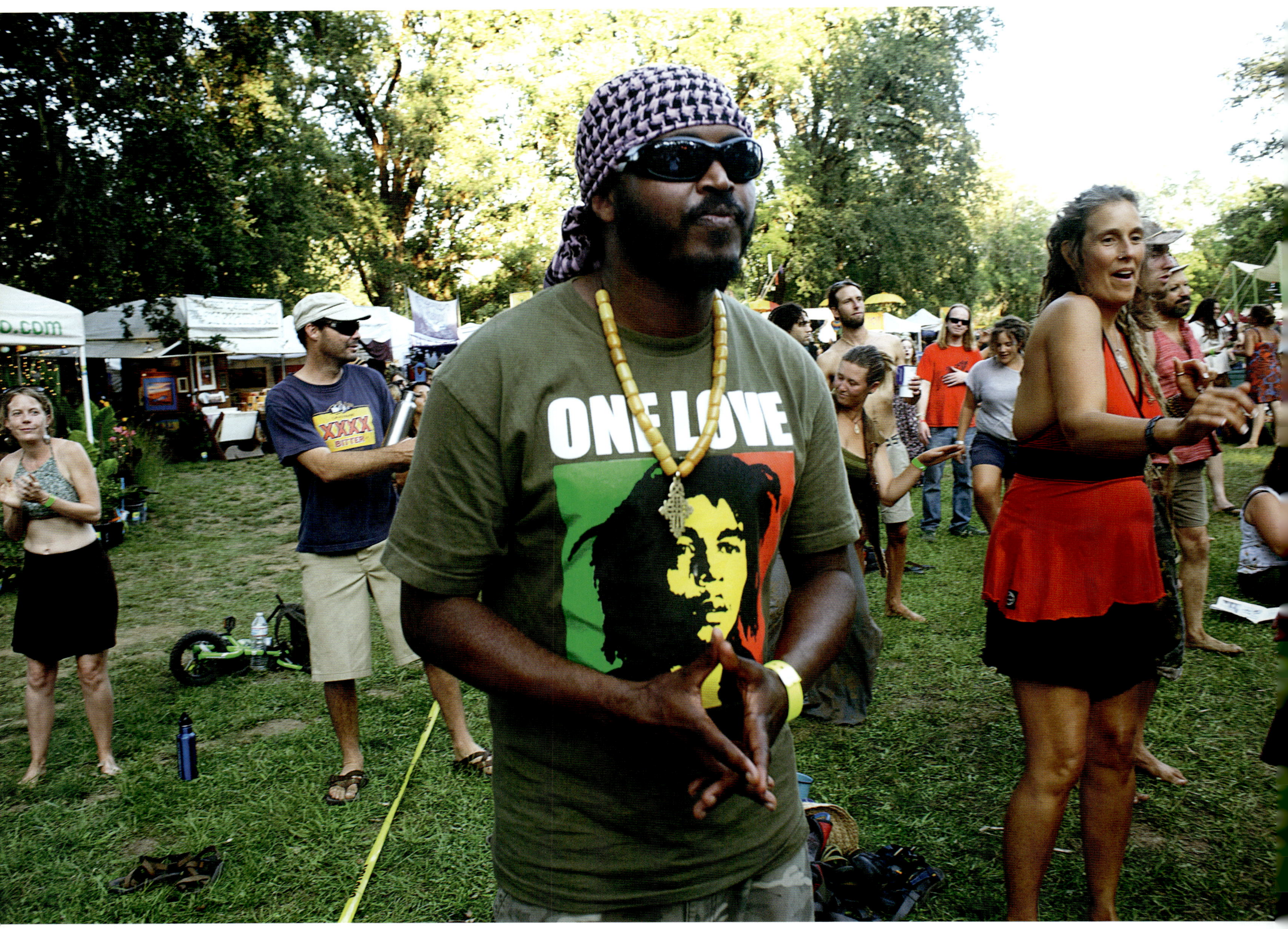

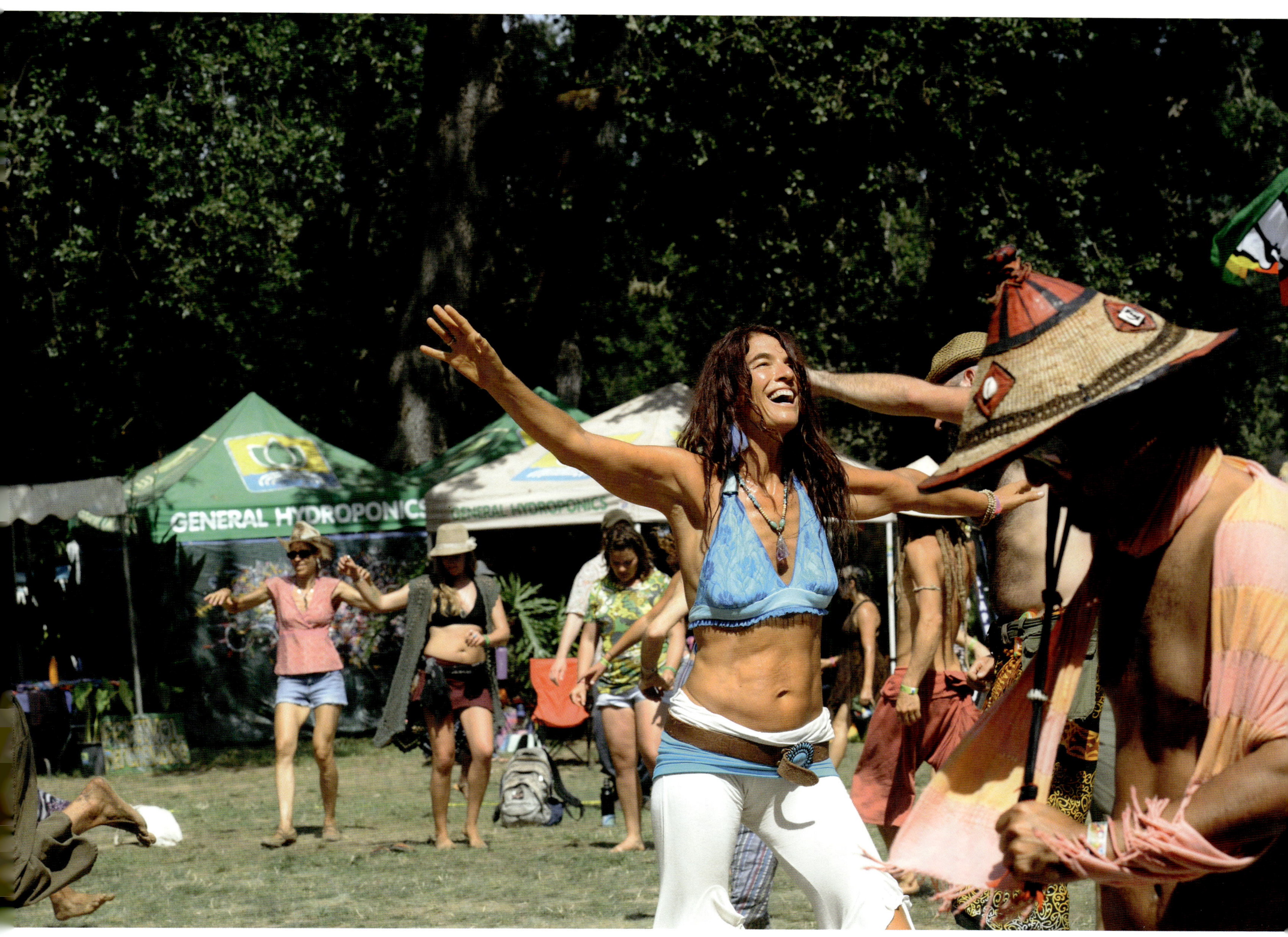

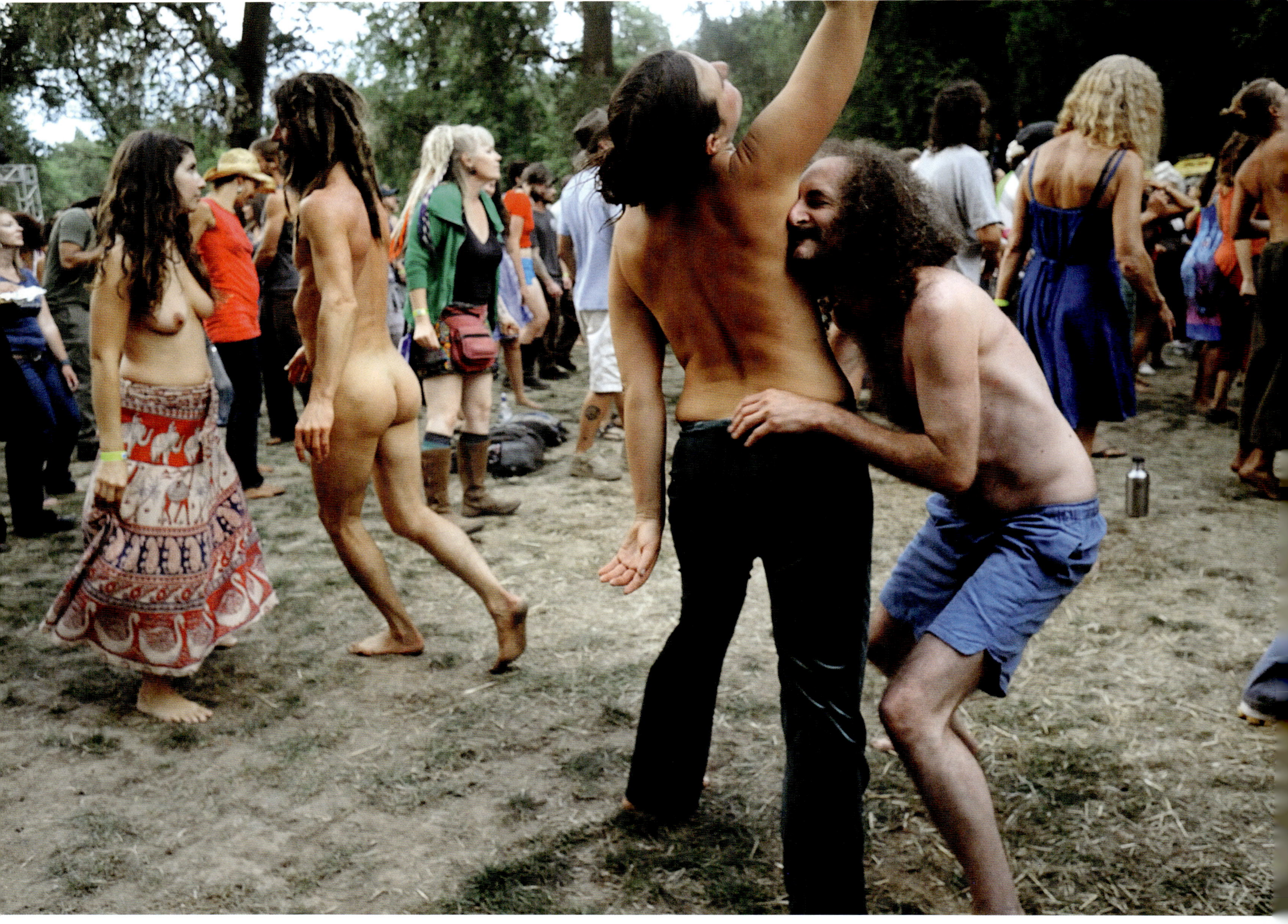

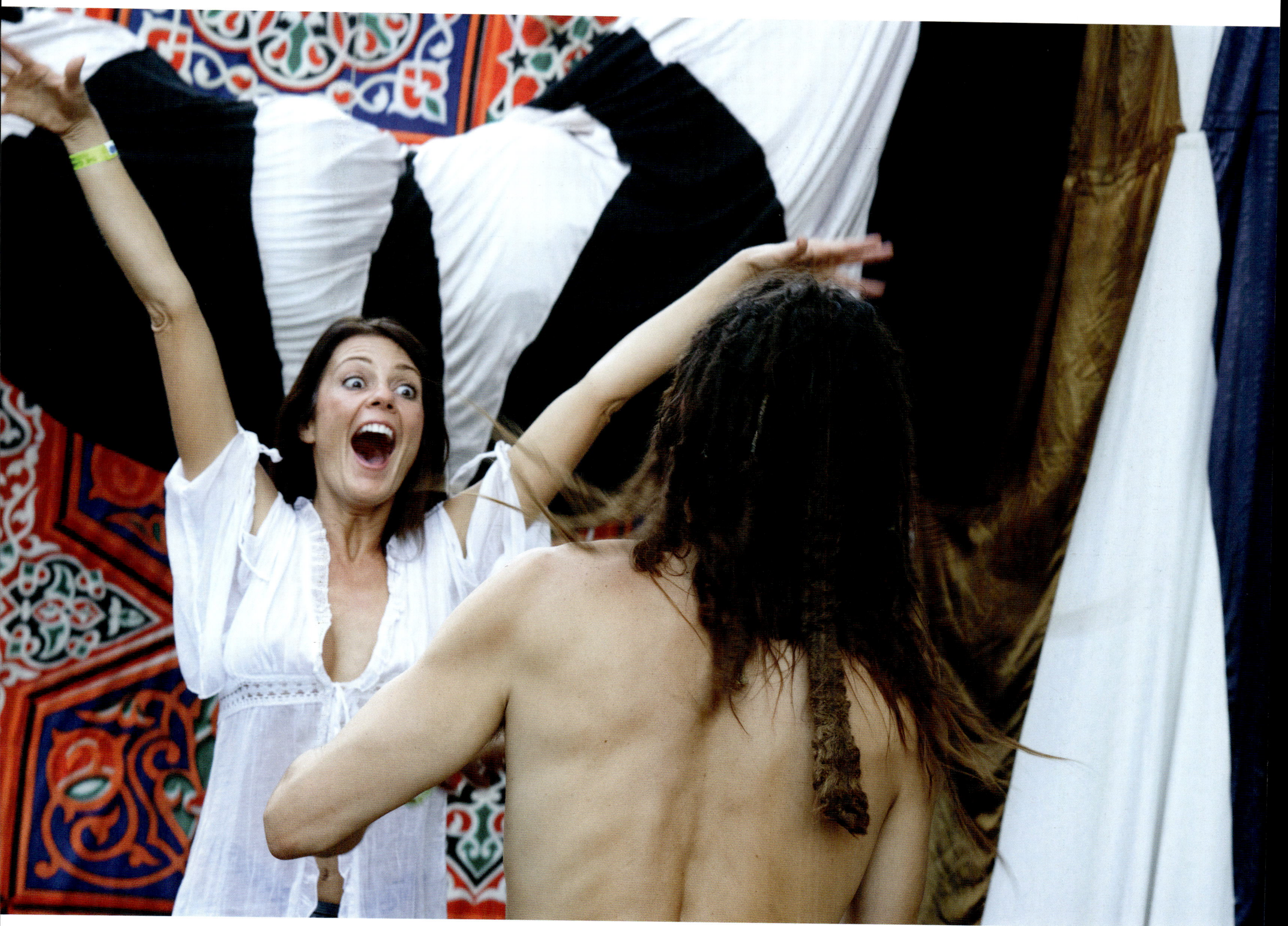

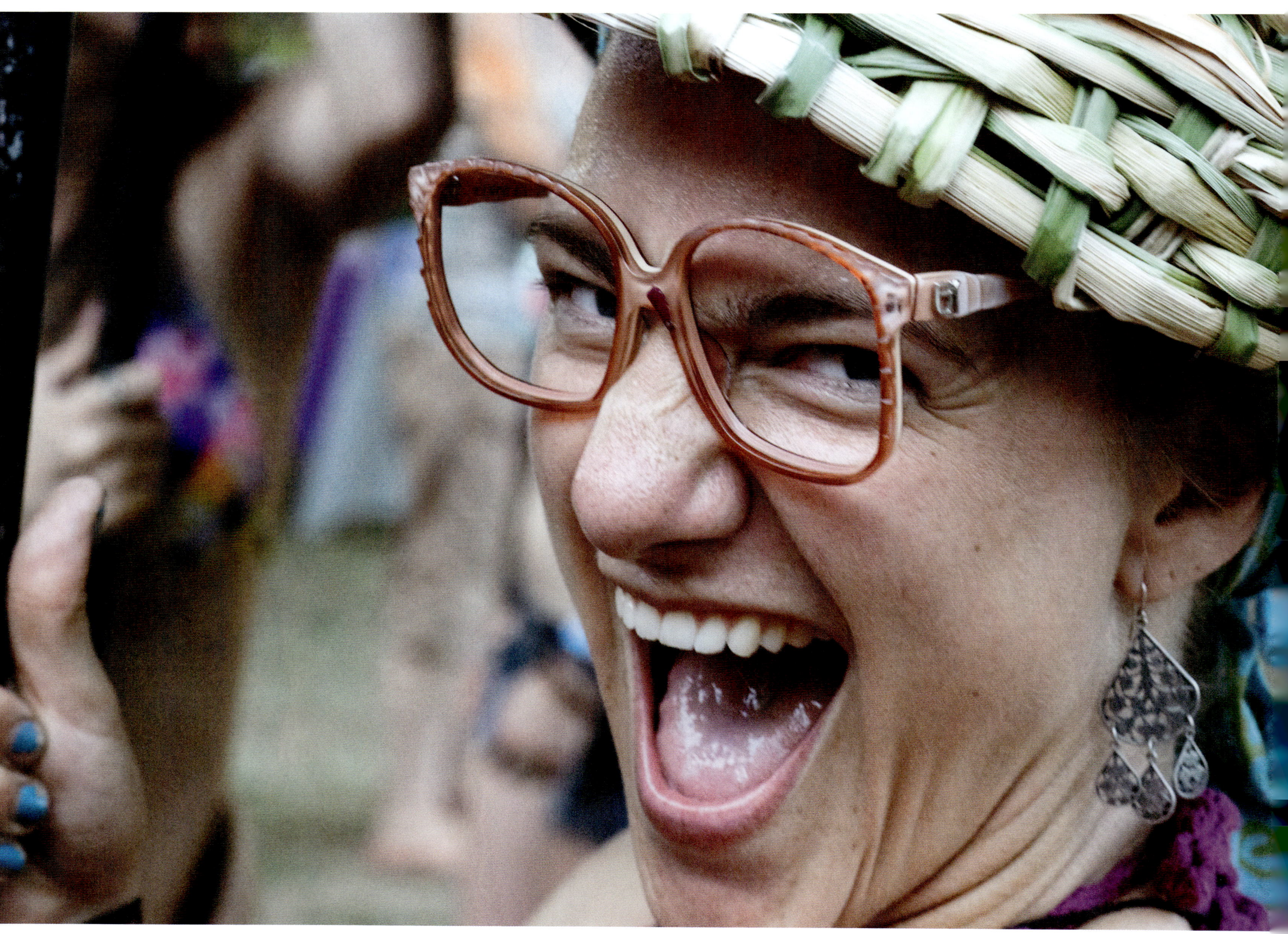

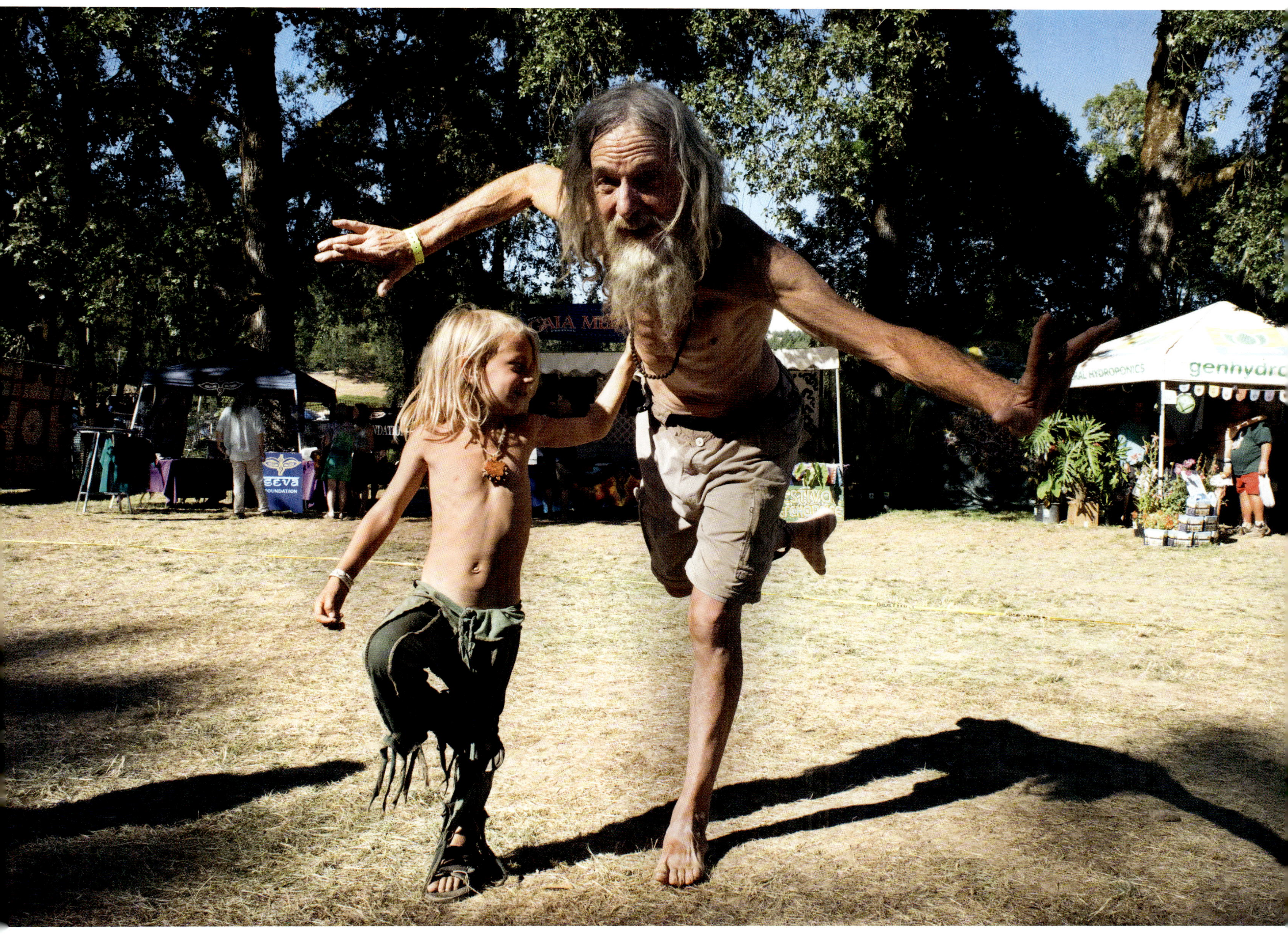

gennydro
HYDROPONICS
seva
FOUNDATION

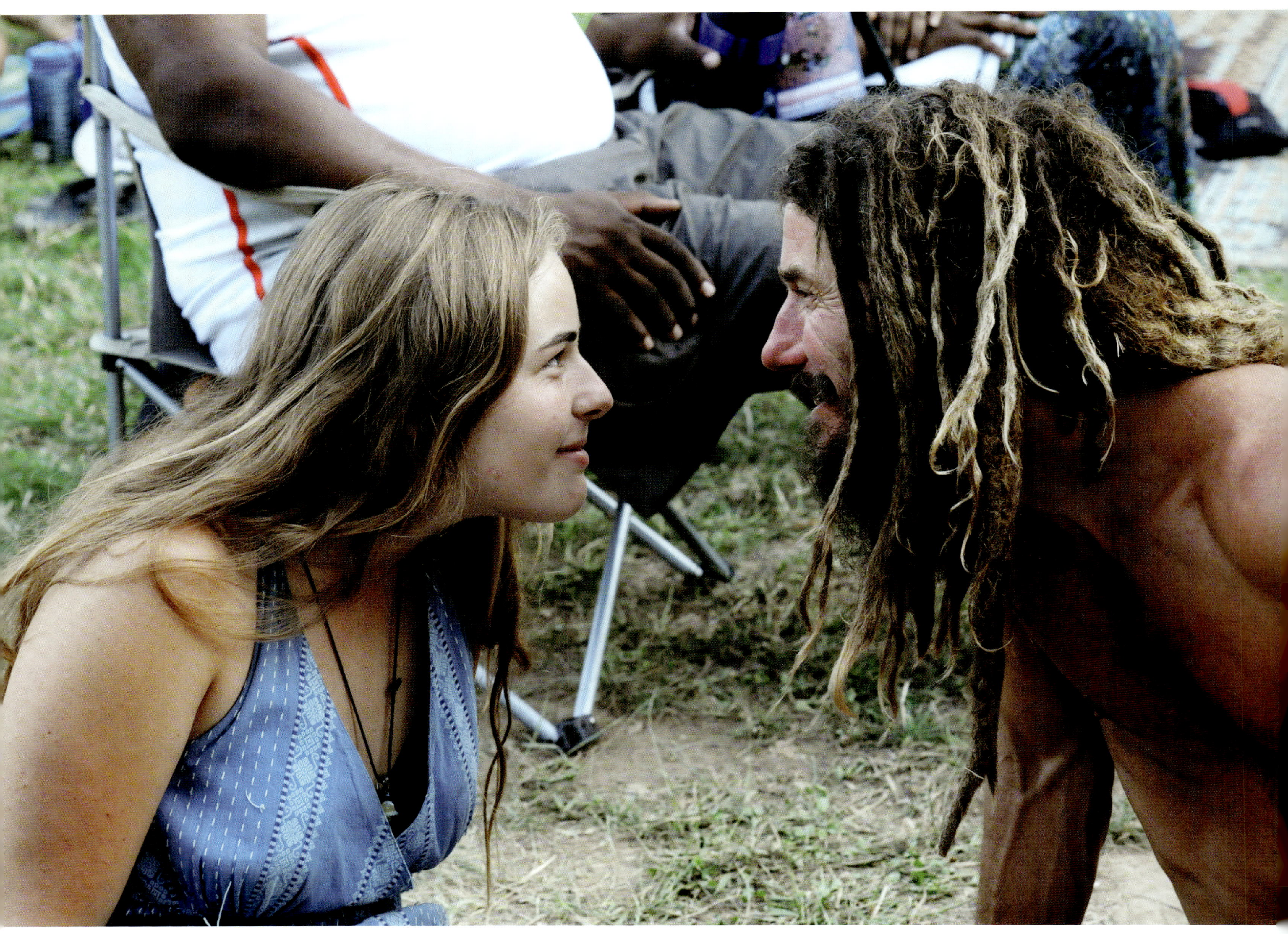

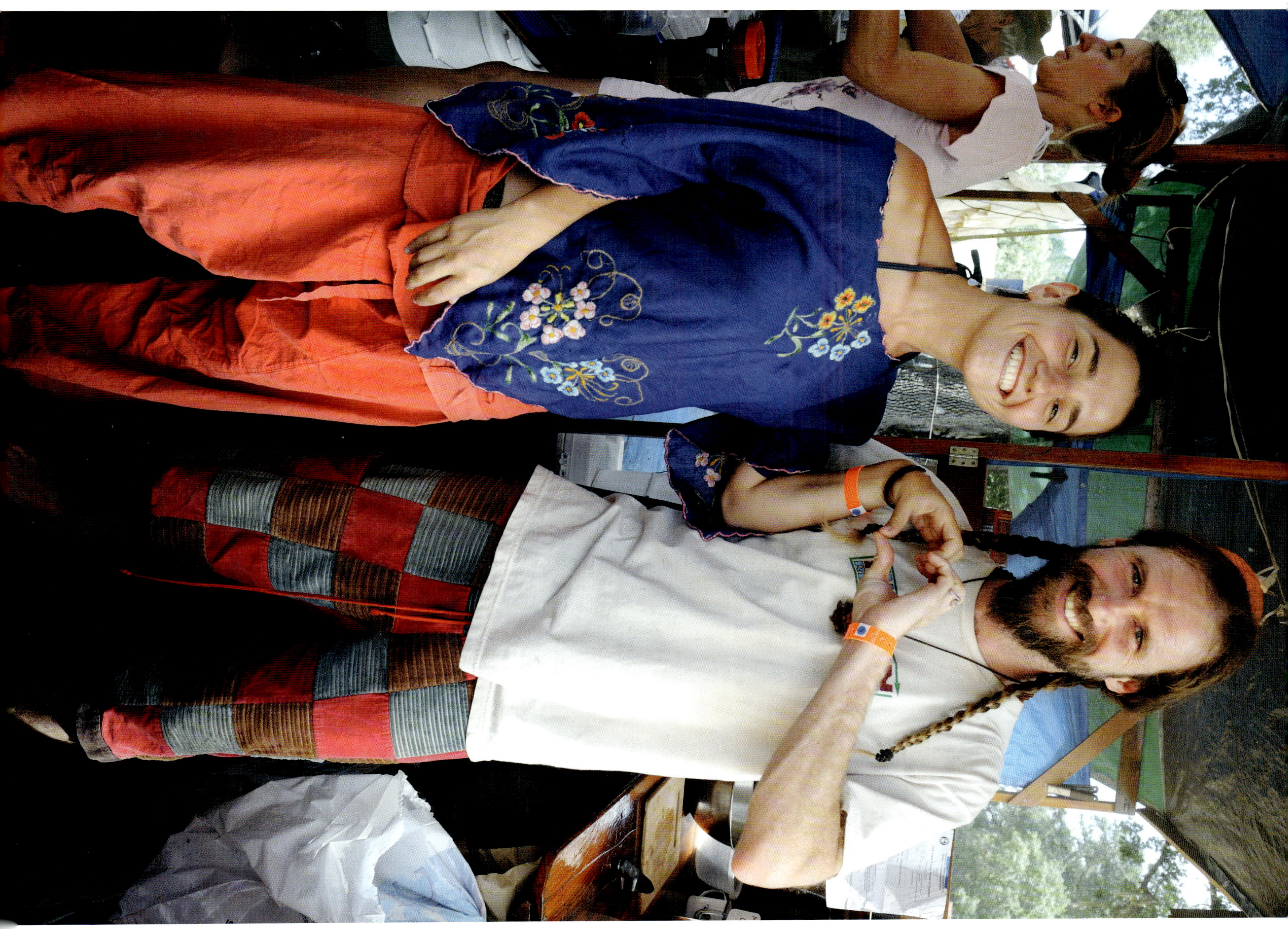

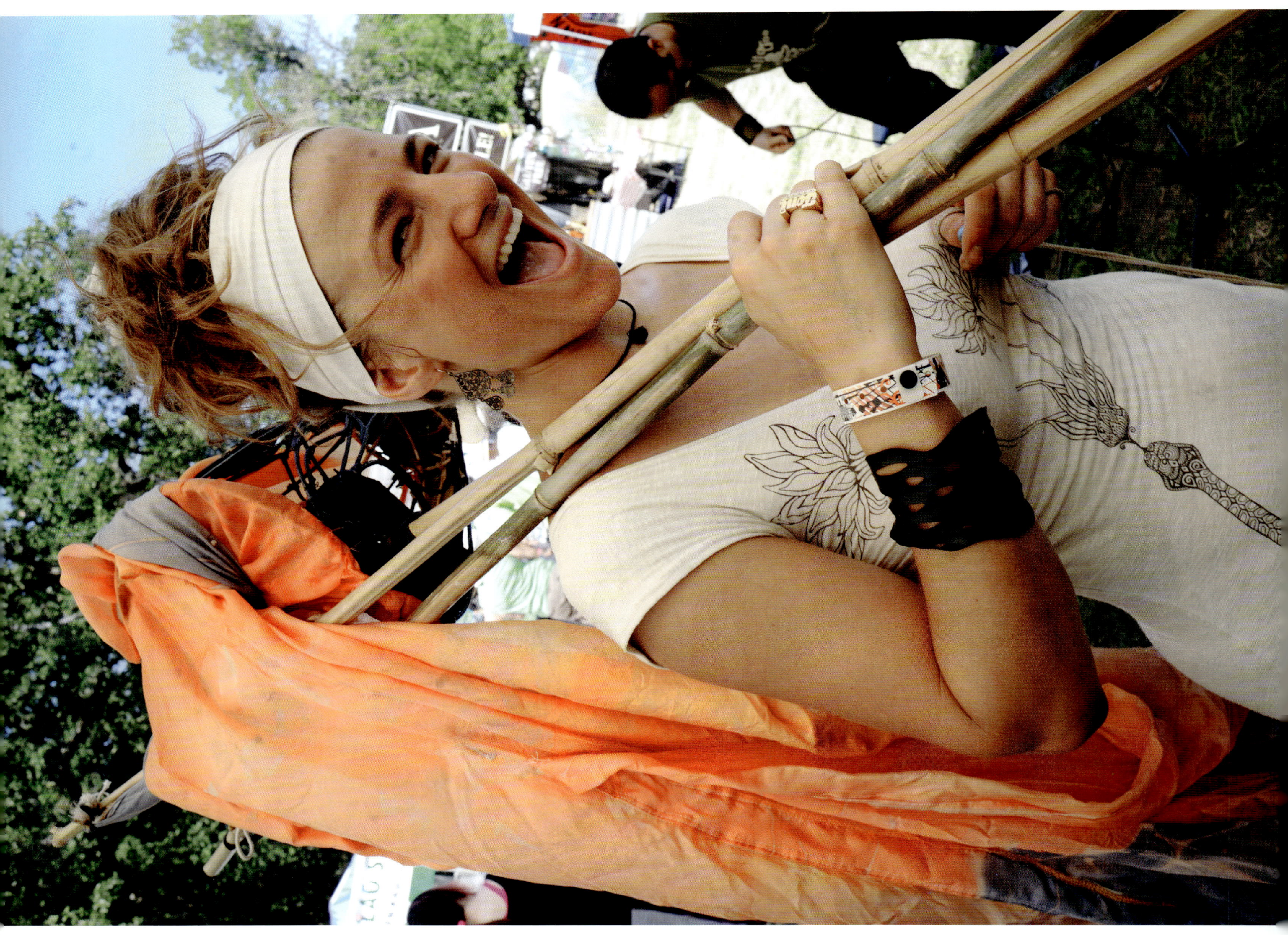

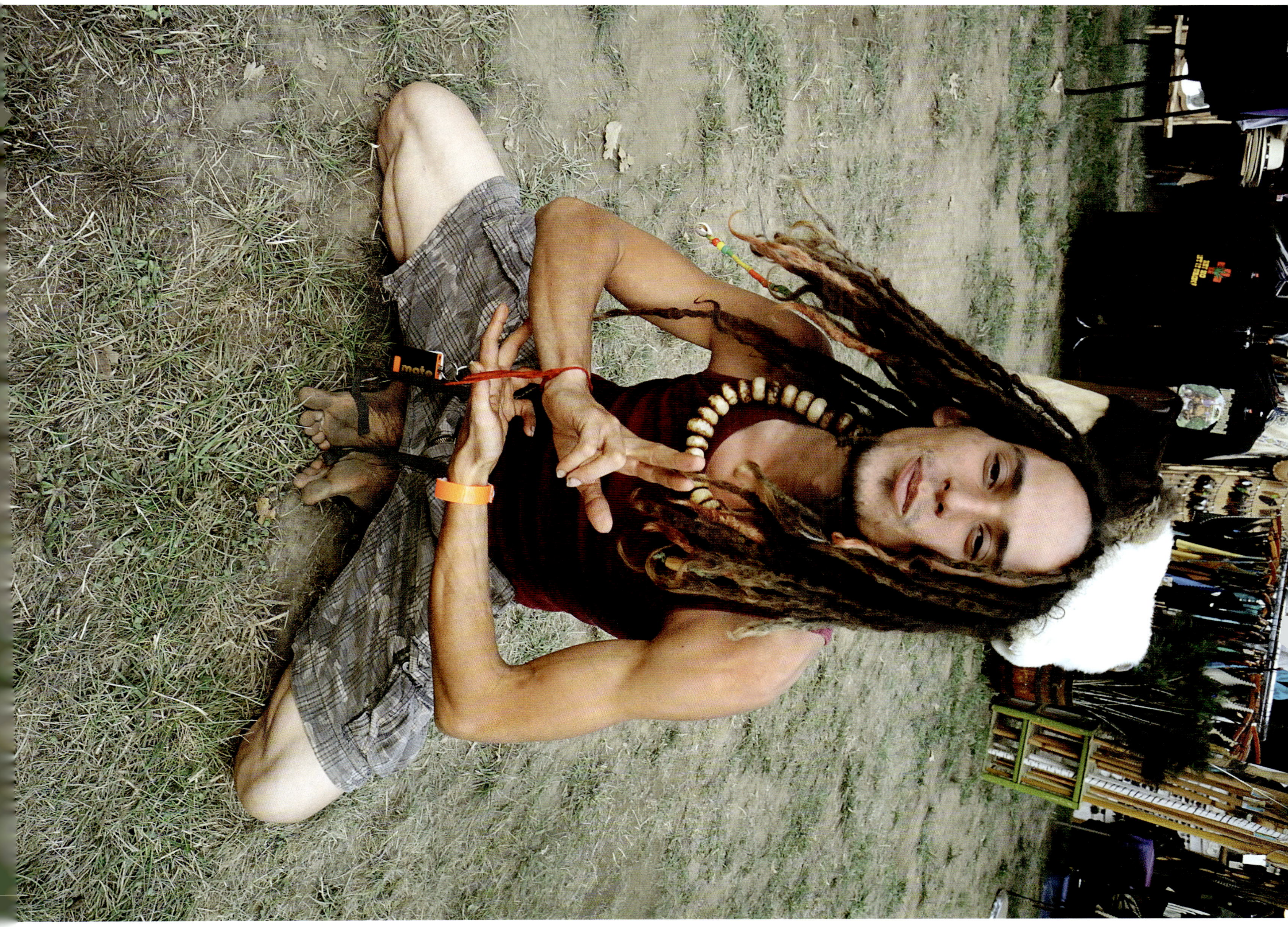

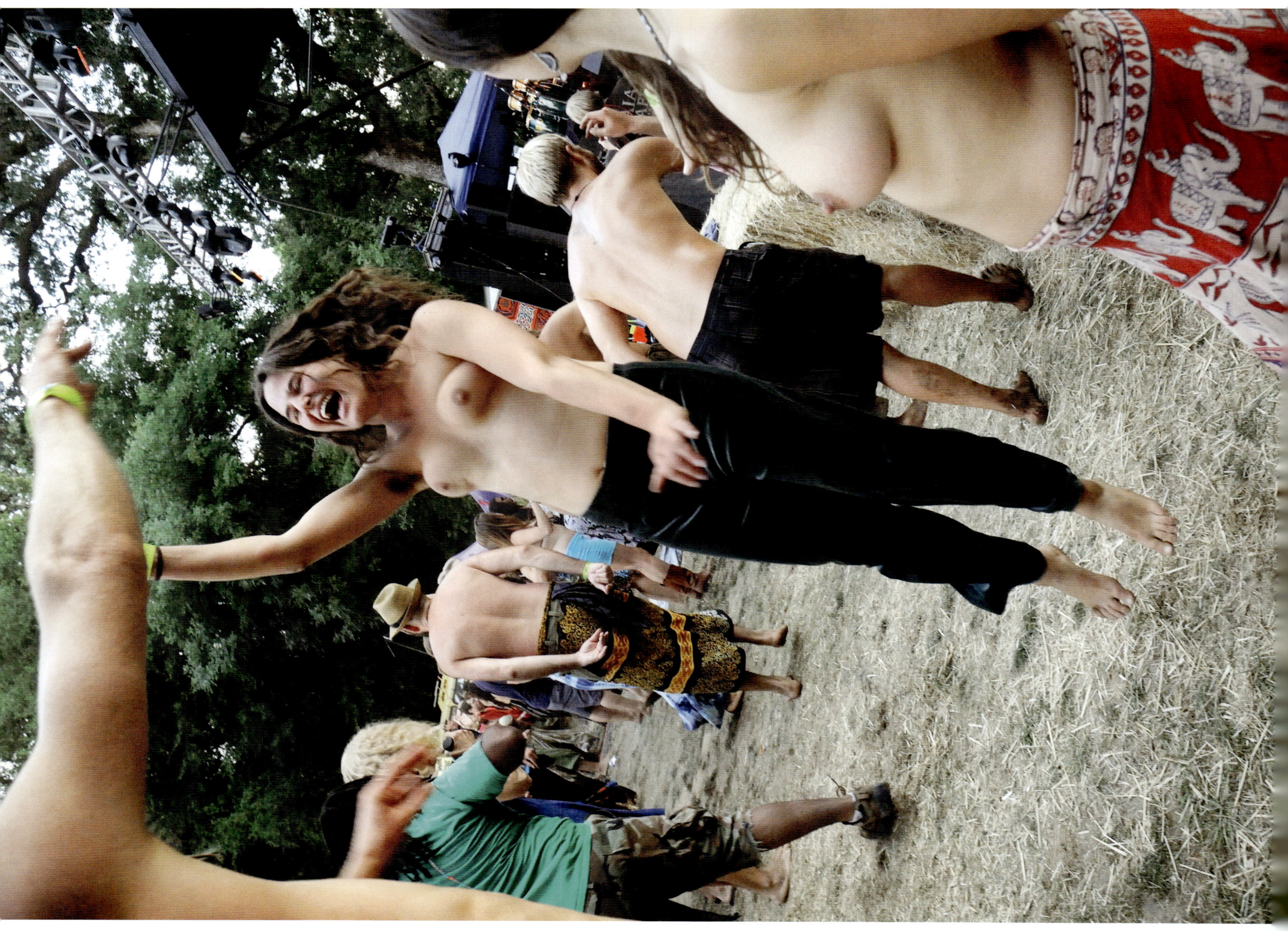

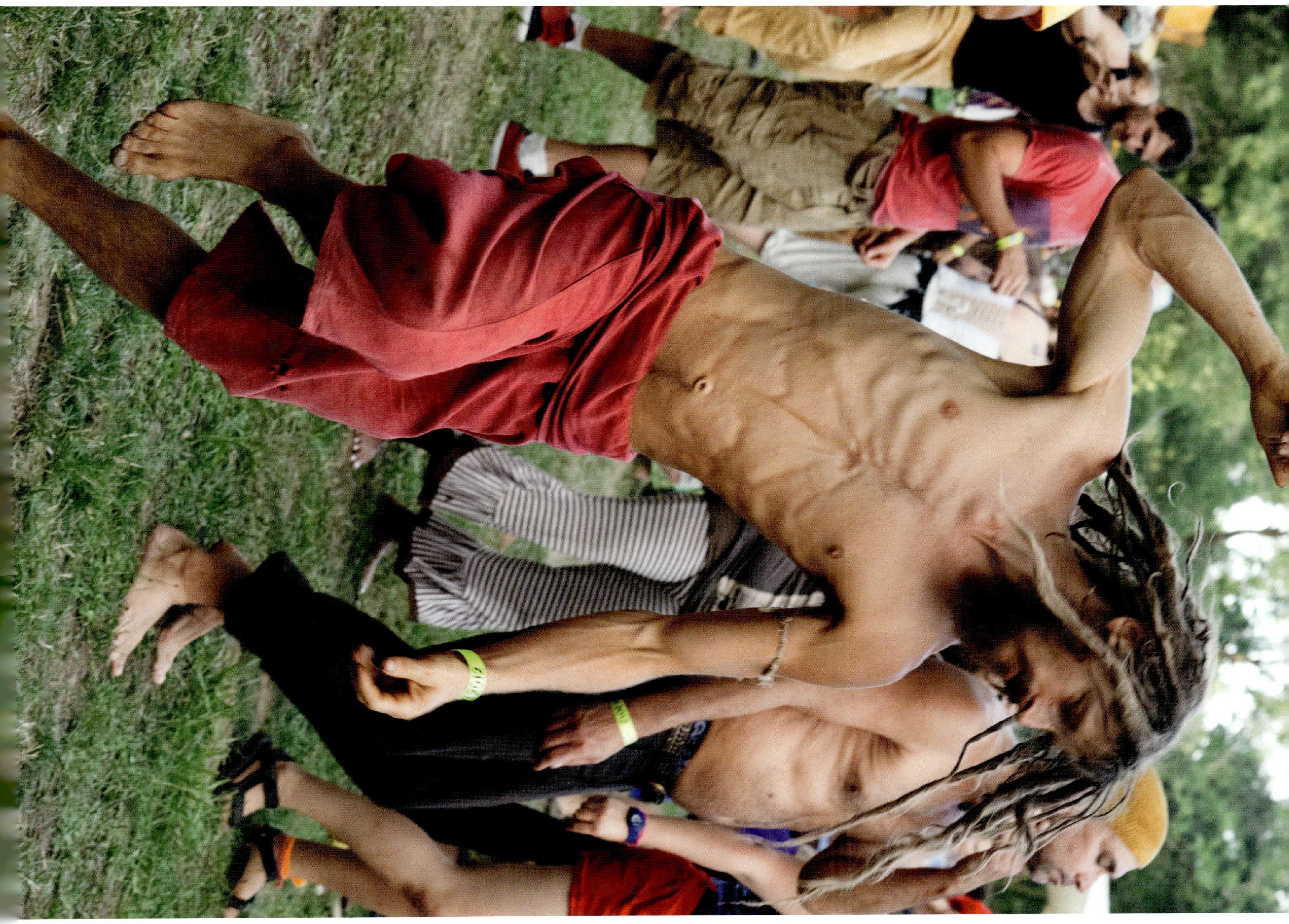

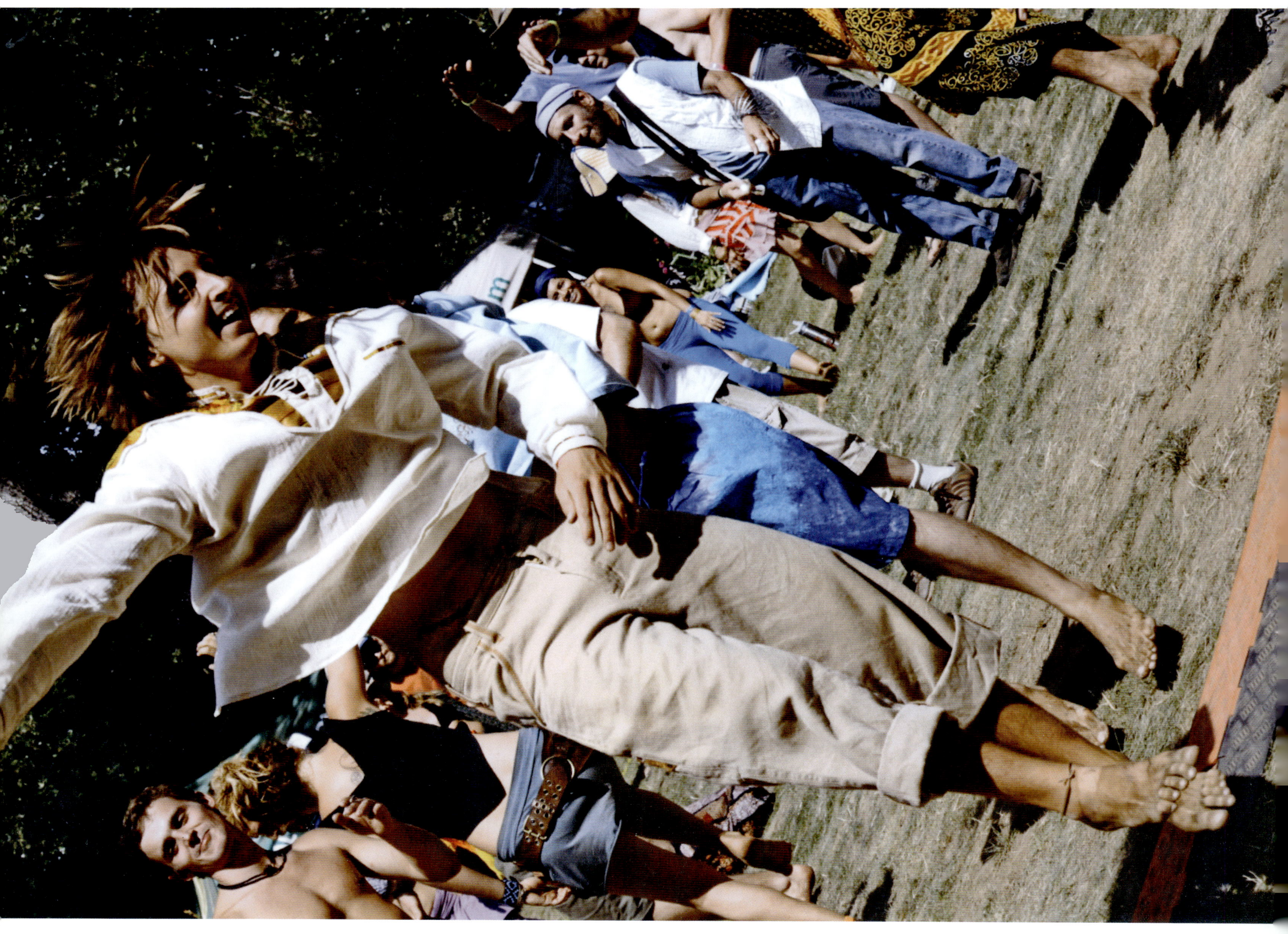

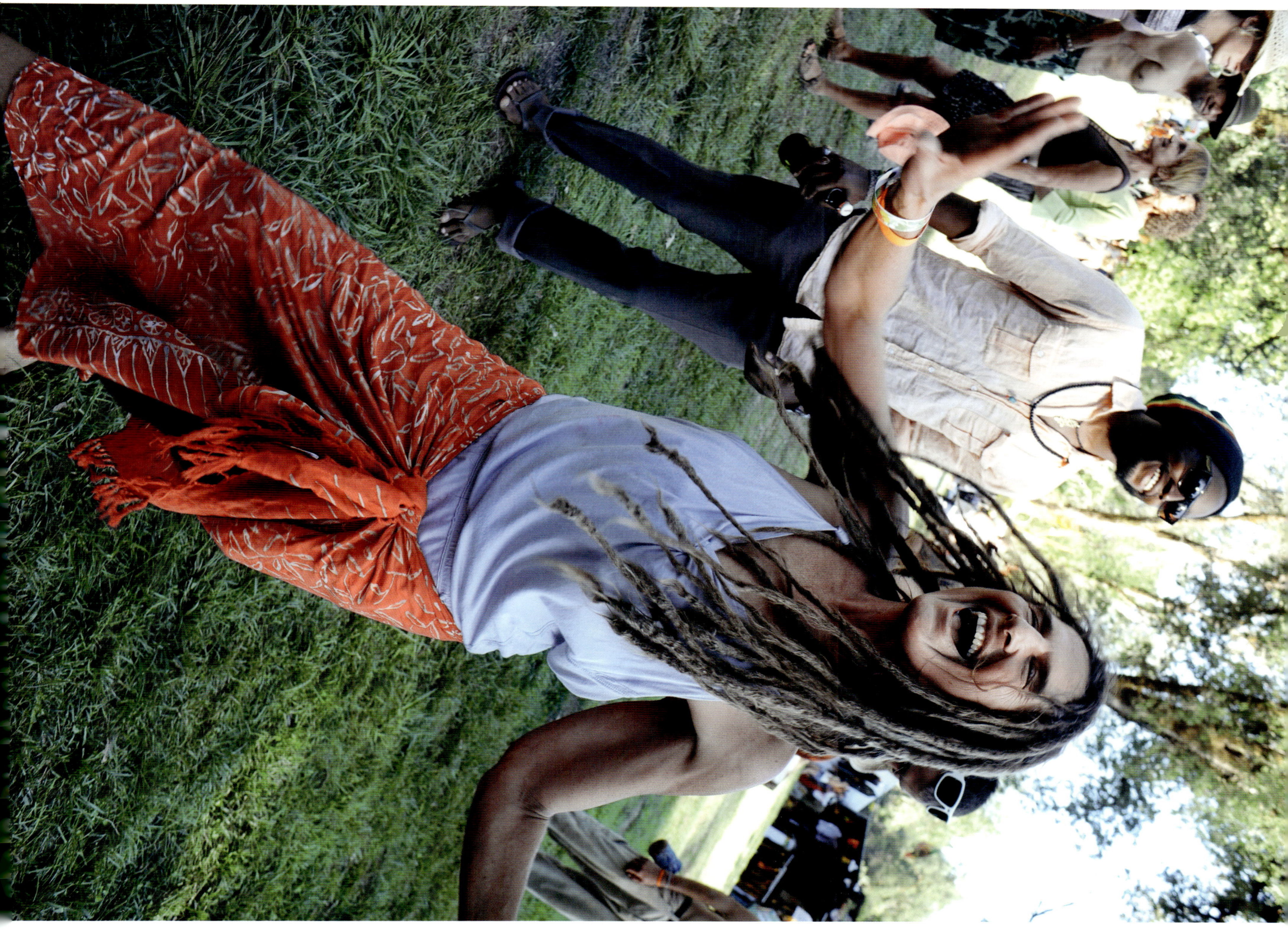

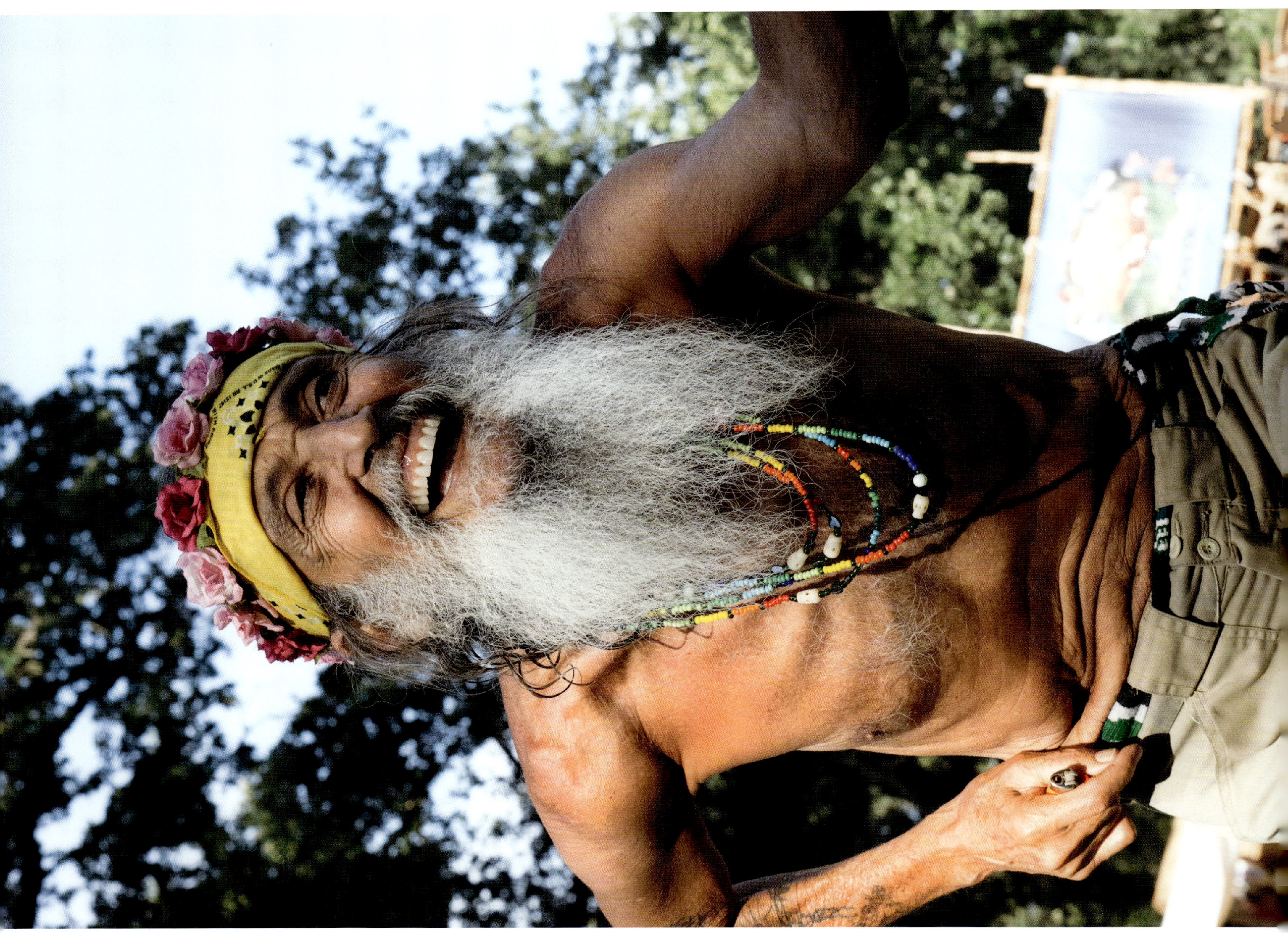

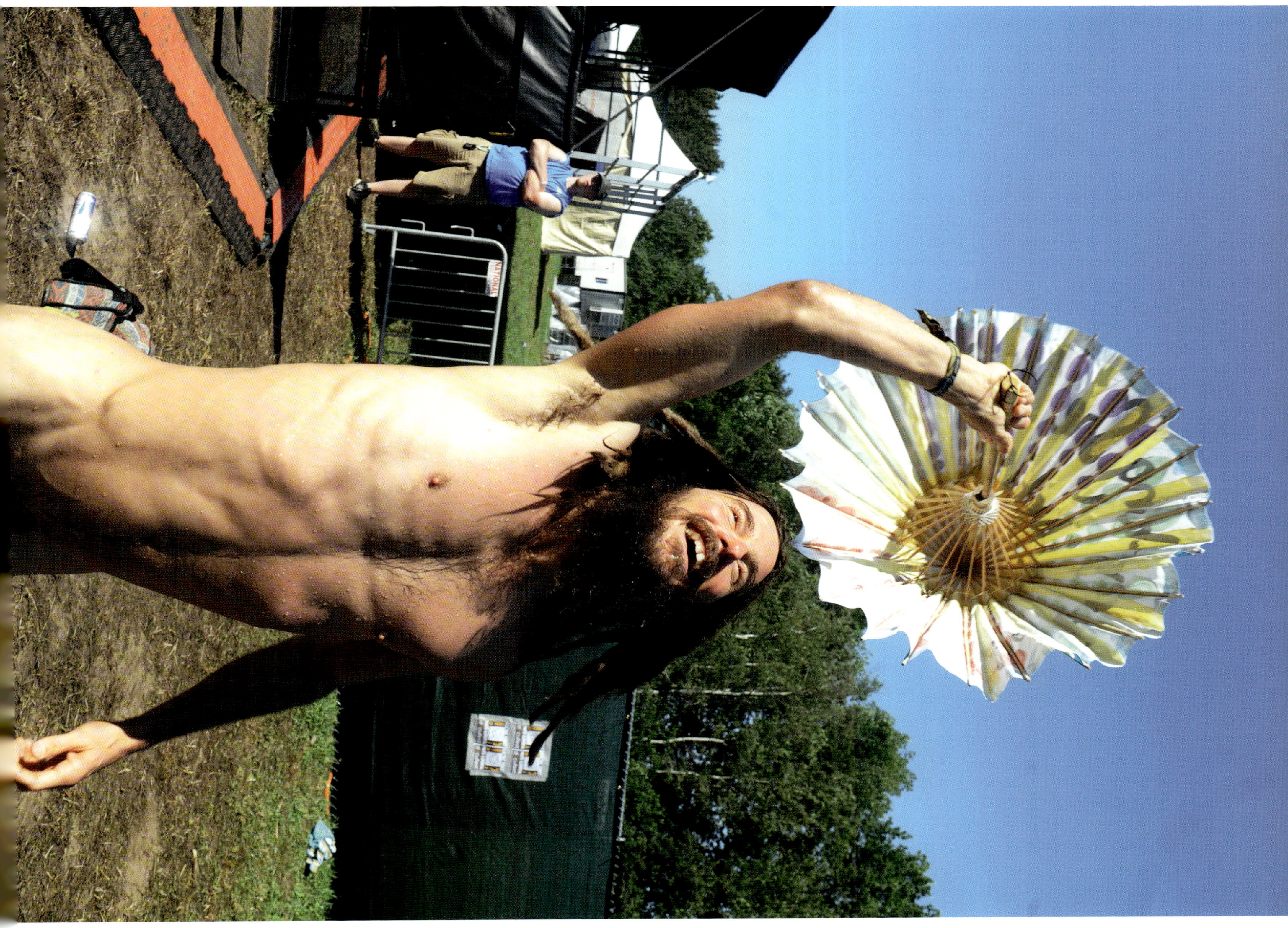

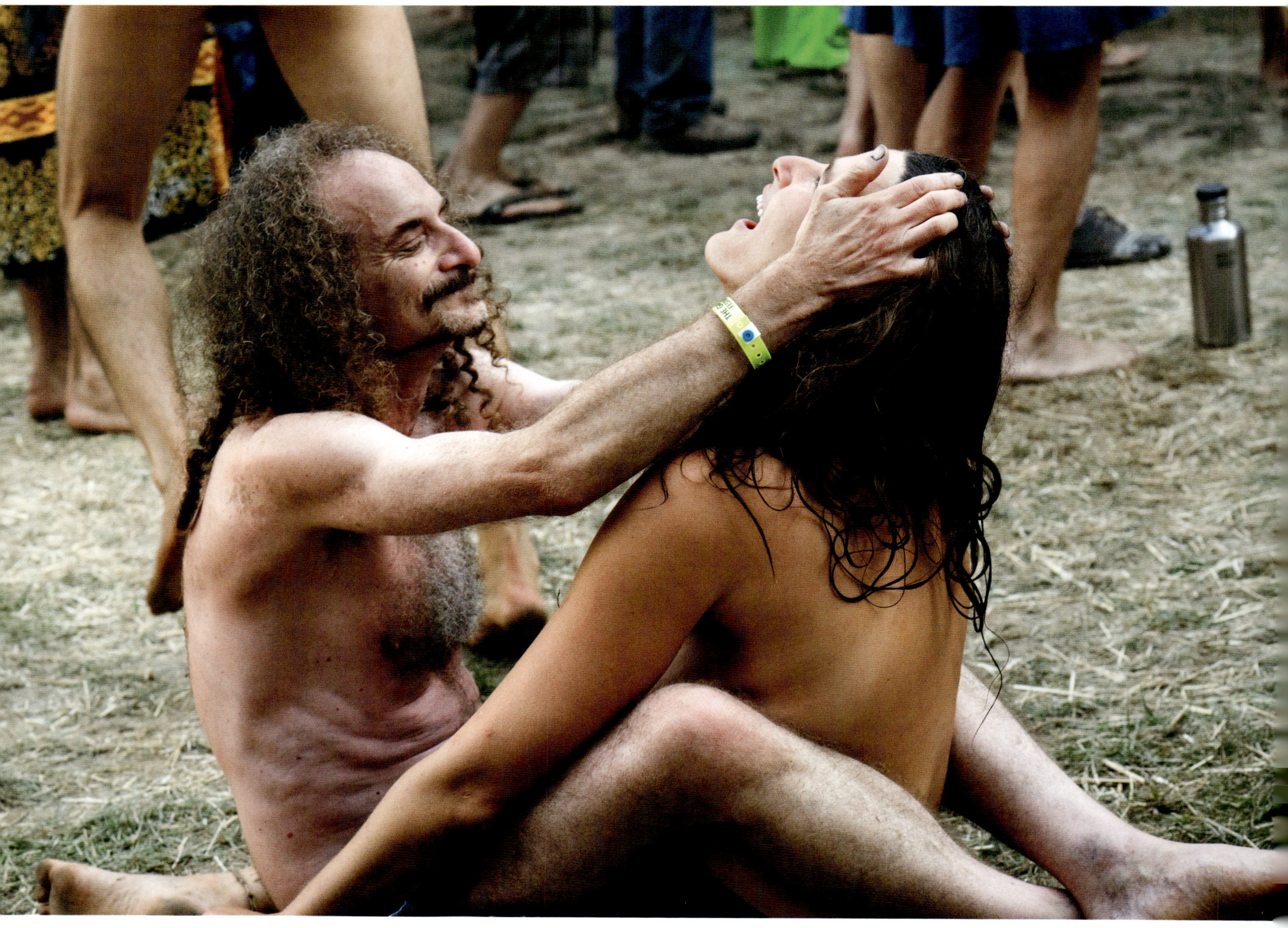

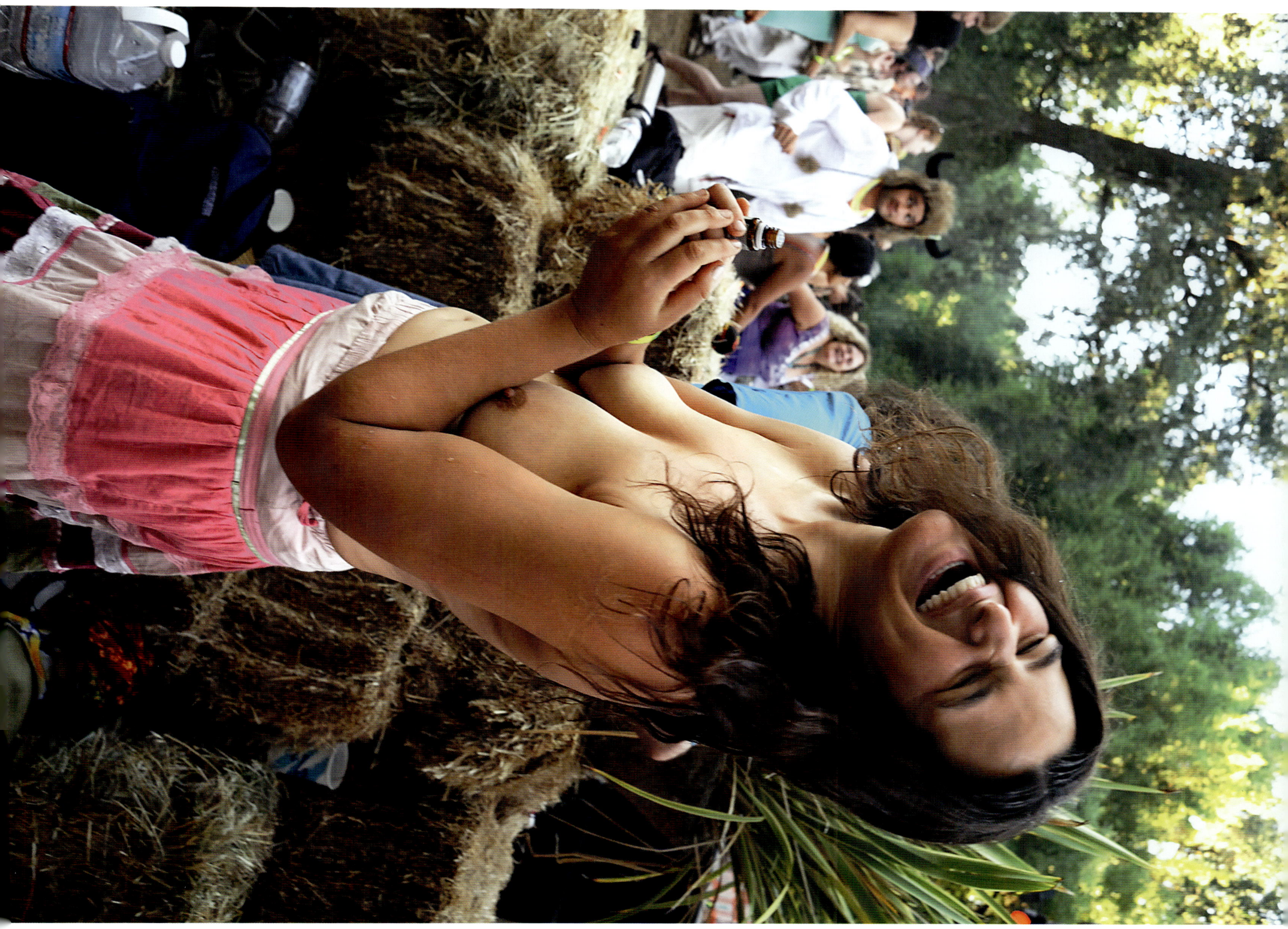

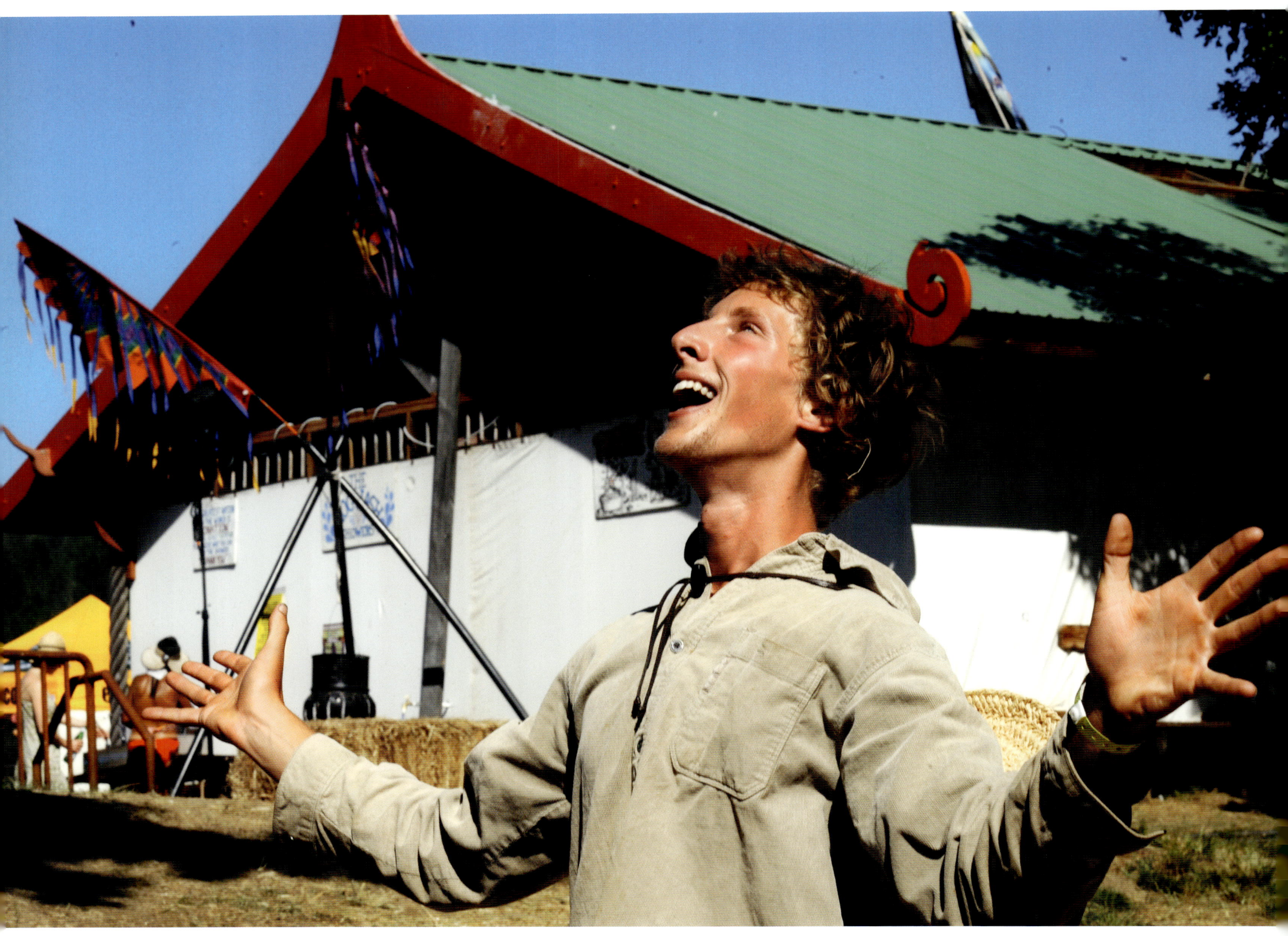

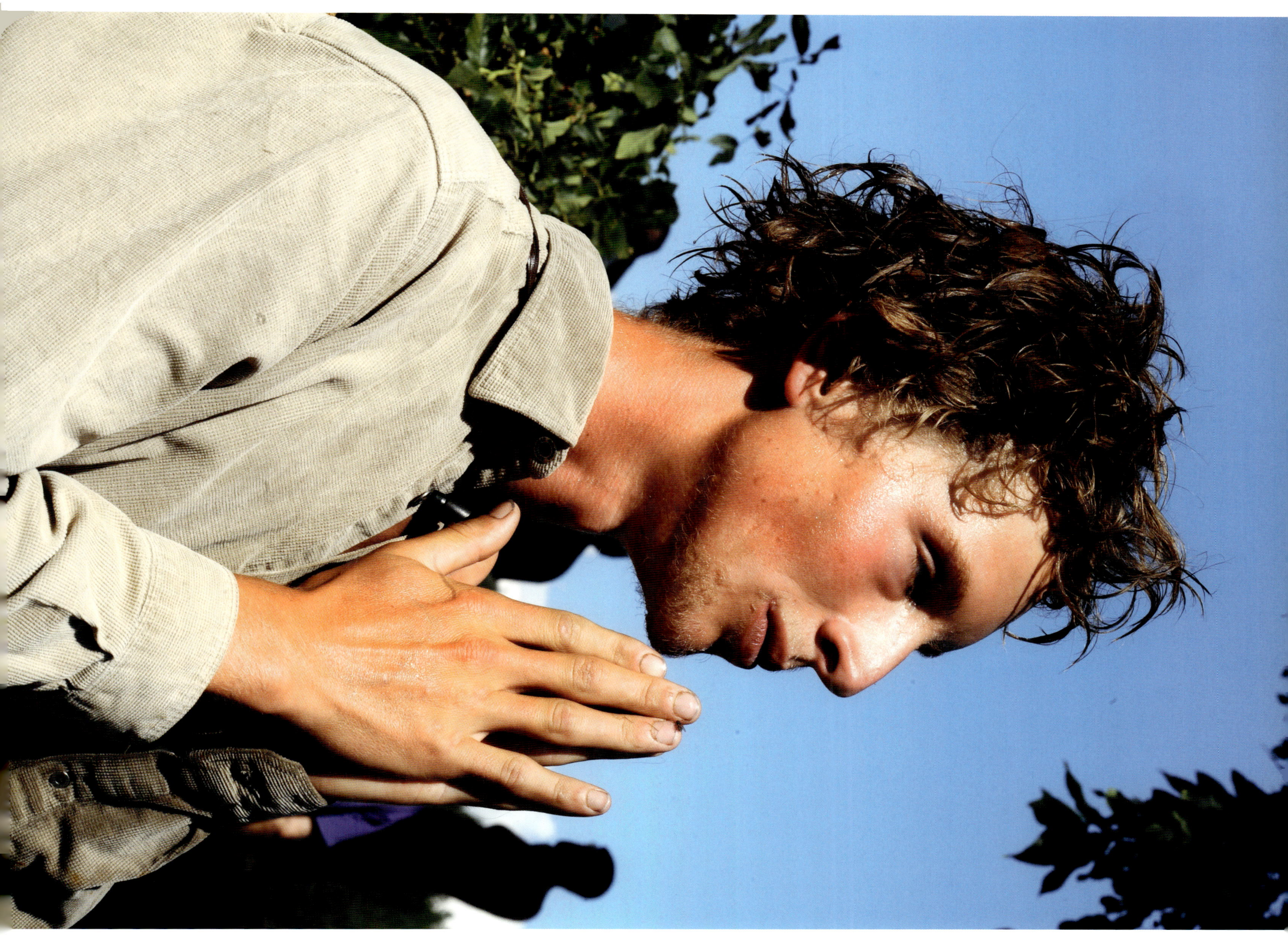

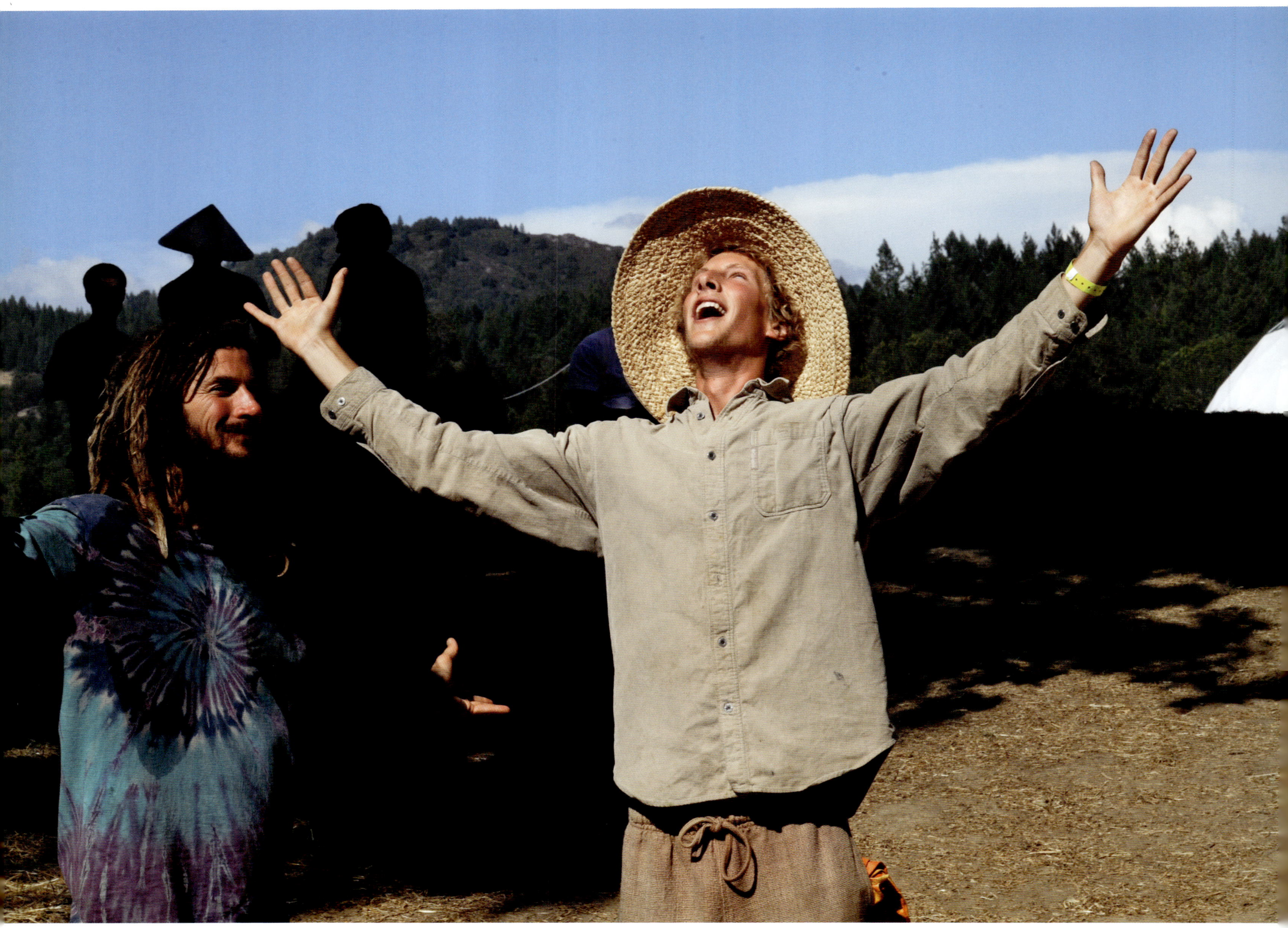

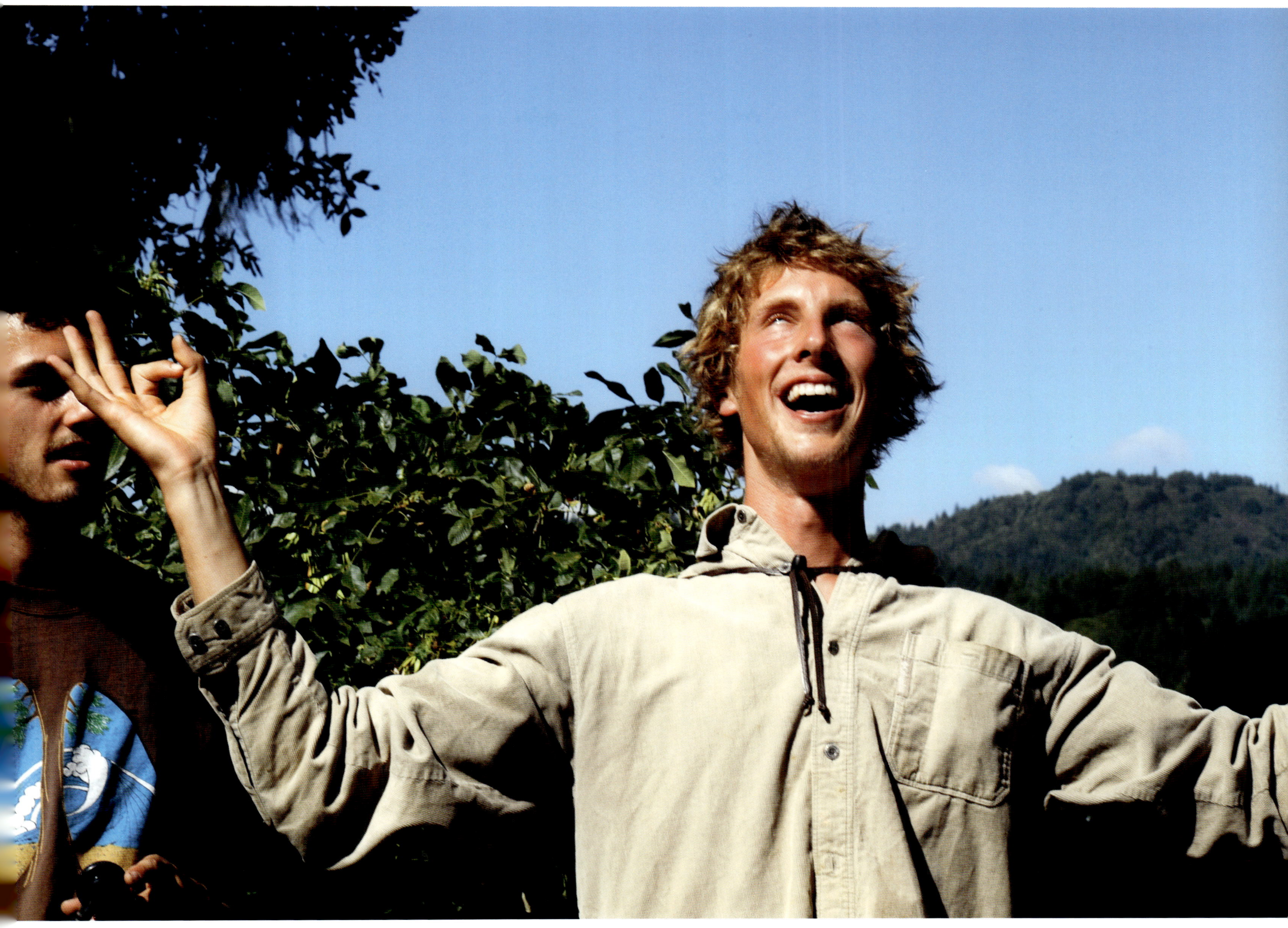

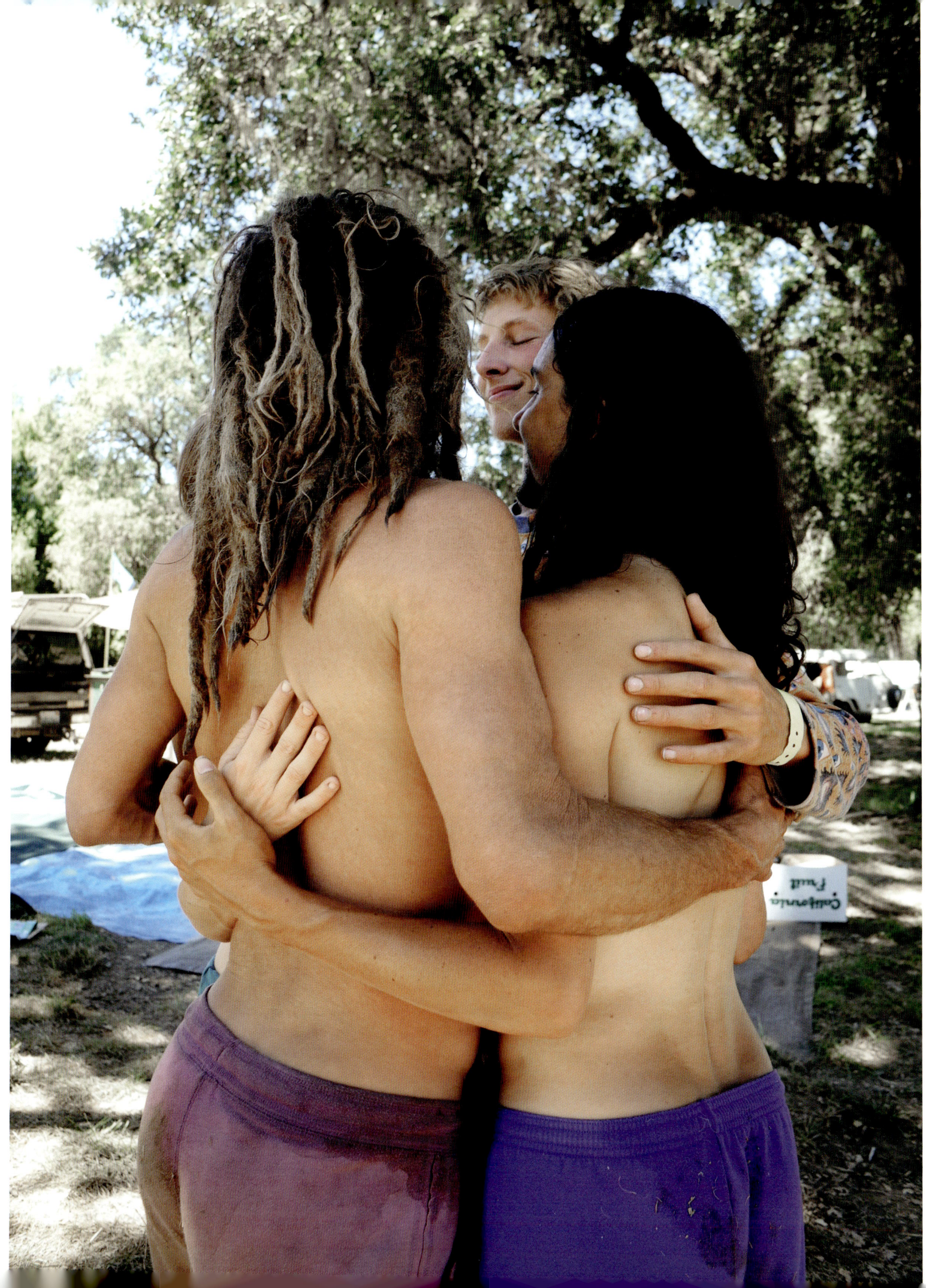

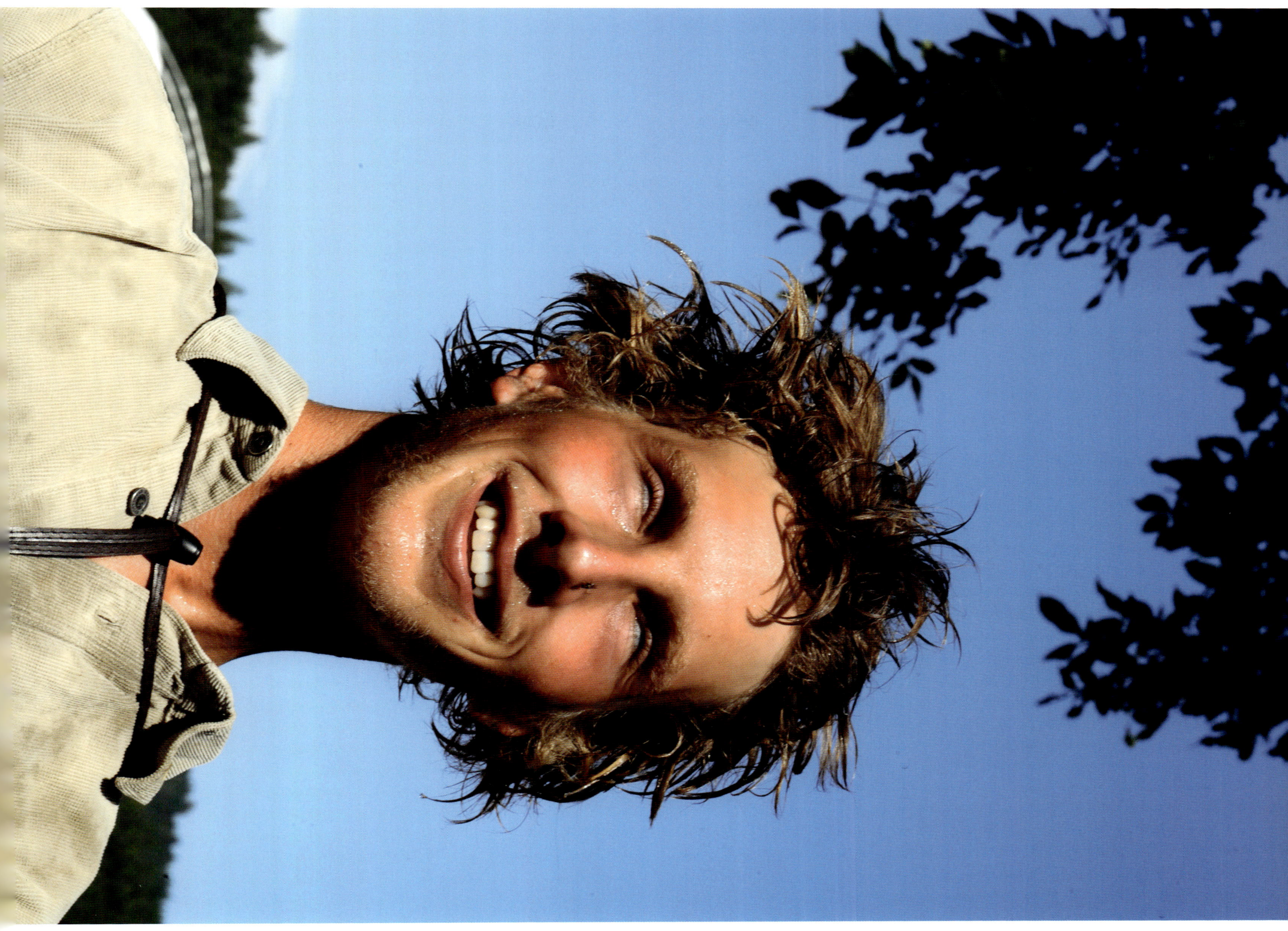

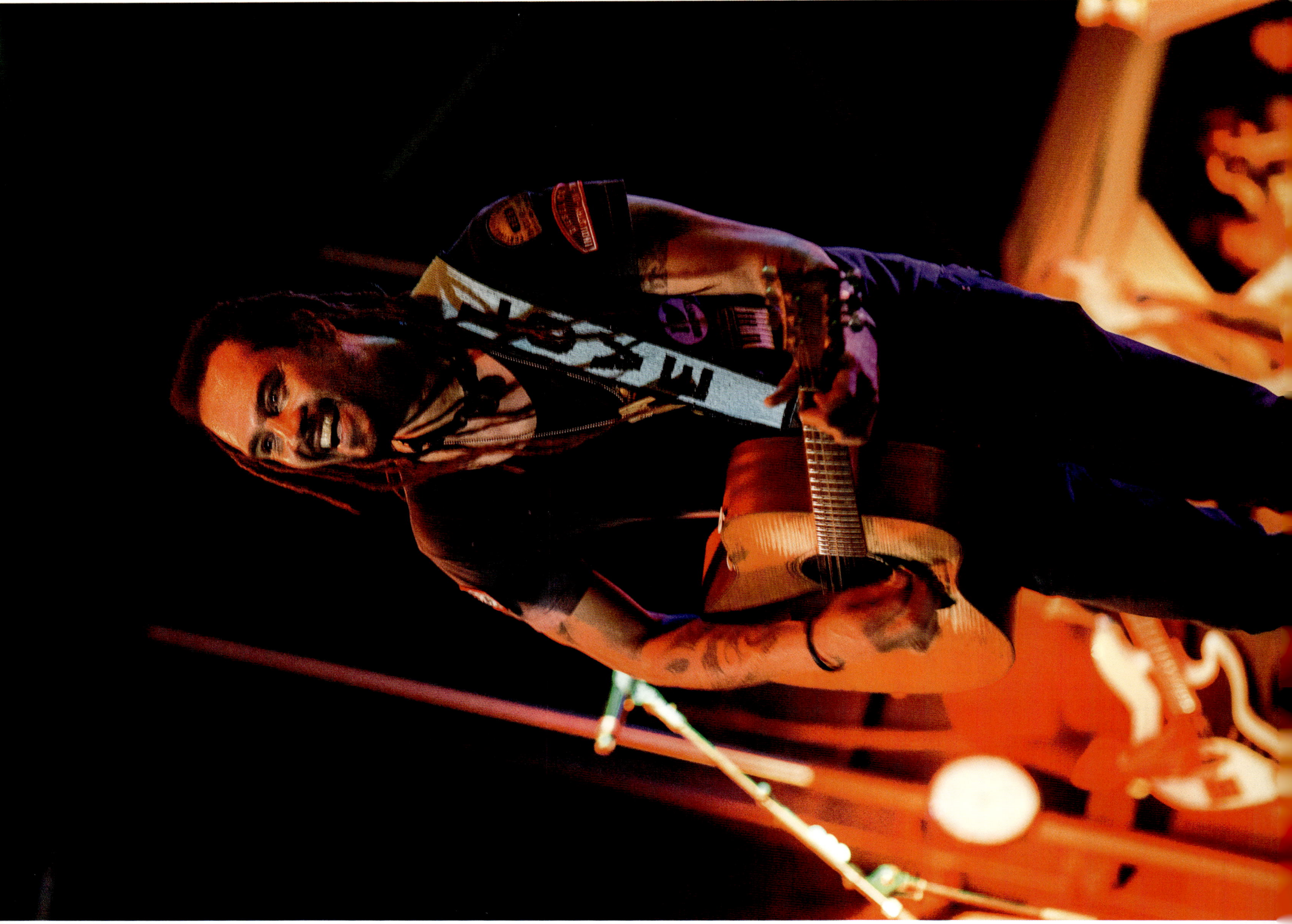

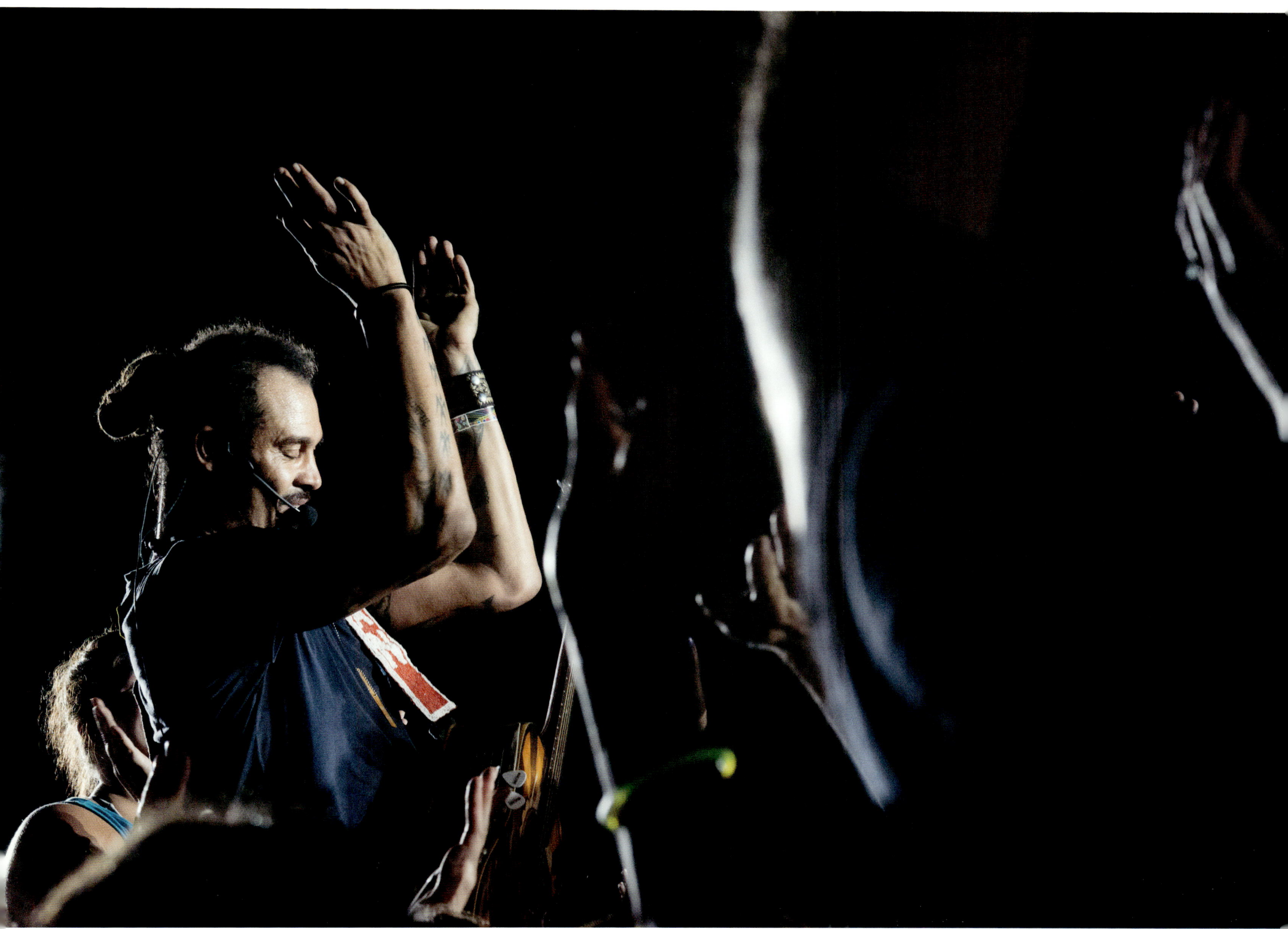

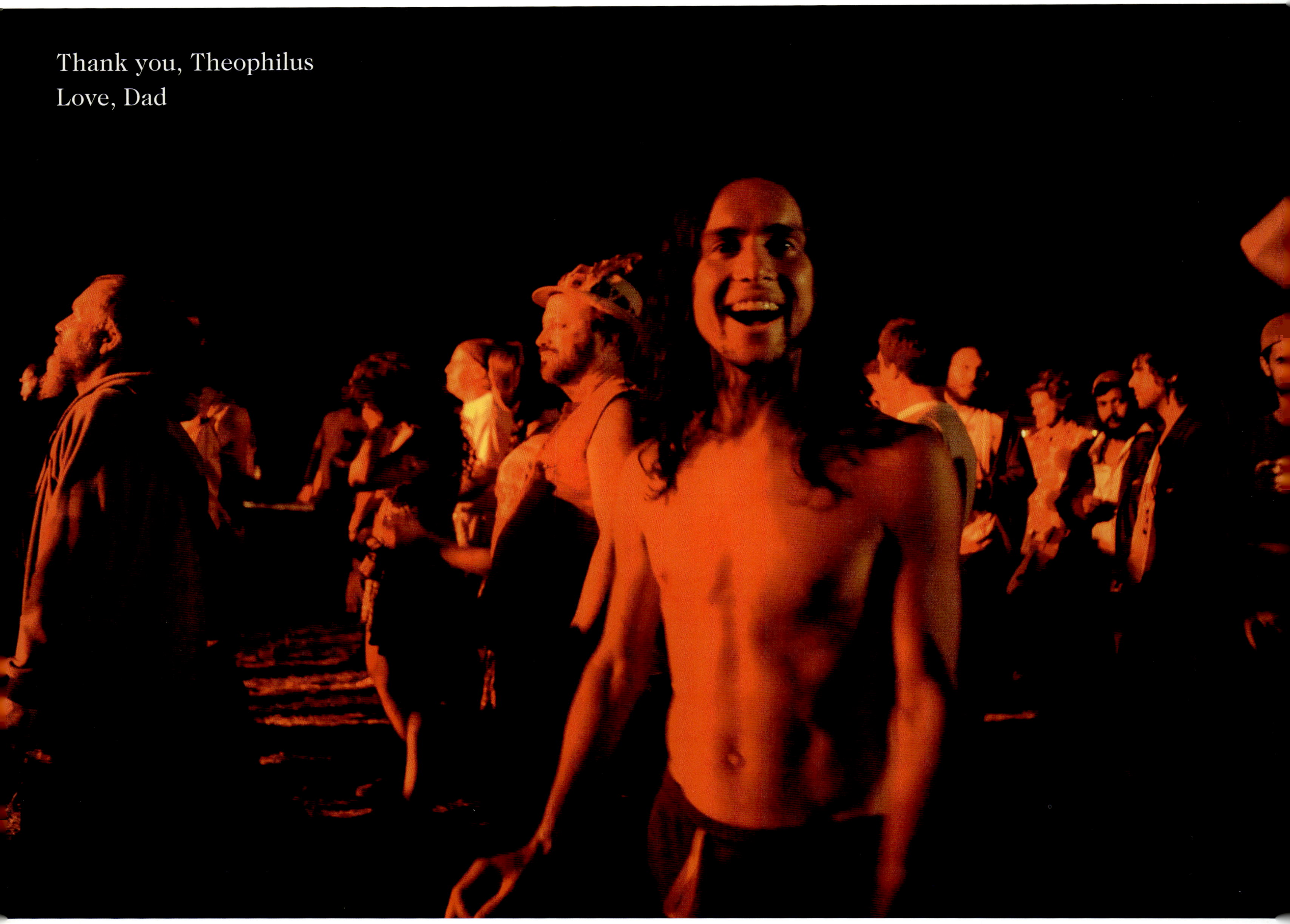

Thank you, Theophilus
Love, Dad

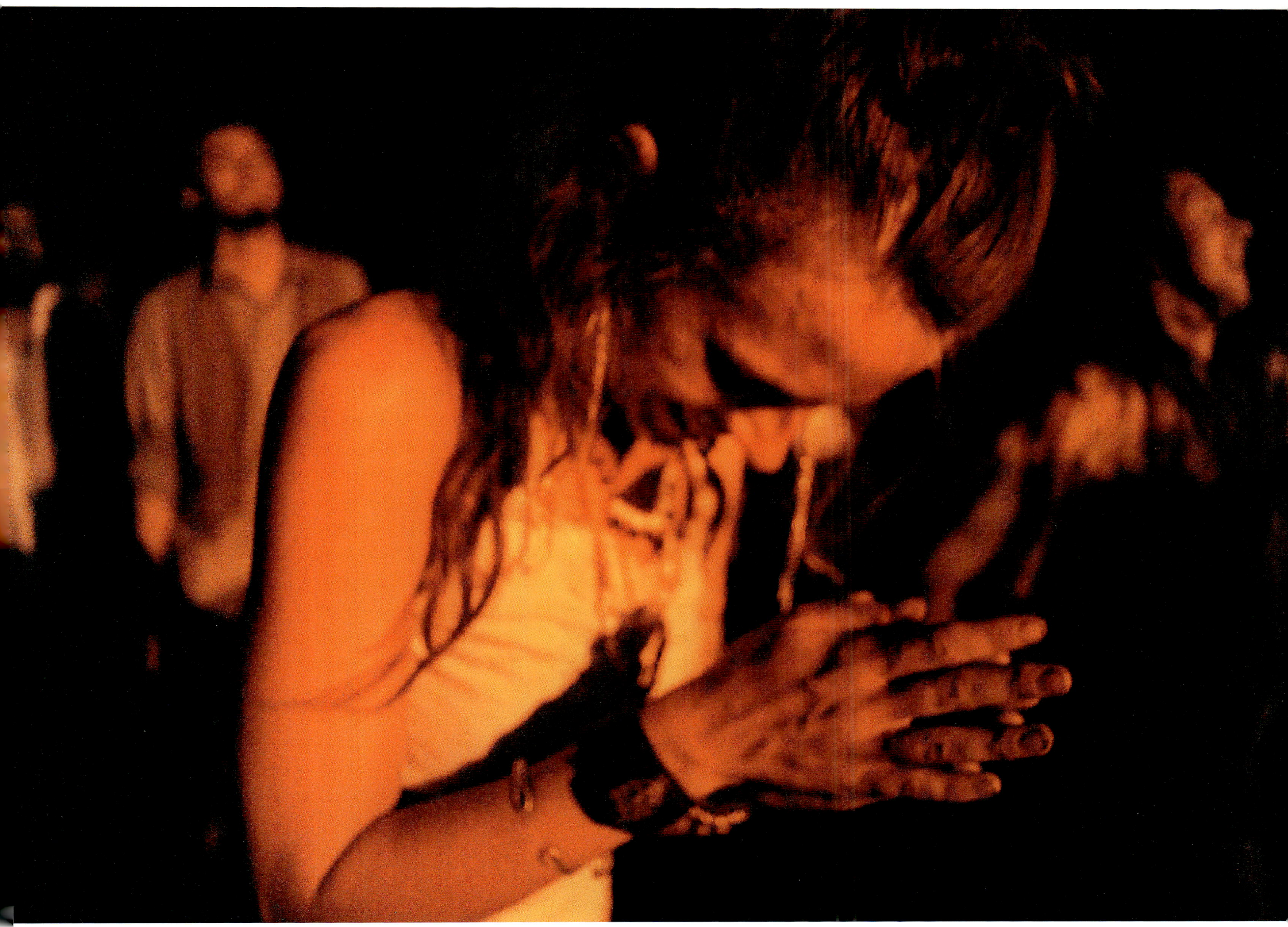

Stories

ERIC OLIVER

I guess you could say it was hereditary, perhaps in my DNA…a handing down of the torch…between my fascination with flipping through old black-and-white prints of my father in his wild, long-haired, round-framed spectacle days… and being awestruck by stories my mother told me about her experiences during the "Summer of Love," at Woodstock… seeing Jimi Hendrix perform his infamous rendition of "The Star-Spangled Banner." I was always a bit of a shaggy-haired youth…in fact by the fifth grade, my hair was grown out well past my shoulders! In a small, conservative New England town, where other kids just weren't expressing themselves in that sort of way… But it was when I was 12 years old and my father took me to see Bob Dylan perform at the local stadium…something clicked dramatically at that show, and I knew my life was changing quickly and would never be the same again… When I was 13 I found a copy of Jerry Rubin's *DO IT* in the basement of my parents' house… as well as a couple of old *Zap Comix*… both of which were profoundly influential on me… That Jerry Rubin book was about the only "textbook" I cared to study whilst in junior high school… The first week of seventh grade I discovered grass…and then life truly changed forever… We had a small group of friends that would get together and "camp out" in the forest usually behind my parents house… We called ourselves the "generation gap."

It wasn't until perhaps the ninth grade when I finally got my hands on some LSD…which further opened up the doors of perception in my world…

I ditched out on the last few days of high school to go see the Grateful Dead play up in Vermont, back when Jerry was still alive…which was my first real adventure out in the world… Really opened up my eyes and heart to the realm of cosmic synchronicities and new possibilities… and after eventually dropping out of high school…I found myself on Furthur tour… on a cross-country sweep of psychedelic bliss and wonderment…it was at the end of this tour that I wound up at my first Rainbow Gathering.

And then it was ON… I was hooked, as it got me off the streets of Babylon and into the sanctum of nature to celebrate bliss and love with all my beautiful brothers and sisters…

Fifteen years later and some 37-odd Rainbow Gatherings and countless festivals and shows…and I've landed in community setting with a handful of folks that have become family to me over the years of synchronistic crossing and sharing of paths…

For me it's always a point of rock-bottom despair in my life that has propelled me to aim higher and find my place of bliss and deeper connection with the universe (God)… It all comes down to doing my very best at all times…even if it hurts at first…and have found that attitude is everything…as well as deep gratitude (great attitude).

And as far as my quest for attaining and maintaining higher states of bliss… for me purity has also become key… sticking to an organic, raw, vegan diet… living substance free…and becoming ultra clear and unclouded…so that I can experience strong interconnectedness

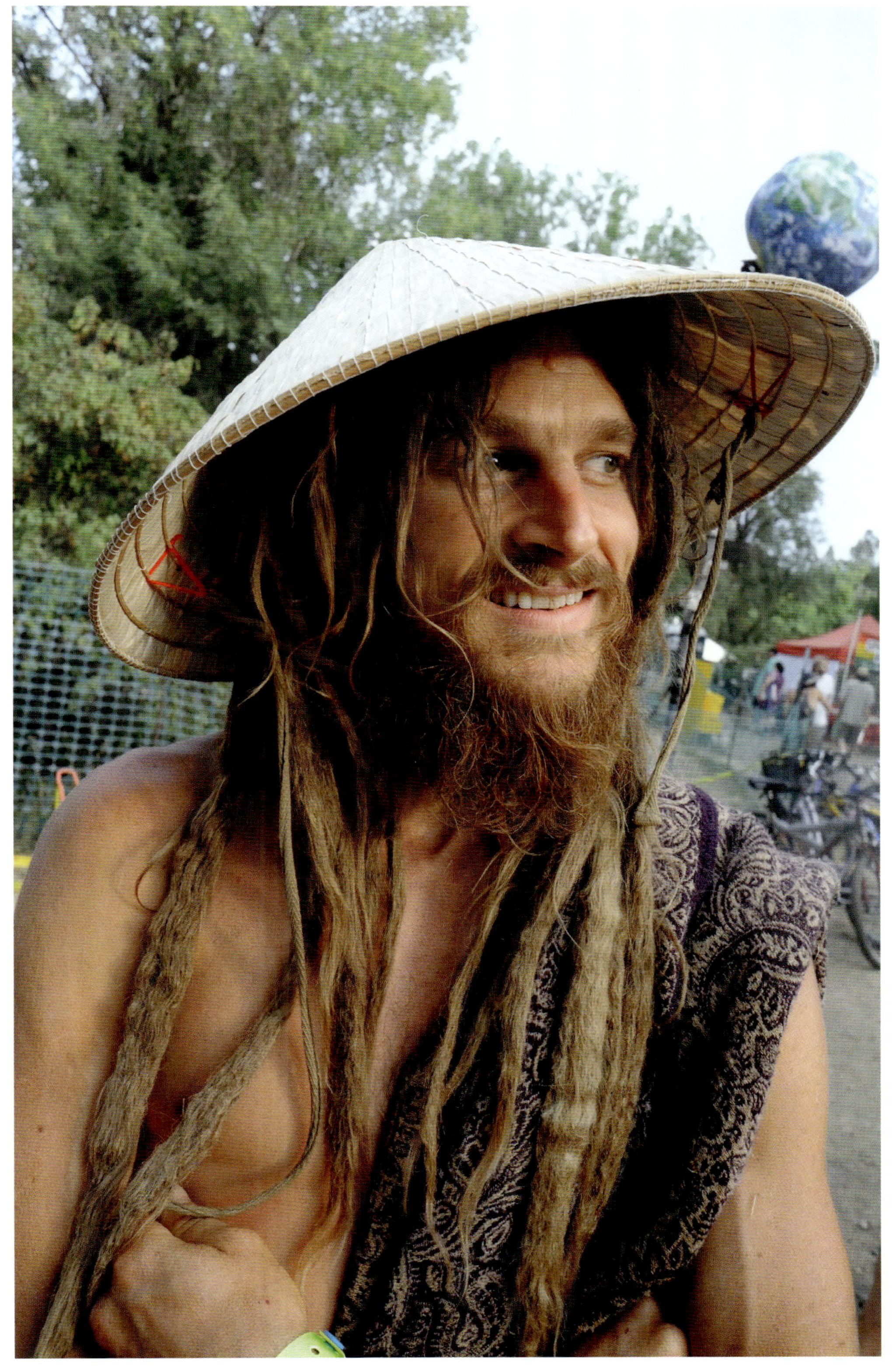

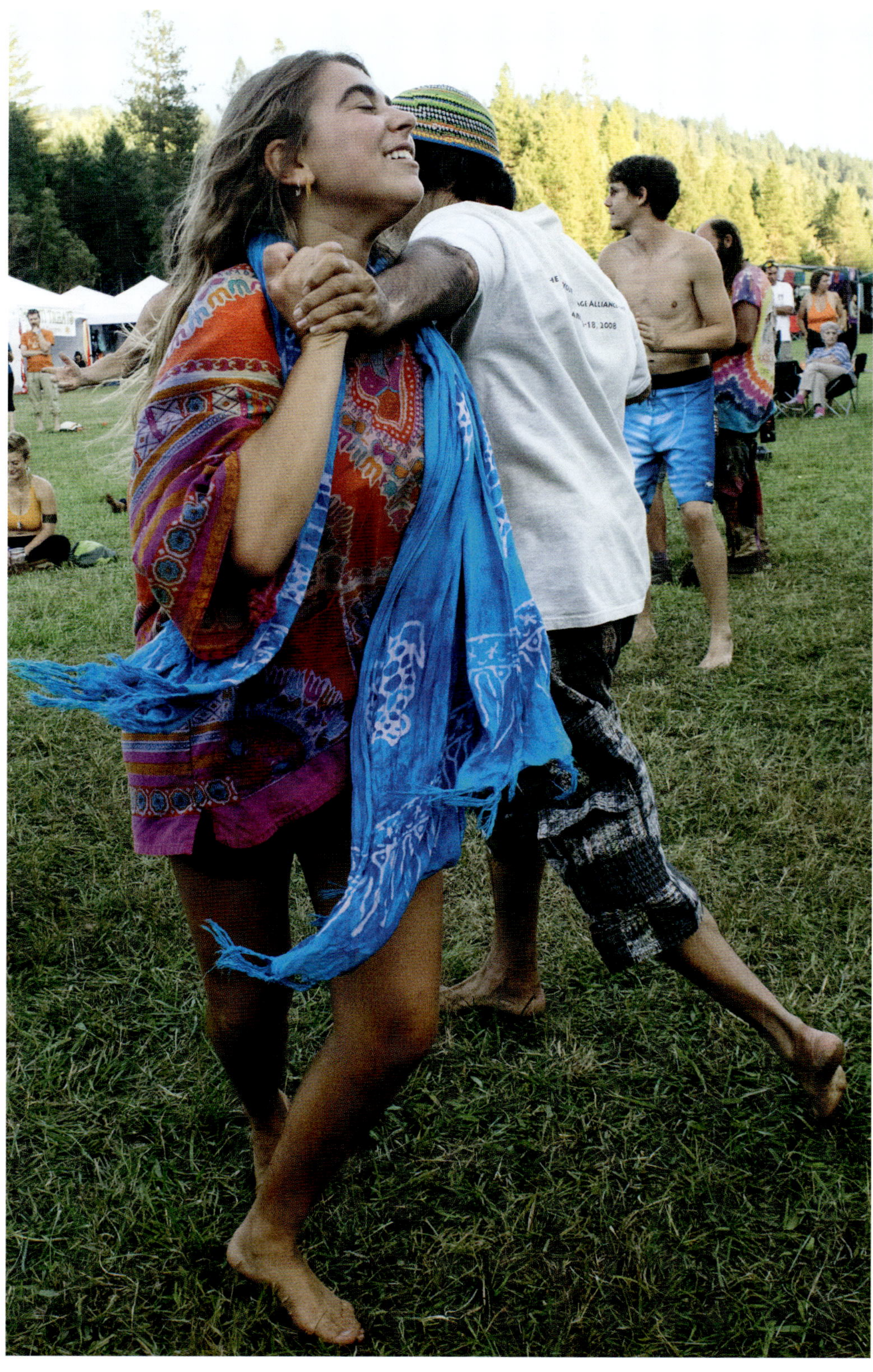

with source (universe) (God) as well as connection with all my brothers and sisters… It's connection that has really brought me the most bliss in life… A strong connection with source brings uncanny synchronicities into one's reality… It's through this "magical" process that I've felt incredible levels of bliss, awe, and wonder with life…and seeing the universe as a whole conscious being of which we are all a part… It's through becoming awakened to your place in the universe…to find your life mission and stick to it steadfastly that has brought me incredible bliss in my adult life… Once you open up and let go and become a co-operating part of the universe, life flows like water…and the natural state of bliss comes into being…

ANDREANNA TERA NARATATMA

Following your own personal sense of Bliss is such a simple and beautiful way to be happy. It is truly living for love, what inspires us and makes us feel most alive. In Bliss, there is no thinking, analyzing, planning, reminiscing. The fabricated realms of "past" and "future" dissolve, and there is only the luminous lucidity of NOW. This is where magic happens, spirit and matter meet, and true living creation happens.

Bliss is what it feels to be truly Alive. My journey back home to the state of ineffable bliss stemmed from the discontent towards the way of life the society I grew up in dictated. Rules, laws, school, work—it all seemed false and lacking the true essence of LIFE. Dreams of the Romantics, Transcendentalists, beatniks, hippies, mystics, and sadhus gave me

a taste of what could be and fueled my search for truth. Psychedelics showered me in kaleidoscopic visions of Love Light Eternal and dedication to practices of Kundalini yoga and meditation focused and directed me to union with the ALL. The sacred taste of Bliss became more and more familiar. With this, any contradictions to Bliss in my lifestyle became more and more apparent and unbearable. This led me to drop out of college and begin to travel. Guided by grace and the intuition of my open heart, I was led to my tribe and embraced by fellow lovers of the lifestyle of freedom and light, dance and music. I give thanks for the sheer joy I have experienced and the amazing ability to share this gift of Love.

DANI'EL LEVITY

At age 22, in Tucson, Arizona, I chose to fast in order to heal from childhood illness. During this fast and yogic cleanse, I had an awesome visionary experience. On the full moon, I went on my rooftop and looked at the moon. In it, all I could perceive was an eye. This eye was so pure. It was open and totally receptive, not knowing or judging, simply embracing. I gazed at this eye, seeing it as the eye of an infant, then of Christ. I saw Christ being staked onto a cross with a crown of thorns, but holding this same gaze, open and embracing. He is the epitome of love and compassion even in this time of bodily torture. I looked at the moon all night, purifying in its light, allowing this eye to become my eye.

During this indescribable experience, I came to understand how all things move with the celestial bodies in perfect

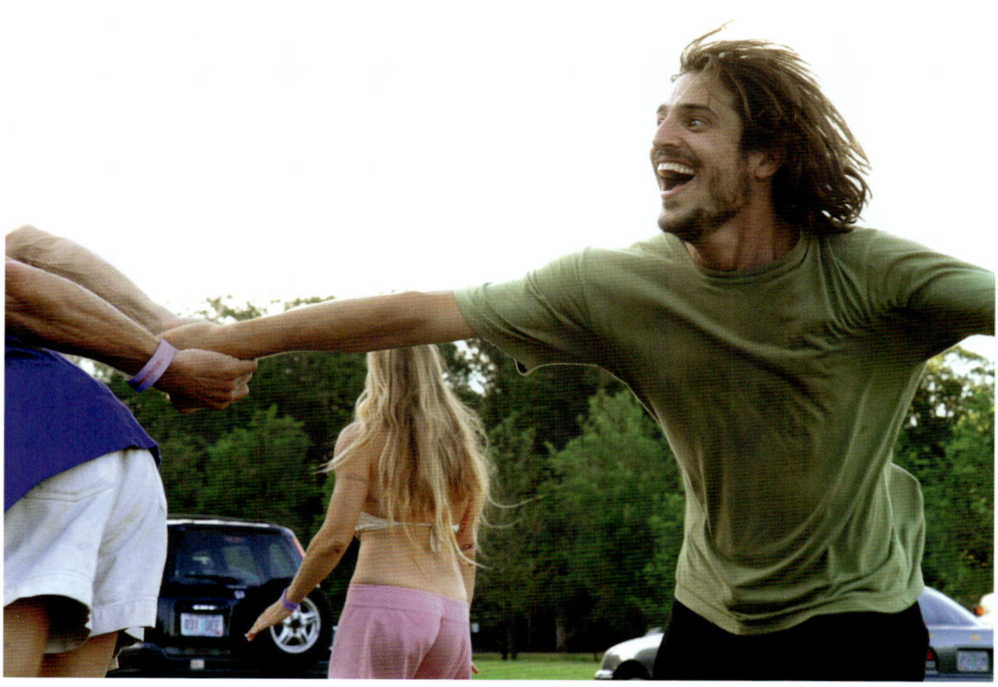

sync with all earth beings and elements. I learned that I, as a child of God, have potential comparative to the Masters, like Christ, and that the universe is working towards the same goals as myself. The message was clear that I am here to serve a unique purpose and that I can choose my path, being totally supported. I felt like a new person. I had been reborn.

In the following days, I had my eyes open and started to become more aware of the synchronic order of events that were continuously flowing. Everything that happened seemed to be vastly significant, unlike what I had ever experienced. I told a local mystic elder about my experience and I accepted his offer to be baptized in a "folk" traditional type manner.

I was given a special book, called *The Ancient Secret of the Flower of Life* with new wisdom about Sacred Geometry in these first days when my heart was tender and just beginning to blossom. The book showed me more about the interconnectedness that I had been experiencing. Specifically, I learned to draw the sacred form known as "The Flower of Life." These patterns quickly ingrained into my psyche, seeing beautiful unfolding lotus patterns in all the colors with my eyes closed, and soon, with my eyes open: in the trees, wind, and people's expressions.

I came to understand that these patterns were the geometries of my light body and I was watching the energy restructure into beautiful purifying formations. I discovered a movement meditation in which I would move physically with the flow of energy around me, like the rhythm of the wind or waves, in every action I'd make. Soon, I began to see these forms, not just as lines and circles, but as human bodies, moving together in sync with the patterns of nature.

I began to share these connective movement ceremonies with my community and found that, upon engaging, most involved would be instantly moved to feeling the infinite bliss of divine presence and experience improved energy sensitivity. I enthusiastically shared this technique with as many people as I could.

One day, after a sauna, I invited two men to join in a connection. We all immediately entered a transcendent state. We set the intention that we were cultivating energy of unconditional love, purity, and bliss. As this energy expanded from our circle, raindrops started to fall upon us. Being in the desert, we all gasped in amazement and broke the connection. I lay back and in this moment declared that I am completely dedicated to cultivating a vibration within myself of unconditional love, purity, and bliss and to share these connective practices with all humanity.

In my mission to share what have come to be called HuMandalas I have traveled to hundreds of gatherings of all style to teach in spontaneity and in workshops. In this quest, I have been guided to live, learn, and teach in many intentional communities and permaculture farms. I often traveled alone, simply with a backpack and did not plan where I would sleep next. I always ended up in the most beautiful of situations and never worried or had any fear. I would simply be patient and allow, not even having to ask. Among many stories, Spirit also led me on an adventure in a purple school bus throughout the western U.S. and Mexico with a crew of seven, all consciously manifesting our experience while sharing connections, song, and joy everywhere we landed.

Currently, I am living simply in Hawaii where I dance, play music, and swim every day. I am always actively creating HuMandala instruction materials, hosting workshops, and sharing HuMandalas on the beach.

DAVID STAR

Take the jump beyond self-imposed human limitation to super consciousness and bliss! Pray to realize the eternal God Self as the goal of life. Some have said Hippie stands for Highly Intelligent Person Pursuing Infinite Enlightenment!

At age 21 I came into conscious contact with Babaji, St. Germain, and other Masters on the inner planes. The teachings of balanced and perfected love and light reached deep inside. I prayed to know if we were all meant to overcome and Ascend like Jesus, and Light greater than I had ever experienced was pressed into the top of my head as by a seeming Master's hand. From then on the practice of prayer and exploring consciousness-raising through music, dance, and meditation became my way of life. I was seeking to have the Holy Spirit guide and move me every moment. I was also attempting to follow Christ's teachings, especially his charge to love God with all our heart, mind, soul, and strength. I decided that giving myself to God and desiring to know more of the spirit, to feel and call upon more light and love for everyone in every situation was the thing to do.

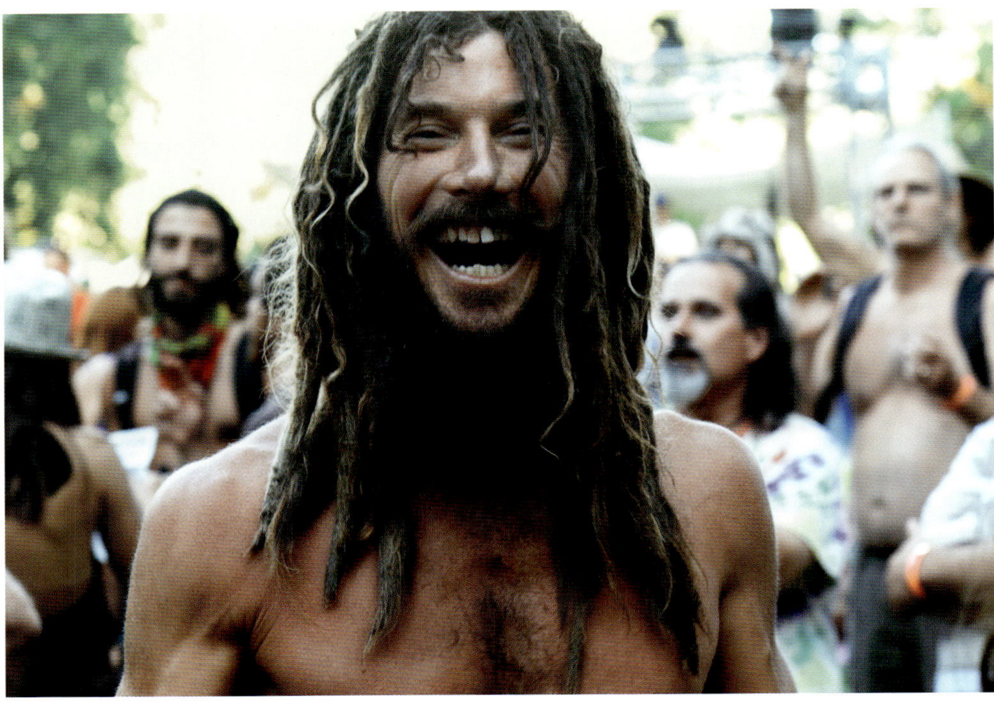

I abandoned all to do this as my work. I went around smiling and raying out love and light to all I could as I walked down the street. I felt my love deepen and pour out more than ever before at Grateful Dead shows. Divine ecstasy flowed from me as I desired to share and dance with it and all. The spirit had me jumping and spinning and rejoicing with all my heart. I was attempting to live in love and be free from fear. It seemed quite necessary to throw my clothes to the wind to experience the natural mystic states I intuited were awaiting humanity.

LARA LOVE

"Follow your bliss,
there's things you'll miss."

I was a Midwestern Jewish girl living in St. Louis. I didn't know what to do with myself after college, so I went to Taos, New Mexico because my friend recommended I do an AmeriCorps teaching program there. One night I went on a pub crawl. At the last bar I went to, there were two hippie guys dancing inside and some hippie circus people fire dancing outside. I was amazed to see the fire dancers and excited to see people actually dancing in the bar. I danced with the two hippie guys and they invited me to come on their school bus with them to a nearby hot springs. I decided to be spontaneous and get on the bus. I soaked in the hot springs with a bunch of hippies from the bus. We went around the circle and talked about our life's dreams. When we got tired, we cuddled on the bus on the beds they had in the back. When I woke up the next morning, I said out loud, "Oh my God! I'm on a hippie bus!" One of the hippie guys on the bus and I started talking and hanging out after the hot springs adventure. We eventually started dating. He taught me a lot about hippie philosophy and lifestyle. A few months later I lived with a bunch of hippies in a communal house. One day we had two hippie "sisters" visit and stay with us. "Can I be part of the rainbow family (hippie culture)?" I asked one of them. "Do you have a belly button? Anyone with a belly button can be in the rainbow family," she said. I began to feel like I belonged and had found my tribe and family. I started calling people sisters and brothers and smiled when people called me their sister. I went with the hippies I had first met on the bus to Hawaii to join another hippie circus troupe and put on a production of Alice in Wonderland. It was the best month of my life and the most free and hippie I have ever lived. I hitchhiked, did work trade to sleep in a barn in the jungle, and had many amazing adventures.

When I returned to the mainland, my aunt offered to let me live with her in Santa Cruz, California. I started going to see live bands play music all over the Bay Area. At a Grateful Dead cover band show in Berkeley, I met the manager of Wavy Gravy. I told him I had just started seeing live music and was interested in arranging tours for bands. He invited me to go to festivals with Wavy and him for the summer. "What's a festival?" I asked.

My first festival was Harmony back in 2005. I had only been to two small festivals in Taos prior to that. So there I was, first time at a big festival, with a backstage pass and free entry to the festival! I had so much fun dancing to bands and made lots of new friends. I went to many festivals that summer all over the country. I even got to stay with Wavy and his manager at a house Bob Dylan used to stay at. I felt like hippie royalty. I loved going to festivals and got hooked on them. I eventually got married (to another hippie) at a festival in Northern California with Wavy Gravy as our Master of Ceremonies. My husband and I went to Rainbow Gatherings in the U.S. and one in Thailand where I learned that the hippie culture has spread all over the world.

I still identify as a hippie and am going to seven festivals this summer. I'm on my way right now with my girlfriend to see the band Phish—a popular jam band. I am a teacher during the school year, so I get to be a free, hippie gypsy every summer. I try to infuse my life with the hippie philosophies I value most: be kind to each other and the earth, live simply, share generously, and above all enjoy life to the fullest!

LARA ON DAVID

I went to my first big "Grateful Dead" show at Bill Graham in San Francisco. I was bouncing to the music and noticed another happy bouncy person jumping to the beat at the same time I was. After a few songs of connecting on the dance floor, I went over to him and we became fast friends. As the weeks went by, he kept telling me about this magical being named David Star, who was traveling around Hawaii at the time. He kept saying, "You HAVE to meet him! He's amazing!"

At my first West Coast festival (Harmony 2005) I saw Shimshai play a beautiful set. I jumped and spun and danced with many people, but especially with this

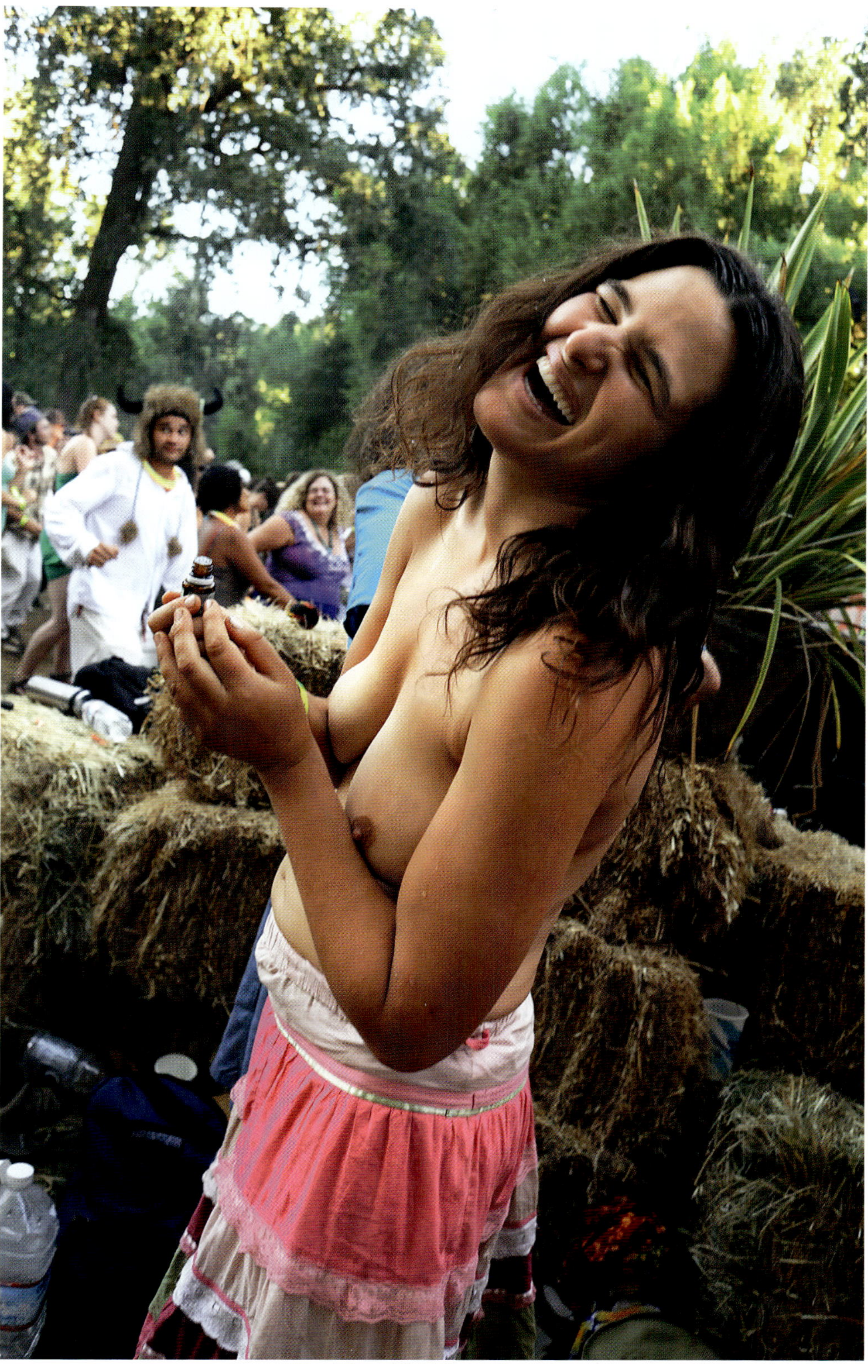

amazingly high, happy, and spiritually connected dready guy. As the show came to an end, I ran around hugging all of the people I had danced with. As I came up to the happy, dancey brother, I thought, "I bet this is David." Sure enough, it was. I love it when Spirit tells me what's up.

David and I have been friends ever since and I currently consider him one of my best friends on the planet. We have had LOTS of adventures together. He has helped me free up in so many ways, for which I am eternally grateful.

THEOPHILUS DONOGHUE

My journey into Bliss really began when I met my friend David Star at the age of 23. I had been on a spiritual path prior to that—meditating, doing Buddhist retreats, reading tons of spiritual books—but, despite enjoying ecstatic dancing, peace as opposed to Bliss had been the key focus of my spiritual life. When I was 19 and studying philosophy in Ireland, I met an incredible spiritual being who taught me the practice of eye gazing. He said that he had met a shaman in Amsterdam who told him that two of the keys to life are slow down and look people in the eyes. By integrating these two practices into his life, this brother had become what felt like an angel on Earth. He introduced me to this spiritual practice in which two people simply stay silent and meditate while looking into one another's eyes. The energy and strength which comes from such a technique felt so incredible compared to the traditional solitary form of meditation I had started learning the year before.

That being said, I was prepared to meet David who tends to replace a traditional "hello" with blissed out eye gazing! We were both at a program for Amma, also known as "The Hugging Saint," in Chicago. He had been dancing joyously in a circle with some friends and seemed to be the Brightest Light in the place! I went up to introduce myself as I was continuously looking for the highest vibrational people to interact with and, instead of talking, we went immediately into this Joyous state of open-eye meditation.

Despite exchanging e-mail addresses and phone numbers, I didn't see or speak to him until the following summer when he returned for Amma's Chicago visit. During the course of that year, I had thought about our interaction a lot and had decided to focus my spiritual life on living the way he lives. I had asked him a couple of questions when I first met him such as, "What do your parents think of how you live?" To which he replied smilingly, "They don't understand it." It was clear that to live in such a free, joyous manner, one would have to step out of one's comfort zone and be free of many restricting social conventions.

After seeing each other at Amma's again, I ended up visiting him in Michigan at the house of his girlfriend's family a couple of weeks later. During that time, David introduced me to the spiritual concept of Ascension which I hadn't really come across in the spiritual books I had read. Ascension can sort of be described as the ultimate purification of oneself—a spiritualizing of the dense, material body so that nothing emanates from one except Purity and Light. He also introduced me to the writings of Annalee Skarin who

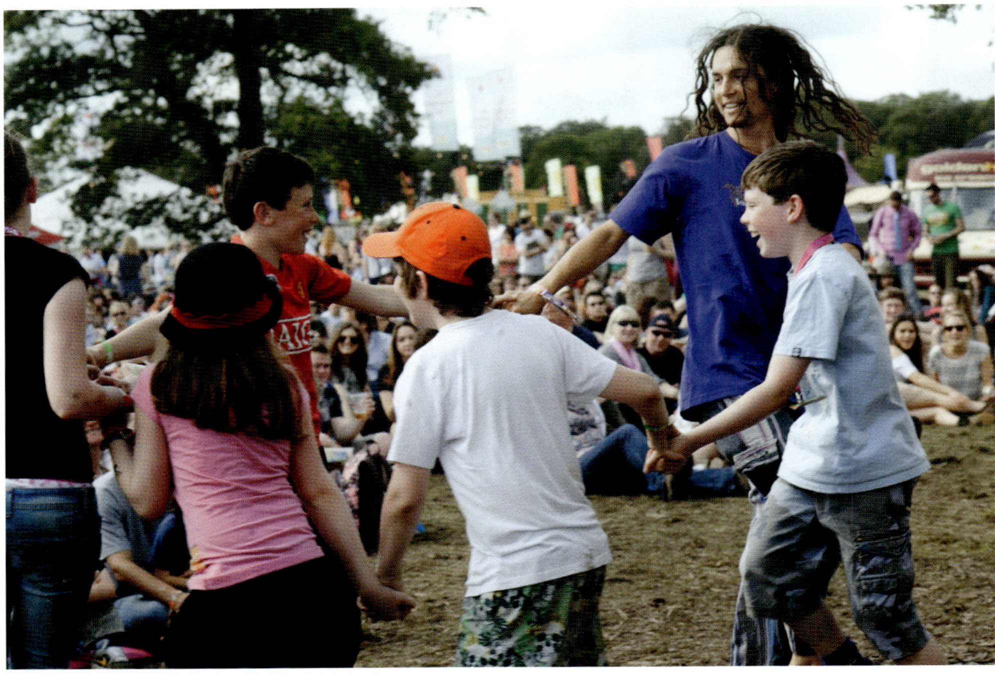

he said had played a primary role in his spiritual development. Annalee's books approach the idea of Spiritual Ascension from a Christian perspective. This was also new to me as Jesus hadn't been at all a part of my spiritual life. I spent the next year reading a lot of the material which David had showed me.

We then became close friends throughout the following years. We spent a blissed out week that following Spring in L.A. when I was there for one of my dad's photo shows. David and I would spontaneously go into these High States of Joy through dancing & open-eye meditation on buses and in grocery stores as well as in the more conventional setting of a Grateful Dead cover band show.

David visited the following summer and stayed with my family in Chicago for a while. We then traveled to Burning Man with my dad and another friend. The adventures continued that winter when I spent some time on the road with him. At a certain point, however, it felt as though something was missing. Jesus had been playing a part in my spiritual life, but He sort of seemed to be another spiritual master among masters. I had been open to worshiping God in the various forms of different religions, but it started to become clear that I needed to commit to Christ as my one and only guru and savior. Such a commitment and newly awakened belief radically altered my approach to spirituality, as service now seemed to be an important factor of the spiritual life which I had been neglecting through my preoccupation with self-growth and the false idea that "you can't liberate anyone else until you yourself are liberated." That maxim may be a bit true, but we can definitely comfort others and that's what Christ calls on us to do.

After this shift happened, I finally read the Bible for the first time—which for some reason had been completely neglected due to all of the other spiritual books I had been reading—and I started to get involved in basic service projects such as soup kitchens, which then eventually led me to doing prison ministry in four different facilities each week and taking on four hospice patients. My main spiritual teaching became Jesus' words in Matthew 25:34, "Come, you who are blessed by my Father; take your inheritance, the kingdom prepared for you since the creation of the world. For I was hungry and you gave me something to eat, I was thirsty and you gave me something to drink, I was a stranger and you invited me in, I needed clothes and you clothed me, I was sick and you looked after me, I was in prison and you came to visit me." Living such a life, however, definitely needs to be balanced by going out regularly to dance in Bliss! I decided to also take time off to travel with my dad for two summers and help him document this not-so-well-known niche of Bliss Ninnies—a sort of counterculture subculture of which I definitely feel a part. I hope this book inspires you and that, regardless of your age, you get a chance to be a part of it at some point in your life's journey as well! Just follow the Rainbow…

MICHAEL QUIJANO

At age 16, living in the State of Florida, I was an average teenager. School, skateboarding, and art were how I used to pass my time. However, it was only through skateboarding that I was brought to an awareness of Self and yoga. Stretching before each session was a vital way to remain fluid and relaxed. Soon enough I had learned some basic yoga asanas that would help my flexibility on the skateboard. This led me to the inquiry of yoga and the true meaning of such a practice or sadhana. I soon came to the realization that I had no idea how I got here, but it all seemed too familiar, a feeling of déja vù, like I had been here before, so I continued with my practice, becoming strict vegetarian, meditating everyday, skateboarding, and reading all kinds of different spiritual books.

The very first spiritual book I ever read was the sixth skanda of Srila Prabhupada's *Srimad Bhagavatam*. Inside, it expressed the salvation of a man by the name of Ajamila, who was saved on his deathbed by calling out one of his sons' names—Narayana, who was named after the lord himself. When calling out for his son, instead the lord appeared and gave him salvation from birth and death. Similarly I had called on the lord for salvation, and he gave me a vision. In that very moment, I renounced everything to which I was attached, engaged myself in austerities and meditation, and went to the West the following year.

It was around this time that I was drawn to see Amma, "The Hugging Saint," from India. My birthday fell on a free program day, so I decided I would go then. I had just enough money for a one-way flight and did not even know anyone personally in California, but it felt in alignment, so I jumped without thinking. I was graced with receiving Amma's darshan on my 18th birthday of June 5, 2011.

There I met many wonderful people and shared many wonderful stories. I met a woman who offered me a ride to a National Rainbow Gathering in the State of Washington. I had been to a small one in Ocala, Florida that wasn't the best, but I didn't lose hope in the pot of gold at the end of the rainbow, so a few weeks after Amma's, I took the ride north on the I-5. It was probably one of the most beautiful experiences I ever had in my life. I had shown up to the gathering with only a jacket on my back, a small shawl, and some cheap china slippers. I was totally unprepared and did not realize there would be snow on the ground with temperatures below freezing. I did not have a tent or own a sleeping bag or blanket. I spent the nights walking from one fire pit to the next trying to stay warm, listening to different musicians play beautiful heart songs around the fire. Sometimes I could only sleep a few hours at most. The days were spent soaking in the hot sun and conversing with thousands of people. As I walked the trails, I would look each person passing by in their eyes with a warm smile. This happened to become very exhausting in itself and became overwhelming very quickly. However, I kept faith and was able to eat two meals a day for free without even having a begging bowl of my own—even the Buddhists monks have at least a bowl. The gathering was coming to an end and it was time to go, so I caught a ride to a hot spring with some sisters who were on their way to a festival in Oregon. I had found out there were a few more festivals in Northern California as well and I could realistically travel from one festival to the next. However, I didn't really

have any specific destination, I was just in the moment, in the flow—this is what made my experience so beautiful and uplifting. I found myself in these wonderful conscious festivals, blissing out to good music, art, raw food, and positive vibes.

In between festivals, many people would converge around Mount Shasta since it's so close to the I-5. There I was the most spiritually connected and felt the most at peace. Deep in nature I was in constant communion, grateful for the grace God had showered upon me, and thankful for the healing waters to shower in.

My journey into Bliss took me next to fruit picking farms for the fall harvest. I was able to earn about two grand in a little over two months of hard work and this time was able to pay for the retreat with Amma for Thanksgiving. I remember I even paid for David, who had helped me so much earlier in the summer. I traveled a few weeks after Amma's during the winter and decided I would use the money to fly to Brazil for the World Rainbow Gathering and to continue the nomadic lifestyle in South America. I spent six months traveling in a caravan with people from all around the world, holding sacred ceremonies, and having wild visions of being in New York City sharing my light in some cliché white garments.

It wasn't until the return of my birthday, during the Transit of Venus, that I would feel an urge to leave South America. The day passed very slowly as I walked around the forests and waterfalls, communing with mother earth. I returned to the village where I had been staying in a small house with some friends. When I arrived they had asked me why I missed

my party. I said, "What party?" and they said, "The one we all planned for you! Everyone was there waiting." I couldn't help but laugh because no one had told me they were planning such an event the days prior. As I was standing outside laughing about the news, I could not stop laughing. It almost became like breathing, when you don't even notice you're breathing. Everything went white and I had blacked out, and next thing I know, I woke up on the floor and the cleaning lady who was sweeping outside was slapping my face saying "My darling, my darling. Are you OK?" but all I could see was Amma standing over me, giving me her darshan.

As I came to, the separation from the divine mother was too much so I asked around online for a sponsor to fly me to California to catch at least the last day of her free programs, Devi Bhava. I got

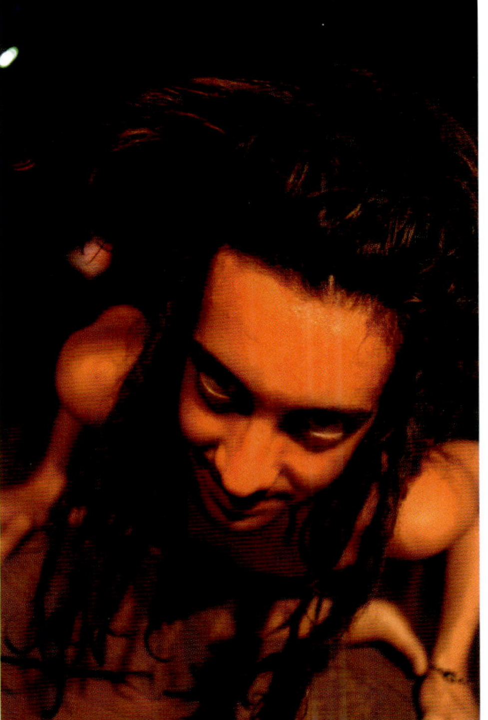

a message five minutes later with an OK and arranged to leave the next day. However, the airport in Brasilia was about 248 kilometers from where I was living, and I only knew one person with a car. I offered to pay him gas money for a lift, but he wouldn't go for it so I caught a cab instead. I had a one day/one night layover in Panama to see my family and landed in SF the next day. I felt so much love when I arrived to the ashram on that last day, and again the sense of déja vù arose, and all seemed in perfect alignment. When the Bhava was over, a friend came and asked me if I would like to do the whole U.S. tour with Amma because he needed riders to split the cost, and I broke down in tears because it was a once-in-a-lifetime opportunity. It wasn't until Amma tour New York when it all made sense to me. There I was, standing in Times Square wearing all white, in the exact place I had seen myself standing when I had the sacred vision in Brazil. I embraced that moment fully and took a big deep breath, "Here I am, there's nowhere else I'd like to be, than right Here right Now in this everlasting moment."

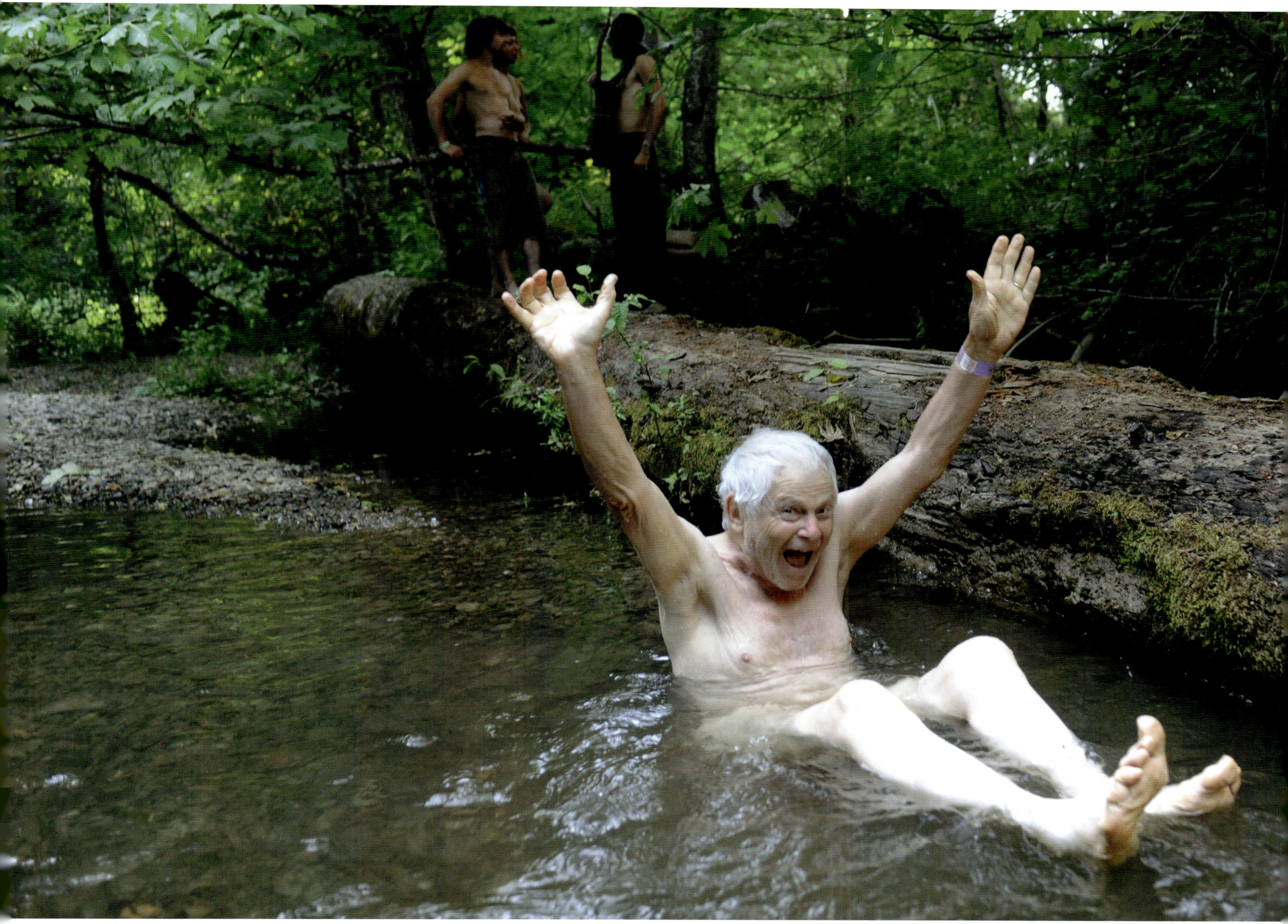

Afterword by WAVY GRAVY

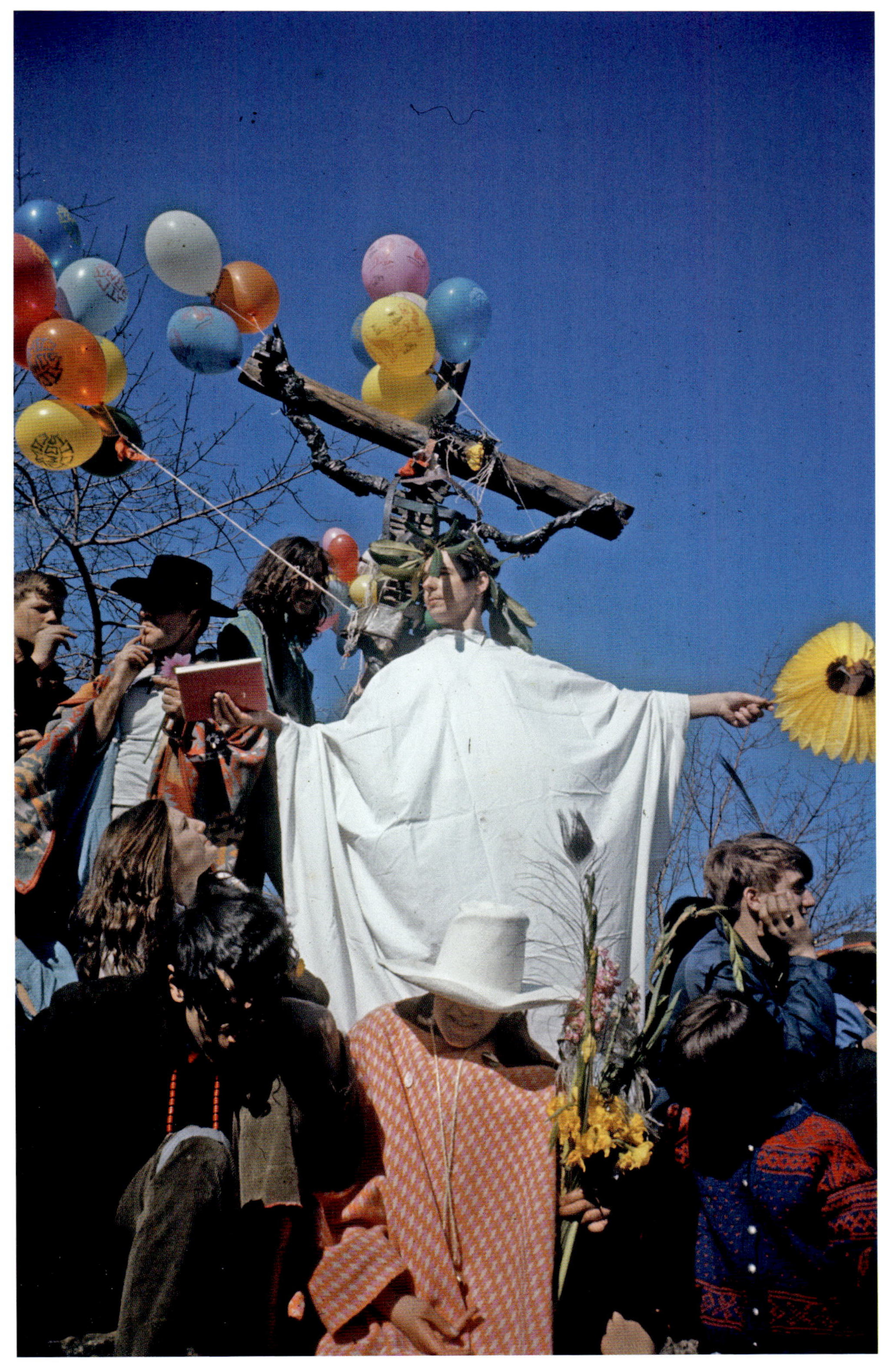

My first blast of bliss was a double-barreled god rant of Rumi, "Follow your bliss, there are a hundred ways to kneel and kiss the ground." Rammed home by Joseph Campbell and The Hero's Journey…Well, sign me up! Kesey said it best. "The trouble with the superhero is what to do between phone booths." This star-spangled word bomb was followed by, "Always put your good where it can do the most." And there you have it…my audio road map to hip hippie heaven…with station stops in the formation of the Hog Farm commune and my life work with the Seva Foundation (Seva.org.) and Camp Winnarainbow (http://www.campwinnarainbow.org/).

Our expanded family's ascension onto the national consciousness came about through our involvement in the Woodstock music festival in the fall of 1969. We had been traveling across America putting on consciousness raising festivals when we were con-tacted by the organizers of this mega music festival. Our commune organized a kitchen, a Please force. The password was "I forgot!," a trip tent where we dealt with bum trips, and I was allowed to make life support announcements, i.e. "Good morning! What we have in mind is breakfast in bed for four hundred thousand." Which is when we introduced hippies

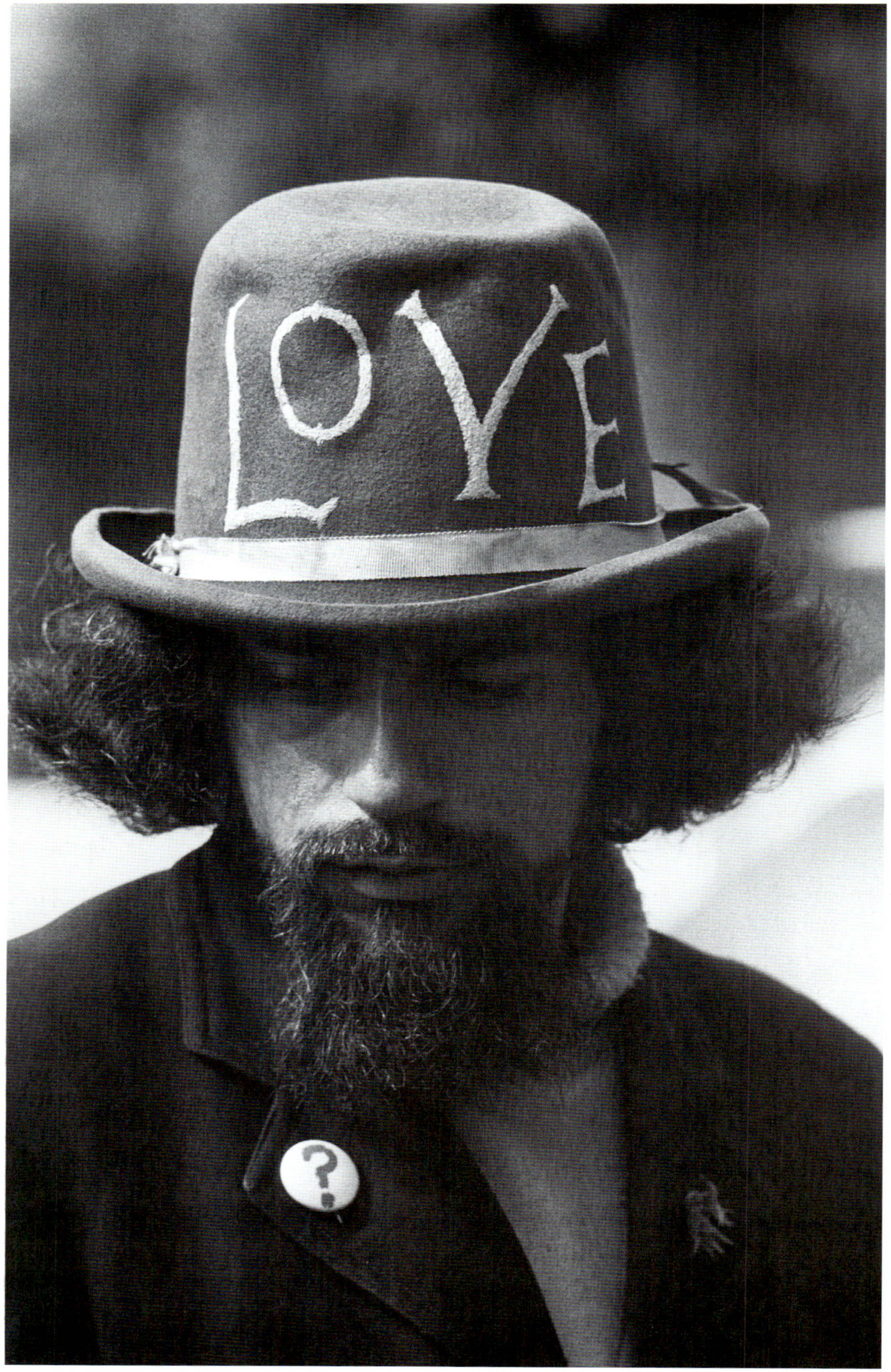

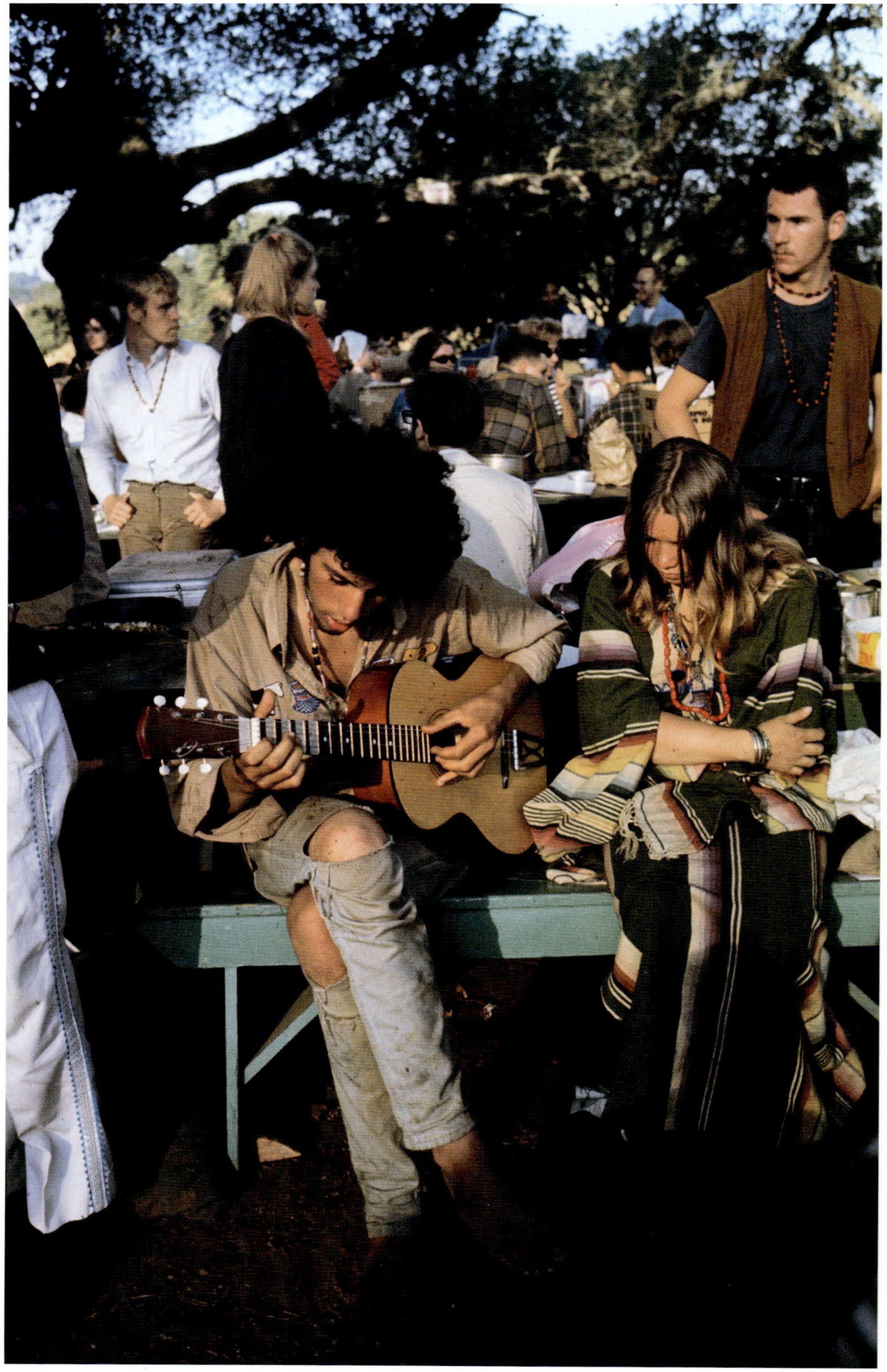

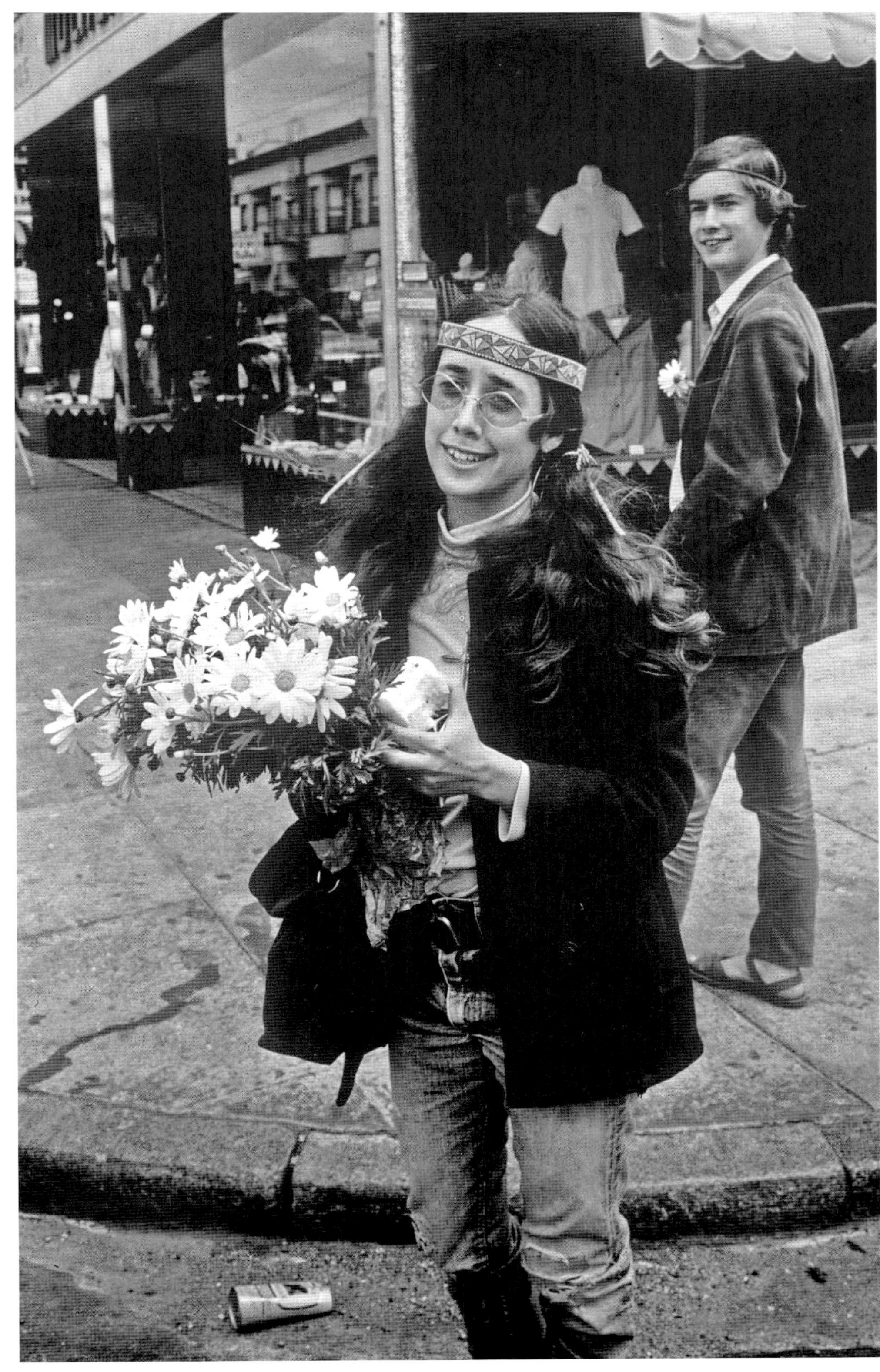

to granola. This was bliss city Blissorama and when adversity came in wind and mud and rain we rose above it and continued to groove to the music and be kind to each other. Janis Joplin said, "If you have any food left share it with your brother and your sister. And that's the person on your left and the person on your right!"

That spirit is alive and well in the here and now. These are the good old days, from Rainbow Gatherings to Burning Man…the beat goes on. There are more communes in America now than there ever were in the 60s… Check out *Communities* magazine for a listing near you!

Just follow your bliss and kiss the ground. The pictures in this book say a million words. Just take them in and turn them into your life. Wavy Gravy sez, "We are all the same person trying to shake hands with ourself." ETERNITY NOW

Left and previous spread:
photographs by Steve Schapiro,
Haight Ashbury, 1967.

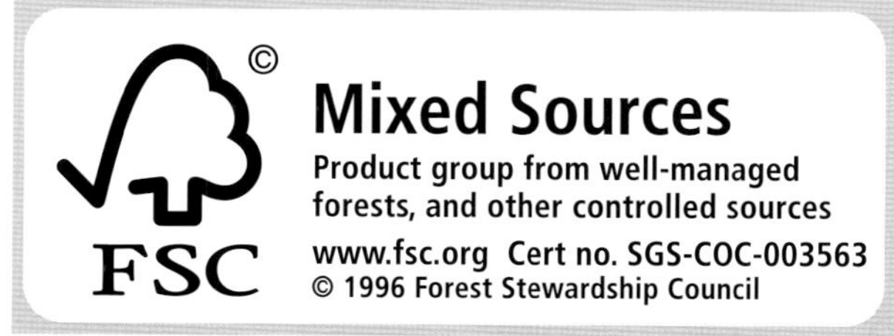
Mixed Sources
Product group from well-managed
forests, and other controlled sources
www.fsc.org Cert no. SGS-COC-003563
© 1996 Forest Stewardship Council
FSC